Meister Eckhart

Meister Eckhart

A Modern Translation

By Raymond Bernard Blakney

HARPER TORCHBOOKS
Harper & Row, Publishers, New York
Grand Rapids, Philadelphia, St. Louis, San Francisco
London, Singapore, Sydney, Tokyo, Toronto

To the friends in the white church of Williamstown who have patiently heard the setting forth of many things contained herein, this book is affectionately dedicated.

CONTENTS

Preface

BEFORE I began to read Meister Eckhart, I shared a common prejudice against medieval thinkers and all their works. I disliked theology in the medieval idiom, regarding it as juiceless and static, and fortunately superseded by more vital modern religious thought. Then, at the behest of a learned friend, I began Eckhart, only to see that what he had to say was indeed like a treasure buried in a field, the more valuable because so rare—and so long neglected. It proved not to be enough merely to read him. The variations among the translations into modern German only suggested a richer treasure behind them all, and the one existing English translation did not help much. This volume, therefore, represents an effort to reread Meister Eckhart with the minute attention a fresh translation requires.

The chief difficulty with reading Eckhart is not linguistic. It is quite possible to overcome the obscurities of his forgotten dialects. Furthermore, his thoughts are simple enough. What makes Eckhart difficult is the moral demand he makes on one: *der warheit bekennet, der weiz daz ich war spriche.* (He who knows the Truth, knows that I am speaking the truth.) He asks of us, not only our minds, but our hearts as well.

It has proved possible to include only about one half of the German works attributed to Meister Eckhart in one volume. Thus I have chosen those most readily authenticated by reference to the *Defense,* which I have included, and which is here translated for the first time, as far as I know, into a modern language. The twenty-eight sermons are arranged to illustrate the movement of Eckhart's inner career. The reader will feel in them a growing sense of a climax which Eckhart reached in Sermon 28. The *Fragments* that follow are bits of sermons offered in lieu of the complete sermons from which they are taken. Some of them have been preserved only as fragments in Pfeiffer; others are selected from the completer texts which Pfeiffer offers.

It appears that Eckhart was sufficiently orthodox in Latin but when he found himself preaching and writing in German, the formal restraints of the official church language seemed to drop off. He not only began to utter "discovered truths" but to give simple, homely words in his native vernacular new meanings—loads they were not accustomed to carry. The identification of these words is made fairly easy by reference to Latin texts of which Eckhart was the author. Certain key words in the German works are literal equivalents of the Latin and their meanings may be determined by studying what they meant in the literature of which Eckhart was undoubtedly a master, such as Plato's *Timaeus*, the writings of Augustine, and Thomas Aquinas. The meanings of these words are also to be determined in the light of Eckhart's own thought scheme. For the reader's convenience, I offer a partial list of them at this point.

ABGESCHEIDENHEIT: Disinterest, disinterestedness. The evidence of Eckhart's life and teaching are against translating this word in the usual senses of "solitude, seclusion," or "detachment." He did not recommend monkish solitude, nor the detachment which suggests lack of interest. See Note 1, to *About Disinterest*. What Eckhart demands is equivalent to what pure science demands of the laboratory investigator. He means to say that the price of truth is self-denial in things spiritual, as well as in things material and intellectual. He asks us to make a careful distinction between what we might desire of the truth and what the truth appears to be. This is disinterest.

BILD: Idea, that is, Plato's ιδέα, from ιδεῖν, to see. Eckhart's Latin word was "ymago," from which he chose the literal "bild" in German. The English word "image," often used in this connection is, however, misleading. See Sermon 11, note 9. See also P. E. More's *Platonism*, Ch. VI, "The Doctrine of Ideas."

EDEL: Aristocratic, of high rank, noble.

GOT: God, god. "god" is the idea of God, perhaps; but the double use of the word suggests Plato, in the *Timaeus*, where "God" and "god" both appear. In this way, Sermon 28 becomes intelligible.

GRUNT: Core, as the core of an apple; "in der sele grunde"—"in the core of the soul," "the little castle in the soul" of Sermon 24. See Evelyn Underhill's *Mysticism*, pp. 64–65, especially the reference to Rudolf Eucken's understanding of "Grund."

INNE SEIN, INNE BLEIBEN: Self-contained, as, for example, "a self-contained person." Literally, "to be in," "to be at home," or as Matthew 6:6 says: "when thou prayest, enter into thy closet." Also, there is the passage in Plato's *Phaedo* 65: "Thought is best when the mind is gathered into herself and none of these things trouble her—neither sounds, nor sights nor pain nor pleasure—when she takes leave of the body and has as little as possible to do with it. . . ." This is Eckhart's meaning.

KRAFT: Agent, in the sense of "chemical agent," or "physical agent," to signify sight, hearing, the will, the intellect, etc., in the phrase "the agents of the soul." Behind Eckhart's German word, there are two Latin words, both of which appear in the *Defense:* (1) "potentia"—which he uses for purely human reference, and (2) "virtus"—which he uses for the divine agent in the soul. See Sermon 6, note 2. The word "agent," used in this sense, is open to objection for novelty but we have no generally accepted word to cover all the psychic functions. There is wide objection now to the older words "faculties," "powers," on account of their static connotations. See, for example, the use of "agent" in Sermon 1. Thomas Aquinas, Eckhart's immediate predecessor, says: "The natural principles of the operations of the soul are the powers, (i.e., the agents) . . ." (*Summa Theologica* I, q. 77, art. 5.) The point is that some vernacular word equivalent to "operator" is required.

MEISTER: Authority, that is, a philosopher or theologian of standing.

NIHTE, NIHTES NIHTE: Nothing, nothing at all; but Eckhart does not literally mean "nothing": his meaning is more akin to the mathematical notion of zero. For example, in Sermon 28, the ultimate condition of the blessed soul comes, superficially, to look very much like "nothing." It is safer, however, to define "nothing" in terms of Eckhart's poverty than his poverty by nothingness. See also Sermon 19.

NU: Now-moment, the point of division between the past and future—without duration—and yet the locus of eternity! See Sermon 15, for example. See also, Psalm 90:4; Augustine, *Confessions* XI, 16 and 20; Plato, *Timaeus* 37b.

SELE: Soul, from which "selig," of the soul, i.e., blessed. This soul is the scholastic "*anima*," which is now Aristotle's ψυχή, which means, roughly, "life," and now Plato's νοῦς, or immortal soul. It is a help to see what

Eckhart's contemporary Dante was writing about the soul in his *Convivio*, Third Treatise, Ch. II.

The complete list of words for which the dictionary meaning seemed inadequate would be too long to include here. Suffice it to say that when I have felt an arbitrary translation necessary, the choice of a modern English equivalent has been made in consideration of Eckhart's total message.

My thanks are due to many persons who have helped in many ways. I am indebted to Professor Maurice W. Avery of Williams College, for help in preparing the translation of the *Defense*; to Professor Karl E. Weston of Williams, for notice of the Cologne school of painting as described in the Introduction; to Mr. Foster Palmer and Mr. Robert H. Haynes of the Harvard University Library, who generously put several indispensable texts into my hands for long periods of time; and to Frau Dr. Elsa Houtermans, who is the learned friend at whose behest I began this work.

RAYMOND B. BLAKNEY

Williamstown, Massachusetts
July, 1941

Introduction

MEISTER ECKHART was born in Germany in 1260, about five years before the birth of Dante in Italy, and died about 1328, or seven years after Dante's death. He has two minor claims to fame. He is said to have done for the German language what Dante did for the Italian. He discussed for the first time the ultimate things of life and death in the medieval German dialects and, having done so with power and clarity, he made German a vehicle for ideas that hitherto had been considered expressible only in Latin.[1]

He is also credited with being the father of German idealism. For example, Franz von Baader writes:[2] "I was often with Hegel in Berlin. Once I read him a passage from Meister Eckhart, who was only a name to him. He was so excited by it that the next day, he read me a whole lecture on Eckhart, which ended with: 'There, indeed, we have what we want!'" Schopenhauer on The Will, and Spinoza on Ethics will have a startling familiarity to one who has just read what the great German monk said or wrote. Of course, the debt goes back much further to the church fathers, the Gospels, and the classic writers of antiquity. The number of authorities Eckhart quotes and uses as springboards for his own thinking is amazing.

Nevertheless, his best contribution was neither literary nor philosophical. It is quite clear that he never thought of himself as a writer. He wrote only when he needed to write to do what he felt ought to be done. It is also clear that he did not regard himself as a thinker. At least he was not self-conscious about it. To be sure, he was a scholastic and an adept at dealing with abstract notions and fine distinctions. Some German critics say that the more abstract an idea the better Eckhart liked it and the more he was given to

xiii

expounding it. That, however, was not Eckhart's point. He was a man of single intent, and that intent was God.

It was in his doctrines of God that he went beyond the tolerance of his time and perhaps beyond the capacity of ours. What he knew of himself, and through himself of all people in all times, and therefore what he discovered about God and the relations of God to man and man to God—this was the gift he wished to give and did give most richly. Certainly he lifted Christianity above any parochial conception and revealed its inner relation to the great, universal spiritual movements which have found expression in many forms. He lived on that high level, on the same highlands of the spirit that were disclosed in the Upanishads and Sufi classics. To go where Eckhart went is to come close to Lao Tzu and Buddha, and certainly to Jesus Christ.

To be sure, the religions that have grown up around these great ones fall with time, each into its own parochial form and idiom, and each acquires its own crust, its own shell which encases one or two germs of the one universal life. But, says Meister Eckhart, "Wiltu den kernen haben, so muostu die schalen brechen."[3] Eckhart was a breaker of shells, not as an iconoclast breaks them, but as life breaks its shells by its own resurgent power.

There is much agreement that Eckhart was not a precursor of the Reformation. That is true in the sense that he had no quarrel with the ecclesiastical institution as such. To the last day of his life he protested that he was a faithful and loving child of the church and what is even more conclusive is the apparent lack of any open attack on the notorious evils of the church of his day. Eckhart was one of the world's great "Yes-sayers," whose deep conviction was that untruth or evil is not to be fought with condemnation or criticism, but that it must be displaced by an overwhelming disclosure of the true and good.

Nevertheless, it is now clear that the ministrations of the church in the latter part of the thirteenth century were unsatisfactory to an ever-increasing number of people. This is eloquently attested by the sporadic but persistent appearances of so-called "wild" religious societies, which preached and propagated alarming and dangerous mysticism, from the point of view of responsible leaders of the church. At no point in Europe did this spontaneous generation of heat well up more conspicuously than in the Rhine valley where Eckhart was born. There were the Beghards, the Beguines, the Friends of God, and so on, whose much-too-exuberant enthusiasm began to find its way into pulpits and monasteries, until the authorities could no longer ignore it and began to take measures to stamp it out.

In defense of the Inquisition, the duty of whose officers it was to check the irregular movements, there is much to be said. Mysticism in the hands of Eckhart is one thing; in the hands of men of comparatively feeble intellect it is something else. This is what the "great priest" of the legend[4] is trying to point out and what many a friendly priest must have argued to Eckhart before the Franciscans got on his trail.

Of the stern realities of the problem the church officials had to deal with, we in the twentieth century should be well aware. Mysticism, like Mother Eve, has two kinds of children, Abel and Cain. For the Abel kind, almost everything good is to be said; for the Cain kind, almost everything evil. Out of mysticism, the great life-giving impulses of civilization come; but out of mysticism of a kind, the National Socialist movement of Germany is also born.

According to the Nazis, Eckhart is a member of their party in good standing. Dr. Alfred Rosenberg praises him, saying that the springs of National Socialism are to be found in the fourteenth century mystic's teachings! In his recent essay, *Germany's New Religion*, Professor Wilhelm Hauer professes to be a disciple of Eckhart, or at least in sympathy with him, and therefore he, too, yearns for a God who is more than God, etc.[5]

Cain, too, is a mystic; but Cain-mysticism is not the fault of Meister Eckhart. It merely illustrates, in Nazi Germany, how great an error can be made by using a noble name to support a partisan purpose, when those who use it have learned nothing from him who bore it. It also illustrates the understandable repugnance of church authorities in Eckhart's time to mysticism in the heads of crude and undisciplined people. That Eckhart himself became the unmeriting victim of that repugnance is, to say the least, a deplorable accident, but in the history of martyrdoms not at all novel.

How deep and how far this fourteenth century mysticism went, may be gauged from the fact that a school of art—the "Cologne school"[6] of which Meister Wilhelm and Stephan Lochner are examples—arose to represent it. These men bear striking testimony in their paintings to the powerful impression made on them. In their work symbolism replaces realism, as indeed it did when Eckhart himself turned the verbal images of Christianity into symbols of the concepts which measure the progress of mankind in spiritual mastery.

What little we know of Eckhart's biography could be put in tabular form. It is derived almost entirely from the juiceless records of the fourteenth century church files, or from headings attached to his works by editors. Of his own personal life hardly a word escaped him to our knowledge. Regret it or not, this is characteristic of the man who forgot himself completely in the pursuit of one great idea. Furthermore, immortality via biography or autobiography would hardly have interested one who believed that heaven was more real and solid than earth.

Nevertheless, since what he wrote and said are inseparable from the few known details of his outward life, it is perhaps better to follow them as an outline. Johannes Eckhart was born in the village of Hochheim, near Gotha, about A.D. 1260. His father was the steward of a knight's castle in the Thuringian forest. Here he acquired a mental image which later he turned to good use: "Look and see: this little castle of the soul is exalted so high above every road . . . that God himself cannot steal into it."[7] Here, too, he acquired his notions of the Aristocrat,[8] who in Eckhart's mature years ceased to be a person as the world sees him and became instead a man as God sees him.

Not earlier than his fifteenth year he entered the Dominican monastery at Erfurt for at least nine years of study required for the priesthood and after that he studied at the "high school" at Cologne, where Albertus Magnus taught until his death in 1280. It is not considered probable that Eckhart sat under this famed teacher but he did come under the influence of Thomas Aquinas, who had just died and whose star was definitely ascending.

Somewhere near the year 1300, he is recorded as "Brother Eckhart,

Great home in humans

Prior of Erfurt, Vicar of Thuringia." His promotion to these distinctions must have come fairly early in his membership in the preaching cloister. It was here, near to the age of forty, that he wrote the pamphlet that has come down to us under the heading *Das sint die rede der unterscheidunge*—"These are the Talks of Instruction that the Vicar of Thuringen, the Prior of Erfurt, Brother Eckhart of the Preaching Order held for such of his spiritual children as asked him about various things as they sat together in evening table-conversation."

The substance of this little book is kindly, straightforward talk that reminds one of Mozart music. It gives us the first glance at Eckhart's inner life. He writes of obedience, self-denial, prayer, work, growth, sin, the will, the blessed life, and devotion as few have ever been able to write of these things, but it is when he speaks of God that the measure and quality of his own soul appear most clearly. "God never tied man's salvation to any pattern of life. . . . So one must be permeated with the divine Presence, informed with the form of the beloved God who is within him, so that he may radiate that Presence without working at it." Already the God who lives yonder, in another world apart, is put aside for the God who is at home in man—not a new idea, except as any idea becomes new when it is taken seriously. And Eckhart took it with shocking seriousness. God is something to any person who is religious, but to Eckhart he was everything. One recent commentator says: "Truly, Eckhart makes it hard for us to penetrate the world of his thoughts, for he demands of us a devotion and a faith such as contemporary man does not possess."[9]

It has been said that in the Talks of Instruction, Eckhart had not yet gone beyond the range of the Catholic piety of his time.[10] In the externals that is true, but on deeper inspection we meet here for the first time an inwardness of the God-conception reminiscent of the life in a seed that is about to burst the shell. Eckhart speaks with earnestness and devotion, but always without fear and trembling, kneeling and bowing.

About the year 1300, the German Dominicans seem to have been well aware of Eckhart's power and he was sent to the world-famed college at Paris on a teaching mission. It is believed that he was to

champion the Dominican point of view against that of the Franciscans.[11] We may estimate the heat generated in this clash from a sentence of a sermon he delivered much later at home: "When I preached
at Paris, I said—and I regard it well said—that with all their science,
those people at Paris are not able to discern what God is in the least
of creatures—not even in a fly!"[12] The enmity of the Franciscans for
Meister Eckhart probably dates from the Paris debate.

It is worth while to pause a moment at this point to notice the
rivalry between the Franciscans and the Dominicans. It was no passing episode and seems to have been a matter of sore perplexity to
some of the popes. Doubtless there was political rivalry in the
church as these two powerful orders competed for prestige and control, but the ostensible basis for their quarrels lay in matters of
philosophy and theology. Theology was, to the medieval man, what
politics is to us today. The issues involved were of immediate,
heated, and personal interest and just as people today may be punished for political views and propaganda believed inimical to some
government or state, wrong theological views, considered inimical
to the church, could be punished then. The rivalry of the orders
lent itself well to this kind of ferocity. A Franciscan would be only
too glad to lend himself to the punishment of a Dominican, as
Meister Eckhart discovered.

What this all adds up to is a simple proposition. At the end of the
Middle Ages, the spiritual world, the world contemplated by theology, was the real world, while the world of politics, over which
we quarrel today, was the nominal world.[13] It is hard for a person
of the twentieth century to conceive that this should be so, but at
the beginning of the fourteenth century the man in the street could
be complacent about the political issues of the state, and even
indifferent to them, whereas he had an opinion about the affairs of
heaven and hell that did make a difference to him and he tended to
belong loosely to the party whose doctrines best suited his taste or
convenience.

It would be clear to us today that this state of mind, coupled with
moral laxity, laziness, and corruption in the church should soon be
shaken by a revolution such as the Reformation, after which religion
would tend to take a more and more subsidiary place in human

culture. What we do not see now is that our present wars over political ideologies, waged for power and prestige, can bring about a reverse revolution, when one side or the other has won a victory such that nothing of the political and economic world is left which is worth possessing, and men's thoughts once more focus on the world to come.

Suffice it to say that six centuries ago in Europe men understood by realism exactly the opposite of what we mean. There were neo-platonist ideas in the air then and, looking at them, the modern man might well feel tempted to call them "the last, the thinnest and the emptiest of all," as Nietzsche did. Only in this way can we understand how, in the Middle Ages, men fought over what we discount as generalizations and abstractions. The modern idea that individual and concrete things alone are real would have seemed to Eckhart a sad vagary, just as to a person with our contemporary scientific background much of what Eckhart proclaimed with such passion would seem like dream ideology—much sound but signifying nothing.

Nevertheless, the Parisians must have been impressed with Eckhart. In 1302 the College of Paris, then the world's most renowned, conferred on him the Licentiate and Master's degree, so that always after he was known as Meister Eckhart. Thereafter he advanced rapidly in preferments. In 1303 he was made Provincial of the Dominican order in Saxony, which then included nearly all of middle and lower Germany. In 1307 the duties of Vicar of Bohemia were added and this serves to inform us that during the great creative period of Eckhart's life, he was a very busy man, apart from his preaching and writing. His duties involved extensive travel, which must have consumed more time than we can imagine, since the roads were extremely bad and the going slow.

From this middle part of Eckhart's life comes his best-attested German work, *The Book of Divine Comfort*, said to have been composed for the Queen of Hungary whose courage had been shattered by a series of sad accidents.[24] If this is so, it seems a little strange to us that the comforter should begin with a good, stiff, philosophical work-out, and only then develop "thirty teachings, any one of which should be enough to solace." It is indeed a strong treatment of suffering and evil and, if I may be permitted a personal testimony, one of the most convincing I have ever seen.

It would seem as if the distress of the Queen of Hungary really provided Eckhart a second occasion for a definitive expression of his thoughts, and this time he is thinking of the essential unity of God and man—for this is the root of his solution of the problem of suffering. We are not God, yet God's blood flows in our veins, so to speak. God is the procreator, the begetter of all that is real and eternal in man. There is nothing new in this idea as it stands: it is one of the leading ideas of the New Testament, derived from Jesus' reference to God as "my father." No idea, as such, ever made more pulses quicken or more eyes shine than the thought that we really are in God's family—the uncreated One, being the head of the house that this world is. With Eckhart, however, there was a difference: with the exception of Jesus himself, no one had ever taken this idea of "blood relationship" to God so seriously or followed its consequences so radically to the last possible deduction. Already, in this *Book of Divine Comfort*, he was moving toward heresy, a heresy of degree if not of idea.

As an example of Eckhart's radicalism—or shall we say *vividness*? —it is worth noting that he works out this "blood relationship" to God by means of the analogy of the sexual relationship in marriage. To be sure, this is never explicit—and perhaps—probably—it is entirely unconscious with him. He illustrates, however, his own oft-avowed law that whatever a man gives up for God's sake he finds again in God a hundredfold.[23] Having given up marriage in the flesh for God's sake, Eckhart finds it again everywhere in God's dealings with himself and mankind. God is a procreator, a begetter, and thus the Father. The soul is the virgin wife, in whom the Son is begotten, and this is the secret of God's eternal delight and man's too. It is God's sole occupation in the "Now" of eternity. It is the mode of creation. God is the tireless lover of the soul.

It could justly be said that Meister Eckhart was a man of one idea —one very great idea, to whom nothing else mattered much. That idea was the unity of the divine and the human. Still we should notice that he never fell victim to the illusion that "I, this earthly individual, whom men call Brother Eckhart, am God." Far from it.

No one ever expressed more decisively than he the immeasurable difference between the Creator and the creature, between God and man. Creatures, of themselves, he was never tired of saying, are nothings.[14]

Still, in spite of their endless differences, if God and man are of the same genus, it must be possible to set free the divine kernel of being in man's inmost self by the ever-increasing conquest of his outer self-identity. This divine kernel, this "little spark"[15] of God which is concealed within the shell of selfhood, is as high above all that is purely human and personal as heaven is high above earth. It is the germ of eternal life and the seed of God, the point of divine grace from which man may derive his worth and hope.

What distinguished Eckhart from all others who strove much to the same point is less the What than the How of his piety: the passionate radicalism of his application of the dogma of the God-man. This alone made him a heretic, that is to say, one dangerous to the church as an institution—as he was. The Reformation can be traced back to Eckhart spiritually and intellectually—if not ecclesiastically. There was enough matter for any reformation to work on in what Eckhart said plainly to whoever would listen to him. He could not be satisfied until he had made certain of the creative, ultimate source of all being, in the only place where it can be immediately known: in the depths of the immaterial self of a man. This is Protestantism.

In the year 1309 he was nominated to the post of Superior of the German Dominican Province but, owing perhaps to his clashes with the Franciscans at Paris and perhaps to a fear of his growing power that was creeping even into Dominican minds, the nomination was not confirmed. He seems then to have had a second Paris visit, during which he began or composed his Latin masterpiece, the *Opus Tripartum*,[16] and by 1313 we find him back at Strassburg as a preacher and prior. It is probable that during this period his preaching gifts unfolded to their highest level. What prestige and respect he must have enjoyed is indicated by the fact that in his sixtieth year he was called to a post reserved for only the most eminent persons: a professorship in the college at Cologne, where the Franciscan Heinrich von Virneberg presided as archbishop and where, much to the archbishop's alarm and distaste, mystical societies proliferated.

Thus it was at this point, at the pinnacle of his career, when he had grown gray in the service of the Word of God, that there broke over him the worst trouble that could come to a medieval priest. He was formally charged with heresy, with teachings that "incited ignorant and undisciplined people to wild and dangerous excesses." In part, this charge refers to the immense popularity of his sermons.

Sadly, however, we possess hardly a sermon of Eckhart's, of which we can assert with confidence that it comes down to us unchanged from the Meister.[17] Of the twenty-eight included in this book the first four, on the birth of the Son of God, may be exceptions. The belief is that he wrote these out fully and, apart from possible editing, they are as he made them. The rest must be regarded as shrunken residues, from which the vitality of the original words is only dimly to be surmised. They have had to be disentangled from notes taken by those who listened to him, or from passages in sermons written by his followers, known to have been lifted from those notes.

It is quite probable that Eckhart did not write his sermons, but spoke from notes or outlines, depending on the gift of the moment for the embodiment of his thought. Thus he found himself saying things that surprised him too, making statements that afterwards he could only describe as "uncovered truths." What made his sermons utterly unique was the genial simplicity with which this man could turn his life inside out, again and again, and divulge the ultimate spiritual facts with childlike frankness. One quotation, translated from Schulze-Maizier's introduction to his edition will suffice, so far as comment may suffice, to indicate what Eckhart means to his countrymen of today:

"What erupts from the mountain peaks of Eckhart's preaching is none other than the secret drive of all human and superhuman desire to step beyond the limits of creaturehood and at last to feel free— free like the creative God. He who does not learn to penetrate to the bottom the frightful driving power of the human soul, to divine the Titanic power that slumbers under all human crusts like lava, will not sense the Titan that storms and presses behind all the calmness and mildness of Eckhart's preaching."[18]

The denouement of the master's career has already been sufficiently foreshadowed. This man who, with moving eloquence, told the common people about the unity of God and man, a unity so intimate that there would be no need for kneeling and bowing, no room for a priest in between, did indeed threaten to burst the ecclesiastical shell. When they overheard him say to great crowds in the churches, "Hier umbe so bite ich got, daz er mich quit mache gotes,"[19] they shook their heads, for they did not understand, or perhaps they understood only too well.

Already in 1325 loud complaints reached Dominican headquarters in Venice, of a Brother in Germany who set forth things in his sermons to the common people "which might easily lead his listeners into error." In vain Eckhart replied: "If the ignorant are not taught, they will never learn and none of them will ever know the art of living and dying. The ignorant are taught in the hope of changing them from ignorant to enlightened people."[20]

The Archbishop of Cologne who, as a Franciscan, was unfavorable to Dominicans anyway, but who was also much perplexed about what to do with the "wild" mystical movements in the Rhine valley, instituted proceedings before the Inquisition—the ecclesiastical Gestapo. Through some connivance, however, a Dominican was assigned to investigate Eckhart, who, after hearing him, acquitted him of all fault.

Needless to say, the Archbishop was annoyed. He finally succeeded in connecting Eckhart with the "Beghard" movements and then the Meister's doom was sealed. This time two Franciscans,[25] learned men, and bloodhounds for error, were turned loose on Eckhart's sermons and pamphlets and soon they had drawn up a formidable list of errors, to which he replied with his now-famous *Defense* (*Rechtfertigungsschrift*), a translation from the Latin of which the reader may consult for himself. It is a touching document—the defense of a fresh and original religious experience before an Inquisition of men who could not sympathize with him because they had had no comparable experience of their own. It is an important document because it has become a means of authenticating and identifying genuine Eckhartiana.

"I may err but I may not be a heretic—for the first has to do with the mind and the second with the will!" That, in one sentence, is his defense. With sufficient sarcasm, he pointed out to his accusers that they were really condemning Cicero, Origen, St. Thomas, other church fathers, and even the Bible itself. He warned them that they themselves might be proved to be the heretics. Then he appealed to Rome, as the privileges of his Order entitled him to do.

It should be emphasized that Meister Eckhart was really horrified by the idea of heresy himself. There was, nevertheless, this paradoxical fact that his own inner certainty was more sacred to him than any outward symbol of religion. The indwelling of the divine in his own heart was more compelling than any church requirement. To those who sought to quicken the imaginations of unimaginative people with bowings and genuflections, he replied: "You worship—you know not what!"[34] If he had stepped over the boundaries of church religion, he had done it, as he said, for the sake of religion.

At the beginning of 1327 (January 24) he was required to answer the charges at the Archbishop's court at Cologne. There he complained of the dilatory course of his case. On February 13, 1327, he preached in the Cologne church and afterwards, in a Latin statement accompanied by a German explanation, defended the faith that was in him. He insisted that he had always avoided all errors of faith and unbecoming moral conduct and said that, if erroneous statements were found in his writings or sermons, he would retract them. This offer gave color to the Pope's claim, in his bull of March 27, 1329, that Eckhart *had* retracted the errors as charged. It was, however, really a grim challenge to debate in which his accusers were reluctant to engage. On February 22, 1327, he was officially notified that his appeal to Rome had been denied. This is the last surviving notice we have of Meister Eckhart as alive. The bull of John XXII, dated March 27, 1329, speaks of him as dead.

He was spared the experience of reading that the Pope, the head of the church, regarded him as having been deceived "by the father of lies who often appears as an angel of light" into "sowing thorns and thistles amongst the faithful and even the simple folk." This would have broken his heart.

Having been condemned posthumously, it is hardly strange that for three centuries there should have been little public notice of the great mystic master. How does it happen that any remains of Eckhart at all have survived to be translated into American English in this particular year of grace—and war?

The answer is first to be sought among the "wild" mystical societies—particularly the "Friends of God," who were not squelched and who, under the leadership of Tauler and Suso, continued to flourish for many years and in one form or another (viz., Anabaptists and Quakers) still continue. We may well believe that Eckhart's remains were secretly cherished among these people, as they will be always among those who grow tired of the negations of institutional minds and hungry for some sure affirmation. Even today the scientific mind, by definition, must be skeptical and perhaps exhaust its powers in justified "No" to this and that. Only the mystic knows something to which he can say "Yes!"

The rest of the story in detail can be read in a variety of works, mostly German, but in some excellent essays on Eckhart by Josiah Royce and Rufus Jones.[21] In the middle of the seventeenth century one Johann Scheffler, whose famed pen name is Angelus Silesius, reduced Eckhart's chief ideas to clever rhymed couplets under the title *The Cherubic Wanderer (Der Cherubinische Wandersmann)*, still published and read in Germany today.[22]

Early in the nineteenth century Franz von Baader, philosophic friend of Hegel, seems to have rediscovered and recognized Eckhart's importance, as I have noted earlier. That was the real beginning of the modern Eckhart renascence. Once Eckhart had got into nineteenth century German idealism, directly or indirectly, the next step was inevitable. In 1857, Franz Pfeiffer published the sumptuous collection of Eckhart remains in the Middle High German, from which, chiefly, the translations of this book are selected. Pfeiffer's collection gave the critics sufficient material to go to work on. Two names in the history of Eckhart scholarship are worth much more than mere mention: the Roman Catholic Father H. S. Denifle (1844–1905) and Philip Strauch, who in his *Meister Eckhart Probleme* established the *Book of Divine Comfort* and *Talks of Instruction* as bases for comparisons and, more striking still, discovered and translated the papal bull in which twenty-six of Eckhart's propositions were condemned. This, together with the discovery of the Latin text of

Eckhart's *Defense*, puts us on a sure footing in the matter of distinguishing the sheep from the goats in the words attributed to the Meister himself.

Perhaps a word as to the leitmotifs of medieval thought, which Eckhart shared with his age, may be helpful to those readers who venture herewith for the first time into the field of his mysticism. The great names of Augustine (354–430), Boethius (475?–525?), and "Dionysius the Areopagite" (5th century) will come often to the eyes of the reader of Eckhart. He had pondered their efforts long and well—and a host of others whom he quotes without identification, merely noting that "an authority says. . . ." I have been able to track down very few of these.

A few remarks, therefore, about the roots of thought from which all medievals fed their minds are to the point. First and foremost was Plato and the Neoplatonist tradition, in the line of which Eckhart surely belongs. Paul Shorey remarks: "*The shortest cut to the study of the philosophy of the Middle Ages is to commit the* Timaeus *to memory.*"[26] At least a reading of this Platonic dialogue would prove helpful. It had been Boethius's chief contribution to translate into Latin—while Latin was still a living language—the *Timaeus* and most of Aristotle's *Logic*, both of which the scholastics studied avidly and pieced out from Augustine's works.[27] Thus, Aristotle set the rules of their reasoning and Plato gave them a physical and mental philosophy. For example, Meister Eckhart undoubtedly drew his notion of "bild" which appears on most of his pages from this source—the Platonic "idea"—a word nearly identical with our word "form" in meaning.

Given these, Eckhart and his age went to work on the Bible, especially on a few passages which incited them to the attack of their main problems. Through Exodus 3 :14, "*Ego sum qui sum*," they got at the problem of being. "Since in fact, God is being *per se*, and since our conception of God excludes all non-being, it follows that in Him, the fullness of existence must be completely realized."[28] This states the fact as surely for Eckhart as it did for his contemporaries.

Next in importance is the citation from Malachi 3 :6, "*Ego Dominus et non mutor,*"[29] from which they deduced that God exists because it is his nature to exist—he *is* existence, they said. This is the seed of the ontological argument for the existence of God as Anselm developed it, and the great Dominican Thomas Aquinas, Eckhart's immediate predecessor, carried it to the conclusion that "all that is not God might not exist." That is to say, the world of creatures has only contingent existence—its existence depends on God. This thought led Eckhart to his most cited heresy: "Creatures of themselves are pure nothings."[30]

Another Bible passage important, not only to the Middle Ages in general, but to Eckhart in particular, is Genesis 1:26-27, "*Let us make man in our own image . . . so God created man in his own image.*' Thence,[31] the chief problem of divine studies became that of Socrates: "*Know thyself.*" Once again the reckless pursuit of this clue led Eckhart to at least a heresy of degree, or of statement: "There is something uncreated, something divine in the soul. . . ."[32]

No reader of Meister Eckhart will understand the foregoing items to underrate the thoroughness and diligence with which he read all the Bible, Old and New Testaments and the Apocrypha alike. No complete estimate of Eckhart will be possible until his Latin commentaries on Genesis, Exodus, and the Gospel of John have been studied and translated. He fed with special appetite on the Wisdom Literature, believing philosophy literally to mean "the love of wisdom"; he quoted much from St. Paul; in his sermons he expounded the Johannine mysticism in season and out. It was not that Eckhart preached doctrines strange to orthodox ears that made him a heretic; it was rather his gift of stamping them with the vivid pattern of his own deep religious experience. He had discovered the truths contained in them within his own soul.

It is often said that the medieval thinkers were not original—and I shall not attempt to defend them against this charge: that they merely worked over the ideas of the great originators. Who ever had a truly original idea? The medievals would have answered unhesitatingly: only God. Plato thought so too. It is our custom to seek the origin of ideas by tracing their seeds in history. It is much better, I think, if one is concerned with "originality" as a virtue, to get at it as Pope did:

> True wit is nature to advantage dress'd,
> What oft was thought, but ne'er so well express'd.[33]

At least that sets forth the virtue of Meister Eckhart. He breathed his own endless vitality into the juiceless formulas of orthodox theology with such charm and passion that even the common people heard them gladly.

The Treatises

"When I preach, I usually speak of disinterest and say that a man should be empty of self and all things;

and secondly, that he should be reconstructed in the simple Good that God is;

and thirdly, that he should consider the great aristocracy which God has set up in the soul, such that by means of it man may wonderfully attain to God;

and fourthly, of the purity of the divine nature."

THESE ARE THE TALKS OF INSTRUCTION THAT THE
VICAR OF THURINGEN, THE PRIOR OF ERFURT,
BROTHER ECKHART OF THE PREACHING ORDER
HELD WITH SOME OF HIS SPIRITUAL CHILDREN,
WHO ASKED HIM ABOUT MANY THINGS AS THEY
SAT TOGETHER AT COLLATION

I

Of *true obedience*

TRUE and perfect obedience is a virtue above all virtues. No great
work can be accomplished without it; nor can there be any task,
however small or insignificant, which will not be done to better
purpose in obedience, whether it be hearing or reading the Mass, or
prayer, or contemplation, or whatever. Take any project you please,
however trifling; it is improved and exalted by obedience. Obedience
brings out the best of everything; it never fails or errs in any matter;
and no matter what you do, if you do it in true obedience, it will not
miss being good.

Obedience has no cares; it lacks no blessing. Being obedient, if a
man purifies himself, God will come into him in course; for when he
has no will of his own, then God will command for him what God
would command for himself. When I give my will up to the care of
my prelate, and have no will of my own, God must will for me; for if
he were to neglect me, he would be neglecting himself. So it is with
everything: where I do not choose for myself, God chooses for me.

What will He choose for me? That I shall not choose for myself.
When I deny myself, his will for me is identical with his will for
himself, just as if it were for him alone; and if he did not so behave,
then by the truth that God is, he would not be just, nor would he
be what it is his nature to be. You will never hear an obedient person
saying: "I want it so and so; I must have this or that." You will hear
only of utter denial of self. Therefore, in the best prayer that man

3

may offer, he will not say: "Give me virtue or a way," nor "Yea, Lord, give me thyself or life eternal," but only "Lord, give me nothing but what thou wilt and dost—Lord, what and how thou wilt in every detail!" This exceeds the first prayer as heaven the earth; and when one has achieved it, he has prayed well. He has given up to God in true obedience and just as there is no "I want this" in true obedience, so he will never be heard saying "I will not"; for "I will not" is the bane of obedience. According to St. Augustine, the true servant of God will not be pleased when someone gives him or says to him what he would like to see or hear; his first and chief care is what pleases God most.

2

Of the strongest prayer and the most exalted work

THE strongest prayer, one well-nigh almighty in what it can effect, and the most exalted work a man can do proceed from a pure heart. The more pure it is, the more powerful, and the more exalted, useful, laudable and perfect is its prayer and work. A pure heart is capable of anything.

What is a pure heart?

A pure heart is one that is unencumbered, unworried, uncommitted, and which does not want its own way about anything but which, rather, is submerged in the loving will of God, having denied self. Let a job be ever so inconsiderable, it will be raised in effectiveness and dimension by a pure heart.

We ought so to pray that every member and faculty, eyes, ears, mouth, heart, and the senses shall be directed to this end and never to cease prayer until we attain unity with him to whom our prayers and attention are directed, namely, God.

3

Of undevoted people who are full of self-will

PEOPLE say: "Alas, sir, but I would prefer to stand well with God, to have the devotion and divine calm of some people," or "I wish I could be like this or as poor as that." Or they say: "It will never do if I cannot be here or there and do thus and so. I must get away—or go into a cloister or a cell."

The truth is that you yourself are at fault in all this and no one else. It is pure self-will. Whether you realize it or not, there can be no restlessness unless it come from self-will, although not every person understands this. This is what I mean: people fly from this to seek that—these places, these people, these manners, those purposes, that activity—but they should not blame ways or things for thwarting them. When you are thwarted, it is your own attitude that is out of order.

Begin, therefore, first with self and forget yourself! If you do not first get away from self, then whatever else you get away from you will still find obstacles and restlessness. People look in vain for peace, who seek it in the world outside, in places, people, ways, activities, or in world-flight, poverty and humiliation, whatever the avenue or degree; for there is no peace this way. They are looking in the wrong direction, and the longer they look the less they find what they are looking for. They go along like someone who has missed his road; the farther they go the more they are astray.

What, then, is to be done?

Let everyone begin by denying self and in so doing he will have denied all else. Indeed, if a man gave up a kingdom, or even the whole world and still was selfish, he would have given up nothing. If, however, he denies himself, then whatever he keeps, be it wealth, honor, or anything else, he is free from it all.

Commenting on St. Peter's words, "See, Lord, we have forsaken all," when he had forsaken nothing but his nets and smacks, a saint named Hieronymous[1] says: "To give up your little bit willingly is to give up not this alone but all that worldly people seek after, indeed all they could possibly desire." To give up one's will and deny self is to forsake all else as completely as if it had been his very own, and he possessed it with full authority. For what you do not desire you let go, and let go for the sake of God. Thus our Lord says: "Blessed are the poor in spirit"—that is, [those devoid] of will and there should be no doubt that if there were a better way, the Lord would have mentioned it. But he said: "If any man will come after me, let him first deny himself." It all comes down to that. Watch yourself, and where you find self [creeping in], reject it; for that is best.

4

Of the usefulness of denial, to be practiced inwardly and outwardly

KNOW that no man in this life ever gave up so much that he could not find something else to let go. Few people, knowing what this means, can stand it long, [and yet] it is an honest requital, a just exchange. To the extent that you eliminate self from your activities, God comes into them—but not more and no less. Begin with that, and let it cost you your uttermost. In this way, and no other, is true peace to be found.

People ought not to consider so much what they are to do as what they *are*; let them but *be* good and their ways and deeds will shine brightly. If you are just, your actions will be just too. Do not think that saintliness comes from occupation; it depends rather on what one is. The kind of work we do does not make us holy but we may make it holy. However "sacred" a calling may be, as it is a calling, it has no power to sanctify; but rather as we *are* and have the divine being within, we bless each task we do, be it eating, or sleeping, or watching, or any other. Whatever they do, who have not much of [God's] nature, they work in vain.

Thus take care that your emphasis is laid on *being* good and not on the number or kind of thing to be done. Emphasize rather the fundamentals on which your work depends.[2]

5

Notice what makes nature and the fundamentals good

THIS is the basis on which human nature and spirit are wholly good, and from which our human actions receive their worth: a mind completely devoted to God. Direct your study to this end, that God shall be great in you, so that in all your comings and goings your zeal and fervor are toward him. In fact, the more you do so, the better your behavior will be, whatever your work. Hold fast to God and he will add every good thing. Seek God and you shall find him and all good with him. Indeed, with such an attitude, you might step on a stone and it would be a more pious act than to receive the body of our Lord, thinking of yourself, and it would distract your soul far less. To the man who cleaves to God, God cleaves and adds virtue. Thus, what you have sought before, now seeks you; what once you pursued, now pursues you; what once you fled, now flees you. Everything comes to him who truly comes to God, bringing all divinity with it, while all that is strange and alien flies away.

6

On solitude and the attainment of God

I WAS asked this question: "Some people withdraw from society and prefer to be alone; their peace of mind depends on it; wouldn't it be better for them to be in the church?" I replied, No! And you shall see why.

Those who do well, do well wherever they are, and in whatever company, and those who do badly, do badly wherever they are and in whatever company. But if a man does well, God is really in him, and with him everywhere, on the streets and among people, just as much as in church, or a desert place, or a cell. If he really has God, and only God, then nothing disturbs him. Why?

Because he has *only* God and thinks only God and everything is nothing but God to him. He discloses God in every act, in every place. The whole business of his person adds up to God. His actions are due only to him who is the author of them and not to himself, since he is merely the agent. If we mean God and only God, then it is he who does what we do and nothing can disturb him—neither company nor place. Thus, neither can any person disturb him, for he thinks of nothing, is looking for nothing and relishes nothing but God, who is one with him by perfect devotion. Furthermore, since God cannot be distracted by the numbers of things, neither can the person, for he is one in One, in which all divided things are gathered up to unity and there undifferentiated.

One ought to keep hold of God in everything and accustom his mind to retain God always among his feelings, thoughts, and loves. Take care how you think of God. As you think of him in church or closet, think of him everywhere. Take him with you among the crowds and turmoil of the alien world. As I have said so often, speaking of uniformity, we do not mean that one should regard all deeds, places, and people as interchangeable. That would be a great mistake; for it is better to pray than to spin and the church ranks above the street. You should, however, maintain the same mind, the same trust, and the same earnestness toward God in all your doings. Believe me, if you keep this kind of evenness, nothing can separate you from God-consciousness.

On the other hand, the person who is not conscious of God's presence, but who must always be going out to get him from this and that, who has to seek him by special methods, as by means of some activity, person, or place—such people have not attained God. It can easily happen that they are disturbed, for they have not God and they do not seek, think, and love only him, and therefore, not only will evil company be to them a stumbling block, but good company as well—not only the street, but the church; not only bad deeds and words, but good ones as well. The difficulty lies within the man for whom God has not yet become everything. If God were everything, the man would get along well wherever he went and among whatever people, for he would possess God and no one could rob him or disturb his work.

Of what does this true possession of God consist, when one really has him? It depends on the heart and an inner, intellectual return to God and not on steady contemplation by a given method. It is impossible to keep such a method in mind, or at least difficult, and even then it is not best. We ought not to have or let ourselves be satisfied with the God we have thought of, for when the thought slips the mind, that god slips with it. What we want is rather the reality of God, exalted far above any human thought or creature. Then God will not vanish unless one turns away from him of his own accord.

When one takes God as he is divine, having the reality of God within him, God sheds light on everything. Everything will taste like God and reflect him. God will shine in him all the time. He will have the disinterest, renunciation, and spiritual vision of his beloved, ever-present Lord. He will be like one athirst with a real thirst; he cannot help drinking even though he thinks of other things. Wherever he is, with whomsoever he may be, whatever his purpose or thoughts or occupation—the idea of the Drink will not depart as long as the thirst endures; and the greater the thirst the more lively, deep-seated, present, and steady the idea of the Drink will be. Or suppose one loves something with all that is in him, so that nothing else can move him or give pleasure, and he cares for that alone, looking for nothing more; then wherever he is or with whomsoever he may be, whatever he tries or does, that Something he loves will not be extinguished from his mind. He will see it everywhere, and the stronger his love grows for it the more vivid it will be. A person like this never thinks of resting because he is never tired.

The more he regards everything as divine—more divine than it is of itself—the more God will be pleased with him. To be sure, this requires effort and love, a careful cultivation of the spiritual life, and a watchful, honest, active oversight of all one's mental attitudes toward things and people. It is not to be learned by world-flight, running away from things, turning solitary and going apart from the world. Rather, one must learn an inner solitude, wherever or with whomsoever he may be. He must learn to penetrate things and find God there, to get a strong impression of God firmly fixed in his mind.

It is like learning to write. To acquire this art, one must practice much, however disagreeable or difficult it may be, however impos-

sible it may seem. Practicing earnestly and often, one learns to write,
acquires the art. To be sure, each letter must first be considered separately and accurately, reproduced over and over again; but once having acquired skill, one need not pay any attention to the reproduction [of the letters] or even think of them. He will write fluently
and freely whether it be penmanship or some bold work, in which his
art appears. It is sufficient for the writer to know that he is using his
skill and since he does not always have to think of it, he does his
work by means of it.

So a man should shine with the divine Presence without having
to work at it. He should get the essence[3] out of things and let the
things themselves alone. That requires at first attentiveness and exact
impressions, as with the student and his art. So one must be permeated with divine Presence, informed with the form of beloved
God who is within him, so that he may radiate that Presence without
working at it.

7

How a person may work most intelligently

THERE are many people who are not hindered by the things they
handle, since those things leave no lasting impression on their minds.
It is a stage easily reached if one desires to reach it, for no creature
may find a place in a heart full of God. Still we should not be satisfied, for we shall profit by assuming that things are as we are, that
they are what we see and hear, however strange and unfamiliar.
Then and not until then shall we be on the right road—a road to
which there is no end—on which one may grow without stopping,
profiting more and more by making true progress.

In all his work, and on every occasion, a man should make clear
use of his reason and have a conscious insight into himself and his
spirituality and distinguish God to the highest possible degree in
everything. One should be, as our Lord said, "Like people always
on the watch, expecting their Lord." Expectant people are watchful,
always looking for him they expect, always ready to find him in
whatever comes along; however strange it may be, they always

think he might be in it. This is what awareness of the Lord is to be like and it requires diligence that taxes a man's senses and powers to the utmost, if he is to achieve it and to take God evenly in all things—if he is to find God as much in one thing as in another.

In this regard, one kind of work does indeed differ from another but if one takes the same attitude toward each of his various occupations, then they will be all alike to him. Thus being on the right track and God meaning this to him, he will shine, as clear in worldly things as heavenly. To be sure, one must not of himself behave intemperately or as being worldly, but whatever happens to him from without, whatever he sees or hears, let him refer it to God. The man to whom God is ever present, and who controls and uses his mind to the highest degree—that man alone knows what peace is and he has the Kingdom of Heaven within him.

To be right, a person must do one of two things: either he must learn to have God in his work and hold fast to him there, or he must give up his work altogether. Since, however, man cannot live without activities that are both human and various, we must learn to keep God in everything we do, and whatever the job or place, keep on with him, letting nothing stand in our way. Therefore, when the beginner has to do with other people, let him first commit himself strongly to God and establish God firmly in his own heart, uniting his senses and thought, his will and powers with God, so that nothing else can enter his mind.

8

Of steady diligence in growing high

No work may be begun so well or done so skillfully that one may feel free and secure in his progress and then let his mind relax or go to sleep. One should always go at his work with the twin agents,[4] mind and will, alert; and thus he will do his best in the highest sense of the word and guard intelligently against apparent and subtle faults. Thus he will avoid mistakes, and progress without faltering to greater things.

9

How the inclination to sin is always beneficial

KNOW that the impulse to wrong is never without use and benefit to the just person. Let us notice that there are two sorts of people involved. One is so constituted that he has little or no impulse to do wrong, whereas the other is often strongly tempted. His outward self is easily swayed by whatever is at hand—swayed to anger, pride, sensuality or whatever, but his better nature, his higher self, remains unmoved and will not do wrong, or be angry, or sin in any way. He therefore fights hard against whichever vice is most natural to him, as people must who are by nature choleric, proud, or otherwise weak and who will not commit the sin to which they are liable. These people are more to be praised than the first kind. Their reward is also greater and their virtue of much higher rank. For the perfection of virtue comes of struggle, or, as St. Paul says, "Virtue is made perfect in weakness."[5]

The impulse to sin is not sin but to consent to sin, to give way to anger, is indeed sin. Surely, if a just person could wish such a thing, he would not wish to be rid of the impulse to sin, for without it he would be uncertain of everything he did, doubtful about what to do, and he would miss the honor and reward of struggle and victory. Because of the impulse to evil and the excitement of it, both virtue and its rewards are in travail born. The impulse to wrong makes us the more diligent in the exercise of virtue, driving us to it with a strong hand, like a hard taskmaster, forcing us to take shelter in doing well. The weaker one is, the more he is warned to strength and self-conquest; for virtue, like vice, is a matter of the will.

10

How the will is capable of anything and virtue lies in the will, if it is just

A MAN has little reason to be afraid of anything if he knows his will to be good and he should not be disturbed if he cannot realize it in deeds. Nor should he despise his virtue, knowing that virtue and every other good depend on good will. If you have good will, you shall lack for nothing, neither love, humility, nor any other virtue; what you will with all your strength you shall have, and neither God nor any creature can deprive you—if, again, your will is sound, divine and wrapt in God. Therefore, do not say "I would"—for that refers to the future; but say "I will"—that it may now be so. For notice this: if I set my heart on something a thousand miles away, it is more really mine than something I hold in my bosom but which I do not want.

Good will is not less powerful for good than bad will is for evil. Be sure of it, that even if I never do evil and yet, if I hold bad will, I shall have sinned just as much as if I had done the deed. With a will that is purely bad, I commit as great sin as if I were to murder all the people in the world, even though I did not lift a finger toward the crime. Why should not the same power reside in good will? It does—and much, incomparably more![6]

In fact, I may do anything at all with my will. I may bear the burdens of mankind, feed the poor, do the world's work and anything else I please. If I lack the power but not the will to do, then before God I have done it and no one may deny or dispute it for a moment. To will to do something as soon as I may, and to have done it, are the same in God's sight. Furthermore, if I choose that my will shall be a match for the total will of the world, and if my desire is perfect and great, then it shall be so; for what I will have I have. And so, if I really want to love as much as the world has ever loved, and thereby I mean to love God, or what you please, then it is so, when my will is perfect.

You may now be asking when the will is perfect.

It is perfect and right when it has no special reference,[7] when it has cut loose from self, and when it is transformed and adapted to the will of God. Indeed, the more like this the will is, the more perfect and true it is. With a will like this, anything is possible, whether love or anything else.

The next question is: How may I have this love when as yet I have no intimation of it, as I see other people have—their impressive actions betraying it—people in whom I discover impassioned devotion and wonder which I certainly have not?

At this point we must observe two things about love. The first is the nature of it and the second is the action which expresses the nature of love. The seat of love is in the will alone. To have more will is to have more love; but no one can tell whether another person has more love—for that is hidden in the soul, just as God lies hidden in the soul's core. Thus love depends altogether on the will; to have more will is to have more love.

There is moreover, the effect or expression of love. It often appears like a bright light,[8] as spirituality, devotion, or jubilation and yet, as such, it is by no means best! These things are not always due to love. Sometimes they come of having tasted nature's sweets. They can also be due to heavenly inspiration or to the senses, and people at their best are not the ones who experience them most. For *if* such things are really due to God, he gives them to such people to bait and allure them on and also to keep them away from [worse] company. But when such people increase in love, such [ecstatic] experiences will come less facilely, and the love that is in them will be proved by the constancy of their fidelity to God, without such enticements.

Supposing, however, that all such [experiences] were really of love, even then it would not be best. We ought to get over amusing ourselves with such raptures for the sake of that better love, and to accomplish through loving service what men most need, spiritually, socially, or physically. As I have often said, if a person were in such a rapturous state as St. Paul once entered,[9] and he knew of a sick man who wanted a cup of soup, it would be far better to withdraw from the rapture for love's sake and serve him who is in need.

No one should think that thereby he will be robbed of grace, for what we forego willingly for love's sake returns in more precious habit, as Christ said: "He who forsakes anything for my sake shall receive again an hundredfold."[10] Yes, indeed, whatever one gives up or lets pass for God's sake, even though it be the consolation he so greatly desires, or the rapture, or the spirituality he has done all he can to get, he shall actually have it as much as if he had always been fully possessed of it and as if it were the only good—especially if, when it seems that God will not give it, he is still cheerful about it, and foregoes it for God's sake.

Having willingly given up and discounted his own convenience for God, he receives again an hundredfold. For what one would like to have, what he takes comfort in and yet forswears for God's sake, whether it is physical or spiritual, he will find again in God, as if he had always had it and given it up of his own accord; for one ought to be willing to be despoiled of *anything* for God's sake and out of love, to let all comfort go and disdain it.

That we should be willing to give up [rapturous] experiences, the loving Paul tells us when he says: "I could wish that myself were cut asunder from Christ for the love of my brethren."[11] And this is what he meant—not love in the first sense of the word—a love from which he could not wish to be cut off even for a moment, for anything that might ever happen in heaven or on earth. He referred, rather, to the consolations [of Christ].

But remember that the friends of God are never without their comfort; whatever God wills is to them most consoling, whether it is comfort or discomfort.

II

*What a person should do on losing track
of God—when God is hidden from him*

You should know too that good will never misses God. To be sure, our mental processes often go wrong, so that we imagine God to have gone away. What should be done then? Do exactly what you would do if you felt most secure. Learn to behave thus even in deepest distress and keep yourself that way, in any and every estate of life. I can give you no better advice than to find God where you lost him. As it was when you last had him, so let it be now that he has disappeared and so you will find him again. Indeed, a *good* will never misses or loses God at all. To be sure, many people say "We have good will," but they have not God's will; they still want what they want and wish to instruct our Lord to do thus and so. But that is not *good* will. We should look for the most loving will in God.

In general, it is the will of God that we surrender our wills. Even though St. Paul talked much with our Lord and our Lord with him, these conversations remained fruitless until St. Paul surrendered his will and said: "Lord, what wilt thou have me to do?"[12] Then the Lord knew very well what was to be done. So it was with our Lady when the angel appeared to her.[13] All that she and he said to each other could never have made her the Mother of God, but as soon as she gave up her will she at once became the mother of the Eternal Word, conceiving God so that he became her natural Son. There is no way of making a person true unless he gives up his own will. In fact, apart from complete surrender of the will, there is no traffic with God. But if it did happen that we gave up completely and dared to put off everything, physical and spiritual, for God's sake—then we should have done all and not before.

Such people are rare. Aware of it or not, people have wanted to have the "great" experiences;[8] they want it in this form, or they want that good thing; and this is nothing but self-will. Yield completely to God and then be satisfied, whatever he does with his own. There are thousands who have died and gone to heaven who never really gave up their own wills. The only true and perfect will is the one that has been merged with the will of God, so that the man has no will of his own. And the more it is so, the more the man himself blends into God. Indeed, a single Ave Maria, said in the spirit of self-denial, is worth more than a thousand Psalms read without it. Indeed, one step taken in surrender to God is better than a journey across the ocean without it.

Thus perfectly to have given up one's own is to be merged with God, and then anyone who will touch the man must first touch God, for he is wholly within God and God is around him, as my cap is around my head, and to touch me one must first touch my clothing.

Similarly, when I drink, the drink must first pass over my tongue and there be tasted; but if my tongue is covered with a bitter coating, then however sweet the wine, it will taste bitter, because of the coating through which it reaches me. This is how it is with the person who, having given up all that is his own, is coated with God, so that no creature can touch him without first touching God, and whatever reaches him must reach him through God. Thus it gets its flavor and becomes divine.

However great an affliction may be, if it comes through God, God is afflicted first. By the truth that God is! There never was a pain that befell a man, no frustration or discouragement, however insignificant, that, transferred to God, did not affect God endlessly more than man and was not infinitely more contrary to him. So, if God puts up with it for the sake of some good he foresees for you, and if you are willing to suffer what God suffers, and to take what comes to you through him, then whatever it is, it becomes divine in itself; shame becomes honor, bitterness becomes sweet, and gross darkness, clear light. Everything takes its flavor from God and becomes divine; everything that happens betrays God when a man's mind works that way; things all have this one taste; and therefore God is the same to this man alike in life's bitterest moments and sweetest pleasures.

The light shines in the darkness and there man becomes aware of it. What is the good of light or learning except it is used? It is when people are in the dark, or suffering, that they are to see the light.

The truth is that the more ourselves we are, the less self is in us. That man who has denied himself will never lose track of God whatever his activity. If he makes mistakes, says bad things or does wrong, if God was at the bottom of it, he will take the blame and therefore these things should never distract us from our work. Illustrations of this are to be found in St. Bernard and many other holy ones. We shall never be free from such episodes in this life and we do not throw away the good grain just because the rats often get into it. To the just man who is well acquainted with God, pains and untoward episodes are quite fruitful, for all things work together for good,[14] as St. Paul and St. Augustine both tell us—and this includes sin too.

12

This is about sin and what one should do when he discovers that he is sinning

TRULY, it is not sin to have sinned and repent of it. Only do not consent to sin—not for anything that might happen in time or eternity—neither to mortal nor to venial sin, nor any other kind. Those who are well grounded in God are always aware that the faithful, loving

God has lifted them out of a life of sin into life that is divine, having changed enemies to friends, and to them that means more than the creation of a new world. This is one of the strongest motives urging man to God and, when he completely denies himself, it is astonishing how much stronger the love and greater love the self-denial will engender.

Indeed, once justly set in the will of God, a man will not wish that the sin he committed had never happened. To be sure, it was contrary to God, but by it he is committed to greater love, being abased and humbled because he did act contrary to [the will of] God. You may, however, fully trust God not to have put the sin upon you, except to bring out the best that is in you. Thus when you rise above sin and turn away from it, God, who is faithful, will act as if you had never sinned at all and not for a moment will He let the former sins count against you.

Even if your sins were as great in number as all mankind's put together, still he would not count them against you and he would still have as much confidence in you as he ever had in any creature. If only he finds you ready, he will pay no attention to what you were before. God is God of the present; as he finds a man, so he takes him and accepts him, not for what he has been but for what he is now. All the evil and outrage done to God in sin, he will gladly suffer and suffer for many years to come, if only he may bring man to a better knowledge of his love, and make man's affection and thankfulness warmer, his struggle more passionate—as so often it is, after one has sinned.

Thus God bears the brunt of sin gladly and puts up with a lot of it. Most often, he causes people to sin when he foresees that by sinning they will move up to higher things. Consider this: who was ever dearer to our Lord, or more intimate with him than the apostles? There was not one of them that did not commit mortal sin; all of them were mortal sinners. In the Old and New Testaments he often indicates that this is true of them that afterwards he will love most dearly. Even today, one seldom hears of people achieving great things without first making mistakes. It is our Lord's intention that thus we shall learn how great his compassion is and be warned to greater humility and devotion. New repentance makes new love and increases it.

13

Of two kinds of repentance

THERE are two kinds of repentance. One is temporal and sensual and the other is divine and supernatural. The first always drags man down, into ever greater woe, causing him to complain, leaving him in doubt; and thus this repentance sticks in misery, getting no further. Nothing comes of it.

Divine repentance, however, is quite different. Displeased with himself, man rises at once to God, turning with unmovable will against all sin. Thence he rises to a lively faith in God and, gaining certainty, he receives that spiritual joy that lifts the soul above all sorrow and complaint and fixes it in God. The frailer one knows himself to be, the more evil he has done, the more reason he has to tie to God with undivided love—to God in whom no sins or frailties are. The best thing one may do when he wants perfect devotion to God is to get rid of his sin by means of divine repentance.

The more grievous a man's sins seem to him, the readier God is to forgive them, to enter the soul and drive them out; for everyone is most diligent in getting rid of what is most disagreeable to him. The more in number a man's sins are, the greater they are, the more immeasurably glad God is to forgive them. The more they irk him, the quicker he is about it. The sooner divine repentance reaches up to God, the sooner the sins are swallowed up in the abyss of God— as quickly as I can shut my eyes. They are annihilated as if they had never happened, if only the repentance be whole.

14

About genuine confidence and hope

TRUE and perfect love is demonstrated when a man has great hope and confidence in God. There is nothing to test the perfection of love better than trust. Wholehearted love for another person carries confidence with it. Whatever one dares to trust God for, he really finds in God and a thousand times more. And just as man can never love God too much, so he can never put too much confidence in God. There is nothing else a man can do that is so beneficial as to put complete trust in God. God never failed anyone who trusted him greatly but rather, by them, he does great things. To have this confidence is also to be aware that it comes of love; for love carries not only trust but true knowledge and undoubting certainty.

15

Of two kinds of certainty of eternal life

IN THIS life there are two kinds of certainty about eternal life. The first is based on the belief that God himself tells man about it, or that he sends word through an angel, or reveals it in some special illumination. These rarely happen, and to few people.

The second kind is incomparably better and more useful and common among people who love wholeheartedly. It is based on the love for God and the intimacy with him which binds man to him, by which he has full confidence in God and is so completely certain of him that he loves God, without making any differences, in all creatures. And even though creatures denied God and forswore him, and even though God denied himself, still he would not mistrust, because love cannot mistrust. Love is confidence itself in the good and therefore there is no need to speak of the Lover and the beloved; for once a man discovers that God is his friend, he knows what is good for him and all that belongs to his happiness. Of this you may be sure, that however dear you are to God, he is immeasurably dearer to you and he trusts you that much more; for he himself is the confidence by which one is sure of him, as sure as all who love him are.

This certainty is far stronger than the first kind, and more perfect, and truer. It does not deceive. Verbal telling might well be deceptive and throw a false light on the whole matter. What is more, this certainty is to be found in all the soul's agents. That is why it will not deceive true lovers of God. They will no more doubt it than they would doubt God himself, for love drives out all fear, or, as St. Paul says, love knows no fear.[15]

It is further written that love hides a multitude of sins.[16] Perfect love and confidence cannot be where sins are, but love does hide sin completely. Love knows nothing of sin—not that man has not sinned—but sins are blotted out at once by love and they vanish as if they had not been. This is because whatever God does he does completely, like the cup running over. Whom he forgives, he forgives utterly and at once, much preferring great forgiveness to little; for complete confidence is like that.

I regard this view as much better—nay, incomparably better—than the first, and more rewarding, more certain. Neither sin nor anything else is an obstacle to it. Those whom God finds alike in love, he rates as equals, whether their misdeeds are great or small. Moreover, to be forgiven much is to love much, as our Lord Jesus Christ said: "He to whom much has been forgiven will love much."[17]

16

About true penitence and the blessed life

IT SEEMS to many people that to be "penitent" they must do striking things, external acts, such as fasting, going barefoot, and the like. The best penitence, however, and the supremely profitable penance, is to turn away, root and branch, from all that is not God and not divine, whether it be in one's self or in other creatures. The true penitence is to face about toward our beloved God, with unwavering affection, so that all we think about and delight in is pregnant with him. However you can accomplish this is the way for you, and the more you do it the more real your penitence or penance will be, the more your sins will be washed away, together with the pain of them. Indeed, if in some moment of time you could turn sheer away from all your sins, with disgust and repugnance for them, and effectually turn to God, then, even if you had committed all the sins since Adam's or all that ever could be committed, you would be forgiven instantly and the pains of them would be remitted, so that if you died then you would rise at once, face to face with God.

True penitence is like this and it appears most exquisitely in the perfect passion of our Lord Jesus Christ. The more one copies that, the more his sins will fall away, together with the pains of them. Make it a life-habit to copy the Lord Jesus Christ, the things he did and forbore to do, his life and passion, and think of him at all times as he did of us.

This penitence is simply a [state of] mind exalted above things to God and whatever the exercises that help you most to keep it, do them most diligently. If there are any that hinder, stop them at once, whether watching, fasting, study, or whatever; and then do not fret about whether or not your penitence is being neglected. God does not look at what you do but only at your love and at the devotion and will behind your deeds. It matters little to him what we do but he does care a lot about the attitudes our deeds express. He is concerned only that we shall love him in all things. A man who is not then satisfied with God is much too greedy. This, then, is the reward of all you do, that God knows about it and that through your deeds you aimed at him. Let that be enough. The more purely and simply you go out to him, the more thoroughly your deeds will wash your sins away.

Remember this too, that God has been the common Savior of the whole world. I am indebted to him for this much more than if he had saved only me. Similarly, you, too, shall be the common savior of all that, in yourself, you have spoiled by sin, when once you are wholly committed to him. For you *have* spoiled all that you are with sin—your heart and mind, body, soul, and faculties. It is all quite sick and decaying. Therefore fly to him in whom there is no wrong, but only good, so that he may be to you the common Savior of all that is spoiled by sin within and without.

17

How to be at peace and to follow after God when you discover that you are not taking the pains and doing as Christ and many of his saints have done

ANXIETY and discouragement may easily come to people when they see how strict and diligent the lives of our Lord Jesus Christ and his saints have been, and that humanly we are not up to their level, nor even much inclined to be. When people find that they are otherwise disposed, they think they are apart from God—so far apart that they cannot follow him. Let no one think that! No one may say at any time that he is apart from God, either because of his faults, or infirmities or anything else. If, however, by reason of a great fault, you are an outcast, so that you are not able to approach God at all, then, of all times, consider that God is near you, for great harm comes of feeling that God is distant. For let a man go away or come back: God never leaves. He is always at hand and if he cannot get into your life, still he is never farther away than the door.

So it is with the strenuous life of discipleship. See how this applies to your discipleship. Notice, as you must have already, just what God exhorts you to do, for all people are not called to God by the same road, as St. Paul says. If you find that your shortest road is not via visible works and great efforts and privations, which things, after all, are of no great importance, unless one is specially required by God to do them—and one is strong enough to take it without disturbing his spiritual life—if, then, you find that this way is not for you, take it calmly and make nothing of it.

Perhaps you will say: If these things make no difference, why did our forebears and many of the saints do them?

Now consider: Our Lord was to them a pattern and also the strength to follow it as they understood it and therefore that was the way they could do their best; but God never tied man's salvation to any pattern. Whatever possibilities inhere in any pattern of life inhere in all, because God has given it so and denied it to none. One good way does not conflict with another and people should know that they are wrong when, seeing or hearing of some good man that his way is not like their own, they say that his is just so much labor lost. Because that person's life pattern does not please them, they decry it, together with his good intentions. That is not right! We ought rather to observe the ways of other good people and despise none of them. Let each keep his own way and absorb into it the good features of other ways and thus include in his own the merits of all. A change of life pattern makes for unstable mind and character. What you get out of one pattern may be worked out in another, provided it, too, is good, praiseworthy and directed toward God only—for not all people may travel the same road.

So it is with following the strenuous way of certain saints. You may admire the pattern of their lives; they may please you immensely; and still you may not be able to go their way.

You may, however, say of the Lord Jesus Christ, that his way was always the highest and that we ought to follow him in it. That may be true, but our Lord should be followed reasonably and not by details. He fasted forty days: no one is called upon to copy him literally in that. There are other things he did, in which he meant us to follow him spiritually and not literally. We should take care to follow him intelligently, for he is much more intent on our love than on our actions. We are always to follow him in our own way.

But how?

The manner and the method must be settled in each situation individually. As I have often said, I regard intelligent action as far better than literal actions. What does that mean?

Christ fasted forty days. Follow him by observing what [bad habit] you are most inclined to and refuse to do that. But look well to yourself: it will profit you more to abstain from that [habit] without regret than to abstain from food completely.

Even so, it is often harder to keep back one word than it is to abstain from speech altogether. Sometimes people find it more difficult to pass over one little spiteful word, unimportant in itself, then to bear a heavy blow for which they are prepared; harder to be alone in a crowd than to be alone in a desert; harder to give up a little thing than a great one; harder to do a little job than one that seems important. So, in his weakness, a man may follow our Lord and not assume that he is far away.

18

How to take fine food, nice clothes, and jolly company as one ought, when they happen to come along

You shall not be concerned about the style of your food and clothing, thus laying too much stress on them, but rather accustom your heart and mind to be exalted above such things, so that nothing may move you to pleasure or to love except God alone. Let your thoughts be above all else.

Why?

Because only a feeble spirit could be moved by the garments of appearance; the inner man should govern the outer, and only this will do for you. But if it happens that you are well off, in your heart be tranquil about it—if you can be just as glad and willing for the opposite condition. So let it be with food, friends, kindred, or anything else that God gives or takes away.

So I hold this to be best, that a man should give himself over to God and let God throw on him what he will, offenses, work, or suffering, and that then he takes them gladly and thankfully, allowing God to put such things upon him even if he does not choose them for himself. To learn from God gladly in all things, and to follow after him only, is to be on the right track. In this frame of mind, a man may enjoy his honor or comfort—if he is just as glad to take hardship and disgrace when they come along. Thus, they may eat with perfect right and good conscience who are as ready and glad to fast.

Probably this is the reason why God spares his friends so many and such great wounds—which his incomparable honor would not otherwise permit: many and great are the blessings to be found in suffering. And while it would not suit God, nor would he wish to withhold any good thing, yet sometimes he does withhold these things, being content with his just good will; and again, he skips

no degree of suffering because of the benefits inherent in it. Therefore, you should be content as long as God is, and inwardly so
responsive to his will as not to be concerned with ways and works.
Avoid especially any singularity in clothes, food, or speech, such
as the use of high-flown language, for example, or eccentric man-
nerisms, which help not at all.

Still, you should know that not all singularity is forbidden. On
many occasions, among many people, you will have to be singular.
There are times when distinctive people cannot avoid standing out
in many ways, for spiritually a man must conform to our Lord Jesus
Christ in all things so that men may see his divine form, the reflection
of him at work. In all you do, keep in yourself as perfect a likeness of
him as possible. You are to sow and he is to reap. Work devotedly,
with wholehearted conviction, and thus train your mind and heart
so that you may represent him at all times.

19

Why God often allows people who are really good to be hindered in doing pious works

THE faithful God often lets his friends fall sick and lets every prop
on which they lean be knocked out from under them. It is a great joy
to loving people to be able to do important things such as watching,
fasting, and the like, besides sundry more difficult undertakings. In
such things they find their joy, their stay and hope. Thus their
pious works are supports, stays, or footings to them. Our Lord wants
to take these things all away, for he would like to be their only
stay. He does this because of his simple goodness and mercy. He
wants nothing more than his own goodness. He will not be influenced in the least to give or do by any act of ours. Our Lord wants
his friends to be rid of such notions. That is why he removes every
prop, so that he alone may support them. It is his will to give
greatly but only because of his own free goodness, so that he shall
be their support and they, finding themselves to be nothing at all,
may know how great the generosity of God is. For the more helpless
and destitute the mind that turns to God for support can be, the

deeper the person penetrates God and the more sensitive he is to God's most valuable gifts. Man must build on God alone.

20

About the body of our Lord, how often
one should partake of it, with what
devotion and in what manner

THOSE who would like to partake of the body of our Lord should not wait until they feel an upsurge of emotion or devotion but let them rather consider their attitude or disposition [toward it]. Attach significance, not to what you feel like, but rather to what you are to receive and to your thoughts about it.

The person who wants to go to our Lord and go with a free heart, must first make sure that his conscience is without reproach. In the second place, his will must point only to God and he must so concentrate on God that he can take pleasure in nothing but God, and so that he will be displeased by all that is not leading to God. This is the test by which one may prove how far away from God he is— or how near—according as he is less or more this way. The third rule is that his affection for our Lord shall grow with each repeated communion and that his reverence for the sacrament does not diminish with familiarity.

It is often true that what is life to one is death to another. Therefore, be careful that your love for God grows and your reverence does not die out. Then, granted that, the oftener you take the sacrament the better off you will be and the more salutary and beneficial you will find it. Thus, do not let any speech or sermon persuade you away from your God, for the more you go the better, and the dearer God will be to you.

For our Lord takes pleasure by living in men and with them. But perhaps you say: "Yes, sir, but I feel so bare and cold and dull that I dare not go to the Lord!" To which I reply:

So much the more your need to go to God! Being joined to him, made one with him, you will be justified; for the grace you shall find in the sacrament will nowhere else be so evident. There, your

physical powers will be assembled and focused by the superlative
power of the presence of our Lord's body, the scattered senses
brought together into unison, and several of them, being aimed too
low, will be lifted up so that they, too, point, like true offerings,
to God.

Then the loving God conditions them to spiritual ways, weans
them from the obstruction of temporal things, makes them adroit
in matters divine, strengthens and renews them by his body. For we
are to be changed into him and sometime made One with him, so
that what is his shall be ours and what is ours, his: our hearts and
his are to be one heart; our body and his, one body. So, too, it shall
be with our senses, wills, thoughts, faculties, and members: they
are all to be transported into him, so that we feel with him and are
made aware of him in every part of the body and soul.

Perhaps you say: "But, sir, I am not aware that I have anything
to offer more impressive than poverty; how then can I go to him?"

My goodness! If you want to exchange your poverty, why not go
straight to that treasury of inestimable value and get rich? For you
ought to know that, as far as you are concerned, his is the only
treasure with which you will be contented or satisfied. Therefore
say to him: "I am coming to you so that your wealth may supply
my poverty, so that the unsearchable You may fill my emptiness
and your unlimited Godhead, more than man may conceive, shall
fulfill my base, spoiled humanity."

"But, sir, I have sinned too much; I shall never be able to atone!"

For that reason, go to him; he has richly atoned for your guilt.
It is your free opportunity to make the best of all offerings for your
guilt to the heavenly Father through him.

"But, sir, I should like to be able to thank God; but I cannot!"

Still go to him, for our Lord alone is agreeable to the divine
goodness and a perfect, unquestionable, and true measure of gratitude
to God. In brief, if you want to be relieved of all your defects and
be clad in garments of virtue and grace, and to be led with joy again
to the Source of your being, plan to partake worthily and often of
the sacrament and so be joined to our Lord, ennobled by his body.

Indeed, the soul, too, may be led so near to God by the body of our
Lord that all the angels, not excepting the Cherubim and Seraphim,

shall not see any difference. For where they touch God they touch the soul, and where they touch the soul they touch God. There never was another such union [as between the soul and God], for the soul is nearer to God than it is to the body which makes us human. It is more intimate with him than a drop of water put into a vat of wine, for that would still be water and wine; but here, one is changed into the other so that no creature could ever again detect a difference between them.

Still you may say: "How can this be? There is nothing in my experience to correspond to it!"

What difference does that make? The less you experience and yet believe such things the more praiseworthy your faith will be, and the more distinctive and worth while; for perfect faith is much more than human illusion. Through our Lord we get certain knowledge. The truth is that we lack nothing but perfect faith. That it seems to us that one thing is better than another is due merely to our physical limitations, for one thing is not more than another. If you have the same faith in everything, you will get as much, and have as much, out of one thing as another.

You might also say: "How may I believe such great things, while I am still so defective and given to so many other matters?"

See! You must observe two things about yourself that our Lord also had to deal with. He, too, had higher and lower powers,[18] each having its own function. By his higher powers, he possessed and enjoyed the bliss of eternity while, at the same time, by his lower powers, he went through much suffering and struggle here on earth, and still this did not inhibit the function of the higher powers. So it should be with you. Your higher faculties should be trained on God, offered up to him and consecrated to him at all times.

Moreover, we should assign suffering solely to the body, the lower faculties and the senses, and with all our strength freely plunge the spirit into God. The spirit will not be tempted by suffering, the senses and [concerns of] the lower faculties. The increasing struggle, becoming ever more fierce, only magnifies the victory and emphasizes the glory of it. The stronger the temptation, the more insistent the impulse to vice, the more genuine man's virtue will be and the dearer to God, once he has overcome it. Therefore, if you wish to receive God worthily, take care that your higher powers are directed toward God, that your will is seeking his; be careful also what you think about him and to fix your faith in him.

One does not receive the true body of our Lord, having this attitude, without receiving a special measure of grace and the more often it is so the better. Indeed, it is possible to receive the body of the Lord with such devotion and consideration, one's life being otherwise well-ordered, that he is received up into the lowest choir of angels. Again, it may so be received that one is raised up into the second choir. Indeed, you may so receive it as to be worthy of the eighth or ninth choir.[19]

Thus, if two persons lived alike and one received the body of the Lord worthily, once more than the other, he would be to that other person like a blinding sun and would have a special unity with God.

This partaking of the blessed body of our Lord and the enjoyment of it consists not only of the visible enjoyment involved, but also of the spiritual partaking of divine unison and devotion by a hungry heart. One may eat of this [inner food] until he becomes richer in grace than any other person on earth. He may eat it a thousand times a day and oftener wherever he wishes, whether sick or well. He may prepare for it as for the sacrament, by means of a well-ordered life and great desire for it. If, however, one is not orderly and has not the desire, he should compel himself to it, and keep at it, until in time he does become holy and in eternity, blessed. May the Lord grant us the truth, the requisite love of purity and life eternal. Amen.

21

About devotion

WHEN taking our Lord's body, one does well not to be worried. Thus it is proper and useful first to go to confession, even if one's conscience does not hurt, just for the sake of the sacrament of confession and its fruits. If, however, a person is guilty and no confessional is available, let him go to God acknowledging his fault with great penitence and rest easy on that score until a confessional is convenient; and meanwhile, if he forgets the reproach of his sins, he may take it that God, too, has forgotten. We ought sooner to confess to God than to men, for if one *is* guilty he is bound to take his confession before God seriously and call himself to order. Also, being in the habit of the sacrament, one should not give it up lightly in order to attend to other affairs, even if, in so doing, his intentions are good, godly, and just.

We ought to learn how to keep a free mind in all we do, but it is rare that an untrained person can do this, so that neither circumstances nor jobs bother him. It requires great diligence. Expert attention is necessary. To be aware of God at all times and to be enlightened by him equally under all circumstances, there are two special requirements. First: be spiritually quite private, guarding the mind carefully against irrelevant ideas, so as to keep them out and not deal in them, giving them no place in your life. The second has to do with the mind's own inventions, whether spontaneous in the mind or representing some object, or whatever their nature. Do not be dissipated in such ideas lest you become lost in the crowd of them. For these two requirements, for this goal, one must focus all his mental powers and train his mind, for he will need to have his wits about him.

You may say: "But when a person has a job to do, he must give attention to it and thus concentrate on external things, for it takes an idea to make a job possible." And that is quite true, but the reference of ideas to things does not belong to the objective world as far as the spiritual [subjective?] man is concerned, for all things are to him simply channels of the divine and spiritual.

And this viewpoint is possible only through discipline and the training of the intellect to the ways of God and, doing this, a man will become, in time, divine within. The mind does not get as close to anything as God does, nor is it so germane to things, nor do they require its presence [as they require God]. Thus, there is no need for the mind to turn elsewhere [than to God] and it never attends to creatures without suffering violence and being hurt and perverted [by the distraction]. When the mind has once been spoiled in youth, or any other age for that matter, every effort should be made to correct it, to withdraw it to its proper sphere and to train it there. However natural and native God is to the mind, once the mind has digressed, taken root in creatures, and been perverted by them and become accustomed to them, it is proportionately infected and enfeebled, handicapped for its nobler functions, so that every effort one may make is always too little to effect the mind's restoration. Then, even if one does succeed, he will require constant protection [against relapse].

Above all a person should take care to discipline himself strictly and thoroughly. It would be fatal for an undisciplined and unskilled person to try to do what an expert may do and, what is more, he would get nowhere by trying. Only when he has been thoroughly weaned away from things and things are alien to him—only then may a man do as he pleases with things, free to take them or leave them with impunity. The undisciplined person, however, cannot take pleasure or indulge in meat or drink or whatever he is fond of, without harm.

We must learn neither to seek nor to take our own advantage in any matter, but always to find and procure the advantage of God. For God does not give gifts, nor did he ever give one, so that man might keep it and take satisfaction in it; but all were given—all he ever gave on earth or in heaven—that he might give this one more: himself. With all his giving, he is trying only to prepare us for the gift that he himself is; and all his works—all that he ever did on earth or in heaven—he did for the sake of this one more: to perfect our happiness. Therefore I say that we must learn to look through every gift and every event to God and never be content with the thing itself. There is no stopping place in this life—no, nor was there ever one for any man, no matter how far along his way he'd gone. This above all, then, be ready at all times for the gifts of God and always for new ones.

Let me tell an anecdote about someone who greatly desired something of our Lord. I told her that she was not ready for it and that if God gave it to her, while still she was not ready, it would hurt her. You ask: "Why was she not ready? Hadn't she goodwill? You say that, given the will, everything is possible and that everything, perfection included, depends on the will."

That is correct; but "will" must be understood in two senses. There is first the contingent and nonessential will and then there is the providential will, creative and habitual. The truth is that it is not enough that the heart of man shall have its detached moments, in which to seek union with God; but there must be a disciplined detachment which precedes and follows [the moment of union] and only in that way may man receive the great things of God and God himself in them. If, however, one is not ready for the gifts, they do harm and God in them. That is why God cannot always give us the things we ask for. The fault is not on his side; he is a thousand times more ready to give than we are to receive. It is we who do violence and wrong him by hindering his natural action with our unreadiness.

We ought to learn through God's gifts to get away from selfishness, to care no more for what we have a right to, to seek nothing for our own, neither instrument, pleasure, spirituality, delight, reward, the Kingdom of Heaven, nor that our wills be done. God never gave himself, nor will he ever, to one whose will is alien to his own. He does not give himself except through his will. Where God finds his will done, there he gives himself and enters [the world] with all that he is, and the more we depart from self, the more this [self-giving of God] will be realized. Therefore it is not enough to surrender self and all that goes with it once. We have to renew the surrender often, for thus we shall be free and unfettered in all we do.

It is also a good thing for a person not to be content merely with entertaining the notion of virtues, such as obedience, poverty, and the like, but to exhibit their fruits in his deeds, often examining himself, with the desire and will that other people shall examine him and put him to the test. Neither is it enough merely to act virtuously, by obeying, or adopting poverty, or being singular, or being humble, or allowing oneself to be neglected. We should keep at it and never cease to do these things until we have acquired the essence of virtue, the root of it. One may test the degree to which he has attained to virtue by observing how often one is inclined to act virtuously rather than otherwise. When one can do the works of virtue without preparing, by willing to do them, and bring to completion some great and righteous matter without giving it a thought

—when the deed of virtue seems to happen by itself, simply because one loved goodness and for no other reason, then one is perfectly virtuous and not before.

Let us learn self-forgetting until we call nothing more our own. Know it or not, the storms of unrest come of self-will. We should commit ourselves and all our minds to the complete undoing of will, to desire only that we may fall in with the good and loving will of God, taking along all we will or want.

A question: "Should even the delight of God-enjoyment be renounced? Would this not mean laziness and weak will Godward?"

Yes, to be sure, if there be no discrimination; but one can tell whether or not this is due to laziness, or true disinterest, or renunciation. When you are in low condition, and feel forsaken, see if you are just as true to him as when your sense of him is most vivid and if you act the same when you think all help and comfort far removed as you do when God seems nearest.

No time will be too little for the just man whose will is good. For when a man will do as much as he can now, and not only now, but as much as he could if he lived a thousand years, his will counts as much as all the deeds he might do in that thousand years; before God, he has done all.

22

*How to follow after God
and some good ways to do it*

WHEN you are about to begin a new life or work, go to God and ask with all your might and devotion that he will make it turn out for the best, as it seems most agreeable and fitting to him and be sure you are not thinking of your own advantage but only of God's dearest will and nothing else. Then whatever God brings about, take it as direct from him—the best as he sees it—and be completely satisfied.

Then afterward, perhaps a better way will occur to you and you should think: "It was this way that God meant for you and so he must think it best." Thus, trust God and gather up each good method as it comes into your one way [your trust in God], and use everything, of whatever kind, accordingly. For the good that God does, the good that he gives in one way, man may discover in a variety of ways. We must see that all good ways belong together in the One Way. That One Way is no specialty.

Still, a man must ever do one thing; he cannot do everything. He must always be one person and yet take everything into himself. For if he tried to do everything, now this, now that, forsaking his own way to take on another which, for the moment, pleased him better, he would soon become quite unstable. One who leaves the world and once and for all time joins an order, will achieve mastery sooner than one who left his own order to join another, however more holy it might be. This follows simply from the change of orders. Let a person choose one good way for himself and stick to it always and co-ordinate other good ways with his own, observing only that they are all God's. Let him not begin with one today and take another tomorrow.

One should not worry that he is missing something this way. For with God one will not miss anything; for as little as God would be likely to overlook, so little may we overlook with him. Therefore, take your own good way as it comes from God and [believe] that it can include all good ways.

If, however, [of two good ways] one is not to be reconciled with another, that is a sure sign that one of them is not from God. One good will not contradict another, as our Lord says: "Every kingdom divided against itself is brought to desolation,"[20] and "He that is not with me is against me; and he that gathereth not with me, scattereth abroad." This is a sure sign: when one good clashes with another or, perhaps, a greater good clashes with a lesser, one of them is not from God. Good builds up and does not destroy.

Briefly, this is true, and not open to doubt: God always gives his best to everybody and he never accepts a person lying down when he could be standing up, for out of his Godhead God knows what is best for each thing.

At that, one may inquire: When God knows which people are going to fall from the grace of their baptism, why does he not take them, so that they die with their infancy before they reach the age of discretion; especially when he knows that they will fall and not rise again? Would this not be better for them?

To which I reply: God is not a destroyer of anything that is good.[25] He is a fulfiller. He is a perfecter of nature and never one to overthrow it. His grace will not negate nature but perfect it until it is at its best. If he were to disorganize nature like that in its beginning, nature would be violated and wronged, which is something he will not do. Man has a free will by which he may distinguish between good and evil and choose which he will. He tells man that death is to result from evil-doing and life from doing good, and otherwise man is free, a master of his actions, who is not destroyed or coerced. Grace does not overcome nature but makes it perfect. There is nothing in God to destroy anything that has the least being. Quite to the contrary, he it is that makes all things right. Thus a greater good or program should never be allowed to destroy a little one or a lesser one but should make each attain to its utmost perfection.

There was some talk about a certain man who wanted to make a fresh start in life and I spoke of it this way: He ought to become a God-seeker in all things and a God-finder at all times. [He should pursue this objective] in all places, among all kinds of people and by every possible method. In this way, he will always make progress and grow, and never come to the end of his way.

23

About activities of the inner life and outer life

IF A person withdraws into himself, with all his powers, mental and physical (i.e., agents of his soul), he comes at last to a condition in which he has no ideas and no limitations and in which he exists without activity of inner or outward life.

He should observe, then, whether or not he is moved to come back to life, but if he finds that he has no urge to get back to work or responsible activity, then he should break loose and get to work of some kind, mental or physical. For a man should never be content [with such indulgence] however good it may be or seem to be, which really does violence to his nature and of which it could be said that he is doing no work, but is merely worked upon, for we must learn to co-operate with God.

Not that one should give up, neglect or forget his inner life for a moment, but he must learn to work in it, with it and out of it, so that the unity of his soul may break out into his activities and his activities shall lead him back to that unity. In this way one is taught to work as a free man should [dispassionately]. Keep your eye on the functioning of your inner life and start from there—to read, or pray, or to do any needed outward deed. If, however, the outward life interferes with the inner, then follow the inner; but if the two can go on together, that is best of all and then man is working together with God.

Comes now the question: How is man thus to work together with God? When a man is rid of self and his own efforts, as St. Dionysius says: "He speaks best of God who in the fullness of his inner riches can best keep silence"? When ideas and efforts fall away and man is given to praise and thanksgiving and such things?

An answer: A single act remains to him, justly and properly his own, and that is, of course, to reduce self to nothingness. Still this annihilation or diminution of self never gets so far that if God did not finish it in himself, it would be imperfect. Humility becomes sufficiently perfect only when God humiliates a man by means of himself. Not until then will he be content or virtue satisfied.

Question: How does God bring the self down to nothing by means of self? It would seem that the reduction of man is the exaltation of God, as the gospel says: "He that humbleth himself shall be exalted."[21]

Answer: Yes and No. Even if a man does humble himself he cannot do it sufficiently, so God has to do it and then the man is exalted. Not that humiliation is one thing and exaltation another, but the highest heights of exaltation lie precisely in the lowest depths of humiliation; for the deeper the valleys go, the loftier the heights that rise above them; the deeper the well, the higher too: for depth and height are the same thing. Therefore the more humble a man may be, the more exalted he will be. Our Lord said: "He that is greatest among you shall be your servant."[22] To be one, you must

be the other too. To be this, you must become that. To become a
servant is to become in fact great so that one who has become a
servant is already a great person. It is thus that the words of the
evangelist are carried out: "He that humbleth himself shall be
exalted." All our being depends therefore on not being.

It is written: "They have become rich in virtue," and that will
never happen except we become poor in things. He who will have all
things must first give them all up. That is fair dealing and a just
bargain, as I said once before. Therefore, if God is to give us himself
and everything else, freely to be our own, he must first take all we
have away. Yes, indeed, for God is not willing that we should keep
even so much as the speck of dust that might lodge in the eye; for of
all his gifts, gifts of nature, gifts of grace, not one was made with
the idea that we should ever regard them as our property. He never
gave on any other condition even to his mother, or to any other person or creature; and in order to teach us that, to impress it on us, he
frequently takes away everything, physical and spiritual. Not even
honor shall be ours but it shall belong to him alone. We are to have
what we have as if it were loaned to us and not given; to be without
proprietary rights to body or soul, mind or faculties, worldly goods
or honors, friends, relations, houses, castles, or anything else.

Why does God stress this point so much?

Because he wants to be ours exclusively. His chief delight and
fun consist of this and the more exclusively he can be our own the
greater his joy is. Thus the more things we keep for ourselves, the
less we have his love; the less we own things, the more we shall own
him and his. When our Lord went to speak of things that are
blessed, he put poverty of spirit at the top of the list and that shows
that all blessings and perfection begin with being "poor in spirit."
In fact, that is the only foundation on which any good may rest;
otherwise, [what seems good is] nothing at all, neither this nor that.
When we get rid of outward things, in return, God shall give us all
that heaven contains, yes, heaven and all its powers, and all that
flows out of God. Whatever the saints and angels have shall be ours
as much as theirs.

If, therefore, I deny myself, God will be mine much more than
any thing could be; he shall be mine as much as his own, neither less

nor more. He will be mine a thousand times more than any personal property one might own and keep in a safe. Nothing was ever owned to the degree that God may be my own, together with all that is his.

We shall merit this divine proprietorship by relinquishing all our rights to what is not God in this world. The purer and more perfect our spiritual poverty becomes, the more our right to him will grow. Still we ought never to think of this as a payment, much less keep it in view as such, casting furtive glances at it as if it were a profit to be made or a gift to be coaxed. It comes only by love of virtue: the poorer, the richer; or, as St. Paul says: "As having nothing, yet possessing all things." He has no sense of proprietorship who wants nothing and does not intend to have anything, either of his own or the world's things about him, no, nor wants even God or anything else.

Do you want to know what a really poor person is like?

To be poor in spirit is to get along without everything not necessary. That person who sat naked in his tub said to the mighty Alexander who had all the world under his feet:[23] "I am a greater Lord than you are, for I have despised more than you have possessed. What you have felt so proud to own, I think too little even to despise." He is far more blessed who gets along without things because he does not need them, than he who owns everything because he needs it all; but best of all is the person who can go without because he has no need. Those, therefore, who can dispense with more and scorn more will have denied themselves more. It looks like a great deed when, for God's sake, someone gives a thousand marks of gold to feed the poor and build convents and cloisters, but much more blessed is he who disdains that much stuff on account of God. A person really has the Kingdom of Heaven when he is wise enough to put off everything for the sake of God.

To which you may say: "Yes, sir, if only it were not for one thing—that my faults prevent me . . ."

If you have faults, then pray often to God to remove them from you, if that should please him, because you can't get rid of them yourself. If he does remove them, then thank him; but if he does not, then bear them for him, not—thinking of them as faults or sins, but rather as great disciplines, and thus you shall merit reward and exercise your patience; but be satisfied whether he gives you what you want or not. For he does give to each, according to what is best for him and what best fits the need. If a coat is to fit, it must be cut to measure, for what fits one will not fit another; each person must be measured if his coat is to fit.

Thus God gives men what is best for them and [he can do so] because he is so near and knows so much. The truth is that, if you trust God in such matters, you will have as much in the meanest as in the most ample circumstances. If it were God's will to give me St. Paul's gift, I should take it gladly because he wished it so; but now that he has not seen fit to give it to me (and he has given it to very few people in this life), he is just as dear to me, and I thank him just the same, and I am just as much at peace, since he has withheld it, as I should be if he had given it. Other things being equal, I am quite content that he did not grant it.

This is the truth: I am to be so content with God's will in every event, so pleased that his will is being done, that this fact means more to me than all he might ever use me for or give to me. In this way, all gifts are mine and all being is God to me. Then, if all creation and God were its best or worst, it could [add nothing to] or subtract nothing from me. What, then, have I to complain about, when all human gifts are mine? Truly, I am so content with all God does, whether he gives or withholds, that there is not a cent's worth of difference between my condition and the best I could imagine for myself.

Now you say: "I am afraid I do not devote enough attention to such matters or bother as much as I might . . ."

Let that be a sorrow to you and bear it as patiently as you may; take even this as discipline and let it go at that. God, too, bears shame and misfortune and is quite willing to forgo his service and praise, if only those who belong to him and think of him may be at peace. Why should we not be at peace, whatever he sends or whatever we have to forgo? It is written that our Lord said: "Blessed are they which are persecuted for righteousness' sake."[24] Truly, if a thief about to be hanged, having justly deserved it for his theft, or a murderer about to be killed because he merited it, could only have this insight, "See, you are suffering in the cause of right now that you get what you deserve," he would immediately be blessed. In fact, however wrong we are, if we accept from God whatever he does or fails to do, as being just because it comes from him, and thus we suffer for righteousness' sake, we shall be blessed. Then do not complain—or, rather, complain only that you still complain and are not yet content. You are permitted to complain only because you have too much; for the right way is to take your losses as you do your profits.

"But see," you say, "how it is that God acts through some people! They are suffused with divine being and thus it is God acting in them and not they themselves!"

Then thank God for that; and if he should ordain that it be so with you, then, in God's name, take it! But if he does not, then do without gladly. Think only of him and do not worry about whether it is God acting through you or you doing it yourself; for if you are thinking only of him, God must be acting through you whether he wills to or not.

Never mind therefore what the nature of anybody's God-given knack may be. If I were so good and holy that men beatified me, there would still be some people who would want to debate whether my saintliness was due to nature or to grace. That is wrong! Let God act through you and let *him* do it. Do not worry about whether it is natural or supernatural; for both nature and grace are his. What difference does it make to you how he likes to operate?—or what he wants to do with you or anyone else? Let him act where and when and how he will.

There was a man who proposed to turn a brook into his garden, who said: "As long as I get my water, I shall not care what kind of channel it flows through—whether it is made of iron or wood or stone or whatever—as long as I get the water!" It is also quite wrong to fret over the mechanism of God's work in man. Whether it be nature or grace, let him go to it and you be at peace.

For you will have peace to the extent that you have God, and the further you are away from God the less you will be at peace. Anything that is at peace has God in it to the extent that it is at peace. Thus you may measure your progress with God by measuring your peace or the lack of it. When you have unrest within you, you will be restless visibly, but the unrest comes from the creature and not from God. There is nothing in him to be afraid of, and nothing to cause sorrow. He is only lovable.

Perfectly to will what God wills, to want what he wants, is to have joy; but if one's will is not quite in unison with God's, there is no joy. May God help us to be in tune with him! Amen.

The Book of Divine Comfort[1]

BENEDICTUS DEUS ET PATER DOMINI NOSTRI JESU CHRISTI.
II Corinthians 1:3

THE noble teacher, St. Paul, writes these words in his epistle: "Blessed be God, even the Father of our Lord Jesus Christ, the Father of mercies, and the God of all comfort; who comforteth us in all our tribulation." There are three kinds of tribulation that may befall one and oppress him in this exile.[2] The first is damage to external goods, and then to friends dear to him, and finally to himself: disgrace, privation, physical pain and mental anguish.

Therefore, I propose to set forth in this book certain doctrines from which comfort is to be derived in every adversity, tribulation, or sorrow, and having gathered from them truth sufficient to comfort one in any kind of trouble, to distinguish thirty teachings, any one of which should be enough to solace. Thereafter, in the third part, examples of words and deeds will be found, such things as the wise have said and done when they suffered.

I

In the first place, it must be clear that wisdom and the wise, truth and the true, goodness and the good, justice and the just are each related to the other.[3] Goodness [for example] is neither made, created nor engendered but itself is the begetter, the procreator of the good; and the good, to the extent that it is good, is not made or created, but is born as if it were the child or son of goodness.[4] Goodness itself is self-begotten and all its works, for it is the essence of good. It pours knowledge, love, and deeds into the good man and he takes his nature, knowledge, love, and works out of the depths of good-

43

ness and only thence.[5] When the good is added to goodness, it is still
only goodness, except that one is begotten of the other, one begetting, the other begotten,[6] as if it were the child of goodness. There
is reality and life in goodness only and so the good man receives all
he is from goodness and in goodness. In goodness he lives, moves,
and has his being and there he finds himself. All he knows and
loves, he knows and loves by virtue of goodness which works in
and through him. It is as the Son says: "The Father that dwelleth
in me, he doeth the works. My Father worketh hitherto, and I
work. All things that the Father hath are mine; and all that is mine
is my father's."[7] His giving is my taking.

Thus, know that the name or word "goodness" stands for nothing
more or less than pure and simple goodness and so, when we speak
of "the good," that should mean goodness infused [into something]
or begotten by the unbegotten goodness. Therefore the gospel says:
"As the Father hath life in himself; so hath he given to the Son to
have life in himself."[8] Note that it says "in himself," and not "of
himself," for the Father has given it him.

All I have just said of goodness and the good holds equally for
truth and the true, for justice and the just, for wisdom and the wise,
for God the Father and God the Son, and for all that is begotten of
God because it has no earthly parent. It is true of everything which
contains no idea that is not God pure and simple, of everything in
which no creature is and in which no creature that is not God is
suggested. As St. John says in his Gospel: "To all gave he power to
become the sons of God . . . which were born, not of blood, nor
of the will of the flesh, nor of the will of man, but of God."[9]

By "blood" he means in man all that is not subject to human
willing. By "flesh" he means in man all that is subject to human
willing and yet, rebelliously, is inclined to fleshly desire; he is
referring to things common to body and soul, not peculiar to the
soul alone, things which account for the fatigue and sickness of the
soul's agents.[10] By the "will of man," St. John means the highest
agents of the soul and person, whose functions are unmixed with
the carnal and which, being segregated apart from time, remain
constant in a pure state in the soul, unlocated and discontinuous
with all that is related to, or tainted with time and space. He refers

to that something in man which is of God's order, which has nothing in common with anything else, and by which man is of the genus and species of God. Yet since these agents of the soul, being created with the soul, are not God, they must be changed, transformed into God, reborn in him and of him, so that only God is Father and they, too, become his sons, his only-begotten sons.

For I am God's son when I have been born and formed in his image. This is how the good sons of goodness, the just sons of justice, become sons of God. To the degree that one is God's son and reproduces the unbegotten as a born son would, one has the same order of reality as justice and walks in the paths of justice and truth. It is from such doctrines, derived from the sacred gospel and certified by the native light of reason, that sure comfort is to be had in every sorrow.

St. Augustine says: "God is not far off nor is he long in coming." If you want not to be far from God nor to wait long for him, then go straight to him, for in him a thousand years are but as yesterday when it is past. I also say that in God there is neither sorrow, nor crying, nor any pain. If you will be rid of pain and suffering, stop where you are and turn to God—but only to him. Surely suffering is due to our failure to aim at him and him alone; for if you are reborn and clothed in justice, then truly nothing could hurt you any more than God's own justice would.[11]

Solomon says that the just are not troubled by anything that befalls them.[12] He does not say "the just person" or the "just angel," nor this nor that instance of justice; for justice, so limited, is only the child of earthly parentage. It is a creature that is made or created as much as its parent is. He is speaking instead of that pure justice whose Father is neither made nor created—the justice that God alone is. That is why sorrow and pain disturb justice as little as they do God. Justice saddens no man; for justice is love, joy, and rapture. If justice could bring the just to grief, itself would have to turn into grief. Injustice and iniquity may by no means sadden a just man, because creature things are far beneath justice; they do not affect or influence it nor come to birth in it, whose Father God is.

Therefore a man should study to discount self and all other creatures and to know no Father except God only. Then nothing may sadden or worry him, neither God nor creature, created or uncreated, and his whole being, life, knowing, and loving will be of God, in God and will be God himself.[13]

There is something else to be known that will comfort a man in tribulation and that is that the just and good person delights incomparably more—may, unspeakably more—in well-doing than he or even the highest of angels delights in his natural estate. That is why the saints so gladly give up their lives for the right.

Now I say that when external harm befalls a good or just person, and he is not excited by it and the peace in his heart remains undisturbed, then what I have been saying is verified: the just are not troubled by anything that befalls them. If, however, a man is troubled by some external harm, then truly it is only fair and just of God to have ordained that the harm befell the man who could believe himself just and yet be upset by so little a thing. And if it is just of God, then truly the man need not mind but he ought far more to rejoice than he does at his own life, at what is to bring more joy and worth to all men than the whole world of itself could bring: for what shall all the world profit a man when he is no more?

The third truth one should and may know is this: the elemental fact is that the only stream, the only living artery of goodness, real truth, and perfect comfort is God, and that whatever is not God bears in itself a native bitterness, discomfort, and sorrow and it can never make for good, the good which is only of God. Rather, it diminishes, covers up and conceals the sweetness, the rapture and comfort of God.

I further maintain that sorrow comes of loving what I cannot have. If I am sad about my losses, that is a sure sign that I love external things and really enjoy my sorrow and dis-ease. What wonder, then, that I grow sad, loving my affliction and sorrow, if my heart seeks what it has lost and my mind attributes to things what belongs to God alone? I turn toward the creature from which discomfort comes in course and turn away from him from whom joy and comfort naturally come. What wonder, then, that I am sad and grow sadder? Truly, it is impossible for either God or the world that any person should ever find true comfort when he looks to a creature for it, but those who love only God in the creature and the creature only in God shall discover real, true, and apposite comfort on all sides.

2

Here follow some thirty arguments, any one of which should be sufficient to comfort an honest person in his distress. The first is that there is no hardship without some comfort; there is no loss that is pure loss. Accordingly, St. Paul says that God's good faith and the essential goodness which characterizes him permit no suffering to be unbearable or any temptation to be overwhelming.[14] He always provides some solace for man's use. Both the saints and heathen masters say that neither God nor nature permits the existence of undiluted evil or suffering.

Let me cite the case of a man who had a hundred dollars and lost forty but still had sixty. If he thinks of the forty he lost all the time, he will be afflicted and full of anguish. How can one whose attention is fixed on his loss and misfortune ever be comforted, especially if he keeps visualizing it, brooding over it, his eyes heavy with sorrow, talking to his loss and the loss persuading him as if they two were persons staring into each other's faces? If he would only look at the sixty dollars he still has and, holding converse with that, forget the lost forty dollars, he would surely find some comfort. What is, and is good, is comfortable; whereas what is not, and is neither good nor yet mine, since I lost it, can only cause a feeling of adversity, discomfort, and trouble.

Thus Solomon says: "In the days of adversity and affliction, forget not the good days and the pleasure of them."[15] That means: when you suffer for things gone wrong, think of good and happy things yet coming to you and let them be of some use. Why not be comforted in the thought of the thousands of people who, if they had the sixty dollars you still have, would think themselves rich lords or ladies and who therefore, would be heartily thankful and glad to God?

The second argument for comfort. Suppose that, being ill, a man is in great pain and yet he has his house, the necessities of food, drink, and medical attention, as well as the attendance of his family and the sympathy and companionship of friends. What should he do? How do the poor make out, who suffer as much or more discomfort with nobody to give them even a drink of cold water? They must seek their dry bread, come rain or snow, in bitter cold, from house to house. If you would be comforted, forget this one who has the best of it and think of those worse off.

Furthermore, I say that sorrow comes of affection and love, for these are the beginning and the end of sorrow. Thus, if I am sad for passing things, not loving God with all my heart nor even giving him the love he might justly expect to meet in me, what wonder if God ordained that I should still suffer loss and pain?

St. Augustine says: "Lord, I did not want to lose you, but I did want to own some creatures besides you. It was because of my greed that I lost you—for it did not please you that anyone should own creatures that are false and at the same time own you who are the truth."[16] He says also, in another place: "He who is not satisfied with God alone is much too greedy." How could the creatures God gives satisfy a man who is not satisfied by God himself?

Things cannot comfort or satisfy a good man but, rather, anything other than God or alien to him will be painful. He will always say: "Lord God, when you send me elsewhere than into your own presence, give me then another *you*; for you are my comfort and I want you only." When our Lord vowed every good thing to Moses in the Holy Land, which here means the Kingdom of Heaven, Moses replied: "Lord, send me not, except you come with me!"[17]

Affections, desires, and loves are due to likeness; for things are always attracted by their own kind, to love them. The pure love purity; the just love justice and are inclined to it, and the mouth of every man utters what is in the man. Thus our Lord said: "Out of the abundance of the heart, the mouth speaketh";[18] and Solomon said: "All the labor of a man is for his mouth."[19] When one longs for outward things, for mortal and temporal creatures to comfort himself, it is a sure sign that God is not in his human heart.

A good man will be ashamed before God and himself when he discovers that God is not in him, that God the Father is not working through him and that it is by miserable creatures that he lives and acts. So David in the Psalter, complains: "Tears have been my meat day and night, while they continually say unto me, Where is thy God?"[20] To long for the pleasure and solace of outward things in adversity, to be eager for them, to talk much about them, is a sure sign that God is neither shining through me nor working in me, and such being the case, I shall be ashamed in the presence of good people who detect my condition. A good man never complains of his misfortunes or distresses; he may only complain of his complaining—that he should be aware of it at all.

Authorities say that immediately under heaven a great fire is raging far and wide and yet heaven is not affected by it in the least.[32] Another writing declares that the lowest part of the soul is above the highest heaven. But how could a man estimate that he is heavenly, or that his heart is in heaven, if it is affected and upset by such little things?

Let me go further. There can be no good man who does not want what God wants, because it is not possible that God should want anything but goodness, and just because of this, when God does want something, it must be not only for the good but for the best. That is why our Lord has taught us, through the apostles, to pray every day that God's will be done. And yet, when the will of God is done, we complain and are sad and troubled.

Seneca, the heathen philosopher, asked what comfort might be best for those suffering misery, said: "It is for a man to take everything that comes as if he had asked for it, nay, as if he had prayed for it"—to be as if you were praying all the time that the will of God be done, so that, when it is done, you will not be put out. There was a heathen authority who said: "Lord, supreme Father and only Master of high heaven, I am ready for anything you will; only give me the will to want what you will."

A good man trusts God, believing and certain in his knowledge that God is good and that because of the divine goodness and love it is impossible that God should let adversity befall anyone, except he intended to spare that person much greater, or to prepare him for a nobler earthly comfort, or he intended something better to come of it, something still more compatible with divine honor. But be that as it may, since it is God's will that this happens, and since the good man's will is at one and united with God, even though it were his undoing, or even his own damnation, he would still agree to it. Thus St. Paul: he was willing to be cut off from God, for God's sake and honor.[21]

A really perfect person will be so dead to self, so lost in God, so given over to the will of God, that his whole happiness consists in being unconscious of self and its concerns, and being conscious, instead, of God, in knowing nothing and wishing to know nothing except the will and truth of God, or "knowing God," in St. Paul's words, "as we are known."[22] God knows what he knows and loves what he loves within himself and his own will, and thus our Lord said: "This is life eternal, to know thee, the only true God."

The authorities say that the Blessed Ones in the Kingdom of Heaven know their creatures apart from [the instrumentality of] ideas, that they know their creatures through their common prototype in God, just as God knows, loves, and wills things. God tries to teach us to long and pray that it may be so with us:

"Our Father, which art in heaven, hallowed be thy name." That means "Be thou alone known." "Thy kingdom come" means "I shall have nothing, know nothing, and value nothing but thy reign." So the gospel also says: "Blessed are the poor in spirit,"[23] meaning those who are poor as regards will of their own. And we pray that God's will be done on earth, meaning in us, as it is in heaven, meaning in God himself. This kind of person[24] is so unified with God and in unison with his will, that he wants what God wants and wants it God's way. Therefore, when betimes it is the will of God that I commit sin, I shall not afterward wish that I had not done it, for thus God's will is done *on earth*, meaning *in misdeeds*, as it is done *in heaven*, meaning *in right deeds*. In this way does without God, for God's sake, and is cut off from him; this is the only true repentance for sin, and by it my sin becomes painful to me but does me no harm, just as all evil is painful to God but does him no harm.

Suffering I have, and my principal pains, because of sin, even though I would not sin for all creation—no, not if a thousand worlds were to be mine through eternity; yet all this does no harm if I accept the suffering and transfigure the pain into the will of God. Suffering thus becomes perfect, when it is due to pure love for the pure good and joy of God. This is how what I am saying in this book is true and to be understood: the good man, to the extent he is good, assumes the character of the goodness that God himself is.[25]

Just think what an amazing life a man might have on earth—a life like God in heaven! There is strange comfort to be had when adversity serves as well as convenience, and pain is like pleasure. If I have the grace and goodness of which I have just been talking, I shall be even-tempered, wholly comfortable and happy, under all circumstances, and if I am not so, I shall do without it, just because it is the will of God. Then if God should grant what I have foregone, I should take it in his name joyfully. If he did not grant it, I should get along without, in the same spirit, for then, evidently, it was not in God's will. Thus I take both the granting and the denial.

What, then, do I lack? The certainty that man gets to God more truly through what he foregoes than what he receives; for if a man takes [something from God], then his reason for being comfortable and glad may be the gifts; but if he receives nothing, his only reason for being happy is God and God's will.[30]

Here is another comfort. Suppose you lose some good thing, such as a friend, a relative, an eye, or whatever, be very sure that if you bear the loss with humility for God's sake, you shall still have that [inward something] to the last drop, for the sake of which you would not willingly have suffered the loss. For example, supposing a person loses an eye, which he would not willingly have lost for a thousand dollars or more, in God's sight he still has [the visual power] because of which he would not willingly have endured his loss. Probably that is what our Lord meant: "It is better for thee to enter into life with one eye, than to be lost with two eyes."[26] Probably, it is also what God means by saying: "Everyone that hath forsaken father or mother, sisters or brothers . . . or whatever . . . shall receive again an hundredfold and life eternal."[27]

It should further be recognized that virtue, and willingness to suffer with patience, have degrees, just as we observe that one person is naturally handsomer or more skillful than another. Therefore, I say that a good man, being good, may nevertheless be affected and shaken by his natural love for his parents, and still not fail of God or goodness. Still, his goodness is to be measured by the extent to which he is comforted by or aware of his natural affection for father and mother, sister, brother, or himself.

As I have said before, if a person could accept it as the will of God (in so far as it is God's will) that since the first man's sin against divine justice, human nature does have sinful weaknesses and, even if this were not the case, he would gladly be without such weakness, were it God's will, then all would be well with him and he would surely find comfort in sorrow. That would mean, as St. John says, that the true light is shining in the darkness,[28] or, as St. Paul says, that "virtue is made perfect in weakness."[29] And if the thief could truly, perfectly, purely, willingly, and gladly suffer death for love of divine justice, by which evildoers are put to death, in accordance with God's will, then surely he would at once be made and kept blessed, for the will of God is our salvation and beatification.

Here is another comforting thought. Probably one could not find anybody who had not someone of whom he was sufficiently fond, to keep whom alive he would not gladly do without his eyes and be blind for a year's time, let us say, if only afterward having saved his friend from death, he could have his eyes back again. Supposing, then, that one could expect to live twenty or thirty years more, if he would do without his eyes one year to save a man from death within the year, then surely it is not unreasonable to expect that he would give up his twenty or thirty years if thereby he might have eternal happiness, and see God in the divine light, and in God behold himself and all other creatures.

Moreover, here is another comfort. The good man who is begotten of goodness in its own image, sees, in proportion to his goodness, that the world of creatures is mean, full of bitterness and hurt, and that to lose the creature is to be free, and rightly understood, to part with sorrow, misery and harm. It is a fact that release from pain is indeed a comfort and, since worldly possessions are nothing but inconvenience, worry, and anxiety, one should not complain of their loss. He should complain rather that he is unacquainted with true comfort and ease, because it cannot reach him. He has far more reason to complain that he is not rid of the idea of creaturehood and therefore not established, not cast in the mold of divine goodness.

Remember that God tells the truth and praises truth by enacting it. If he failed to keep his word, to tell the truth, he would fail in Godhood and could not be the God whose Word is Truth. He has promised that our sorrow shall be changed to joy. Now if I knew it for the truth that all my stones were to be changed into pure gold, the more stones I had and the larger they were the gladder I should be. Here, I say, is great comfort for anyone in his trouble or misery.

There is another point similar to that. No cask holds two kinds of drink at the same time. If the cask is to hold wine, its water must first be poured out, leaving the cask empty and clean. If you are to have divine joy, all your creatures must first be poured out or thrown out.

On this point St. Augustine says: "Pour out, that you may be filled; learn not to love [this] that you may love [that]; turn away from thence that you may turn thither." Plainly, he means that to accept or receive you must be empty. Authorities tell us that the eye, if it had color of its own, would not be able to detect it or any other color, but being free of color, it distinguishes them all. The wall is colored and therefore distinguishes neither its own color nor any other and takes no pleasure in colors, insensitive either to gold or black. But the eye has it not and therefore really has it, detecting it accurately with pleasure and delight.

Thus, the freer and more immaculate the agents of the soul, the wider their range and the more accurately they function in perception. The more they can be identified with the objects of their concern, the more delight is in them. This [principle] can be extended to the highest agents of the soul, which are innocent of creatures and have nothing in common with anything else and are therefore able to take in God—no less!—as he really is, in himself. Authorities all agree that no rapture is to be compared to this union with God and penetration of his nature.

Our Lord speaks pointedly in the gospel, saying: "Blessed are the poor in spirit." He is poor who has nothing; and that spirit is poor which, like the eye that is poor, being devoid of color, is very sensitive to it. To be poor in spirit is to be sensitive to other spirits. God is a spirit and the fruits of his spirit are love, peace and joy.[31] Empty poverty that owns nothing and is clean, changes nature; the

pure can make water flow uphill and do other wonders of which I
may not tell you now.

If, therefore, you will find perfect comfort and joy in God, see to
it that you are innocent of creatures and creature comforts. Certainly,
as long as you can find comfort in creatures, you cannot find the true
comfort. It is only when nothing but God can console you, then he
will be a real consolation and you will find delight in him and with
him. If what God is not gives you comfort, you are neither here nor
there [i.e., neither of the world nor of heaven]; but when creatures
are no longer comforting and suit you not at all, then both here and
there are yours.

If it were possible and a person knew how to empty a vessel and
keep it empty of everything that could fill it, even of air, doubtless
the vessel would forget and belie its normal nature and rise up to the
sky. Analogously, the soul that is empty of creatures is lifted up to
God.[30] Likeness and heat are also entities that lift things up. We
ascribe likeness to the Son in the Godhead and heat, love, to the
Holy Spirit. All likeness among things, but especially in the divine
nature, is born out of the Oneness [of the Godhead] and this likeness,
begotten of the One, and in and of the One, is the beginning, the
source of that glowing flower: love. The One itself, however, is a
source that had no beginning, a source to which all likeness looks
as to its origin, and for the fact of its existence and beginning. In
contrast, love's nature is such that it appears only where two are;
but itself turns out to be one and uniform and never twofold; for
love cannot exist divided. In love's nature, two function as one, and
there is ardor, willing, and longing.

Solomon observes that a stream, like all other creatures, flows
hurriedly by, runs back to its origin, and this suggests that what I
have just said must be true. Likeness and love hurry upward like
flames, to bring the soul to its origin, in the One that is our heavenly
Father, who is one in heaven and on earth. So I say that likeness
born of the One leads the soul to God, for he is One, unbegotten
unity, and of this we have clear evidence. When physical fire kindles
and burns wood to sparks, the wood absorbs the fire's nature and
becomes like the pure fire that hangs immediately under heaven.
[The burning wood] suddenly forgets and abandons its father and

mother, brothers and sisters on earth and hurries upward to seek its father in the sky.[32] Here below, its father is the fire, its mother is the wood, its brother and sisters are other sparks. It does not wait for them, but hurrying up, it mounts to its true father in the sky. He who knows the truth knows that physical fire is not the true father of the spark; the real, the true father of all fire is above.

It is necessary therefore to notice another item: it is not only father and mother on earth that the spark forsakes and forgets but rather it denies and forgets itself, because of a natural affection, to get to its sky-father, even though it has to be extinguished in the cold of the air between.

I have spoken heretofore of emptiness, that is, of innocence, to the effect that the more innocent and poor the soul is, the less it has to do with creatures, the emptier of things that are not God, the more surely it takes to God, gets into him and is made One with him, itself becoming God.[30] Then, to use St. Paul's words, the soul sees God face to face and no longer as an idea or image.

So, now, I shall speak of likeness [relation?] and the fire of love. The more one thing is like another, the more it pursues it, and swiftly follows its scent, and the sweeter and more delightful the pursuit becomes. The farther it leaves its former self behind, departing from all that its object is not, the more unlike its old self it becomes, the more it grows like the object it so hotly pursues. And since likeness flows from the One, drawing, attracting with power borrowed from the One, there can be neither rest nor satisfaction, either for the attracter or for the attracted, until at last they are united in the One. Therefore our Lord spoke through the prophet Isaiah, saying in effect that "neither height, nor depth, nor likeness, nor love's peace shall satisfy me until I myself appear in my Son and I kindle and burn in the Holy Spirit."[33]

Our Lord Jesus Christ besought his Father that we should be made one—not merely united—but joined together in him and with him in the one single One.[34] We have an open parable and revelation of the truth of this saying in nature, most obvious in the case of fire. When fire goes to work on wood,[32] kindling it to burning, the fire first fills the wood with desire for its own dissimilar nature, by taking away from the wood its solidity and coldness, its hardness

and watery moisture. Thus the fire makes the wood more and more
like itself and still neither can rest, be satisfied or quieted in mere
warmth, heat or likeness. The fire begets itself in the wood, giving
the wood its own fiery nature, even its own being, so that wood may
be identical with the fire and neither more nor less distinct. Before
this can happen, there is always a smoking, crackling struggle
between wood and fire, but when all unlikeness is removed and done
away, the fire quiets and soothes the wood. I say further, and it is a
fact, that there is a power in nature which hates even a covert likeness between things—especially when it brings out differences and
bifurcations. That power seeks oneness instead of likeness and loves
things only for the sake of the One in them, as the mouth likes wine
for its sweetness and flavor only. If water had the flavor wine has,
the mouth would not prefer one to the other.

Thus I have argued that the soul hates likeness; it has no love for
likeness in and of itself, but loves likeness for the sake of the unity
that lies hidden in it, the unity that is its Father, in whom is the
beginning of everything in heaven and on earth. I have said that as
long as there is mere likeness, as between wood and fire, there can
be neither true pleasure nor quiet, neither rest nor contentment.
Thus the authorities[32] say that fire is a process of conflict, change,
and movement in time but that the birth of fire, as of desire, is independent of either time or distance. No one finds pleasure tedious,
or joy remote. What I have been saying was implied by our Lord
when he said: "A woman, when she is in travail hath sorrow . . .
but as soon as she is delivered of the child, she remembereth no
more the anguish. . . ."[35] Thus, too, God bids us in the gospel to
pray the heavenly Father that our joy may be full.[36] And to the
same point, Philip: "Lord, show us the Father and it sufficeth us."
Here "Father" means the One, in which all likeness is hushed and
all that has being and desire is made still.

Now we may see clearly why we are discomforted in our pain,
anguish, and hurt. It is due simply to our human way of living on
the outside of things, far away from God, and not being empty or
innocent of creatures, not being like God, and to our being cold to
divine love.

There is, however, another consideration which, when you know it and think it over, will give you reasonable comfort in external damage, pain, and discomfort. A man travels by a certain road, or takes up or quits a certain job. Then he gets hurt, breaks a leg or an arm, loses an eye or gets sick. Then he is likely to think: Ah!—if you had only gone the other way or had done or not done that job, this wouldn't have happened to you; and so he continues to be distressed and is bound to suffer. He would do much better to think: if you had gone by another road, taken up or quit another job, still greater damage or harm might have been your portion. Thus he might reasonably find comfort and be glad at heart.

Or consider this. You have lost a thousand dollars. Stop weeping over the thousand you lost and, instead, thank God that he gave you a thousand to lose and let go, so that you might be exercised in patience and virtue and be worthy of life eternal—as many thousands of people are not. Or take this to your comfort. A man who has been well-off for many years, loses it all. He ought then to reflect wisely and thank God for his misfortune and loss, for only then will he realize how well-off he was before. He ought to thank God for the well-being he enjoyed so many years—and not growl about it.

He might well remember that naturally man has nothing of himself but faults and naughtiness. What is good about him was lent him by God—not given. To know the truth is to know that God gave all that is any good to his Son and to the Holy Spirit. He gives no good to the creature but merely lends it good, on trust. The sun gives heat to the air, but the light it only lends. As soon as the sun has set, the light is taken away but the heat remains because it is given the air to keep.

Thus, the authorities say the heavenly Father-God is the Son's Father—not his Lord—nor is he master of the Holy Spirit. God, the Father, Son, and Holy Spirit, is the Lord—but the Lord and master of creatures. We say that, from eternity, God has been and is our Father but since he made creatures, he is their master, and owner. If then, it is true that all that is any good for comfort is lent to man to care for it, what complaint has he when God wants to take it back? Let him rather thank God that he lent it so long. Let him also be thankful that God did not take back all of his loan all at once, for it would be quite reasonable of God to withdraw everything from the man who gets angry because God takes what never belonged to man, things of which man was never the master and owner. Jeremiah does well in the midst of his sufferings and lamentations, to exclaim: "O how great are God's manifold mercies that we are not destroyed altogether."[37]

If a man who has lent me his coat, sweater, and overcoat takes back his overcoat, but leaves me the coat and sweater against the frost, I ought to be very glad and thankful to him. It is noteworthy how wrong it is to be angry and complain when something is lost: that bears the presumption that that good thing was given us instead of being lent, that we were its owners, the perfect Sons of God by nature instead of God's Sons by grace only. [By contrast] it is the property of the Son of God and the Holy Spirit to be evenly disposed under all circumstances.

We should also remember that natural human virtues have superior strength.[38] No visible efforts are great enough or strenuous enough to give them full scope for expression. For that reason there is an inward or spiritual effort to be made, not limited by time or encompassed by place, an effort in which one discovers God, the divine and godlike—all too much for time and space. That effort is being made everywhere equally and at all times and in this it is much akin to God; for no creature may ever realize the goodness of God perfectly or imagine it. That is why there must be something higher and more spiritual, some entity in which the heavenly Father is perfectly revealed, poured out and made manifest: the Son and the Holy Spirit.

Nothing can hinder this inner effort of virtue any more than God himself can be hindered.[38] It is a process that shines and gives light day and night. It praises and sings God's glory in a new song, as David says: "Sing unto the Lord a new song, for his praise is from the ends of the world."[39] God does not love the effort, the process which is limited by time and place, the narrow job that cramps and constrains the man, the work in which one grows old and tired in the doing of it. The real job is to love God, to will goodness and the good to such purpose that all the good man has ever wanted, or still wants with a pure and perfect will, he has done already; for this way he would be like God. Of him, David writes that all he ever thought of doing is done.[40]

Of this doctrine, we have a good parable in the stone, whose apparent work it is to fall down and lie on the ground. Its action, of course, may be hindered, since a stone cannot always fall to earth without interruption. There is, however, another action more essential to the stone than falling. It is the constant downward tendency ingrained in it and which neither God nor man nor creature can take away. The stone does its work day and night. It if lay on the ground a thousand years, it would press downwards as much or as little as it did on the first day.

I may say the same of virtue. It, too, has an inner function: to will and tend toward all good and to resist and struggle against all evil and bad, against all that is unconformed to God and goodness. The more evil the deed, the more incompatible it is with God, the stronger the reaction of virtue will be; but the greater the deed, the more agreeable to God it is, the easier, the more pleasant and agreeable virtue's effort is. Her only complaint and sorrow is—if virtue can know sorrow—that her suffering for God is little and that there is so little that may be done in time by which she may be expressed or represented. In action she grows stronger, in devotion richer. She wishes that she had not suffered and grieved beyond suffering and grief; it was always her desire to suffer without ceasing for God and goodness. Her happiness consists in suffering, for God, and not in having suffered.

Thus our Lord says: "Blessed are they that suffer for righteousness' sake." He did not say: "they that *have* suffered." They [the blessed ones] hate past suffering. It is not the suffering they love. It is suffering that has been taken away and is thus a damage to suffering for God—which they love. I say also that the blessed ones also hate future suffering, for that also is not suffering now. Still, they hate it less than suffering which is past; for the latter is over and gone and not to be compared with any present pain—far from it —whereas anticipated suffering still has some sting—and they love that!

St. Paul says that he would gladly get along without God for God's sake, if that would promote God's glory. They say that St.

Paul said this before he had become perfect, but I think that these words could have come only out of a perfect heart. They also say that he meant that he would gladly be cut off from God for a little while. I say that a perfect person would be as loath to be cut off from God for an hour as to be separated from him for a thousand years. The pain would be no less. Even so, if it were God's will and for his glory that one should be cut off from him, a thousand years or eternity would be just as easy as a day or an hour.

The inner process [of virtue] is also divine.[38] It is of God's kind and shares the divine character; to have God plus all creatures of a thousand worlds would be to have nothing more than God alone. Thus I say, as I have before, that visible deeds do not increase the goodness of the inner life, however long or broad, whatever their number or dimension; its goodness is its own. The visible deeds of virtue can never be worth much, if the inward process is small or nonexistent, or they can never be little worth, if the inward process exists and is great. The inner process of virtue goes on perpetually, draws its value from God—from the very heart of God, for it is regarded by God as a Son and it is born as a Son from the heavenly Father's heart.

It is not so with visible actions, for they derive their goodness from the inner process of virtue. They fall like a cataract from the Godhead, all clad in distinctions, multiplicity, and division, all of which are far from the likeness of God in which they originated, and yet they all depend on their good Original. The creature, however, is always blind to the goodness and light within itself, blind to that one thing that God begets as his only-begotten Son, by which children of the divine come to being and are born God's Sons. Here, too, is the source of the Holy Spirit, by whom alone, since it is God's spirit and one with him, the Son is conceived in man. Here, too, is the point of origin of all who are Sons of God, according as they are more or less purely born of him and in his manner, or are transformed into his likeness, having put away multiplicity—which, however, is still to be found to some degree even in the most exalted of angels.

Fully to know this inner work of virtue, however, one must be estranged even from good, truth, or anything else which, in thought or by name, implies the light or shadow of distinction. He must entrust himself to that pure One, which has been purified of multiplicity and division and which is One even as the Father, Son and Holy Spirit are one. It is this One that makes us blessed and the further we are from it, the less we are Sons, and the less the Holy Spirit flows through us. The closer we are to that One, the more we are Sons and the Holy Spirit is flowing through us. And this may explain what the Son of our God divinely says: "Whosoever shall drink of the water that I shall give him shall never thirst; but the water that I shall give him shall be in him a well of water springing up into eternal life."[41] St. John says that he was speaking of the Holy Spirit.

The [term] "Son," in the Godhead, properly speaking, denotes only sonship, "born-of-God-ness"—the spring, the brook, the stream which is the Holy Spirit, the love of God. It denotes a full, true, and satisfying taste of the one heavenly Father. Therefore the voice of the Father calls down to the Son: "Thou art my beloved Son in whom I am beloved, at home, and well pleased."[42]

We do not doubt that God can love no one purely and perfectly who is not a Son of God,[43] for love, which is the Holy Spirit, originates in the Son and the Son loves himself in the Father and the Father in himself. Thus our Lord says very well that they are blessed who are poor in spirit, that is, people having no human spirit of their own and thus come in purity to God. As St. Paul says: "God has revealed it to us in his Holy Spirit."[44]

St. Augustine says that one gets the best understanding of the Scriptures by studying them without prejudice for the truth they contain, which is to say, in the spirit of God. St. Peter says that "holy men of God spake as they were moved by the Holy Ghost."[45] St. Paul says: "No one may know what is in the man except the human mind; and no one may know what God is save the mind of God."[46] There is a gloss which also puts the matter well: "No one can understand or teach the doctrine of St. Paul except he have the mind by which St. Paul spoke and wrote." It is my complaint that crude people, quite innocent of the spirit of God, who have not even turned in his direction, proceed to judge what they hear or read in the Scriptures, when the Scriptures were spoken or written by men moved by the Holy Spirit. They never consider what is written, that what is impossible to man is possible to God—nay, even common or natural to him. Things impossible in nature may be usual or natural in a realm above nature.

Let us therefore look again at what I have just been saying about the good man, born the Son of God, how he loves God for his own sake. There are many other related things which I have already put down, among which is the following: a good man, born into God and Goodness, partakes of all the properties of the divine nature.[25] According to Solomon, it is the property of God to do everything for his own sake, which is to say that he pays no attention to anything but himself. He loves and acts only for himself. Therefore, if one loves himself and what he does—not for honor, reward, or comfort—but for [the implicit] God and for the glory of God only, that is a sign that he is a Son of God.

Again, God loves for his own sake, acts for his own sake: that means that he loves for the sake of love and acts for the sake of action. It cannot be doubted that God would never have begot his Son in eternity if [for him to think of a] birth were not [the same as actual] birth. The saints, therefore, say that God's Son is born eternally so that God may be born incessantly. So, too, God would never have created the world if [his idea of] creation were other than [his act of] creation. Thus God created the world so that he might keep on creating. The past and future are both far from God and alien to his way.

To be the born Son of God, therefore, is to love God for himself, that is, to love him for the sake of loving God, to act only for the sake of acting for God and one who does so will never be tired of love or work and it will be all one to him what he loves. This indicates what God-love is like and that, as I said above, the good man will always want to suffer for God[47] and will not be impatient to get his pain over. He will suffer because he likes to suffer for God and to bear God's will and he thus ends in being God's Son, transformed by God into God. He will love God through himself, through his own affections and work, the work he has to do, and thus God will always love him and act in his nature; his being, his life, and his blessedness will be God's work. So finally, the good man, to the degree that he is the Son of God, will suffer for God and act for God and that will be to him existence, life, work, beatitude. That is [in part] what our Lord meant by saying: "Blessed are they that are persecuted for righteousness' sake."

In the third place, I say that this good man, to the extent he is good, has the properties of God,[48] not only because in his loving service he is loving and serving God, but he loves and serves of himself. He, the lover, is the born Son of God; the object of his love is [to him] the Father God not yet born and thus the Son is in the Father and the Father in the Son and together they are One in the Holy Spirit. (At the end of this exposition, in the piece named *The Aristocrat*, you will find out how the inmost and highest part of the soul creates and receives God-sonship and becomes the Son of God in the bosom or heart of the heavenly Father.)

It should also be understood that in nature the influence and expression of a higher power is pleasanter and more delightful to each thing than its own way or essence. [For example,] it is the way of water to flow downwards into the valley and that is its custom; but under the influence and action of the moon up in the sky, water forsakes and forgets its own way and flows uphill and its rising is easier than its downflow.

A person may conclude from this that it is right for him, too, to be glad, consciously, to suspend his own natural will and to deny himself and always to forego selfishness in whatever God gives him to bear. That makes good sense of what our Lord said: "If any man will come after me, let him deny himself and take up his cross"[49] —meaning that a man shall lay down and put away all the cross stands for in the way of suffering. For surely there can be no more crucifixion in suffering and pain for the man who has denied and forgotten self. To him it is all joy, delight, and heart's content. He really is following God and nothing can make this man suffer or be sorry any more than it can God.

Therefore, when our Lord says: "If any man will come to me, let him deny himself and take up his cross and follow me," that is not merely a command as some people think and say commonly; it is a faith—it is divine instruction as to how the suffering, work, and life of man may be filled with joy and delight: it is more a reward than a command. The person who does what our Lord requires has all he wants and still wants no evil thing, and that is the blessing of which our Lord spoke, saying: "Blessed are they which are persecuted for righteousness' sake."

When he said: "Let him deny himself and take up his cross and follow me," it was as if He said: "so that he might become a Son even as I was born one." For God is that same One that I am, the One I create in my nature by remaining in the bosom and heart of the Father. The Son also says: "Father, I will that they who come and follow me shall be where I am,"[50] but no one comes to the Son except by becoming the Son himself and no one can be where the Son is except he is in the Father's heart and bosom, one in the One as the Son is.

"I," says the Father, "will allure her . . . into a wilderness and there speak to her heart."[51] Heart to heart—for God loves One to one and hates everything alien or otherwise. He gathers all up into unity, the unity which all creatures really seek, even the meanest of his creatures. That the highest creatures can and do find this unity when they are lifted above their own natures, and transformed, is expressed, perhaps, in what the Son Jesus Christ says in his Godhead: "Father, where I am, there shall my servants be who have followed and come to me."[52]

There is another comfort we ought to know. It is impossible to break, spoil, or disturb nature except when a better good is intended—better than nature's present good. Nature is never satisfied to repeat her patterns; she always wants to improve on them. A wise physician does not disturb a man's sore finger merely to hurt him, especially if he cannot make the finger better and thus improve the whole man, doing good to him. If he can do the man and his finger good, he is glad, but if not, he cuts the finger off for the man's own welfare. It is better to lose the finger and keep the man than to ruin both the finger and the man. Better one hurt than two, especially if one is more serious than the other.

It is also well to remember that the finger and hand or any other bodily part would give up its own existence gladly and without thought in case of need, preferring the whole man to itself. It is certainly the truth to say that the member cares not for itself, but only for the body of which it is a member. Therefore, it stands to reason and is natural and right that we should care for ourselves not at all, except as God and in God. Then whatever God's will in us or for us, it is all so easy and delightful, especially if we know and are certain that God would allow incomparably less hurt or harm if he did not know that a great benefit was involved. Truly, if a man does not trust God, it is only natural that he should have much pain and misery.

There is another matter of comfort. St. Paul says that God chastises those he loves and accepts as Sons. [53] It follows that to be a Son of God is to suffer. It was not possible that the Son of God should suffer in eternity and therefore the heavenly Father sent him into time to become human and suffer. If you think you can be God's Son and not suffer, you are mistaken. It is written in the Book of Wisdom that God tries and proves the just man as gold is tried in the burning of the furnace. [54] When the king or prince sends a knight to the front line of battle, it is a sign of trust. I have seen one lord who, when he chose a household retainer, would ride out at night to meet and fight the candidate and it happened once that he was nearly killed one night by someone he was putting to the test and that knight was afterwards very dear to him and highly valued.

We read that St. Anthony once suffered greatly in the desert because of evil spirits and that when he had overcome his difficulty, our Lord appeared, visible and joyous. Then the saint said: "Ah, Lord, where were you just now when I needed you so much?" Our Lord replied: "I was here just as I am now but I did want the pleasure of seeing how stanch a person you are." Silver and gold may be pure, but when it comes to making a cup from which a king is to drink, it is burnt far longer than for other purposes. Thus the apostles wrote that they rejoiced at being worthy to suffer contempt and misery for God. [55]

He who was naturally the Son of God, because of his grace, willed to become human so that he might suffer for you. How is it, then, that you wish to become the Son of God so that you need not suffer, either for God or for yourself? If people could only know and consider how great the joy that God [in his own way], the angels,

and all who know and love God, have in human patience, by which
a man bears pain, misery, and loss for God's sake, they would find
in that knowledge sufficient reason to be comforted. A man will
forego his own good and endure adversity for a friend if in so doing
his friend might be rejoiced and shown affection. Suppose, however,
that his friend were suffering pain and misery for him, then certainly it would be only reasonable for him to go to that friend and
comfort the friend with his presence and consolations as much as he
could. Thus our Lord says in the Psalter, speaking of the good man,
that he will be with him in trouble.[56] From these words, seven
lessons and grounds for comfort are to be drawn.

First. St. Augustine says that when suffering for God, patience is
better, nobler, and more sublime than the sacrifice of any amount of
worldly goods involuntarily. Among those who love this world,
there are none so rich that they would not gladly go through much
weary hardship and misery if in so doing they might become masters
of the world.

Second. I shall not keep to the literal text of God's word which
says that he is with man in his suffering, but I shall pursue its meaning by saying: If God is with me when I suffer, what else shall I
want? If I am right, I shall want nothing else, nothing but God. St.
Augustine says that a man who is not satisfied with God is foolish
and far too greedy. How can one be satisfied with the spiritual or
material gifts of God if he is not satisfied with God himself? Thus
he says elsewhere: "Lord, if you send us away, give us another you,
for we want only you."

It is written in the Book of Wisdom: "With God, the eternal
wisdom, all good things have come to me at once."[57] One meaning
of this is that apart from God nothing is good or can be good and
that with God anything is good—good simply because it comes
with him. But aside from God himself, if the essence God gives to
creatures were taken from them, they would be pure nothings, un-
pleasant, worthless, and hateful. The text has also another noble
meaning which waits to be expressed: all good comes with God.
Our Lord says: "I will be with man in trouble," and St. Bernard's
comment is: "Lord, if you are with me in trouble, let me be in

trouble all the time; be in me always and with me, so that I may save you.''

Third. I say that, since God is with us when we suffer, he suffers with us. He really knows the truth who knows that what I am saying is true. God, suffering with man, suffers incomparably more in his own way than man suffers for him. It is therefore quite fair that I should suffer if God is willing to, for it is only right that I should be willing for all that God wills. I pray all day as God directs: Thy will be done. And yet when God wants suffering, I complain and that is wrong. So I say certainly, that God suffers gladly, with us and for us, but that he suffers without anguish when we suffer only for his sake. Suffering is then bliss to him and gives him no agony. If, therefore, we were what we should be, we should find in suffering, not anguish, but blessing and comfort.

Fourth. I note that misery is diminished by the sympathy of a friend, but if I can be comforted by human sympathy, how much more shall I find comfort in the compassion of God!

Fifth. If I am ready to suffer with a person I love, and who loves me, I shall justly and gladly suffer with God, as he is involved, when he suffers with me and because of his love.

Sixth. I maintain that, since God goes through my pain before I do, then if I suffer for him, then my agony, however great and manifold it may be, is a comfort and a joy and very easy. Naturally, when one person does something for another, the one for whom it was done is nearer the doer's heart than the deed done and the deed means nothing to the doer except as it affects him for whom it was done. The builder, hewing wood and stone for a house he builds against the summer heat and winter frost, thinks first and always of the house-to-be, except for which he would not be hewing stone or doing any of this work.

Now it is clear that a sick person who drinks sweet wine and thinks it bitter, and says so, is right, in that the wine loses its sweetness in the bitter coating of his tongue, before it has a chance to get into the soul and be recognized and approved. It is incomparably more so with the man who acts only for God. God is his medium, the environment of his soul, so that nothing gets to him without first losing its bitterness while going through God's sweetness. It all has to lose its bitterness and become pure sweetness before ever it can influence or affect that man's heart.

The authorities say that underneath heaven and around it there is a fire,—[2] such that rain or wind or storm or foul weather cannot enter to influence or affect heaven, as it does beneath the sky. These weather conditions are all consumed and destroyed before they can get in. So I say that all a man suffers and does through God will be sweetened with his sweetness before it can reach his emotions, if he acts and suffers for God alone. We say "through" God and that means that something reaches the emotions only through God's sweetness, after having been purified in the hot fire of divine love, in which the heart of the good man is wrapped.

It is now clear how the good man, justly and in many ways, finds comfort in trouble, work, and suffering. If he works and suffers through God, that is one way. If he is wrapped in God's love, that is another. This is the way, then, that one may know whether or not he is doing his all through God. If one finds that he is suffering without comfort, he may know that he is not working through God only, and he is not wrapped in divine love. King David says: "A fire comes with God and from God, surrounding all that is disagreeable to him and unlike him and burning it up."[58] That [fire] is pain, misery, and bitterness.

There remains the seventh lesson of the text "God is with us when we suffer and suffers with us." It is of the greatest comfort: God's property it is, to be pure One, in whom there is no contingent distinction,[59] intellectual or otherwise, such that everything in him is God himself. If that be true, I say that whatever the good man suffers he suffers for God and in God and God suffers with him, [and he speaks of] "my suffering in God" and "my suffering God." Suffering thus loses its anguish; how, then, should it bother me? I suffer in God; my suffering is God. If, for example, God is truth, then where I find truth I find him as truth. Similarly, where I find pure suffering for God and in God I find that suffering to be my God. If anyone cannot understand this, let him blame his own blindness and not blame me or truth.

Suffer, then, gladly and with friendship for God; for suffering is a useful blessing, as our Lord said: "Blessed are they that suffer for righteousness' sake." How could the loving God bear that good people, his friends, should ever be without suffering? Suppose a man had a friend who could suffer for one short day, with such great profit as to earn lasting honor and comfort, and suppose that man hindered his friend from suffering or caused his suffering to be prevented; one would hardly call him a friend or think him very fond. Very likely that is why God cannot permit his friends, the good people, to be without some suffering, even if they have suffered and might now do without it.

As I said above, the benefits of suffering ebb and flow with the goodness of the will. Therefore, whatever the good man is ready to bear and desires to bear for God, in God's sight, he has already borne in God and through God. King David says in the Psalter: "I am ready to be stricken down and my sorrow is continually before me."[60] St. Jerome says that an empty vessel, well made and good, ready for any use as required, is already endowed with all the properties one may expect of it, even if no one ever puts them to use; and as I said above, a stone is not less heavy because it rests on the earth: its weight consists in its tendency to fall or readiness to continue falling. That is why I have just said that a good man has done already everything he has willed to do on earth or in heaven and in this he is like God.

Thus we may observe and understand the dullness of those people who, when they see a good man bearing pain and misery, are astonished and full of surmises that his pains are due to obscure sins. They remark from time to time, "Ah! I thought he was such a good man! If I was right in believing him so faultless, how does he happen to have such pain and misery to bear?"[61] And of course, if it were pain and misery and only these that the man felt, he would not be good or without sin; but if a person is good, his suffering does not mean pain, unhappiness, or misery to him but rather a great delight and blessing. The Lord says: "Blessed are they that suffer for God and righteousness."

Thus the Book of Wisdom says that the souls of the just are in God's hands.[62] Foolish people think, as it seems to them, that the just die but they really go to peace, rapture, and blessing. St. Paul, in writing of the many sufferings of the saints, says that the world was not worthy of them. [63] Correctly analyzed, this saying means three things. The first is that the world was not worthy of the presence of these excellent persons. The second is better, that goodness is contrary to the way of the world and valueless to it; thus the saints are worthy of God and of worth to him only, as goodness has value only to God. It is, however, the third meaning that I now have in mind. People who love the things of this world are not worthy to bear pain and misery for God. It is written that the holy apostles rejoiced to be accounted worthy to bear hardships in God's name. [55]

I have now said enough. In the third section of this book, I shall mention several of the comforts available to the good man in adversity, comforts to be found in the deeds as well as the words of the good and the wise.

3

We read in the Book of Kings that someone cursed David the King, [64] offering him a gross insult; whereupon one of David's friends expressed a desire to kill the cur. But the king said: "By no means! Do him no harm. It may be that the Lord will requite me good for this cursing."

Also, in the Book of Patriarchs, we read that someone complained to a holy father that he was in trouble. The father said: "My son, do you want me to pray God to take it from you?" "No, father," he replied. "It is good for me, as I am well aware; but pray God to grant me grace to bear it wisely and with patience."

A sick man was asked why he did not pray God to make him well. He said that he was loath to do that, for three reasons. First, he was convinced and sure that the loving God would never have permitted him to be sick unless it was best for him. The second reason was that if a man is good, he will not want God to do what he wants done, for that would be wrong; he will rather want what God wants. Thus "if he wants me to be sick—and I should not be sick, except it were his will—it is not for me to want to be well. Without doubt, if it were possible for God to cure me against his own will, it would turn out to be unfortunate and bad for me." The will to suffer comes of love; the will not to suffer comes of want of love [unlove]. I much prefer, and it is better and more useful to me, to love God and be sick, rather than to be sound of body and not love God. What God loves is something; what he does not love is nothing.

It says in the Book of Wisdom—and there is some truth in it—that when God wills a thing—by the very fact that he wills it—it is good. Humanly speaking, I should prefer that a rich and powerful person such as a king, loved me, even if he gave me nothing for a while, rather than to have him summon me for a gift when he did not love me—provided he refrained from giving me anything because, loving me, he proposed at some later time to endow me more richly and more substantially. Furthermore, I take it that a man who loves me and gives me nothing—not even considering a present to me—may presently think better of it and make me a gift. Thus I must wait patiently, especially when he is to give of his own free grace and his gift is undeserved. It is also only fair that he should give me nothing and hate me and leave me to my fate, when I have no regard for his love and oppose my will to his, except when I want to get something from him.

The third reason why I am loath to ask God to give back my health is that I will not and ought not to ask the rich, loving, and bountiful God for so small a thing. Suppose that I traveled a hundred or two miles to see the Pope and, coming before him, I said: "My Lord, holy father, I have traveled nearly two hundred miles at great cost and I pray you, since I have come so far, to give me a bean!" Of course, he and all who heard it would be correct in saying that I was a great fool. Now this I say, and it is a sure matter, that compared to God all good things, even all creation, is less than a bean. Therefore, with good reason, if I am a good and wise man, I shall be ashamed if I pray to be made well again.

In passing, let me also say that it is a sign of inward infirmity that any person should be glad or sad about the passing things of this world. If one is even aware of them, he should be deeply ashamed before God, the angels, and people, even as one feels shame enough over some [trifling] facial defect that is visible to all. But why say more? The books of the Old and New [Testaments], the saintly fathers, and heathen virtuosi, all abound [with instances of] how devout people, either for God, or by reason of native virtue, have willingly surrendered their lives and denied themselves.

One of the heathen, Socrates, says that virtue makes the impossible possible and even easy and pleasant. [In that connection] I must not forget that blessed lady, of whom Maccabees tells,[65] who looked on one day while frightful punishments of inhuman cruelty were inflicted on her seven sons and heard their cries. Gaily she watched, encouraging them and counseling them severally to have no fear and willingly to surrender body and soul for God's justice.

When I have mentioned two more points, that will be enough. This is the first. When a good and godly person sees how a huckster will dare the uncertainties of a distant country, make toilsome journeys over mountains and valleys, deserts and seas, risking the robbery of his goods and the murdering of his body, suffering dire want of food and drink, sleep and other comforts, all for the sake of making a little money, gladly forgetting it all for his small, uncertain profit, he should feel quite bad and greatly ashamed that he, a good man and godly, should ever be excited about suffering. A knight risks his goods, his body, and his soul in a fight, hoping for a brief, passing glory—and yet we think we are great when we endure a little pain for God and hope for the eternal blessing.

The other matter I have in mind is that stupid people say that many of the ideas I have set down in this book and elsewhere are not true. I reply to them with St. Augustine's words in the first book of his *Confessions*.[66] He says that God is doing today all that shall be done in the thousands upon thousands of years of the future—if the world is to last so long—and that God is still doing today all he ever did in the many thousands of years of the past. What can I do about it, if anyone does not understand that? He also says elsewhere that it is pure self-love when people try to blind others to conceal their own blindness. I am satisfied that what I say is true in myself and in God. Someone might look at a shaft stuck down into the water and think it crooked even though it is straight, because the water is denser than the air; but the shaft is always straight to him who sees it only in the rarer air.

St. Augustine says that to apprehend apart from thought, apart from spatial forms and imagination, without [depending on] abstracting what is seen, is to know the truth of things. Those who do not know this way will laugh and mock at me and I shall pity them. They like to look at eternal things and consider divine works and to stand in the light of eternity, while their hearts still flutter about in yesterday and today, in space and time.

Seneca, a heathen philosopher, says: "A man should speak of great and high matters with intent that is great and high and with an exalted soul; and further, it should be said that such learning should not be exposed before the uncultured either in speech or in writing." To which I reply: If ignorant people are not taught, they will never learn, nor will they ever know how to live or die.[67] For this the unlettered man is taught: to change him from an ignorant to a cultured person. If there were nothing new there could be nothing old, and so our Lord said: "They that are whole have no need of the physician."[68] It is the physician's point in being, to make the sick well.

If these words are misconstrued, what can one who puts their right construction on them do about it? St. John proclaims his holy Gospel to all believers, and to unbelievers so that they may become believers, and yet he begins by speaking of God in terms higher than anyone had ever used before. And his words, as indeed the words of our Lord, are often misconstrued.

May the loving and compassionate God, who is the truth itself, grant to me and to all who read this book an inward awareness of truth.

The Aristocrat[1]

OUR LORD says in the gospel: "A certain nobleman went into a far country to receive for himself a kingdom, and to return."[2] In these words our Lord teaches how noble man is by nature created and how divine, by grace, he may aspire to be. This is the point of a major part of the Holy Scriptures.

To begin with, let us recognize the obvious fact that man has two natures, the body and the spirit. As one writer puts it: "To know one's self is to know all creatures; for they are all either body or spirit." Similarly, the Scriptures say of human beings that there is an outward man and, along with him, an inner man.

To the outward man belong those things that depend on the soul but are connected with the flesh and blended with it, and the cooperative functions of the several members such as the eye, the ear, the tongue, the hand, and so on. The Scripture speaks of all this as the old man, the earthy man, the outward person, the enemy, the servant.

Within us all is the other person, the inner man, whom the Scripture calls the new man, the heavenly man, the young person, a friend, the aristocrat. And that is what our Lord meant when he said that an aristocrat went into a far country and got himself a kingdom and returned.

In this connection, it is worth noting what Jerome says and what the authorities usually teach, that every man, because he is a man, has within him a good spirit, an angel, and also an evil spirit, a devil. The good angel is always counseling him and alluring him toward the good and the divine, toward the virtuous, the heavenly, and the eternal. The bad spirit advises and tempts the man always toward the temporal and passing, to all that is sinful, evil, and devilish. The bad spirit keeps a rendezvous with the outward man, through whom it is insinuated to the inner man, as the snake had its assignation with Lady Eve, and through her with Mr. Adam. Adam is the inner person—the man in the soul. He is the good tree of which our Lord speaks, the tree that always brings forth good fruit. He is the field in which the good seed was sowed, the field in which God planted his own idea and likeness, the root of all wisdom, all knowledge and virtue and goodness. He is the seed of the divine nature. The seed is God's Son, God's word!

But the outward man is hostile to him, wickedly sowing the tares. St. Paul speaks of *him*: "I find in myself something that hinders and is contrary to the command and counsel of God"[3]—to what God has commanded and ordained and still ordains in the highest part, the core of my soul. Elsewhere he complains: "O wretched man that I am, who shall deliver me from the body of this death-bringing flesh?" In still another passage he writes that the human spirit and flesh are constantly at war with each other.[4] The flesh advises vice and evil; the spirit, the counsel and love of God and his peace and joy and other virtues. To be obedient to the spirit's counsel, and to live by it, is to have eternal life; but to obey the flesh is to die. Our Lord is speaking of the inner man when he says that an aristocrat went into a far country. The inner man is also the good tree that our Lord says always bears good fruit and never bad; for the inner man always wants the good, tends toward goodness, and soars into the good, unconcerned about this or that. The outward man is the bad tree that cannot bear good fruit.

Relative to the aristocracy of the inner, spiritual man and the commonalty of the outward, physical person, the heathen philosophers, Tully and Seneca, maintain that no rational soul is without God.[5] The seed of God is in us. Given an intelligent farmer and a diligent fieldhand, it will thrive and grow up to God whose seed it is and, accordingly, its fruit will be God-nature. Pear seeds grow into pear trees; nut seeds into nut trees, and God-seed into God!

But if the good seed has a foolish farmer and a bad cultivator, weeds grow up with it, covering it and crowding it so that it gets no light and cannot grow. Still, Origen, a high authority, says: "Even though it is covered up, because it is God that has sowed this seed in us, pressed it in, begotten it, it cannot be extirpated or die out; it glows and sparkles, burning and giving light, and always it moves upward toward God."

For the inner man, the new man—says St. Augustine—the first grade is living according to the ideas of good and saintly people but he is still childish, dependent and like an infant at the breast.

In the second grade, he no longer attends only to the examples of good people but he runs in hot pursuit of instruction, the counsel of God and divine wisdom, turning his back on the human and his face toward God, crawling out of his mother's lap and smiling at the heavenly Father.

In the third grade, he begins to leave his mother's bosom, straying farther and farther from her, escaping her care and putting fear away. And then, even if it were possible for him to be unjust or cruel to others with impunity, he would not be satisfied to do so. He is taken up with the love of God, trusting him with such zeal that at last he is established in joy and delight, so that whatever is unlike God, or alien to him, or unseemly in his presence has become disagreeable.

In the fourth grade he keeps growing and becomes sufficiently rooted in God's love to be ready always to encounter temptation in any shape, to be put to the test, and is willing to suffer and to suffer gladly, with desire and joy.

In the fifth grade, he is at peace with himself and the world, at rest in the riches and delight of the highest, unspeakable wisdom.

In the sixth grade, he is "disformed" and transformed in the divine eternal nature, having achieved full perfection. He has forgotten the things of this passing temporal life and has been caught up into the likeness of God, having become a child of God. There is no higher grade, nothing beyond this. It is eternal rest and blessing —the final end of the inner and new man, eternal life.

As for this inner aristocrat, stamped with the likeness of God, in whom the divine seed is sown, sometimes this seed and likeness of the divine nature appears, and one is aware of it; and then again it goes into hiding. Origen, that eminent authority, treats this [phenomenon] with a simile: God's Son or Idea is like a flowing spring in the core of the soul. If you throw earth over it, that is, earthly desires, it will be choked up and covered so that you may not know where it is or be aware of it any more. It is still flowing, however, and if the dirt that has been thrown over it is removed, it will be discovered again and one will know about it. He says further that the Book of Genesis is hinting at this when it tells how Abraham dug a well in his field.[6] Bad people filled it up again with earth but when the earth was again thrown out, the running spring appeared as before.

Another simile to the same point: The sun is constantly shining but when clouds or mist are between us and the sun, we do not get the sunshine. So, too, when eyesight fails or the eye is hurt, we do not see daylight. Sometimes I have used this illustration. When an artist makes a sculpture out of wood or stone, he does not put his idea into the wood but, rather, he chips away the material that has been hiding it. He does not impart something to the wood but cuts the covering away and removes the tarnish so that what was hidden there may shine. This is "the treasure hid in a field" of which our Lord speaks in the Gospel.[7]

St. Augustine says that when the human soul is fully devoted to eternity, turned to God alone, the divine image appears in it shining. When, however, the soul turns away, even if it be to outward deeds of virtue, the divine image is covered up. This is suggested by St. Paul's doctrine that a woman's head should be covered, while men are uncovered. That to which the soul inclines tends always to become like a cover or a hood; but in being lifted up, the soul is made naked before the idea of God, for God's begetting; the image of God is unveiled and free in the open soul of the aristocrat; and the Son of God, the seed of the divine nature is not extinguished even though it be covered up. David says in the Psalter that, even if vanity and suffering and sorrow are the portion of man, still he remains in the image of God and God's image in him.[8] The true light shines in the darkness even though no man is aware of it.

As the Book of Love has it: "Look not upon me because I am brown; I am comely and beautiful—it is only that the sun hath altered my color."[9] The sun is the light of this world and so it means that even the best and highest of creatures will encrust the idea of God within us and discolor it. "Take away the dross from the silver," says Solomon, "and the purest of vessels will shine forth and sparkle"[10]—the idea of God in the soul.

That is also what our Lord meant when he said in the text that an aristocrat went out. For a man has to go outside any form or self and be alien to it and unlike it, if he really wants to become a Son, and receive Sonship in the bosom and heart of the Father. Anything that interferes [between the soul and God] is foreign to God.

God says: "I am the first and the last."[11] There are no distinctions in God and no differences between the divine persons, since they are to be regarded as one in nature. The divine nature is Oneness and each person is One, the same One in nature. The distinction between being and existence is referred back then to the One, where they are the same thing. When that oneness is no longer in oneself, then division has crept in. Since we find God in oneness, that oneness must be in him who is to find God. Our Lord says that "a man went out." Neither the One, nor being, nor God, nor rest, nor blessedness, nor satisfaction is to be found where distinctions are. Be therefore that One so that you may find God. And of course, if you are wholly that One, you shall remain so, even where distinctions are. Different things will all be parts of that One to you and will no longer stand in your way. The One remains the same One in thousands of thousands of stones as much as in four stones: a thousand times a thousand is just as simple a number as four.

A heathen authority says that the One is born of the supreme God. Its property is to be the one in One; to look for unity short of God is to be self-deceived. The same authority, to whom I now refer for the fourth time, says that this One is a friend only to persons of chaste and virgin hearts, or, as St. Paul says: "As a chaste virgin I have given you in marriage."[12] This is how man is to be united to the One that only God is.

"A man went out," says the Lord. The true meaning of the word "man" in Latin, according to one interpretation, is a person who submits completely to God, giving up all he is and has, a person who looks up to God, disregarding the self which he has left beneath and behind him. That is genuine and perfect humility. Man gets his name from the earth[13] but I shall say no more about that here. "Man" also means that which is above nature and time and spatial and corporeal things but which is subject to time, and is temporary because it is spatial and physical.

When this man "goes out" still farther on his way, he has nothing more to do with vanity, in the sense that he does not copy anything else and there is nothing like him. There is no vanity to be found in him, for vanity has been removed from him to the extent that he is now pure being, goodness and truth. To be like this is to be an aristocrat and nothing else.

Our Lord uses still another interpretation or doctrine of the aristocrat. It should be remembered that those who know God through his disguises know creatures, too, in the same way. Since knowledge is the light of the soul, naturally everybody wants it; there is nothing better. Knowledge is good. Thus, the authorities teach that when one knows creatures as they are in themselves, that is "twilight knowledge," in which creation is perceived by clearly distinguished ideas; but when creatures are known in God, that is "daybreak knowledge," in which creatures are perceived without distinctions, all ideas being rejected, all comparisons done away in that One that God himself is. This is the knowledge that characterizes the aristocrat, of whom our Lord says that he "went out." He is aristocratic because he is One and knows God and creatures as they are One.

I shall offer still another explanation of what an aristocrat is. I say that when a man looks at God [in soul and spirit], he knows it and knows that he is the knower. That is to say, he knows it is God he is looking at and knows that he knows him. Now some people wish it to appear that the flower, the kernel of blessing is this awareness of the spirit, that it is *knowing* God. For if I have rapture and am unconscious of it, what good would it do and what would it mean? I cannot agree with this position.

For granting that the soul could not be happy without it [consciousness of its own processes], still its happiness does not consist in that; for the foundation of spiritual blessing is this: that the soul look at God without anything between; here it receives its being and life and draws its essence from the core of God, unconscious of the knowing-process, or love or anything else. Then it is quite still in the essence of God, not knowing at all where it is, knowing nothing but God.

When, however, the soul is aware that it is looking at God, loving

him and knowing him, that already is a retrogression, a quick
retreat back to the upper level of the natural order of things. For no
one can know that he is white except a person who is white. To
know, therefore, that you are white is to overlay your being white
with something extraneous to it; your knowledge [of your white-
ness] is therefore not immediate; you do not get it unconsciously
from the color; but your soul gets its perception, its awareness [of
your whiteness] not from the actual color but from something [the
idea of whiteness?] made white and thus a man thinks himself
white.[14] To know that one is white is far short of being white, and
quite external to it. The wall is something quite different from the
foundation on which it is built.

The authorities teach that the agent of the soul which enables the
eye to see is one thing, and that the agent which enables one to know
that he sees is quite another. Take the former case—in which the
eye sees. This depends entirely on color and not on the thing colored.
It is independent of whether the thing colored is a stone or wood, a
person or an angel; if only it has color, that is all that matters.

So I say that the aristocrat is one who derives his being, his life,
and his happiness from God alone, with God and in God and not at
all from his knowledge, perception, or love of God, or any such
thing. Thus our Lord says very well that life eternal is to know God
as the only true God[15] and not that it is knowledge that God may be
known. A person can hardly know that he knows God when he does
not know himself! This much is certain: when a man is happy, happy
to the core and root of beatitude, he is no longer conscious of himself
or anything else. He is conscious only of God.

To be conscious of knowing God is to know *about* God and self.
As I have just been explaining, the agent of the soul which enables
one to see is one thing and the agent by which one knows that he
sees is another. Of course, in this world, it is only just that the
agent which makes us conscious of seeing should rank above the
agent of vision itself, for nature begins its work with lowliest
things, whereas God begins with those things that are most perfect.
Nature makes the man from the child, and the hen from the egg, but
God makes the man and then the child, the hen and then the egg.
Nature first makes the wood warm, then hot, and only then gives

the wood over to fire, but God begins by giving creatures existence. That is where time comes in, and all the properties of things which belong to time—existing beside the timeless. So, too, God gives out the Holy Spirit, before the gifts of the Holy Spirit.

Thus, then, I say: there will be no blessing except a man be conscious of his vision and knowledge of God but it is not the will of God that I be blessed on that basis. If anyone will have it otherwise, let him do so; I can only pity him. The heat and the essence of fire are two different things, far apart in nature, yet close together in space and time. So, too, God's sight and mine are far different—utterly dissimilar. . . .

Our Lord well says that "an aristocrat went into a far country to receive a kingdom for himself, and to return." For a man must himself be One, seeking unity both in himself and in the One, experiencing it as the One, which means that he must see God and God only. And then he must "return," which is to say, he must have knowledge of God and be conscious of his knowledge.

The prophet Ezekiel has already pointed out all that I have said here: "A great eagle, with great wings, long wings full of feathers of divers colors, came to the undefiled mountain and seized the culmen of the highest tree, breaking it off and bearing it down. . . ."[16] What our Lord calls an aristocrat, the prophet calls a great eagle. Who ranks above him? For he is born, on one side, from the highest and best in the domain of creatures and on the other side, from the inmost core of the divine nature in its solitude.

Our Lord speaks in the prophet Hosea: "I will allure her—the soul of the aristocrat—into the wilderness and there speak to her heart"[17]—that is, One to one, one from One, one in One and the One in one, eternally.

About Disinterest[1]

I HAVE read much of what has been written, both by heathen philosophers and sages and in the Old and New Testaments. I have sought earnestly and with great diligence that good and high virtue by which man may draw closest to God and through which one may best approximate the idea God had of him before he was created, when there was no separation between man and God; and having delved into all this writing, as far as my intelligence would permit, I find that [high virtue] to be pure disinterest, that is, detachment from creatures. Our Lord said to Martha: "*Unum est necessarium*,"[2] which is to say: to be untroubled and pure, one thing is necessary and that is disinterest.

The teachers praise love, and highly too, as St. Paul did, when he said: "No matter what I do, if I have not love, I am nothing."[3] Nevertheless, I put disinterest higher than love. My first reason is as follows. The best thing about love is that it makes me love God. Now, it is much more advantageous for me to move God toward myself than for me to move toward him, for my blessing in eternity depends on my being identified with God.[4] He is more able to deal with me and join me than I am to join him. Disinterest brings God to me and I can demonstrate it this way: Everything likes its own habitat best; God's habitat is purity and unity, which are due to disinterest. Therefore God necessarily gives himself to the disinterested heart.

In the second place, I put disinterest above love because love compels me to suffer for God's sake, whereas disinterest makes me sensitive only to God. This ranks far above suffering for God or in God; for, when he suffers, man pays some attention to the creature from which his suffering comes, but being disinterested, he is quite detached from the creature. I demonstrate that, being disinterested, a man is sensitive only to God, in this way: Experience must always be an experience of something, but disinterest comes so close to zero[5] that nothing but God is rarefied enough to get into it, to enter the disinterested heart. That is why a disinterested person is sensitive to nothing but God. Each person experiences things in his own way and thus every distinguishable thing is seen and understood according to the approach[6] of the beholder and not, as it might be, from its own point of view.

The authorities also praise humility above other virtues, but I put disinterest above humility for the following reasons. There can be humility without disinterest but disinterest cannot be perfect without humility; perfect humility depends on self-denial; disinterest comes so near to zero that nothing may intervene. Thus, there cannot be disinterest without humility and, anyway, two virtues are better than one!

The second reason I put disinterest above humility is that in humility man abases himself before creatures, and in doing so pays some attention to the creatures themselves. Disinterest, however, stays within itself. No transference of attention [such as humility] can ever rank so high that being self-contained[7] will not go higher. As the prophet puts it: "*Omnis gloria filiae regis ab intus,*"[8] which means, "the glory of the king's daughter comes from within her." Perfectly disinterested, a man has no regard for anything, no inclination to be above this or below that, no desire to be over or under; he remains what he is, neither loving nor hating, and desiring neither likeness to this or unlikeness to that. He desires only to be one and the same; for to want to be this or that is to want something; and the disinterested person wants nothing.[9] Thus everything remains unaffected as far as he is concerned.

Someone may say: Surely our Lady had all the virtues and therefore she must have been perfectly disinterested. If then, disinterest ranks above virtue, why did the Lady glory in her humility rather than in disinterest? She said: "*Quia respexit Dominus humilitatem ancillae suae.*" That means: "He hath regarded the low estate of his handmaiden."[10]

I reply by saying that in God there is both disinterest and humility as well, to the extent that virtues may be attributed to God. You should know that it was loving humility that made God stoop to human nature, the same humility by which he created heaven and earth, as I shall later explain. And if our Lord, willing to become man, still remained unaffected in his disinterest, our Lady must have known that he desired this of her, too, and that therefore he would have regard to her humility rather than to her disinterest. Thus she continued, unmoved in her disinterestedness, and yet she gloried in humility.[11]

If, however, she had said: "He hath regarded my disinterest," her disinterest would have been qualified by the thought and not perfect, for she would have departed from it. Any departure from disinterest, however small, disturbs it; and there you have the reason why our Lady gloried in humility rather than in disinterest. The prophet says: "*Audiam, qui loquatur in me Dominus Deus,*"[12] which means "I will be silent and hear what God the Lord will utter within me"—as if to say, "If God the Lord wants to speak to me, let him come in, for I shall not go out." As Boethius puts it: "Ye people, why do you seek without for the blessing that is within you?"[13]

I also put disinterest above mercy, for mercy is nothing but a man's going out to the want of a fellow and the heart is disturbed by it. Disinterest, however, is exempt from this, being self-contained and allowing nothing to disturb. To speak briefly: When I survey the virtues, I find none as flawless, as conducive to God as disinterest.

A philosopher named Avicenna[14] said: "The rank of a disinterested mind is so high that what it sees is true, what it desires comes to pass, what it commands must be done." You may take this for the truth, that when a free mind is really disinterested, God is compelled to come into it; and if it could get along without contingent forms, it would then have all the properties of God himself. Of course, God cannot give his properties away and so he can do nothing for the disinterested mind except to give himself to it and it is then caught up into eternity, where transitory things no longer affect it. Then the man has no experiences of the physical order and is said to be dead to the world, since he has no appetite for any earthly thing. That is what St. Paul meant by saying: "I live; yet not I, but Christ liveth in me."[15]

You may ask: "What is this disinterest, that it is so noble a matter?" Know, then, that a mind unmoved by any contingent affection or sorrow, or honor, or slander, or vice, is really disinterested—like a broad mountain that is not shaken by a gentle wind. Unmovable disinterest brings man into his closest resemblance to God. It gives God his status as God. His purity is derived from it, and then his simplicity and unchangeable character. If man is to be like God, to the extent that any creature may resemble him, the likeness will come through disinterest, and man proceeds from purity to simplicity and from simplicity to unchangeableness, and thus the likeness of God and man comes about. It is an achievement of the grace that allures man away from temporal things and purges him of the transitory. Keep this in mind: to be full of things is to be empty of God, while to be empty of things is to be full of God.

Bear in mind also that God has been immovably disinterested from the beginning and still is and that his creation of the heavens and the earth affected him as little as if he had not made a single creature. But I go further. All the prayers a man may offer and the good works he may do will affect the disinterested God as little as if there were neither prayers nor works, nor will God be any more compassionate or stoop down to man any more because of his prayers and works than if they were omitted.

Furthermore, I say that when the Son in the Godhead willed to be human and became so, suffering martyrdom, the immovable disinterest of God was affected as little as if the Son had never become human at all.

Perhaps, then, you will say: "I take it, therefore, that prayers and good works are so much lost motion; God pays no attention to them and will not be moved by them. And yet they say that God wants us to pray to him about everything."

Now pay close attention and understand what I mean, if you can. When God first looked out of eternity (if one may say that he ever *first* looked out), he saw everything as it would happen and at the same time he saw when and how he would create each thing. He foresaw the loving prayers and the good deeds each person might do and knew which prayers and which devotions he would heed. He foresaw that tomorrow morning you will cry out to him in earnest prayer and that tomorrow morning he will not heed you because he had already heard your prayer in his eternity, before you became a person; and if your prayer is neither honest nor earnest, he will not deny it now, for it is already denied in eternity. In that first eternal vision, God looked on each thing-to-be and therefore he does what he now does without a reason. It was all worked out beforehand.

Still, even if God remains forever unmoved, disinterested, the prayers and good works of people are not lost on that account, for well-doing is never without its reward. Philippus[16] says: "God the Creator holds things to the course and order he ordained for them in the beginning." To God there is neither past nor future and he loves the saints, having foreseen them before ever the world began. Then, when events, foreseen by God in eternity, come to pass in time, people think that God has taken a new departure, either to anger or toward some agreeable end; but it is we who change, while he remains unchanged. Sunshine hurts ailing eyes but is agreeable to sound ones, and yet it is the same sunshine in both cases. God does not see through time, nor does anything new happen in his sight.

Isidore[17] makes the same point in his book on the highest good. He says: "Many people ask what God was doing before he created heaven and earth. Where did he get his new impulse to make creatures? This is the answer: There never was a departure in God, nor a change of intention, and if there ever was a time when creatures did not exist as they do now, still they existed forever in God, in the mind of God." God did not make heaven and earth as our time-bound speech describes creation; they came into being when He spoke the word out of eternity. Moses said to our Lord, "Lord, if Pharaoh asks who you are, what shall I tell him?" The Lord replied: "Tell him that *he-who-is* sent you." We might say: The unchanging One hath sent me!

Someone well may ask: had Christ this unmoved disinterest when he said: "My soul is sorrowful even unto death"?[18] Or Mary, when she stood underneath the cross?[19] Much has been made of her lamentations. How are such things compatible with unmoved disinterest?

On this point the authorities say that a person is not one, but two people. One is called the outward man—the sensual person. He is served by the five senses, which function by means of the soul's agents. The other is the inner man—the spiritual person. But notice this, that a man who loves God prefers not to use the agents of the soul in the outward man any more than necessary and then the inner man has recourse to the five senses only to the degree to which he can guide and lead them. He guards them against animal diversions —such as people choose when they live like animals without intelligence. Such people are more properly called animals than persons.

Whatever strength the soul possesses, beyond what it devotes to the five senses, it gives to the inner man. If this inner man is devoted to some high and noble enterprise, the soul recalls its agents and the person is said to be senseless or rapt because his enterprise or object is an unintelligible idea or is unintelligible without being an idea. Remember that God requires of every spiritual person a love which includes all the agents of the soul. Thus he said: "Love your God with all your heart."

There are people who squander the strength of their souls in the outward man. These are the people, all of whose desires and thoughts turn on transient goods, since they are unaware of the inner person. Sometimes a good man robs his outward person of all the soul's agents, in order to dispatch them on some higher enterprise; so, conversely, animal people rob the inner person of the soul's agents and assign them to the outward man. A man may be ever so active outwardly and still leave the inner man unmoved and passive.

Now both in Christ and our Lady, there was an outward man and an inner person and, while they taught about external matters, they were outwardly active but inwardly unmoved and disinterested.[20] This is how it was when Christ said: "My soul is sorrowful even unto death." And whatever the lamentations and other speeches of our Lady, inwardly she was still unmoved and disinterested. Take an illustration. A door swings to and fro through an angle. I compare the breadth of the door to the outward man and the hinge to the inner person. When the door swings to and fro, the breadth of the door moves back and forth, but the hinge is still unmoved and unchanged. It is like this here.

Now I ask what the object of pure disinterest is. I reply that it is neither this nor that. Pure disinterest is empty nothingness,[21] for it is on that high plane on which God gives effect to his will. It is not possible for God to do his will in every heart, for even though he is almighty, he cannot act except where he finds preparations made or he makes them himself. I say "or makes them" on account of St. Paul, for God did not find him ready; he prepared St. Paul by an infusion of grace.[22] Otherwise, I say that God acts where he finds that preparations have been made.

God's activity is not the same in a man as in a stone; and there is a simile for that, too, in nature. If a bake oven is heated and lumps of dough are put into it, some of oatmeal, some of barley, some of rye, and some of wheat, then, even though there is only one heat for all in the oven, it will not act the same way on the various doughs; for one turns into a pretty loaf, another to a rough loaf, and others still rougher. That is not due to the heat but to the material, which differs. Similarly God does not work in all hearts alike but according to the preparation and sensitivity he finds in each. In a given heart, containing this or that, there may be an item which prevents God's highest activity. Therefore if a heart is to be ready for him, it must be emptied out to nothingness, the condition of its maximum capacity. So, too, a disinterested heart, reduced to nothingness, is the optimum, the condition of maximum sensitivity.

Take an illustration from nature. If I wish to write on a white tablet, then no matter how fine the matter already written on it, it will confuse me and prevent me from writing down [my thoughts]; so that, if I still wish to use the tablet, I must first erase all that is written on it, but it will never serve me as well for writing as when it is clean. Similarly, if God is to write his message about the highest matters on my heart, everything to be referred to as "this or that" must first come out and I must be disinterested. God is free to do his will on his own level when my heart, being disinterested, is bent on neither this nor that.

Then I ask: What is the prayer of the disinterested heart? I answer by saying that a disinterested man, pure in heart, has no prayer, for to pray is to want something from God, something added that one desires, or something that God is to take away. The disinterested person, however, wants nothing, and neither has he anything of which he would be rid. Therefore he has no prayer, or he prays only to be uniform with God. In this sense we may understand the comment of St. Dionysius[23] on a text of St. Paul—"they which run in a race run all, but one receiveth the prize"—that is, all the soul's agents race for the prize but only the soul's essence receives it. Thus, Dionysius says: "This race is precisely the flight from creatures to union with the uncreated." When the soul achieves this, it loses its identity, it absorbs God and is reduced to nothing, as the dawn at the rising of the sun. Nothing helps toward this end like disinterest.

To this point we may quote a saying of St. Augustine: "There is a heavenly door for the soul into the divine nature—where some-things are reduced to nothings." On earth, this door is precisely disinterest, and when disinterest reaches its apex it will be unaware of its knowledge, it will not love its own love, and will be in the dark about its own light. Here, too, we may quote the comment of an authority: "Blessed are the pure in heart who leave everything to God now as they did before ever they existed." No one can do this without a pure, disinterested heart.

That God prefers a disinterested heart for his habitation may be seen from the question: "What is God looking for in everything?" I reply with these words from the Book of Wisdom: "I seek peace in all things."[24] There is, however, no peace except in disinterest. Therefore God prefers it to any other condition or virtue. Remember, too, that the more his heart is trained to be sensitive to divine influences, the happier man is; the further he pushes his preparation, the higher he ascends in the scale of happiness.

But no man can be sensitive to divine influence except by conforming to God, and in proportion to his conformity he is sensitive to divine influence. Conformity comes of submission to God. The more subject to creatures a man is, the less he conforms to God, but the pure, disinterested heart, being void of creatures, is constantly worshiping God and conforming to him, and is therefore sensitive to his influence. That is what St. Paul means by saying: "Put ye on the Lord Jesus Christ"[25]—that is, conform to Christ! Remember that when Christ became man, he was not one man but took all human nature on himself. If you get out, therefore, and clear of creatures, what Christ took on himself will be left to you and you will have put on Christ.

If any man will see the excellence and use of perfect disinterest, let him take seriously what Christ said to his disciples about his humanity: "It is expedient for you that I go away: for if I go not away, the Comforter will not come unto you"[26]—as if he said: "You take too much pleasure in my visible form and therefore the perfect pleasure of the Holy Spirit cannot be yours." Therefore discard the form and be joined to the formless essence, for the spiritual comfort of God is very subtle and is not extended except to those who despise physical comforts.

Heed this, intelligent people: Life is good to the man who goes, on and on, disinterestedly. There is no physical or fleshly pleasure without some spiritual harm, for the desires of the flesh are contrary to those of the spirit, and the desires of the spirit are contrary to the flesh. That is why to sow the undisciplined love of the flesh is to be cut off by death, but to sow the disciplined love of the spirit is to reap of the spirit, life eternal. The less one pays attention to the creature things, the more the Creator pursues him.

Listen to this, man of intelligence: If the pleasure we take in the physical form of Christ diminishes our sensitivity to the Holy Spirit, how much more will the pleasure we take in the comfort of transitory things be a barrier against God? Disinterest is best of all, for by it the soul is unified, knowledge is made pure, the heart is kindled, the spirit wakened, the desires quickened, the virtues enhanced. Disinterest brings knowledge of God; cut off from the creature, the soul unites with God; for love apart from God is like water to a fire, while love with God is the honeycomb in the honey.

Hear this, every intelligent spirit: The steed swiftest to carry you to perfection is suffering, for none shall attain eternal life except he pass through great bitterness with Christ. Nothing pierces man like suffering and nothing is more honey sweet than to have suffered. The surest basis on which perfection rests is humility, and he whose nature kneels in deepest lowliness—*his* spirit shall rise up to the heights of divinity; for as love brings sorrow, sorrow also brings love. Human ways are various: one person lives thus and another so.

For him who wishes to attain the utmost in life in his time, I set down here several aphorisms, much abbreviated, and taken from many writings.

Among men, be aloof; do not engage yourself to any idea you get; free yourself from everything chance brings to you, things that accumulate and cumber you; set your mind in virtue to contemplation, in which the God you bear in your heart shall be your steady object, the object from which your attention never wavers; and whatever else your duty may be, whether it be fasting, watching, or praying, dedicate it all to this one end, doing each only as much as is necessary to your single end. Thus you shall come to the goal of perfection.

Someone may ask: "Who could long endure this unwavering contemplation of the divine object?" I reply: No one living in such times as these. I tell you privately about these things only to have you know what the highest is, so that you may desire it and aspire to it. And if this vision is withdrawn from you, if you are a good man, the withdrawal shall be to you as if the eternity of bliss were taken away, but you must return at once to the pursuit of it, so that it may return to you. Even so, set a perpetual watch over yourself and your thoughts and let your refuge be in this [vision], in which you abide as constantly as possible. Lord God, be thou praised forever! Amen.

The Sermons

"Someone complained to Meister Eckhart that no one could understand his sermons. Whereupon he said: 'To understand my preaching, five things are needed. The hearer must have conquered strife; he must be contemplating his highest good; he must be satisfied to do God's bidding; he must be a beginner among beginners; and denying himself, he must be so a master of himself as to be incapable of anger.' "

"Some said, He is a good man: others said, Nay; but he deceiveth the people."   John 7:12

This is Meister Eckhart from whom God hid nothing[1]

DUM MEDIUM SILENTIUM TENERENT OMNIA ET NOX
IN SUO CURSU MEDIUM ITER HABERET. . . .

(Wisdom of Solomon 18:14)

"FOR while all things were wrapped in peaceful silence and night was in the midst of its swift course . . ."

Because the same One, who is begotten and born of God the Father, without ceasing in eternity,[2] is born today, within time, in human nature, we make a holiday[3] to celebrate it. St. Augustine says that this birth is always happening. And yet, if it does not occur in me, how could it help me? Everything depends on that.[4]

We intend to discuss, therefore, how it does occur in us, or how it is made perfect in a good soul, for it is in a good soul that God the Father is speaking his eternal word. What I shall say applies to that perfect person who has turned to the way of God and continues in it, and not to the natural undisciplined person who is far from this birth and ignorant of it. This, then, is the saying of the wise man: "While all things were wrapped in peaceful silence . . . a secret word leaped down from heaven, out of the royal throne, to me."[5] This sermon is to be on that word.

Three points are, then, noteworthy. The first is: where does God the Father speak his word in the soul, or where does this birth take place—or what part of the soul is susceptible to this act? It must be in the purest, noblest, and subtlest element the soul can provide. Truly, if God[6] could give the soul anything rarer out of his omnipotence, and if the soul could have received into its nature anything nobler from him, he must have awaited its coming to be born. Therefore the soul in which this birth is to happen must have purity and

95

nobility of life, and be unitary and self-contained;[7] it must not be dissipated in the multiplicity of things, through the five senses. What is more, it must continue to be self-contained and unitary and of the utmost purity, for that is its station and it disdains anything less.

The second part of this sermon will discuss what one should do about this act of God, this inward utterance, this birth: whether it is necessary to co-operate in some way to merit and obtain the birth. Should one construct an idea in his mind and thinking-process and discipline himself by meditating upon it, to the effect that God is wise, almighty, and eternal? Or should one withdraw from all thought and free his mind of words, acts, and ideas, doing nothing but being always receptive to God and allowing him to act? How shall one best serve the eternal birth?

The third part [of this sermon will discuss] the profitableness of this birth and how great it is.

In the first place, please note that I shall support what I have to say by citations from nature, which you may check for yourselves. Even though I believe more in the Scriptures than I do in myself, I shall follow [this policy] because you will get more out of arguments based on evidence.

Let us take first the text: "Out of the silence, a secret word was spoken to me." Ah, Sir!—what is this silence and where is that word to be spoken? We shall say, as I have heretofore, [it is spoken] in the purest element of the soul, in the soul's most exalted place, in the core, yes, in the essence of the soul. The central silence is there, where no creature may enter, nor any idea, and there the soul neither thinks nor acts, nor entertains any idea, either of itself or of anything else.

Whatever the soul does, it does through agents.[8] It understands by means of intelligence. If it remembers, it does so by means of memory. If it is to love, the will must be used and thus it acts always through agents and not within its own essence. Its results are achieved through an intermediary. The power of sight can be effectuated only through the eyes, for otherwise the soul has no means of vision. It is the same with the other senses. They are effectuated through intermediaries.

In Being, however, there is no action and, therefore, there is none in the soul's essence. The soul's agents, by which it acts, are derived from the core of the soul. In that core is the central silence, the pure peace, and abode of the heavenly birth, the place for this event: this utterance of God's word. By nature the core of the soul is sensitive to nothing but the divine Being, unmediated. Here God enters the soul with all he has and not in part. He enters the soul through its core and nothing may touch that core except God himself. No creature enters it, for creatures must stay outside in the soul's agents, from whence the soul receives ideas, behind which it has withdrawn as if to take shelter.

When the agents of the soul contact creatures, they take and make ideas[9] and likenesses of them and bear them back again into the self. It is by means of these ideas that the soul knows about external creatures. Creatures cannot approach the soul except in this way and the soul cannot get at creatures, except, on its own initiative, it first conceive ideas of them. Thus the soul gets at things by means of ideas and the idea is an entity created by the soul's agents. Be it a stone, or a rose, or a person, or whatever it is that is to be known, first an idea is taken and then absorbed, and in this way the soul connects with the phenomenal world.

But an idea, so received, necessarily comes in from outside, through the senses. Thus the soul knows about everything but itself. There is an authority who says that the soul can neither conceive nor admit any idea of itself. Thus it knows about everything else but has no self-knowledge, for ideas always enter through the senses and therefore the soul cannot get an idea of itself. Of nothing does the soul know so little as it knows of itself, for lack of means. And that indicates that within itself the soul is free, innocent of all instrumentalities and ideas, and that is why God can unite with it, he, too, being pure and without idea or likeness.

Whatever skill a master teacher may have, concede that skill to God, multiplied beyond measure. The wiser and more skillful a teacher is, the more simply, and with less artifice, he achieves his ends. Man requires many tools to do his visible work and, before he can finish it as he has conceived it, much preparation is required. It is the function and craft of the moon and sun to give light and they do it swiftly. When they emit their rays, all the ends of the world are filled with light in a moment. Higher than these are the angels who work with fewer instruments and also with fewer ideas. The highest seraph has only one. He comprehends as unity all that his inferiors see as manifold. But God needs no idea at all, nor has he any. He acts in the soul without instrument, idea or likeness. He acts in the core of the soul, which no idea ever penetrated—but he alone—his own essence. No creature can do this.

How does God beget his Son in the soul? As a creature might, with ideas and likenesses? Not at all! He begets him in the soul just as he does in eternity—and not otherwise.[2] Well, then, how? Let us see.

God has perfect insight into himself and knows himself up and down, through and through, not by ideas, but of himself. God begets his Son through the true unity of the divine nature. See! This is the way: he begets his Son in the core of the soul and is made One with it. There is no other way. If an idea were interposed, there could be no true unity. Man's whole blessedness lies in that unity.

Now you might say: "Naturally! But there is nothing to the soul but ideas." No! Not at all! If that were so, the soul could never be blessed, for even God cannot make a creature in which a perfect blessing is found. Otherwise, God himself would not be the highest blessing,[10] or the best of ends, as it is his nature and will to be—the beginning and the end of everything. A blessing is not a creature nor is it perfection, for perfection [that is, in all virtues] is the consequence of the perfecting of life, and for that you must get into the essence, the core of the soul, so that God's undifferentiated essence may reach you there, without the interposition of any idea. No idea represents or signifies itself. It always points to something else, of which it is the symbol. And since man has no ideas, except those abstracted from external things through the senses, he cannot be blessed by an idea.

The second point [of this sermon] is this: What should a man do to secure and deserve the occurrence and perfection of this birth in his soul? Should he co-operate by imagining and thinking about God, or should he keep quiet, be silent and at peace, so that God may speak and act through him? Should he do nothing but wait until God does act? I repeat, as I have said before, that this exposition and this activity are for those good and perfect persons only, who have so absorbed the essence of virtue that virtue emanates from them without their trying to make it do so, and in whom the useful life and noble teachings of our Lord Jesus Christ are alive.[11] Such persons know that the best life and the loftiest is to be silent and to let God speak and act through one.

When all the agents [of the soul] are withdrawn from action and ideation, then this word is spoken. Thus he said: "Out of the silence, a secret word was spoken to me." The more you can withdraw the agents of your soul and forget things and the ideas you have received hitherto, the nearer you are to [hearing this word] and the more sensitive to it you will be. If you could only become unconscious of everything all at once and ignore your own life, as St. Paul did when he could say: "Whether in the body, or out of it, I cannot tell: God knoweth!"[12] His spirit had so far withdrawn all its agents that the body was forgotten. Neither memory nor intellect functioned, nor the senses, nor any [of the soul's] agents which are supposed to direct or grace the body. The warmth and energy of the body was suspended and yet it did not fail during the three days in which he neither ate nor drank. It was also this way with Moses, when he fasted forty days on the mountain and was none the worse for it. He was as strong on the last day as on the first. This is the way a man should diminish his senses and introvert his faculties until he achieves forgetfulness of things and self. So one authority said to his soul: "Draw back from the unrest of external actions," and also: "Fly from the storm of visible works and inward thoughts and hide yourself, for they only make turmoil."

Therefore, if God is to speak his word to the soul, it must be still and at peace, and then he *will* speak his word and give himself to the soul and not a mere idea, apart from himself. Dionysius[13] says: "God has no idea of himself and no likeness, for he is intrinsic good, truth, and being." God does all that he does within himself and of himself in an instant. Do not imagine that when God made heaven and earth and all the creatures, that he made one today and another tomorrow.[14] To be sure, Moses describes it thus, but he knew much better! He put it this way on account of the people who could neither understand nor conceive it otherwise. God did nothing more about it than just this: he willed and they were! God acts without instrumentality and without ideas. And the freer you are from ideas the more sensitive you are to his inward action. You are nearer to it in proportion as you are introverted and unself-conscious.

It was to this point that Dionysius instructed his disciple Timothy, saying: "My dear son Timothy, you should soar above self with untroubled mind, above all your faculties, characteristics, and states, up into the still, secret darkness, so that you may come to know the unknown God above all gods. Forsake everything. God despises ideas."

But now, perhaps you say: "What can God do in the core and essence [of the soul] without ideas?" I couldn't possibly know, for the agents of the soul deal only in ideas, taking things and naming them, each according to its own idea. A bird is not known [as such] on the human idea [pattern],[15] and thus, since all ideas come from the outside, [what God is doing in the core of my soul] is hidden from me and that is a great benefit. Since the soul itself does not know, it wonders and, wondering, it seeks, for the soul knows very well that something is afoot, even though it does not know how or what. When a person learns the cause of anything, he soon grows tired of it and looks for something else to work out, and is constantly uneasy until he knows all about that, and thus he lacks steadfastness. Only this unknown knowledge keeps the soul steadfast and yet ever on the search.

The wise man said: "In the middle of the night, while all things were wrapped in silence, a secret word was spoken to me." It came stealthily, like a thief. What does he mean by a word that is secret or hidden? It is the nature of a word to reveal what is hidden. "It opened and shone before me as if it were revealing something and made me conscious of God, and thus it was called 'a word.' Furthermore it was not clear to me what it was, because it came with stealth like a whisper trying to explain itself through the stillness." See! As long as it is concealed, man will always be after it. It appears and disappears, which means that we shall plead and sigh for it.[16]

St. Paul says that we are to hunt it and track it down and never give up till we get it. Once he was caught up into the third heaven[17] of the knowledge of God and saw everything. When he came back, he had forgotten nothing but it had so regressed into the core of his soul that he could not call it up to mind. It was covered up. Thus he felt constrained to pursue it within [his soul] and not without. It is always within and never outside—but always inward. When he was convinced of that, he said: "I am persuaded that neither death . . . nor any affliction can separate me from what I find within me."[18]

One heathen authority once said something fine about this to another: "I am aware of something in myself *whose shine is my reason.* I see clearly that something is there, but what it is I cannot understand. But it seems to me that, if I could grasp it, I should know all truth." To which the other authority replied: "By all means keep after it! For if you do grasp it, you will possess the totality of all goods and life eternal!" St. Augustine also has something to say about this: "I am aware of something in myself, like a light dancing before my soul, and if it could be brought out with perfect steadiness, it would surely be life eternal. It hides, and then again, it shows. It comes like a thief, as if it would steal everything from the soul. But since it shows itself and draws attention, it must want to allure the soul and make the soul follow it, to rob the soul of self." One of the prophets also has something to say about this: "Lord, take from them their spirit and give them instead thy spirit!" This is what that loving soul[19] meant when she said: "When Love said that word, my soul melted and flowed away. Where he comes in, I must go out!" That is also what Christ meant, when he said: "Whosoever shall forsake anything for my sake, shall receive again an hundredfold and whosoever will have me, must deny himself of everything and whosoever will serve me must follow me and not seek his own."[20]

Now perhaps you are saying: "My dear sir! You are trying to reverse the natural course of the soul. It is the soul's nature to take things in through the senses and convert them into ideas. Do you want to reverse that sequence?"

No! But how do you know what precious things God has stored up in nature which have not yet been described—things still hidden? Those who write about the aristocracy of the soul can get no further than their natural intelligence will take them. They cannot get into the core and therefore much must remain hidden from them and unknown. The prophet said: "I will sit and be silent and listen to what God shall say in me." That this word comes "at night and in the darkness" is expressive of its hiddenness. St. John says: "The light shone in the darkness. It came unto its own. And to as many as received it, to them power was given to become the Sons of God."[21]

See now the profit and fruit of this secret word and this darkness. Not only the Son of the heavenly Father is born in the darkness which is his own, but you, too, are born there, a son of the same heavenly Father, and to you also he gives power. Now see how great the profit is! For all the truth the authorities ever learned by their own intelligence and understanding, or ever shall learn up to the last of days, they never got the least part of the knowledge that is in the core [of the soul]. Let it be called ignorance or want of knowledge, still it has more in it than all wisdom and all knowledge without it, for this outward ignorance lures and draws you away from things you know about and even from yourself. That is what Christ meant when he said: "Whosoever forsaketh not himself and mother and father and all that is external is not worthy of me." It was as if he would say: "Whosoever will not depart from the externality of creatures cannot be born or received in this divine birth." By robbing yourself of self and all externalities you are admitted to the truth.

And I really believe it, and am sure that the person who is right in this matter will never be separated from God by any mode [of action] or anything else. I say that there is no way he can fall into deadly sin. He would rather suffer the most shameful death than commit the least of mortal sins, as did the saints. I say that he could not commit even a venial sin nor consent to one in himself or other people, if it could be prevented. He is so strongly attracted and drawn and accustomed to this way of life that he would not turn to another. All his mind and powers are directed to this one end.

May God, newly born in human form, eternally help us, that we frail people, being born in him, may be divine. Amen.

2.

This is another sermon[1]

UBI EST QUI NATUS EST REX JUDAEORUM?

(Matthew 2:2)

"WHERE is he that is born king of the Jews?" Now let us see where this birth takes place. It takes place, as I have so often said before, in the soul, exactly as it does in eternity and with no difference, for it is the same birth and occurs in the essence, the core of the soul.[2]

This raises questions. Granted that God is Mind in all things and is more intimate to each than anything is to itself—and more natural—and granted that where God is, knowing himself, he acts by the utterance of his word:[3] what special right has the soul to this act of God more than other creatures of reason, in which he also is? Let us study the distinction.

God in things is activity, reality, and power, but in the soul he is procreative. For creatures are only God's footprints, but by nature, the soul is patterned after God himself. This pattern must be adorned and fulfilled by divine conception and no other creature except the soul is adapted to such a function. In fact, whatever the perfection that may come to the soul, let it be divine light, or grace, or any other blessing, it cannot come except by birth. No other way is possible. Cherish in yourself the birth of God, and with it all goodness and comfort, all rapture, reality, and truth will be yours. Reject it and you reject all goodness and blessing; but given the birth of God, whatever comes your way will bring with it unsullied reality and stability. Whatever you try to get without it will come to nothing, try how you will. It alone gives blessing. All else corrupts. Moreover, in this birth you will have a part in the divine stream [that flows into life] and will share its benefits. But the creature in which God's idea[4] is not to be found is not eligible [to these benefits]. It is the soul that is especially designed for the birth of

103

God and so it occurs exclusively in the soul, where the Father's child is conceived in the core, the inmost recess, where no idea ever glowed or agent of the soul crept in.

The second question is this. Let us say that this act of conception takes place in the core or essence of the soul. It must then take place in the sinner as well as the saint. How, then, does it add grace or benefit me? For [saint or sinner], the cores of their beings are both alike. Indeed, even in hell, the aristocratic element in one's nature persists eternally. But we should notice that the divine birth has the distinctive property of being always accompanied by new light. To the soul it brings a great light, because it is the way of goodness to diffuse itself. In this birth God pours himself into the soul, and the light at the core of the soul grows so strong that it spills out, radiates through the soul's agents, even passing the outward man. This is what happened to Paul when God touched him with light on the road [to Damascus] and spoke to him. A semblance of this light appeared outwardly, so that his companions saw it enveloping Paul as it does with saints. The light in the soul's core overflows into the body, which becomes radiant with it. The sinner is not adapted to this, nor is he worthy of it when he is filled with sin or wickedness, which is a kind of darkness.

As he [John 1] says: "The darkness neither received nor comprehended the light." There is the obstacle! The avenue by which the light ought to get in is littered and barricaded by falseness and darkness, for light and darkness are incompatible, like God and creature. If God is to get in, the creature must get out. This light is well known to man. When one turns to God, a light at once begins to glimmer and shine within, instructing one in what to do and what not to do, and giving lots of intimations of good, of which, previously, one was ignorant and understood nothing.

"How do you know that?" For example, suppose you are moved to turn away from the world. How could such a thing happen without this enlightenment? It is so tender and so delightful that it makes you disdain anything but God or the divine. It coaxes you Godward and you become aware of many good impulses even though you are unaware of their origin. This inward constraint can by no means be due to creatures nor can it be instigated by them, for the effects of creatures and their suggestions come altogether from the outside. Nevertheless, the core of the soul is affected by creatures and the freer you keep yourself from them the more light, truth, and discernment you will have. Therefore, no one will err in anything unless first he loses track of this [inward light] and then puts too much emphasis on externalities.

St. Augustine says: "There are many people who have sought light and truth, but they look for it outside themselves, where it is not."[5] Thus, at last, they get so far off the track that they cannot find their way back to the core of their souls and they never discover the truth, for truth is at the core of the soul and not outside the man. To be enlightened and discerning, cherish the birth of God's Son in the core of the soul and then the soul's agents will be illuminated, and the outward man as well.

When God touches the soul with truth, its light floods the soul's agents[6] and that man knows more than anyone could ever teach him. Thus the prophet says: "I know more than I was ever taught." See! God's Son cannot be born in sinners because this light cannot shine in them. It is incompatible with the darkness of sin because it occurs in the essence of the soul and not in the agents.

Here, too, is another question. If God begets his Son only in the soul's essence, and not in the soul's agents, what have the agents to do with it all? Is their function to be voided by idleness? Of what use is the birth if it does not affect the soul's agents? The question is well put, but let us notice some distinctions.

Each creature works toward some end. That end comes first in its intentions and last in execution. So God, too, intends a blessed end in all his works, that is, in himself. It is the aim of all God does that the agents of the soul should be redirected inward, toward himself, by means of the birth of his Son. He waylays everything in the soul and invites it to his convocation or feast, but if the soul is scattered among its agents and spread out in externalities, the agent of sight in the eyes, of hearing in the ears, of taste in the tongue, then its inward action is feebler because scattered forces do not fulfill [their mission]. Therefore if the inward work of the soul is to be efficient, it must recall its agents and gather them in from their dispersion to one inward effort.

St. Augustine says: "There is more to the soul when it loves than there is when it give life to the body." An illustration: There was once a heathen scholar who was devoted to the study of mathematics and he was sitting by the embers [on his hearth] making the calculations his art required. Then someone came along who did not know that he was a scholar and, brandishing his sword, he said: "Tell me your name. Out with it! Or I'll kill you!" But the scholar was so absorbed that he did not hear what the enemy said, or notice what he threatened to do. And so the enemy shouted at him for some time until, getting no response, he struck off the scholar's head. Now, this was due to a secular pursuit.

How incomparably much more we ought to be absorbed away from things and focus all our faculties on the contemplation, the knowing of the unique, immeasurable, uncreated, eternal truth! Focus all your intelligence and all your capacities to this end. Turn them on the core of the soul in which all this buried treasure lies, but know, if you wish to do this, that you must drop all other activities and achieve unself-consciousness, in which you will find it.

Another question still. Is it not better for each agent of the soul to continue with its own activity, neither of them hindering the other and none of them hindering God? Can there be not creature-knowledge in me, except it be a hindrance, just as God knows everything and his knowledge does not hinder him—for it is so with the saints. But notice this distinction. The saints see in God an idea, and in that idea all things are comprehended—and the same is true of God, who sees everything in himself. He does not need to turn from one thing to the other, as we do. If, during this life, we always had a mirror before us—a mirror in which we saw everything all at once, and seeing all, knew all, then neither activity nor knowledge would be a hindrance, but as it is, we have to turn from one thing to the other and therefore we cannot pay attention to one without depriving the other. Furthermore, the soul is so bound up with its agents, that where they go the soul must go too and be present when and where they function, overseeing their work, for otherwise nothing would come of what they do. If then the soul goes out to attend to external activities, it will necessarily be the weaker in its inward efforts and for this birth in the soul God will and must have a pure, free, and unencumbered soul, in which there is nothing but him alone, a soul that waits for nothing and nobody but him.

Thus Christ says: "Whosoever loves another more than me and is attached to father and mother and many other things, is not worthy of me. . . . I have not come into the world to bring peace, but the sword, so that I may cut off everything, and separate brother, child, mother and friend who are the real enemies."[7] If your eye sees everything, your ear hears everything, and your heart remembers everything, then truly in all these things your soul is destroyed.

Thus, too, there is an authority who says: "To accomplish the inward act [of God] a person must withdraw all his soul's agents, as it were, into a corner of the soul, and conceal himself from all ideas and forms, and then he may do it." It must be done by means of forgetting and losing self-consciousness. It is in the stillness, in the silence, that the word of God is to be heard. There is no better avenue of approach to this Word than through stillness, through silence. It is to be heard there as it is—in that unself-consciousness, for when one is aware of nothing, that word is imparted to him and clearly revealed.

But you may be saying: "Sir, you make our salvation depend entirely on ignorance. That sounds wrong. God made man so that he could know, as the prophet says: 'Lord, make them to know!' Where there is ignorance there is error and vanity. The ignorant person is brutal. He is an ass and a fool, as long as he remains ignorant." And that is true. But one must achieve this unself-consciousness by means of transformed knowledge. *This* ignorance does not come from lack of knowledge but rather it is from knowledge that one may achieve this ignorance. Then we shall be informed by the divine unconsciousness and in that our ignorance will be ennobled and adorned with supernatural knowledge. It is by reason of this fact that we are made perfect by what happens to us[8] rather than by what we do.

One authority says: "The power of hearing is better than the power of seeing, for one learns more wisdom by listening than by looking, and listening, he learns better to live by wisdom." It is said of a heathen scholar, who lay dying, that his disciples were discussing his great art when he died, and he raised his head and exclaimed

"O let me learn still more of this great art that I may practice it eternally." Hearing brings more into a man, but seeing he gives out more, even in the very act of looking. And therefore we shall all be blessed more in eternal life by our power to hear than by our power to see. For the power to hear the eternal word is within me and the power to see will leave me; for hearing I am passive, and seeing I am active.

Our blessedness does not depend on the deeds we do but rather on our passiveness to God. For as God is more exalted than creatures, so his work is higher than mine. Indeed, out of his unmeasurable love God has set our blessedness in passivity, in bearing rather than doing, and incomparably more in receiving than in giving. Each of his gifts only prepares us afresh to receive another, a new gift, and more and more gifts. Each divine gift only increases our sensitivity and desire to receive another, which is greater still. On this point, some of the authorities say that in this way the soul is made equal to God. For, just as there is no end to God's gifts, there is no end to the soul's power to receive them. As God is almighty in action, the soul also is boundless in its capacity to take, and thus it is transformed with God and in God. It is necessary that God should both be active and passive in order that he may know and love himself in the soul, and the soul may know as he knows and love as he loves. It is for this reason that the soul is more blessed by what is his than by what is its own, and for this reason its blessing depends more on what he does than on anything we can do.

St. Dionysius' disciples asked him how Timothy came to outstrip them all in perfection. Dionysius replied: "Timothy is a man who is passive to God. He who is skilled in this will outstrip all men." In this sense, your ignorance is not a fault but your chief virtue and your passivity is the chief of your actions. In view of this, you ought to put an end to all your efforts, silence all your faculties,[9] and then you will really discover this birth [of God's Son] in yourself. If you will find him who is born king, pass by everything else you might find and leave it behind. That we *may* pass by and leave behind all that is not pleasing to this king, may he help us, who therefor became the child of man that we might become the children of God. Amen.

3

This, too, is Meister Eckhart who always taught the truth[1]

IN HIS, QUAE PATRIS MEI SUNT, OPORTET ME ESSE.

(Luke 2:49)

"I MUST be about my Father's business!" This text is quite convenient to the discussion in which I shall now engage, dealing with the eternal birth, which occurred at one point of time, and which occurs every day in the innermost recess of the soul—a recess to which there is no avenue of approach. To know this birth at the core of the soul it is necessary above all that one should be about his Father's business.

What are the attributes of the Father? More power is attributed to him than to the other persons [of the Trinity]. Accordingly, no one can be sure of the experience of this birth, or even approach it, except by the expenditure of a great deal of energy. It is impossible without a complete withdrawal of the senses from the [world of] things and great force is required to repress all the agents of the soul and cause them to cease functioning. It takes much strength to gather them all in, and without that strength it cannot be done. So Christ said: "The kingdom of heaven suffereth violence and the violent take it by force."[2]

Now it may be asked about this birth: does it occur constantly or intermittently—only when one applies himself with all his might to forgetting the [world of] things while yet knowing that he does so?

There are certain distinctions to be made. Man has an active intellect, a passive intellect, and a potential intellect. The presence of the active intellect is indicated by [the mind] at work, either on God or creature, to the divine honor and glory. It is characterized

109

chiefly by its drive and energy and therefore is called "active." But when the action at hand is undertaken by God, the mind must remain passive. On the other hand, potential intellect is related to both. It signifies the mind's potentialities, what it has the capacity to do, what God can do. In one case, the mind is at work on its own initiative; in the other, the mind is passive, so that God may undertake the work at hand, and then the mind must hold still and let God do it, but before the mind can begin and God can finish, the mind must have a prevision of what is to be done, a potential knowledge of what may be. This is the meaning of "potential intellect," but it is much neglected and therefore nothing comes of it. But when the mind goes to work in real earnest, then God is enlisted and he is both seen and felt. Still, the vision and experience of God is too much of a burden to the soul while it is in the body and so God withdraws intermittently, which is what [Christ] meant by saying: "A little while, and ye shall not see me: and again, a little while, and ye shall see me."[3]

When our Lord took three disciples up the mountain and showed them the transfiguration of his body, made possible by his union with the Godhead—which shall come to us also in the resurrection of the body—St. Peter at once, when he saw it, wanted to stay there with it forever.[4] In fact, to the extent that one finds anything good, he never wants to part with it. What one grows to know and comes to love and remember, his soul follows after. Knowing this, our Lord hides himself from time to time, for the soul is an elemental form of the body, so that what once gains its attention holds it. If the soul were to know the goodness of God, as it is and without interruption, it would never turn away and therefore would never direct the body.

Thus it was with Paul. If he had remained a hundred years at that point where he first knew God's goodness, even then he would not have wanted to return to his body and would have forgotten it altogether. Since, then, the divine goodness is alien to this life and incompatible with it, faithful God veils it or reveals it when he will, or when he knows it will be most useful and best for you that he do so. He is like a trustworthy physician. The withdrawal does not depend on you but upon him whose act it is. He reveals himself or not as he thinks best for you. It is up to him to show himself to you or not, according as he knows you are ready for him, for God is not a destroyer of nature but rather one who fulfills it, and he does this more and more as you are prepared.

You may, however, say: Alas, good man, if, to be prepared for God, one needs a heart freed from ideas and activities which are natural to the agents of the soul, how about those deeds of love which are wholly external, such as teaching and comforting those who are in need? Are these to be denied? Are we to forgo the deeds that occupied the disciples of our Lord so incessantly, the work that occupied St. Paul on behalf of the people, so much that he was like a father to them? Shall we be denied the [divine] goodness because we do virtuous deeds?

Let us see how this question is to be answered. The one [contemplation] is good. The other [deeds of virtue] is necessary. Mary was praised for having chosen the better part but Martha's life was useful, for she waited on Christ and his disciples.[5] St. Thomas [Aquinas] says that the active life is better than the contemplative, for in it one pours out the love he has received in contemplation. Yet it is all one; for what we plant in the soil of contemplation we shall reap in the harvest of action and thus the purpose of contemplation is achieved. There is a transition from one to the other but it is all a single process with one end in view—that God is, after which it returns to what it was before. If I go from one end of this house to the other, it is true, I shall be moving and yet it will be all one motion. In all he does, man has only his one vision of God. One is based on the other and fulfills it. In the unity [one beholds] in contemplation, God foreshadows [variety of] the harvest of action. In contemplation, you serve only yourself. In good works, you serve many people.

The whole life of Christ instructs us in this matter, and the lives of his saints as well, all of whom he sent out into the world to teach the Many the one truth. St. Paul said to Timothy: "Beloved, preach the word!"[6] Did he mean the audible word that beats the air? Certainly not! He referred to the inborn, secret word that lies hidden in the soul. It was this that he preached, so that it might instruct the faculties of people and nourish them, and so that the behavior of men might proclaim it and so that one might be fully prepared to serve the need of his neighbor. It should be in the thoughts, the mind, and the will. It should shine through your deeds. As Christ said: "Let your light so shine before men!"[7] He was thinking of people who care only for the contemplative life and not for the practice of virtue, who say that they have no need for this, for they have got beyond it. Christ did not include such people when he said: "Some seed fell in good ground and brought forth fruit an hundredfold."[8] But he did refer to them when he spoke of "the tree that does not bear fruit and which shall be hewn down."

Now some of you may say: "But, sir, what about the silence of which you have said so much?" Plenty of ideas intrude into that. Each deed follows the pattern of its own idea, whether spiritual or external, whether it be teaching, or giving comfort, or what not. Where, then, is the stillness? If the mind goes on thinking and imagining, and the will keeps on functioning, and the memory: does not this all involve ideation? Let us see.

We have already mentioned the passive and active intellects. The active intellect abstracts ideas from external things and strips them of all that is material or accidental and passes them on to the passive intellect, thus begetting their spiritual counterparts there. So the passive intellect is made pregnant by the active and it knows and cherishes these things. Nevertheless, it cannot continue to know them without the active intellect's continuing, renewing enlightenment. But notice this: all the active intellect does for the natural man, God does and much more too for the solitary person. He removes the active intellect and puts himself in its place and takes over its complete function.

Now, if a person is quite unoccupied, and his mind is stilled, God undertakes its work, and becomes controller of [the mind's] agents and is himself begotten in the passive intellect. Let us see how this is. The active intellect cannot pass on what it has not received, nor can it entertain two ideas at once. It must take first one and then the other. Even if many forms and colors are shown up by light and air at the same time, you can perceive them only one after the other. It is the same with the active intellect when it acts—but when God acts in lieu of it, he begets many ideas or images at one point. When, therefore, God moves you to a good deed, your [soul's] agents organize at once for good and your heart is set on goodness. All your resources for good take shape and gather at the same instant to the same point. This shows clearly and beyond doubt that it is not your own mind that is working, because it has neither the authority nor the resources required for that. Rather, it is the work which is begotten of him who comprehends all ideas within himself simultaneously. St. Paul says: "I can do all things through him that strengtheneth me and in him; I am not divided."[9] Thus you may know that the ideas back of good deeds are not your own but are from the Superintendent of nature, from whom both the deed and the idea proceed. Do not claim as your own what is his and not yours. It is given you for a little while, but it was born of God, beyond time, in the eternity that is above all ideas or images.

You may, however, ask: "What is to become of my mind, once it has been robbed of its natural function and has neither ideas nor anything else to work on? It must always consist of something and the soul's agents are bound to connect with something on which they will go to work, whether the memory, the reason, or the will."

Here is the answer. The object and existence of the mind are essential and not contingent. The mind has a pure, unadulterated being of its own. When it comes across truth or essence, at once it is attracted and settles down to utter its oracle—for it now has a point of reference. If, however, the intellect does not discover any essential truth or touch some bedrock, so that it can say "this is this and therefore not something else," if has to continue searching and expecting, arrested or attracted by nothing, it can only work on until the end, when it passes out, still searching and still expecting.

Sometimes a year or more is spent in working over a point about nature to discover what it is, and then an equal period has to be spent whittling off what it is not. Having no reference point, the mind can make no statement all this time, for it has no real knowledge of the core of truth. That is why the mind can never rest during this lifetime. For let God reveal himself here ever so much, it is nothing to what he really is. There is Truth at the core of the soul but it is covered up and hidden from the mind, and as long as that is so there is nothing the mind can do to come to rest, as it might if it had an unchanging point of reference.

The mind never rests but must go on expecting and preparing for what is yet to be known and what is still concealed. Meanwhile, man cannot know what God is, even though he be ever so well aware of what God is not; and an intelligent person will reject that. As long as it has no reference point, the mind can only wait as matter waits for form. And matter can never find rest except in form; so, too, the mind can never rest except in the essential truth which is locked up in it—the truth about everything. Essence alone satisfies and God keeps on withdrawing, farther and farther away, to arouse the mind's zeal and lure it on to follow and finally grasp the true good that has no cause. Thus, contented with nothing, the mind clamors for the highest good of all.

Now you may say: "But, sir, you have often told us that the agents should all be still and yet here you have everything setting up a clamor and covetousness in the mind where quiet should be: there is a great hubbub and outcry for what the mind has not. Whether it be desire, or purpose, or praise, or thanks, or whatever is imagined or engendered in the soul, it cannot be the pure peace or complete quiet, of which you have spoken. Rather, the mind is despoiled of its peace."

This requires an answer. When you get rid of selfishness, together with things and what pertains to them, and have transferred all to God, and united with him, and abandoned all for him in complete trust and love, then whatever your lot, whatever touches you, for better or worse, sour or sweet, none of it is yours but it is all God's to whom you have left it.

Tell me: whose is the Word that is spoken? Is it his who speaks, or his who hears it? Even though it come to him who hears it, it still is his who speaks or conceives it. Take an illustration. The sun radiates its light into the air and the air receives it and transmits it to the earth, and receiving it, we can distinguish one color from another. Now, although light seems to be everywhere in the air, it is really in the sun. The rays are really emitted by the sun and come from it—not from the air. They are only received by the air and passed on to anything that can be lighted up.

It is like this with the soul. God begets his Son or the Word in the soul and, receiving it, the soul passes it on in many forms, through its agents, now as desire, now in good intentions, now in loving deeds, now in gratitude or whatever concerns it. These are all his and not yours at all. Credit God with all he does and take none for yourself, as it is written: "The Holy Spirit maketh intercession for us with groanings which cannot be uttered."[10] It is he that prays in us and not we ourselves. St. Paul says that "no man can say that Jesus is the Lord but by the Holy Ghost."[11]

Above all, claim nothing for yourself. Relax and let God operate you and do what he will with you. The deed is his; the word is his; this birth is his; and all you are is his, for you have surrendered self to him, with all your soul's agents and their functions and even your personal nature. Then at once, God comes into your being and faculties, for you are like a desert, despoiled of all that was peculiarly your own. The Scripture speaks of "the voice of one crying in the wilderness." Let this voice cry in you at will. Be like a desert as far as self and the things of this world are concerned.

Perhaps, however, you object: "What should one do to be as empty as a desert, as far as self and things go? Should one just wait and do nothing? Or should he sometimes pray, read, or do such virtuous things as listening to a sermon or studying the Bible—of course, not taking these things as if from outside himself, but inwardly, as from God? And if one does not do these things, isn't he missing something?"

This is the answer. External acts of virtue were instituted and ordained so that the outer man might be directed to God and set apart for spiritual life and all good things, and not diverted from them by incompatible pursuits. They were instituted to restrain man from things impertinent to his high calling, so that when God wants to use him, he will be found ready, not needing to be brought back from things coarse and irrelevant. The more pleasure one takes in externalities the harder it is to turn away from them. The stronger the love the greater the pain of parting.

See! Praying, reading, singing, watching, fasting, and doing penance—all these virtuous practices were contrived to catch us and keep us away from strange, ungodly things. Thus, if one feels that the spirit of God is not at work in him, that he has departed inwardly from God, he will all the more feel the need to do virtuous deeds—especially those he finds most pertinent or useful—not for his own personal ends but rather to honor the truth—he will not wish to be drawn or led away by obvious things. Rather, he will want to cleave to God, so that God will find him quickly and not have to look far afield for him when, once more, he wants to act through him.

But when a person has a true spiritual experience, he may boldly drop external disciplines, even those to which he is bound by vows, from which even a bishop may not release him. No man may release another from vows he has made to God—for such vows are contracts between man and God. And also, if a person who has vowed many things such as prayer, fasting, or pilgrimages, should enter an order, he is then free from the vow, for once in the order, his bond is to all virtue and to God himself.

I want to emphasize that. However much a person may have vowed himself to many things, when he enters upon a true spiritual experience he is released from them all. As long as that experience lasts, whether a week, or a month, or a year, none of this time will be lost to the monk or nun, for God, whose prisoners they are, will account for it all. When he returns to his usual nature, however, let him fulfill the vows appropriate to each passing moment as it comes, but let him not think for a moment of making up for the times he seemed to neglect, for God will make up for whatever time he caused you to be idle. Nor should you think it could be made up by any number of creature-deeds, for the least deed of God is more than all human deeds together. This is said for learned and enlightened people who have been illumined by God and the Scriptures.

But what shall be said of the simple fellow who neither knows nor understands [the meaning of] bodily disciplines, when he has vowed or promised something such as a prayer or anything else? This I say for him: If he finds that his vow hinders him and that if he were loosed from it he could draw nearer to God, let him boldly quit the vow; for any act that brings one nearer to God is best. That is what Paul meant when he said: "When that which is perfect is come, then that which is in part shall be done away."[12]

Vows taken at the hands of a priest are very different. They are as binding as those vowed directly to God. To take a vow with the good intention of binding oneself to God is the best one can do at any time. If, however, a man knows a better way, one that experience has taught him is better, then the first way is at once superseded.

This is easy to prove, for we must look to the fruits, the inward truth, rather than to outward works. As St. Paul says: "The letter killeth (that is, all formal practices) but the spirit maketh alive (that is, inner experience of the truth)."[13] Realize this clearly, that whatever leads you closest to this inner truth, you are to follow in all you do. Let your spirit be uplifted and not downcast, burning and yet pure, silent and quiet. You need not say to God what you need or desire, for he knows it all beforehand. Christ said to his disciples: "When ye pray, use not vain repetitions as the heathen do: for they think that they shall be heard for their much speaking."[14]

That we may follow this peace and inward silence, that the eternal word may be spoken in us and understood, and that we may be one with him, may the Father help us, and the Word, and the spirit of both. Amen.

4

Eternal birth

ET CUM FACTUS ESSET JESUS ANNORUM DUODECIM, ETC.

(Luke 2:42)

WE READ in the gospel that when our Lord was twelve years old he went to the temple at Jerusalem with Mary and Joseph and that, when they left, Jesus stayed behind in the temple without their knowledge. When they got home and missed him, they looked for him among acquaintances and strangers and relatives. They looked for him in the crowds and still they could not find him. Further-more, they had lost him among the [temple] crowds and had to go back to where they came from. When they got back to their starting point, they found him.

Thus it is true that, if you are to experience this noble birth, you must depart from all crowds and go back to the starting point, the core [of the soul] out of which you came. The crowds are the agents of the soul and their activities: memory, understanding, and will, in all their diversifications. You must leave them all: sense perception, imagination, and all that you discover in self or intend to do. After that, you may experience this birth—but otherwise not—believe me! He was not found among friends, nor relatives, nor among acquaintances. No. He is lost among these altogether.

Thence we have a question to ask: Is it possible for man to experience this birth through certain things which, although they are divine, yet they come into the man through the senses from without? I refer to certain ideas of God, such as, for example, that God is good, wise, merciful, or whatever—ideas that are creatures of the reason, and yet divine. Can a man have the experience [of the divine birth] by means of these? No! Truly no. Even though [these ideas] are all good and divine, still he gets them all through his senses from without. If the divine birth is to shine with reality and purity, it must come flooding up and out of man from God within him, while all man's own efforts are suspended and all the soul's agents are at God's disposal.

This work [birth], when it is perfect, will be due solely to God's action while you have been passive. If you really forsake your own knowledge and will, then surely and gladly God will enter with his knowledge shining clearly. Where God achieves self-consciousness, your own knowledge is of no use, nor has it standing. Do not imagine that your own intelligence may rise to it, so that you may know God. Indeed, when God divinely enlightens you, no natural light is required to bring that about. This [natural light] must in fact be completely extinguished before God will shine in with his light, bringing back with him all that you have forsaken and a thousand times more, together with a new form to contain it all.

We have a parable for this in the gospel. When our Lord had held friendly conversation with the heathen woman at the well, she left her jug and ran to the city to tell the people that the true Messiah had come. The people, not believing her report, went out to see for themselves. Then they said to her: "Now we believe, not because of thy saying: for we have seen him ourselves."[1] Thus it is true that you cannot know God by means of any creature science nor by means of your own wisdom. If you are to know God divinely, your own knowledge must become as pure ignorance, in which you forget yourself and every other creature.

But perhaps you will say: "Alas, sir, what is the point of my mind existing if it is to be quite empty and without function? Is it best for me to screw up my courage to this unknown knowledge which cannot really be anything at all? For if I know anything in any way, I shall not be ignorant, nor would I be either empty or innocent. Is it my place to be in darkness?"

Yes, truly. You could do not better than to go where it is dark, that is, unconsciousness.[2]

"But, sir, must everything go and is there no turning back?"

Certainly not. By rights, there is no return.

"Then what is the darkness? What do you mean by it? What is its name?"

It has no name other than "potential sensitivity" and it neither lacks being nor does it want to be. It is that possible [degree of] sensitivity through which you may be made perfect. That is why there is no way back out of it. And yet, if you do return, it will not be for the sake of truth but rather on account of the world, the flesh, and the devil. If you persist in abandoning it, you necessarily fall [a victim to spiritual] malady and you may even persist so long that for you the fall will be eternal. Thus there can be no turning back but only pressing on to the attainment and achievement of this potentiality. There is no rest [in the process] short of complete fulfillment of Being. Just as matter can never rest until it is made complete by form, which represents its potential Being, so there is no rest for the mind until it has attained all that is possible to it.

On this point, a heathen master says: "Nature has nothing swifter than the heavens, which outrun everything else in their course." But surely the mind of man, in its course, outstrips them all. Provided it retains its active powers and keeps itself free from defilement and the disintegration of lesser and cruder things, it can outstrip high heaven and never slow down until it has reached the highest peak, and is fed and lodged by the highest good, which is God.[3]

Therefore, how profitable it is to pursue this potentiality, until empty and innocent, a man is alone in that darkness of unself-consciousness, tracking and tracing [every clue] and never retracing his steps! Thus you may win that [something] which is everything, and the more you make yourself like a desert, unconscious of everything, the nearer you come to that estate. Of this desert, Hosea[4] writes: "I will allure her, and bring her into the wilderness, and speak to her heart." The genuine word of eternity is spoken only in that eternity of the man who is himself a wilderness, alienated from self and all multiplicity. The prophet longed for this desolated alienation from self, for he said: "Oh that I had wings like a dove! for then would I fly away, and be at rest."[5] Where may one find peace and rest? Really only where he rejects all creatures, being alienated from them and desolate. So David said: "I would choose rather to sit at the threshold of the house of my God than to dwell with great honor and wealth in the tents of wickedness."[6]

But you may say: "Alas, sir, does a man have to be alienated from creatures and always desolate, inwardly as well as outwardly, the soul's agents together with their functions—must all be done away? That would put one in a hard position—if then God should leave him without his support, and add to his misery, taking away his light and neither speaking to him nor acting in him, as you now seem to mean. If a person is to be in such a state of pure nothingness, would it not be better for him to be doing something to make the darkness and alienation supportable? Should he not pray, or read, or hear a sermon or do something else that is good to help himself through it?"

No! You may be sure that perfect quiet and idleness is the best you can do. For, see, you cannot turn from this condition to do anything, without harming it. This is certain: you would like in part to prepare yourself and in part to be prepared by God, but it cannot be so, for however quickly you desire or think of preparing, God gets there first. But suppose that the preparation could be shared between you and God for the [divine] work of ingress—which is impossible—then you should know that God must act and pour in as soon as he finds that you are ready. Do not imagine that God is like a carpenter who works or not, just as he pleases, suiting his own convenience. It is not so with God, for when he finds you ready he must act, and pour into you, just as when the air is clear and pure the sun must pour into it and may not hold back. Surely, it would be a very great defect in God if he did not do a great work, and anoint you with great good, once he found you empty and innocent.

The authorities, writing to the same point, assert that when the matter of which a child is made is ready in the mother's body, God at once pours in the living spirit which is the soul—the body's form. Readiness and the giving of form occur simultaneously. When nature reaches its highest point, God gives grace. When the [human] spirit is ready, God enters it without hesitation or waiting. It is written in the Revelation that our Lord told people: "I stand at the door and knock and wait. If any man let me in, I will sup with him."[7] You need not look either here or there. He is no farther away than the door of the heart. He stands there, lingering, waiting for us to be ready and open the door and let him in. You need not call to him as if he were far away, for he waits more urgently than you for the door to be opened. You are a thousand times more necessary to him than he is to you. The opening [of the door] and his entry are simultaneous.

Still you may ask: "How can that be? I do not sense his presence." But look! To sense his presence is not within your power, but his. When it suits him, he shows himself; and he conceals himself when he wants to. This is what Christ meant when he said to Nicodemus: "The wind [Spirit] bloweth where it listeth, and thou hearest the sound thereof but canst not tell whence it cometh and whither it goeth."[8] There is an [apparent] contradiction in what he says: "You hear and yet do not know." When one hears, he knows. Christ meant: by hearing a man takes in or absorbs [the Spirit of God]. It was as if he wanted to say: You receive it without knowing it. But you should remember that God may not leave anything empty or void. That is not God's nature. He could not bear it. Therefore, however much it may seem that you do not sense his presence or that you are quite innocent of it, this is not the case. For if there were any void under heaven whatever, great or small, either the sky would have to draw it up to itself or bend down to fill it. God, the master of nature, will not tolerate any empty place. Therefore be quiet and do not waver lest, turning away from God for an hour, you never return to him.

Still you may say: "Alas, sir, you assume that this birth is going to happen and that the Son [of God] will be born in me. But by what sign shall I know that it has happened?"

Yes! Certainly! There may well be three trustworthy signs, but let me tell about one of them. I am often asked if it is possible, within time, that a person should not be hindered either by multiplicity or by matter. Indeed, it is. When this birth really happens, no creature in all the world will stand in your way and, what is more, they will all point you to God and to this birth. Take the analogy of the thunderbolt. When it strikes to kill, whether it is a tree or an animal or a person, at the coming of the blow, they all turn toward it and if a person's back were turned, he would instantly turn to face it. All the thousands of leaves of a tree at once turn the required sides to the stroke. And so it is with all who experience this birth. They, together with all around them, earthy as you please, are quickly turned toward it. Indeed, what was formerly a hindrance becomes now a help. Your face is turned so squarely toward it that, whatever you see or hear, you only get this birth out of it. Everything stands for God and you see only God in all the world. It is just as when one looks straight at the sun for a while: afterwards, everything he looks at has the image of the sun in it. If this is lacking, if you are not looking for God and expecting him everywhere, and in everything, you lack the birth.

Still you might ask: "While in this state, should one do penances? Isn't he missing something if he doesn't?"

The whole of a life of penitence is only one among a number of things such as fasting, watching, praying, kneeling, being disciplined, wearing hair shirts, lying on hard surfaces, and so on. These were all devised because of the constant opposition of the body and flesh to the spirit. The body is too strong for the spirit and so there is always a struggle between them—an eternal conflict. The body is bold and brave here, for it is at home and the world helps it. This earth is its fatherland and all its kindred are on its side: food, drink, and comforts are all against the spirit. Here the spirit is alien. Its race and kin are all in heaven. It has many friends there. To assist the spirit in its distress, to weaken the flesh for its part in this struggle so that it cannot conquer the spirit, penances are put upon the flesh, like a bridle, to curb it, so that the spirit may control it. This is done to bring it to subjection, but if you wish to make it a thousand times more subject, put the bridle of love on it. With love you may overcome it most quickly and load it most heavily.

That is why God lies in wait for us with nothing so much as love. Love is like a fisherman's hook. Without the hook he could never catch a fish, but once the hook is taken the fisherman is sure of the fish. Even though the fish twists hither and yon, still the fisherman is sure of him. And so, too, I speak of love: he who is caught by it is held by the strongest of bonds and yet the stress is pleasant. He who takes this sweet burden on himself gets further, and comes nearer to what he aims at than he would be means of any harsh ordinance ever devised by man. Moreover, he can sweetly bear all that happens to him; all that God inflicts he can take cheerfully.

Nothing makes you God's own, or God yours, as much as this sweet bond. When one has found this way, he looks for no other. To hang on this hook is to be so [completely] captured that feet and hands, and mouth and eyes, the heart, and all a man is and has, become God's own.

Therefore there is no better way to overcome the enemy, so that he may never hurt you, than by means of love. Thus it is written: "Love is as strong as death and harder than hell."⁹ Death separates the soul from the body but love separates everything from the soul. It cannot endure anything anywhere that is not God or God's. Whatever he does, who is caught in this net, or turned in this direction, love does it, and love alone; and whether the man does it or not, makes no difference.

The most trivial deed or function in such a person is more profitable and fruitful to himself and all men, and pleases God better, than all other human practices put together, which, though done without deadly sin, are characterized by a minimum of love. His rest is more profitable than another's work.

Therefore wait only for this hook and you will be caught up into blessing, and the more you are caught the more you will be set free. That we all may be so caught and set free, may he help us, who is love itself. Amen.

5

The love of God[1]

IN HOC APPARUIT CARITAS DEI IN NOBIS . . .

(I John 4:9)

"IN THIS was manifested the love of God toward us, because that God sent his only begotten Son into the world, that we might live [with him, in him and][2] through him."

Suppose that a rich king had a beautiful daughter and gave her to the son of a poor man. Every member of the poor family would be honored and ennobled by the gift. There is one authority[3] who says: "Since God became man, the whole human race has been lifted up and ennobled—wherefore we may all rejoice that Christ, our brother, of his own power, has risen above the choir of angels to sit at the right hand of God the Father." This is well said, but even then, it does not mean much to me. For what good would it do me to have a brother who is rich, while I remain poor, or a brother wise, when I am foolish? I should rather put it this way, and say, not only that God became man but that he has taken human nature upon himself—for this is more to the point.

Authorities usually teach that all persons are of equal rank by nature, but I say emphatically that all the worth of the humanity of the saints, or Mary, the mother of God, or even Christ himself, is mine too in my human nature.[4] But this might prompt you to ask: If, in my present nature, I already have all that Christ achieved in his, why should he be exalted and honored as the Lord and God? Because he was a messenger from God to us, who carried a blessing that was to be ours. There in the inmost core of the soul, where God begets his Son, human nature also takes root. There, too, it is one and unanalyzable. Anything that might appear to belong to it, and yet could be distinguished from it, would not be of that unity. But now I shall say something further that is more difficult. To live by this pure essence of our nature, one must be so dead to all that is personal, that he could be as fond of persons long dead[5] as he is of familiar and homely friends. As long as you are more concerned for yourself than you are for people you have never seen, you are wrong, and you cannot have even a momentary insight into the simple core of the soul. You may have a symbolic idea of the truth,[6] but this is by no means best.

In the second place, you must be pure in heart, for his heart alone is pure, for whom creatures are as nothing.

In the third place, you must have got rid of all "Not."[7]

They ask, what is burned in hell? Authorities usually reply: "This is what happens to willfulness."[8] But I say it is this "Not" that is burned out in hell. For example: suppose a burning coal is placed on my hand. If I say that the coal burns me, I do it a great injustice. To say precisely what does the burning: it is the "Not." The coal has something in it that my hand has not. Observe!—it is just this "Not" that is burning me—for if my hand had in it what the coal has, and could do what the coal can do, it, too, would blaze with fire, in which case all the fire that ever burned might be spilled on this hand and I should not [feel?] hurt.

Likewise, I should say that because God and all who live in his presence have something like true blessedness in them, such as those who are cut off from God have not, it is only the "Not" [—the need or want of blessing] that punishes souls in hell, rather than any willfulness or other kind of fuel. Truly I say that to the extent "Not" exists in you, you are imperfect, and if you would be perfect you must get rid of it.

Thus my text says: "God sent his only begotten Son into the world"— and by that you must not understand the external world, in which he ate and drank with us, but you should know that it refers to the inner world. As sure as the Father, so single in nature, begets his Son, he begets him in the spirit's inmost recess—and that is the inner world. Here, the core[9] of God is also my core; and the core of my soul, the core of God's, and here, I am independent as God himself is independent.[10] If one could peek into this core [of the soul] even for an instant, he would afterwards think no more of a thousand pounds of beaten red gold than of a counterfeit farthing.

Do all you do, acting from the core of your soul, without a single "Why."[11] I tell you, whenever what you do is done for the sake of the Kingdom of God, or for God's sake, or for eternal blessing, and thus really for ulterior motives, you are wrong. You may pass for a good person, but this is not the best. For, truly, if you imagine that you are going to get more out of God by means of religious offices and devotions, in sweet retreats and solitary orisons, than you might by the fireplace or in the stable, then you might just as well think you could seize God and wrap a mantle around his head and stick him under the table! To seek God by rituals[12] is to get the ritual and lose God in the process, for he hides behind it. On the other hand, to seek God without artifice,[12] is to take him as he is, and so doing, a person "lives by the Son," and is the Life itself.

For if Life were questioned a thousand years and asked: "Why live?" and if there were an answer, it could be no more than this: "I live only to live!" And that is because Life is its own reason for being, springs from its own Source, and goes on and on, without ever asking why—just because it is life. Thus, if you ask a genuine person, that is, one who acts [uncalculatingly] from his heart: "Why are you doing that?"—he will reply in the only possible way: "I do it because I do it!"

Where the creature ends, there God begins to be. God asks only that you get out of his way, in so far as you are creature, and let him be God in you. The least creaturely idea that ever entered your mind is as big as God. Why? Because it will keep God out of you entirely. The moment you get [one of your own] ideas, God fades out and the Godhead too. It is when the idea is gone that God gets in.

God desires urgently that you, the creature, get out of his way[13] —as if his own blessedness depended on it. Ah, beloved people, why don't you let God be God in you? What are you afraid of? You get completely out of his way and he will get out of yours—you give up to him and he will give up to you. When both [God and you] have forsaken self, what remains [between you] is an indivisible union. It is in this unity that the Father begets his Son in the secret spring of your nature. Then the Holy Spirit blooms and out of God there comes a will which belongs to the soul. As long as this will remains uncorrupted by creatures, it is free. Christ says:[14] "No man riseth to heaven but he that came from heaven." All things were created out of nothingness and thus their true origin is the "Not."[15] That is why the aristocratic[16] [free] will, to the extent it condescends to created things, lapses at last with them to their nothingness.

It is sometimes asked whether this noble will may lapse so completely that it cannot recover. The authorities usually teach that, if it has lapsed for some time, there is no recovery. But I say, if [your] will is directed back again, to its secret source, it will once again be as it was, formally free and really free, and at once all the time that was lost will be made up.

People often say to me: "Pray for me!" At that I have to wonder: Why did you ever leave him? And why not be your true self and reach into your own treasure? For the whole truth is just as much in you as in me!

That we all may similarly remain close to this treasure, that we all may know the truth blessedly, without anything separating us from it, or standing in between, may God help! Amen.

6

The Kingdom of God is at hand[1]

SCITOTE, QUIA PROPE EST REGNUM DEI.

(Luke 21:31)

OUR beloved Lord says that the Kingdom of God is at hand. Indeed, the Kingdom of God is within us; and St. Paul says that our salvation is nearer than we think. Now you shall hear how the Kingdom of God is at hand, and to this end we must note what is meant with great care.

If I were a king, and were not aware of the fact, I should not be king. But if I were sure that I was a king and everybody else shared this conviction, and I knew that people everywhere thought so and believed it, then I could be a king and all the wealth of the kingdom could be mine. Yet if I lacked even one of these three, I could not be a king at all. Even so, man's blessedness depends on his awareness and recognition of the highest good: God himself.

There is an agent[2] in my soul which is perfectly sensitive to God. I am as sure of this as I am that I am alive: nothing is as near to me as God is. God is nearer to me than I am to myself. My being depends on God's intimate presence. So, too, he is near to a stick or a stone but they do not know it. If the stick knew God and recognized how near he is, as the holy angels know such things, the stick would be as blessed as the angels. For that reason, a person may be more blessed than a stick, in that he recognizes God and knows how near he is. And the more he knows it, the more blessed he is; the less he knows it, the less his blessing. Man is not blessed because God is in him and so near that he *has* God—but in that he is aware of how near God is, and knowing God, he loves him.

When I think about the Kingdom of God, I am struck dumb by its grandeur; for the Kingdom of God is God himself with all his fullness. The Kingdom of God is no small thing: all the worlds one could imagine God creating would still not be as the Kingdom of God. When the Kingdom appears to the soul and it is recognized, there is no further need for preaching or instruction: it is learnéd enough and has at once secured eternal life. To know and see how near God's Kingdom is, is to say with Jacob: "God is in this place and I did not know it."[3]

God is equally near to every creature. The wise man says: "God has spread his nets and lines out over all things, so that he may be found in any one of them and recognized by whoever chooses to verify this." One authority says: "To see God aright is to know him alike in everything. To serve God with fear is good; to serve him out of love is better; but to love him while fearing is best of all." It is good to have a peaceful life in rest with God; it is better to bear a life of suffering with patience; but to find rest in a life of suffering is best of all. To walk through the fields and say your prayers, and see God, or to sit in church and recognize him, and to know God better because the place is peaceful: this is due to man's defective nature and not to God. For God is equally near to everything and every place and is equally ready to give himself, so far as in him lies, and therefore a person shall know him aright who knows how to see him the same, under all circumstances.

St. Bernard asks: "Why do my eyes behold the sky and not my feet? It is because my eyes are more like the sky than my feet." If then my soul is to see God, it must be heavenly. How shall the soul be prepared so that it may see God and know him in itself—how near he is? Now listen! Heaven may not receive any alien impress; neither pain nor want, brought from without, may be stamped upon it. Even so, the soul that is to know God must be so firm and steady in God that nothing can penetrate it, neither hope nor fear, neither joy nor sorrow, neither love nor suffering, nor any other thing that can come in it from without.

So, too, heaven is equidistant from earth at all places. Likewise, the soul ought to be equidistant from every earthly thing,[4] so that it is not nearer to one than to the other and behaves the same in love, or suffering, or having, or forbearance; toward whatever it may be, the soul should be as dead, or dispassionate, or superior to it. Heaven is pure and clear and without spot, touching neither time nor space. Corporeal things have no place in it. It is not inside of time; its orbit is compassed with speed beyond belief. The course of heaven is outside time—and yet time comes from its movements.[5] Nothing hinders the soul's knowledge of God as much as time and space, for time and space are fragments, whereas God is one! And therefore, if the soul is to know God, it must know him above time and outside of space; for God is neither this nor that, as are these manifold things. God is One!

If the soul is to see God, it must not look again on any temporal thing, for as long as the soul dwells on time or space or any image of them it may never know God. If the eye is to distinguish colors, it must first be purged of them all. If the soul is to see God, it must have nothing in common with things that are nothings. For to see God is to know that all creatures are as nothing. Compare one creature to another, and it appears to be beautiful and is something; but compare it with God and it is nothing!

Further, I say that if the soul is to know God, it must forget itself and lose [consciousness of] itself, for as long as it is self-aware and self-conscious, it will not see or be conscious of God. But when, for God's sake, it becomes unself-conscious and lets go of everything, it finds itself again in God, for knowing God, it therefore knows itself and everything else from which it has been cut asunder, in the divine perfection. If I am to know the highest good or the eternal goodness, then surely I must know it where it is good in itself and not where its goodness is separate. If I am to know true being, I must know it where it is being itself, and that is in God and not where it is divided among creatures.

The whole divine being is in God alone. The whole of humanity is not in one man, for one man is not the whole of humanity. But in God all humanity is known to the soul, and all things else, in their highest [reality], for in him they are known as beings.

If a person lived in a beautifully decorated home, he would know much more about it than one who never entered it, but who enjoys talking about it. Thus I am as sure as I am that I live and God lives, that if the soul is to know God it must know him above space and time. And such a soul [thus acquainted with God] knows him, and is aware of how near his kingdom is, that is, God with all his fullness. The authorities in the schools ask often how it is possible for the soul to know God. It is not from God's strictness that he requires so much of man, but rather from his kindness that he expects the soul to progress to that point where it may receive much, as he gives so much to it.

No one ought to think that it is hard to attain this, however hard it sounds and however hard it may be at first to cut one's self asunder and be dead to everything. But once you have come in, no life is easier, nor pleasanter, nor lovelier, for God is very anxious at all times to be near to people, and to teach them how to come to him, if they are only willing to follow him. Nobody ever wanted anything as much as God wants to bring people to know him. God is always ready but we are not ready. God is near to us but we are far from him. God is within; we are without. God is at home; we are abroad.[6]

The prophet says: "God leads the righteous through a narrow way out onto a broad street, so that they may come into his wide and open spaces"—which is to say, into the true freedom of the spirit which has become one spirit with God. May God help us all to follow as he leads us to himself. Amen.

7

Youth remains in the soul[1]

ADOLESCENS, TIBI DICO, SURGE!

(Luke 7:14)

WE READ in the gospel what My Lord St. Luke writes of a youth who was dead. When the Lord came across him, he went up to him and had compassion on him, and touched him, saying: "Young man, I tell you—I command you to get up!"

Know, then, that God is present at all times in good people and that there is a Something in the soul in which God dwells. There is also a Something by which the soul lives in God, but when the soul is intent on external things that Something dies, and therefore God dies, as far as the soul is concerned. Of course, God himself does not die. He continues very much alive to himself.

When the soul is separated from the body, the body is dead and yet the soul lives on by itself. Thus God may be dead to the soul and yet alive to himself and one knows that there is an agent of the soul which reaches farther than broad heaven—so incredibly far that the distance is beyond telling. It goes even farther than that.

Good enough! Then listen carefully. The Father speaks through this noble agent[3] and says to his only begotten Son: "Get up, young man!" Thus God—and the unity of God with the soul—is so complete as to seem incredible, since he is so high himself as to be beyond the reach of intelligence. Nevertheless, this agent reaches farther than heaven, yes, farther than the angels, whether or not it was by an angelic spark that life first came to earth. We want to reach far—far beyond measure—and yet we find that all that is to be understood or desired is still not God, but that where mind and desire end, in that darkness, God shines.

Thus our Lord says: "Young man, I tell you to get up!" Indeed, if I am to hear God speak in me, I must be as much alienated from all

133

that is mine as I am from things beyond the sea—and especially from time. The soul is as young intrinsically as it was when created, for age concerns only the soul's use of the bodily senses. One authority says: "If an old man had a young man's eyes, he would see as well as the youngster." Yesterday as I sat yonder I said something that sounds incredible: "Jerusalem is as near to my soul as this place is."[2] Indeed, a point a thousand miles beyond Jerusalem is as near to my soul as my body is, and though I am as sure of this as I am of being human, it is something even learned priests seldom understand. See! My soul is as young as the day it was created, yes, and much younger. I tell you, I should be ashamed if it were not younger tomorrow that it is today.

The soul has two agents which are not connected with the body and these are *intelligence* and *will*—agents which function apart from time. Oh—if only the soul's eyes were opened so that it might see the truth! Believe me, it would then be as easy for one to give up everything as it would be to give up peas and lentils. Yes—by my soul—the world of things would be as nothing at all to such a person. Now, there are certain people who give up this or that for love's sake, feeling that their sacrifice is important. But to him who sees the truth it does not matter in the least if he gives up the whole world and himself with it. And yet, living so, the whole world belongs to him anyway.

There is one agent of the soul[3] to which everything is equally sweet. The worst and the best are both alike to it, but it looks at them apart from the here and now. "Now" is time, and "here" is place. On this spot where I now stand, if I got away from self and at the same time were completely pure, the Father in heaven would beget his only Son in my spirit with such purity that my spirit might beget him in return in God. To tell the truth, if I were as well prepared as the Lord Jesus Christ, the Father could function as clearly in me as he did in him, and no less, for he loves me with the same love he has for himself.

St. John says: "In the beginning was the Word, and the Word was with God, and the Word was God."[4] Indeed, he who is to hear this Word [where all is quiet] must be quite quiet himself and void of ideas—yes, of forms too. He must be joined to God so genuinely that nothing can happen to make him sad or glad. He should take everything as it comes from God.

He says: "Young man, I tell you, get up!" God wants to work for you. If someone tells me to carry stone, he could tell me to carry a thousand stones—if he intends to do it all himself. Or let there be a hundredweight to be carried: it could as well be a thousandweight, if another is to take it. God wants to do your work himself, and will if you will only obey and resist him not at all. Let your soul stay where it belongs[5] and then everything will be with you.

There is an agent of the soul—no, not an agent but something more, a Being—yet not a Being, but something more than Being liberates—something so pure, sublime, and precious that no creature can get into it to stay except God himself. To tell the truth, not even God himself could get in there if he were creaturelike. There is no device or condition by which God can enter there, save as he comes in the naked divinity of his nature.[6]

But now look. Notice that he says: "Young man, I tell you." What is God's telling? It is God's work, his function, and this function is so precious and so sublime that God alone can do it. We should know that our whole perfection and blessing depends on our stepping across or beyond the estate of creaturehood, time, and Being and on getting at last to the Cause that has no cause. We pray our dear Lord God that we may be one with him and that he may dwell in us. So help us God. Amen.

The fruits of good deeds live on![1]

MEISTER ECKHART once said, when he stood up to preach: I once declared in a sermon that I want to teach people, who do good deeds while under mortal sin, how their good deeds, performed while under deadly sin, may be brought to life[2] again, together with the interval of time in which they were done. And now I shall set forth the facts of the matter, for I have been asked to explain the meaning of my assertion.

The authorities all say that when a person is under grace, the deeds he does are worthy of eternal life. And that is true, for God works through grace;[3] and I agree with them. Generally speaking, the authorities also assert that, if one falls into mortal sin, his deeds are then dead, as he himself is dead, and none of them merit eternal life, because he is no longer under grace. In some sense this, too, is true, and I agree. They say further, that when God returns his grace to persons who have suffered for their sins, those deeds they did before they sinned mortally, live again in the new grace as they did before—and here, too, I agree.

But when they say that good deeds done by one in mortal sin are lost eternally, time and deeds together, then I disagree. I, Meister Eckhart, assert as follows: Of all the good deeds a man does while in mortal sin not one is lost, once he has been restored to grace, no, nor even the interval of time in which they were done. See! This is contrary to all living authorities.[4]

Now pay close attention to what I am going to say and you will understand what I mean.[5]

I say, categorically, that all the good deeds anyone ever did or might do, together with the time used in doing them, are both lost, time and deeds, all together. I say also that no deed was ever either sacred or blessed and that no interval of time was ever sacred or blessed, nor did it hold more good than any other. And if they are neither sacred nor blessed, nor intrinsically good, how could either be preserved? Since good deeds pass away, along with the time consumed in doing them, how could the deeds done under mortal sin, or the time consumed in doing them, be restored? I say that both are lost, one with the other; deeds and time together, the bad with the good, deed for deed, and time for time, are lost forever.

Then we should raise the question: Why should deeds be qualified, so that one is "good," another "sacred," and another "blessed," and so on; and why speak in similar terms of the times at which they were done? See! As I have said, neither the deed nor the time may so be qualified. "Holy," "blessed," and "good," are terms applied gratuitously either to deeds or time and do not necessarily belong to the nature of either.

Why? A deed, as a deed, is nothing in itself. It did not happen by any will of its own, nor did it happen just by itself. Itself, it knows nothing. Therefore, it is neither good, nor sacred, nor blessed nor unblessed, for these terms apply only to the spirit in which a deed is done, and the spirit is exempt from form, and does not appear after the deed itself. As soon as a deed is done it becomes nothing at all, together with the time consumed in doing it. It is neither here nor there, for the spirit has nothing more to do with the deed. Henceforth, whatever the spirit may do, it must appear in another deed at another time.

For this reason, deeds and time pass away. Bad and good, they are all lost together, for they have no duration in the spirit, nor in their own right, nor have they a place of their own. They are lost because God needs them not at all. If one does a good deed, he is purified, and by this purification he is made more as he was when he was born. To that extent, he is more blessed and better than he was before. This is why we say that a deed is sacred or blessed, or speak so of the time at which it happened. Still, this is not accurate, for the deed knows nothing, nor does the time of its occurrence, and it all passes away. Therefore, the deed itself is neither good, nor sacred, nor blessed, but rather, he is blessed in whom the fruit of good deeds remains—not as times or deeds, but rather as the capacity to do good, which belongs always to the spirit. For the spirit is in the doing of good and is the good itself.

See! In this way, a good deed is never lost, no, nor the time consumed in doing it—not that it is stored up as time or deed but it is stored up apart from time and deed, in the spirit, which is eternal. Then let us see how this applies to deeds done while under mortal sin. As deeds and time, these good deeds are lost, deeds and time together, but then, I have also said that deeds and time are nothing of themselves. And if they are nothing in themselves, then the person who loses them loses nothing! It is true. Still, I have gone further; neither time nor deed has any being or place of itself. In fact, they only issue from the spirit out into time. Whatever the spirit does afterwards, it must be in another deed at another time, and neither of these can ever get into the spirit in so far as it is either deed or time. Neither can it penetrate God, for no temporal deed ever got into him, and for this reason alone it becomes as nothing and is lost.

But now I have said that of all the good deeds a person does while under mortal sin not a single one remains, neither deeds nor time, and that is true in the meaning which I have just explained. I want to make it perfectly clear to you, even though it is contrary to every authority alive.

Now for a brief word about my meaning and why it is true. When a person does a good deed while under mortal sin, he does not do it because of the sin, for his deed is as good as the sin is bad. Rather, he does it because of his basic nature [the core of the soul] which is naturally good, even though he is not under grace and his deeds do not serve to bring in the Kingdom of Heaven at the time he does them. That, however, does not harm the spirit at all, for the fruit of the deed, quite apart from the fact or the time of it, remains in the spirit and is spirit with spirit and can be destroyed as little as the spirit can put itself out of existence. What is more, the spirit purifies itself when it gets rid of the act, which is the image of its own goodness under grace, and in this way is prepared for unity and equality [with God][6] in which neither deeds nor time are of further use. The more a person purifies himself and gets rid of his images, the nearer he is to God, who himself is altogether free of them. The more a man forgets his deeds, as well as the occasion of their performance, the purer he is.

If and when grace comes again [to the mortal sinner], all that by nature is his partakes of grace. To the extent he has purified himself by doing good, even while under mortal sin, he has struck a blow for his ultimate union with God, which might not have been possible if he had not purified himself by doing good under mortal sin. He will need time to get rid of his images [the remembered good deeds], but if he has so purified himself while under mortal sin, he has saved some time in which he may do more good, now that he is pure—good that will further unite him with God. The fruits of deeds remain in the spirit. Only the deeds themselves and the time of them are not eternal. So the spirit lives on, out of which deeds are born and the fruit of the deeds, apart from either deeds or time, is full of grace as the spirit is also.

Now, then, we have set forth the meaning of my assertion clearly and it really is true. All who contradict it are hereby contradicted in return, for Truth itself bespeaks the truth of what I have said. If people really understood what spirit is, what deeds and time are, and how deeds are related to the spirit, they would never say that any good deed could ever be lost or go astray. Only the deed passes away with the time and is made nothing, but its result is that the spirit is ennobled by the deed it has projected. That is the power of deeds and why they are done. Their fruits remain in the spirit and can never be taken away. They will never be lost to the spirit itself. If you understand that, how could it ever be possible to assert again that a good work goes amiss, as long as the spirit has being and lives anew under grace?

That we may come to be one spirit with God and be found under grace, may God help us all! Amen.

9

Now I know[1]

NUNC SCIO VERE, QUIA MISIT DOMINUS ANGELUM SUUM, ET ERIPUIT ME
DE MANU HERODIS, ET DE OMNE EXSPECTATIONE PLEBUS IUDAEORUM.

(Acts 12:11)

WHEN Peter was set free from the bonds of his captivity, by the power of the supreme God, he said: "Now I know of a surety that the Lord hath sent his angel and delivered me out of the power of Herod and out of the hand of the enemy."[1]

We shall turn this expression around and say: "When God has sent his angel to me, then I know of a surety." Let Peter stand for knowledge. On other occasions I have said that knowledge and intellect[2] unite the soul to God. Intellect falls within [the category of] pure Being, but knowledge precedes it—precedes it and breaks out the way—so that God's only begotten Son can be born. Our Lord says in the Gospel of St. Matthew,[3] that no one knows the Father but the Son. The authorities declare that knowledge is limited [by the requirement of] likeness.[4] For that reason, some of them say that the soul is composite of everything, because it can understand everything. This sounds foolish but it is true. They say that what I am to know must be present in me already and like what I know. Moreover, the saints say that the Father has power, the Son, likeness, and the Holy Spirit, unity;[5] so that if the Father is completely represented by the Son and Son is always like him, no one can possibly know the Father but the Son.

"Now I know of a surety," exclaims St. Peter. How does anyone know with certainty? Because there is a divine light that deceives nobody, and in that light things are seen clearly, without coatings, and undisguised. St. Paul says that "God lives in a light to which there is no approach."[6] The authorities again assert that the wisdom we acquire here we shall keep in heaven; but Paul says that "it shall vanish away."[6] One authority says: "Pure knowledge, even in this present body, is so pleasant that all the delights of creation are as nothing to the pleasure it unfolds." And yet, noble as our knowledge may be, it is still contingent, and compared to the uncoated, pure Truth; all the wisdom one may acquire here is as insignificant as one small word would be against the whole world. Thus Paul says: "It shall vanish away." And even if it did not, it would become like foolish vanity when compared to that pure, uncoated Truth which is yet to be known.

The third reason why we shall know with certainty up yonder is that those things which are here seen to be so changeable and changing are known there as changeless and perceived at a given time as undivided and almost as if they were one. Things that are widely separate here are near together there, where everything is present at once. What happened on the first day, and shall happen at the latter day, happen all together in one present there.

"Now I know of a surety that the Lord hath sent his angel to me." When God sends his angel to the soul, it becomes the one who knows for sure. Not for nothing did God give the keys into St. Peter's keeping, for Peter stands for knowledge, and knowledge has the key that unlocks the door, presses forward and breaks in, to discover God as he is. Then it tells its partner, the will, what it has taken possession of, for it had already taken charge of the will. For what I will, that I seek after, but knowledge goes before. It is like a princess seeking to rule in the prince's place, in that virgin realm which she proclaims to the soul, and the soul to the nature and the nature to the physical senses. Still, at its highest and best, the soul's rank is such that no scholar can find a name for it. They call it the "soul," since it gives being to the body.

The authorities teach that next to the first emanation, which is the Son coming out of the Father, the angels are most like God. And it may well be true, for the soul at its highest is formed like God, but an angel gives a closer idea of him. That is all an angel is: an idea[7] of God. For this reason the angel was sent to the soul, so that the soul might be re-formed by it, to be the divine idea by which it was first conceived. Knowledge comes through likeness. And so, because the soul may know everything, it is never at rest until it comes to the original idea, in which all things are one. And there it comes to rest in God. No creature is more respected than another by God.

The authorities say that being and knowing are identical,[8] because if a thing does not exist no one knows it, but that whatever has most being is most known. Because God's being is transcendent, he is beyond all knowledge, as I said the day before yesterday in my former sermon. There, where the soul is informed with the primal purity, stamped with the seal of pure being, where it tastes God himself as he was before he ever took upon himself the forms of truth and knowledge, where everything that can be named is sloughed off—there the soul knows with its purest knowledge and takes on Being in its most perfect similitude. St. Paul says of the matter: "God dwells in the light no man can approach unto."[6] God is one and lives within his own pure being, which contains nothing else. All alloy must be done away. He himself is a pure presence in which there is neither this nor that, because what is in God is God![1]

One heathen says: "The agents of the soul which are under God's suasion, belong in God, for however freely they may exist, their inner connection is with that which has neither beginning nor end and nothing alien may intrude in God." Heaven is an example of this. Heaven will receive nothing alien, as an alien. Thus, by the same token, whatever comes to God is changed. However mean it may be, let it be brought to God and it will no longer be what it was. Take, for example: I may have wisdom, but I am not wisdom myself. I can acquire wisdom and also lose it. But what is of God is God![1] And it can never fall away from him. It is implanted in the divine nature and the divine nature is so stable that whatever gets into it is part of it forever—either that, or it stays out altogether. Then listen, and be astonished! If God so changes little things, what do you think he will do with the soul, which he has already fashioned so gloriously in his own likeness?[9] . . .

10

God laughs and plays

LAUDATE COELI ET EXULTET TERRA.
EGO SUM LUX MUNDI.

(Isaiah 49:13)
(John 8:12)

I HAVE read two texts in Latin. One is in the lection for today and is quoted from the prophet Isaiah: "Sing, O heavens; and be joyful, O earth; for the Lord hath comforted his people and will have mercy on his afflicted." The other is from the Gospel and quotes our Lord: "I am the light of the world: he that followeth me shall not walk in darkness, but shall have the light of life."

Now, notice the first text in which the prophet is quoted: "Rejoice, O heavens and earth." Truly! Truly! By God! By God! Be as sure of it as you are that God lives: at the least good deed, the least bit of good will, or the least of good desires, all the saints in heaven and on earth rejoice, and together with the angels, their joy is such that all the joy in this world cannot be compared to it. The more exalted a saint is, the greater his joy; but the joy of them all put together amounts to as little as a bean when compared to the joy of God over good deeds. For truly, God plays and laughs in good deeds,[1] whereas all other deeds, which do not make for the glory of God, are like ashes before him. Thus he says: "Rejoice. O heavens! For the Lord hath comforted his people!"

Notice that he says: "God hath comforted his people and will have mercy on his afflicted—his poor ones." The poor are left to God alone, for no one bothers with them. If one has a friend who is poor, he does not open his heart to him; but if he is good and wise, he says: "You belong to my crowd!"—and quickly opens his heart to him. But to the poor, they say: "God take care of you!"—and are ashamed of them. The poor are left to God and wherever they go

143

they find him, and everywhere he is theirs.[2] God takes charge of them because they are given to him. That is why the gospel says: "Blessed are the poor."

Now let us look at the text in which he says: "I am the light of the world." "I am" has to do with essence. The authorities say that any creature at all could say "I," for that word is general property, but the word "*sum*—am" belongs to God alone, and none may use it but he. *Sum* expresses the thought of one thing containing all good. To creatures this is denied, so that none of them may have what is exclusively assigned to persons for their comfort. If I had all I could wish for, and yet hurt my finger, I should not have this *all*, for my finger would be hurt and complete comfort would not be mine as long as that was the case. Bread is comfortable to people who are hungry, but if they are thirsty they get as little comfort out of bread as they would out of a stone. It is the same with clothing when one is cold, but when one is hot he gets little comfort out of clothing. So it is with all kinds of creatures: they all have a certain bitterness in them and as surely they contain a certain comfort, like the sweetness of honey, to be skimmed off the surface.[3] But among other things, all that is good in creatures, all their honey-sweetness is from God. Thus it is written in the Book of Wisdom: "All the good of my soul comes from thee."

Creature comfort is never perfect. It is faulty and never comes unmixed. God's comfort is pure and without any admixture. It is full and complete and he needs so much to give it that he can do nothing else until he has. So prodigal is God with his love for us that it might seem as if he had forgotten about the Kingdoms of Heaven and earth, all the blessing of his Godhead, and could have nothing to do with anything else than me alone,[4] so that he might be free to give me all my comfort requires. And to me he gives it— constantly—completely and perfectly—in its purest form—and so he gives it to every creature.

He says: "He that followeth me shall not walk in darkness." Notice that "he that followeth me." The authorities say that the soul has three agents. The first is always seeking what is sweetest. The second is always seeking the highest. The third always seeks the best, for the soul is too aristocratic ever to rest except at its own point of origin,[5] from which there drops what makes for goodness. See, so sweet is God's comfort that every creature is looking for it, hunting it.[6] I shall go even further and say that their very existence and life depend on their search for it, their hunting it.

But you may ask: "Where is this God, after whom all creatures seek and from whom they have their life and being?" (I prefer to speak of the Godhead, from whence all our blessings flow.) The Father says: "My Son, I have begotten thee today in the light reflected from the saints." Where is this God? "I am caught in the perfection of the saints." Where is this God? In the Father. Where is this God? In eternity. Just as a man who is hiding clears his throat and thus reveals his whereabouts, so it is with God. Nobody could ever find God. He has to discover himself.[6]

A saint says: "Sometimes I feel such a sweetness in my soul that I forget everything else—and myself too—and dissolve in thee. But when I try to catch it perfectly, O Lord, thou takest it away. Lord, what do you mean by that? You entice me. Then why do you withdraw? If you love me, why do you run away? Ah, Lord, you do this because you want me to have a lot of experience with you!"

The prophet says: "My God!"

"Who told you that I am your God?"

"Lord, I cannot rest except in you and nothing goes well with me except in you."[7]

That we may ever seek God like this, and even find him, may God the Father, the Son, and the Holy Ghost help us! Amen.

11

Honor thy father[1]

HAEC DICIT DOMINUS: HONORA PATREM TUUM.

(Matthew 15:4)

THIS text which I have read in Latin, from the Gospel, quotes our Lord, and it means in English:[2] "Honor thy father and mother." Another commandment quotes the Lord our God: "Thou shalt not covet thy neighbor's goods, nor his house, nor his farm, nor anything that is his."[3] A third selection is to the point that the people went to Moses and said:[4] "You speak to us, for we cannot hear God." A fourth is that the Lord our God said: "Moses, make me an altar of earth, on the earth and all you offer on it shall be burned completely."[5] A fifth is that Moses went up into the clouds and walked on the mountains and there he found God.[6] In that darkness he found the true light.

My Lord St. Augustine says: "Where the lamb sinks, the ox and the cow swim. Where the cow swims, the elephant runs ahead and the water is only up to his neck." This is a fine simile from which one may draw many thoughts. St. Augustine means that the Scriptures are like deep water. The little lamb signifies humble or simple persons who may be drowned in the Scriptures. By the ox who swims, we may understand [a reference to] those rude people who take what they like out of their reading. In the elephant that runs ahead we have a reference to intelligent people who search the Scriptures and forge ahead in them.

I wonder at the Scriptures that they contain so much, but the authorities say that they should not be interpreted literally and that, when a passage occurs that is crude and simple, it must be read in its higher significance. That calls for [another] simile. "The first went up to his ankles, the second to his knees, the third to his waist, but the fourth went in over his head and sank at once."

Now what does this mean? St. Augustine says that at first the Scriptures will attract and amuse children, but that at last, when one tries to fathom them, they make fools of the wise. There are none so simple mentally that they cannot find their needs met there and none so wise that when they try to touch bottom in the Scriptures, they will not find them deep, and perhaps too deep. All we read and hear from them has a second or hidden meaning, for [the literal] reading of the Scriptures differs from what they really intend and from what they mean to God, as if they did not exist at all.

Now back to the text: "Honor thy father and mother"—and in its literal sense, this does mean father and mother. We are to honor them and all who have spiritual power, as well as those from whom you get your living. Thus one can wade here and there and touch bottom but get little out of it. It is a woman who says: "And if we are to honor those from whom our external goods come, how much more we ought to honor him from whom man gets everything!"

All that appears outwardly so manifold is still one in essence. Now listen closely and observe how this uniformity[7] is related to the Father. I was thinking tonight how all uniformity is intended to lead to him. Therefore, in the second place, honor the Father who is your father in heaven from whom you have your very being.

Who honors the Father? No one except the Son: he alone honors him. And no one honors the Son except the Father. Our Father's total pleasure, affection, and enjoyment are focused on the Son. Except for the Son, the Father is not conscious of anything.[8] He takes such great pleasure in his Son that he can do nothing but beget him, for he is a perfect likeness and image of the Father.

Our authorities[9] say that nothing can thus be born or known but an idea. They say therefore that if the Father is to beget his only Son, he must beget him as the idea of his own nature, the fundamental idea which will reproduce what he himself eternally is (*formae illius*), giving into form what must always remain his own. It is natural to teach—and yet, it seems to me unsuitable—that man must demonstrate God by this or that analogy. For after all, God is neither this nor that and nothing satisfies him but withdrawal into the innermost core of his own being, the kernel of his own Fatherhood, where he has dwelt through all eternity within himself, functioning only as a Father, and finding companionship within his own unique unity.

Here is the unity of blades of grass and bits of wood and stone, together with everything else. This is the optimum about which I myself have often been deceived. For its sake, all that nature tries to do is to plunge on into that unity, into the Father-nature, so that it all may be one, the one Son, and outgrowing everything else, to subsist in his Fatherhood, or if this cannot be done, at least to look like his oneness. Nature, coming from God, does not seek its externals [as ends]. Indeed, nature itself, the *Ding an sich* has nothing to do with its adornments [colors] but rather it aims at nothing short of the likeness of God.[15]

I have been thinking tonight that each analogy [of things spiritual] is like an outer gate. I cannot see anything unless it bears some likeness to myself, nor can I know anything unless it is analogous to me. God has hidden [the essence of] all things in himself. They are not [as they seem to be] this and that, individually distinct, but rather, they are one with [his] unity. Because the eye itself has color, the eye perceives color and the ear does not. The ear perceives tones and the tongue flavors. Each takes what it can identify in itself.

That is why the idea of the soul and the idea of God are identical: we are Sons [of God]. And if I had neither eyes nor ears, I should still be like him. Thus, to take away my eyes or my ears would not mean taking away my life, for the heart is the seat of life. If someone strikes at my eyes, I put up my hands to ward off the blow. If someone strikes at my heart, I set my whole body to protect its life. But if anyone should try to strike off my head, I should throw up my arms at once in order to save my life.

And so, as I have often said: "The shell must be cracked apart if what is in it is to come out; *for if you want the kernel, you must break the shell.*"[10] And therefore, if you want to discover nature's nakedness, you must destroy its symbols and the farther you get in, the nearer you come to its essence. When you come to the One that gathers all things up into itself, there your soul must stay. Who honors God? He who intends to honor God in everything he does.

Many years ago, I did not exist, but shortly thereafter, because of

my father and mother who ate bread and meat, and garden vege-
tables, I became a person. To this end, my parents were not able to
contribute much but God made my body without any help and
created my soul like that which is supreme. Thus I came to possess
life (*possedi me*).

One seed grain grows to be rye. The nature of another causes it to
grow into wheat and never to stop until its end has been achieved.
But this grain has the [ultimate] capacity to turn into everything
and so it submits, and goes to its death, in order to change into
everything.[11] And this metal, [a piece of] copper, can be changed
into gold and it will never stop [changing] until its end has been
attained. Indeed, wood may become stone, but even more than that,
it may become anything at all by being put into the fire and burned
up. It will take on the fire's nature if only it may be united to the
One and thus come to its eternal essence. Indeed, wood and stone,
bone and grasses, all began in one essence. And if it is like this with
[visible] nature, what shall it be like with that nature which is so
pure that it seeks neither this nor that, but only to outgrow [all it
forms] and hurry on to its primitive purity?

I have been reflecting tonight on the many wonders of heaven.
Now, there are many unbelieving people who do not think that the
bread on the altar can be changed or that God can do it. But if God
has given nature the power to become anything at all, how much
more possible it is for him to take this bread and change it into his
body! If frail nature can make a man out of a leaf, isn't it much
more possible for God to make his own body out of this bread?
Who honors God? He who intends to honor God in everything.
This meaning of the text is more obvious, albeit the first is better.

The fourth point[12] is that "they stood afar off and said to Moses:
You speak to us, for we cannot hear God." They stood afar off and
that is the reason they could not hear God.

"Moses went up into the clouds and walked on the mountains
and there he saw the divine light." One really finds light best in the
darkness. Thus when a man suffers and knows discomfort, he is
nearest to the light. Let God do his best or his worst, he must give
himself to us whether we are in trouble or discomfort or not. There
was once a saintly woman whose sons they sought to kill. With a

smile, she said [to her sons]: "Don't worry, but rejoice and think of your heavenly Father, for you have received nothing from me!"[13] It was as if she had said: "You have received your existence directly from God."

This applies to us, too. Our Lord said: "Your darkness [that is, your suffering] shall be changed into clear light."[14] But I must not love it or covet it. Another authority in another place said: "The mysterious darkness of the invisible light of the eternal Godhead is unknown and shall never be known." And the light of the everlasting Father has shined eternally in that darkness and the darkness comprehended it not. Now may God help us to come to the eternal light. Amen.

12

When God shows himself[1]

ELIZABETH IMPLETUM EST TEMPUS PARIENDI ET PEPERIT FILIUM.

(Luke 1:57)

"Now Elizabeth's full time came that she should be delivered and she brought forth a son" and named him John. Then the people said: "What wonders shall come of this child, for the hand of the Lord is with him!" One Scripture says that God's greatest gift is that we are his children and that he begets his Son in us. Nothing else may be born in the soul that is to be God's child or in whom his Son is to be begotten. The supreme purpose of God is birth. He will not be content until his Son is born in us. Neither will the soul be content until the Son is born of it. That is the wellspring of grace by which grace is poured on us. Grace does no work, for its work is to come to be. It flows out of the essence of God, into the essence of the soul but not into the soul's agents.

In the fullness of time, grace was born. The fullness of time is when time is no more. Still to be within time and yet to set one's heart on eternity, in which all temporal things are dead, is to reach the fullness of time. Once I said: "They are not always happy who set their hearts on time." St. Paul says: "Rejoice in the Lord always."[2] [St. Augustine says] "To rejoice always is to find your joy above or beyond time." One Scripture says that three things there are, that prevent a person from knowing anything about God at all. The first is time, the second, materiality, the third, multiplicity. As long as these three are in me, God is not mine nor is his work being done. Thus St. Augustine says: "The soul is greedy, to wish to know so much, and to have and hold it, and so, grasping for time, materiality and multiplicity, we lose what is uniquely our own."[3] As long as [the spirit of "Give me"] "More and More!" is in man, God can neither live nor work. All these things must be got rid of before God comes in and then you may have them in a higher and better way, namely, that the many are made one in you. Thus, the more multiplicity there is, the more you will require unity in yourself, if one is to be changed into the other.

I once said that unity changes the Many into One but that multiplicity does not produce unity. If we have risen above [the world of] things, if we are completely exalted, we cannot be cast down. I am not depressed by things beneath me but if I were purely God-minded, so that I had nothing above me but God himself, nothing would be hard for me any more and I should not be troubled so easily. To this end, St. Augustine says: "Lord, when I bow to thee, hardship, suffering, and labor are lifted from me." Once we get beyond time and temporal things, we are free and joyous and then comes the "fullness of time" when the Son of God is born.

I said once that in the fullness of time God sent his Son. If anything other than the Son is born in you, neither the Holy Spirit nor grace is at work.[4] The Son is the source of the Holy Spirit. If there were no Son, there could be no Holy Spirit. The Holy Spirit cannot put forth its blossoms except from the Son. When the Father gives us his Son, he gives all he has of essence or nature and in the giving of the gift, the Holy Spirit buds.

God intends to give himself wholly.[5] To put it in a simile: in order that fire may catch wood and penetrate it completely, time is required because the wood and fire are so dissimilar. At first, the fire warms the wood and then makes it hot, and then smoking and crackling, because the two are so dissimilar, but as the wood gets hotter it gets quieter. The more the wood gives up to the fire, the more peaceful it is, until at last it really turns to fire. If the fire is to change the wood into itself, all dissimilarity must be removed.

In truth, which is God, if you are intent on anything other than God, if you expect anything else than God, whatever your work may be, it is neither yours nor God's. Your true work is the purpose you intend by your efforts. It is my Father who works in me and I am subordinate to him. There cannot be two Fathers in nature: always be sure that you have only one, so that when everything else is out of the way and time is "full," the birth [of God] may occur.

When one thing fills another, their boundaries are all mutual and in contact with each other and there is no space in between. It has breadth and length, depth and height. If it had height, and not breadth and length and depth, it could not fill anything. St. Paul says: "Pray that ye may be able to comprehend with all the saints, what is the breadth and length and depth and height [of Christ in you]."[6]

These three dimensions[16] represent three kinds of knowledge. The first is sensual: the eye sees things at a distance. The second is intellectual and is much higher in rank. The third represents [the function of] that aristocratic agent of the soul, which ranks so high that it communes with God, face to face, as he is.[7] This agent has nothing in common with anything else. It is unconscious of yesterday or the day before, and of tomorrow and the day after, for in eternity there is no yesterday nor any tomorrow, but only Now, as it was a thousand years ago and as it will be a thousand years hence, and is at this moment, and as it will be after death. This agent reaches God in his closet, or as the Scripture says: in him, above him and through him.[8] "In him"—that is, in the Father. "Above him"—that is, above the Son. "Through him"—that is, through the Holy Spirit.

St. Augustine has a saying that sounds different from this but really agrees: "There is no truth that does not include all truth."[9] This agent takes everything in truth [as it really is]. Nothing is covered or hidden from it. There is a Scripture which says: the heads of men shall be bare and those of women covered.[10] The women are the lower agents which are to be covered. The man is to represent the agent which goes uncovered.

"What wonders shall come of this child!" Recently, I spoke in opposition to certain people who, very likely, are here today, saying: "There is nothing covered that shall not be revealed."[11] Worthless things[12] shall be laid to one side and so covered up that they will not be thought of again. Unconscious of all that is worthless, we shall have nothing in common with it. Creatures, for example are really nothings.[13] When, then, "here and there" cease to be, and creatures are forgotten, being shall be fulfilled. At that time, I said that we should hide nothing but always be discovering [what we are] to God and always giving up to him. Whatever we may discover in ourselves, be it strength or weakness, love or sorrow, or any other inclination, we should get rid of it, for the truth is that if we discover all to him, he will discover his all to us and conceal nothing over which he holds control, neither wisdom, nor truth, nor holiness, nor Godhead, nor any other thing.[14] This is as much a fact as that God exists. We must discover everything to him. If we fail to do so, it will be no wonder if he does not reveal anything to us; for it must be an equal exchange, we to him and he to us.

It is a pity that some people should rate themselves so high, so one with God, and yet be so impatient, clinging to little things with much love and sorrow. They are very far from being what they think they are. They are full of notions and wants. Sometimes I say: if a person is looking for nothing, what right has he to complain if he finds nothing? He gets what he expects. Of course, he who means to get this or that thing will be getting nothing and that is why to pray for something is to get nothing. But to seek nothing and to set out only for God himself, is to discover God who gives the seeker all that is in his divine heart, so that it will be as much his as God's—and neither more nor less, if he sets his heart directly on God.[15]

What wonder is it if a sick man relishes neither food nor wines? He cannot taste either as they are, because his tongue is covered with a coating that cloaks the taste and his victuals taste bitter in proportion to his illness. The food cannot get to the tongue that would taste it and therefore the taste during sickness is always bitter. And the sick man is right, for the taste is bitter, on account of the coating that comes between the tongue and the food. Get rid of the coating and food will taste as it should. As long as there is such a coating between us and God, his flavor will never be to us as it should be and life will often be hard and bitter.

I once said that virgins[17] follow the lamb wherever it goes and stay close behind it. Many of them are virgins but many others who think they are, are not. Wherever the lamb goes, the maiden follows it—if it goes through sweet and pleasant places. But when it goes through [the valley of] suffering, sorrow, and trouble, they turn back and no longer follow it. These are really not virgins, whatever they may appear to be. Certain people say, I will go with you to comfort, honors, and riches. Dreamers! If the Lamb so lived, and so leads you, I wish you well in so following him! The true virgins follow the Lamb through the highways and byways, wherever it may go.

When time was full, then grace was born. That everything in us may be made perfect, that the divine grace may be born in us, may God help us all! Amen.

13

Truth is not merchandise[1]

INTRAVIT IESUS IN TEMPLUM DEI ET EJICIEBAT OMNES
VENDENTES ET EMENTES, ETC.

(Matthew 21:12)

WE READ in the holy Gospel that our Lord went into the temple and
drove out all those that bought and sold, and said to the venders of
doves: "Get these things out of here!" He gave them clearly to
understand that he wanted the temple pure, just as if he had said:
"I have a right to this temple and I alone will be in it, to have control of it."

What does that tell us? The temple in which God wants to be
master, strong to work his will, is the human soul, which he created
and fashioned exactly like himself. We read that the Lord said:[2]
"Let us make man in our own image." And he did it. He made the
human soul so much like himself that nothing else in heaven or on
earth resembles him so much. That is why God wants the temple to
be pure, so pure that nothing shall be in it except he himself. And
that is the reason he is well pleased with it when it is really prepared for him, and why he takes such comfort there—when he is
there alone.

Now let us see who the people were that bought and sold—and
who they still are, but understand me correctly, I shall now speak
only of the good people.[3] Nevertheless, at this time I shall indicate
who the merchants were that bought and sold, whom our Lord
struck and drove out of the temple. He is still doing just that to
those who buy and sell in it. He will not allow a single one of them
to be there. See! The merchants are those who guard against mortal
sins, who would like to be good people and do their good deeds to
the glory of God, such as fasting, watching, praying and the like—
all of which are good—and yet they do these things so that the

156

Lord will give them something they want in exchange, or do something they ardently want to have done.

They are all merchants. That is plain to see. They want to give one thing for another and to trade with our Lord but they will be cheated out of their bargain—for all they ever have or attain is *given* them by God and they do what they do only by means of God, and thus he is obligated to them for nothing. He will give them nothing and do nothing for them that he would not do or give of his own free will anyway. What they are they are because of God, and whatever they have they have from God and not by their own contriving. Therefore God is not in the least obligated to them for their deeds or their gifts. By reason of his grace, he will like to do for them, of his own free will—but certainly not for the sake of any act they perform or offering they bring. For [in these things] they are not giving what is their own and their acts do not come out of themselves. For God himself says: "Without me, ye can do nothing."[4]

They are very foolish people who want to trade with our Lord and they know little or nothing of the truth. Therefore, God strikes them and drives them out of the temple. Light and darkness cannot exist side by side. God is the truth and a light in himself. When he enters the temple, he drives out ignorance and darkness and reveals himself in light and truth. Then, when the truth is known, the merchants must begone—for truth wants no merchandising!

God does not seek his own. In all his acts, he is innocent and free and acts only out of true love. That is why the person who is united to God acts that way—he, too, will be innocent and free, whatever he does, and will act out of love and without asking why, solely for the glory of God, seeking his own advantage in nothing—for God is at work in him.

And what is more, as long as a man is looking for pay for what he does, or wants to get from God anything that God could or would give, he is like a merchant. If you want to be rid of the commercial spirit, do all you can in the way of good works, solely for the praise of God, and efface yourself as completely as if you did not exist. Whatever you do, you shall not ask anything in return for it and then your efforts will be both spiritual and divine. Then only are the merchants driven out of the temple and God is alone in it—when a person thinks only of God. See! This is how the temple is cleared of merchants: the man who thinks only of God, to revere him, is free and innocent of any mercantilism in his various acts, for he "seeketh not his own."

Furthermore, as I said, our Lord spoke to the people who trafficked in doves, saying: "Get these all out of here!" Take them away! But in scolding and driving them out, he was really not too severe. Rather, he spoke quite kindly: "Take it all out!"—meaning, perhaps, "this is not so bad in itself, but it does constitute a hindrance to the simple truth." They were all good people, working impersonally for God and not for themselves, but they were working under their own limitations of time and number, antecedent and consequence. In their varied efforts, they are kept from the highest truth, from innocence and freedom such as our Lord Jesus Christ had. He was incessantly refreshed in spirit by his heavenly Father apart from time, and reborn into the perfection of his Father with each eternal moment—each passing Now.[5] His praise to the father-like Highest was gratitude for like dignity.

Everybody who wants to be sensitive to the highest truth must be like this, conscious of neither "before" nor "after," unhindered by their past records, uninfluenced by any idea they ever understood, innocent and free to receive anew with each Now-moment a heavenly gift, and to consecrate them to God in the same light, with thankful praise to our Lord Jesus Christ. Thus the doves are cleared out, that is, the hindrances, the good deeds that smack of selfishness, which are good enough in their way to enable one to get what he wants for himself. But of these our Lord spoke gently, saying: "Take them all out—get rid of them!" He may have meant merely: "No harm done—but they are just some more obstacles."

When the temple is cleared of every hindrance, that is, of strangers and their properties, its appearance is beautiful and it shines so clear and pure above all, and in all God has created, that no one but the uncreated God can be reflected in it. To be sure, nothing is like this temple but the uncreated God himself. Nothing lower than the angels can be compared to it. In some ways, but not in all, the highest angels are comparable to this temple—the aristocratic soul.[6] That they are like the soul at all is due to knowledge and love, but a limit is set for them, beyond which they cannot go. Only the soul may surpass that limit; for let the soul be equated to the highest element in human nature existing within time: a person with his possibility of freedom may rise unspeakably higher than the highest angel, in every Now-moment—moments without number and without specified nature[7]—rising above the angels and all creature minds. Since God alone is free and uncreated, he is like the soul in being free—but not in uncreatedness, for the soul is created.

Comes then the soul into the unclouded[8] light of God. It is transported so far from creaturehood into nothingness[9] that, of its own powers, it can never return to its agents or its former creaturehood. Once there. God shelters the soul's nothingness with his uncreated essence, safeguarding its creaturely existence. The soul has dared to become nothing, and cannot pass from its own being into nothingness and then back again, losing its own identity in the process, except God safeguarded it. This must needs be so.

As I said before, Jesus went into the temple and drove out those that bought and sold and began to say to the others: "Take this all away!" See! I have it in these words: "Jesus went in and began to say: 'Take all this away!'—and they took it away." Observe, too, that then there was nobody left but Jesus, and being alone, he began to speak in the temple of the soul. Observe this also, for it is certain: if anyone else is speaking in the temple of the soul, Jesus keeps still, as if he were not at home. And he is not at home in the soul where there are strange guests—guests with whom the soul holds conversation. If Jesus is to speak in the soul and be heard, then the soul must be alone and quiet. So he got in, and began to talk. What does Jesus say then?

He says that he is![10] Then what is he? He is the Father's Word. In this Word, God expresses himself, together with all the divine Being, all that God is, as only he can know it. And he knows it as it is, because he is perfect in knowledge and power. Therefore, he is also perfect in self-expression. When he utters his Word, he expresses himself and everything else in a second Person, to whom he gives his own nature. He speaks, and all intelligent spirits, re-echoing the Word, repeat his idea, just as rays shining from the sun bear the sun in themselves. So each intelligent spirit is a Word in itself; even though it is not like God's Word in all respects, it has received the power to become a likeness of the Word of God, full of grace.[11] And thus the Father has completely expressed his Word, as it really is, with all that is in him.

Since, then, the Father has expressed himself, what does Jesus say in the soul? As I have said, the Father utters the Word and speaks in the Word and not otherwise. But Jesus speaks in the soul. What he says is a revelation of himself and all the Father has said to him, in proportion as one's soul is sensitive to it. He reveals the Father's majesty with unmeasured power. If, in his spirit, one discovers this power in the Son, he will have like power in whatever he does, power for all virtue and purity. Neither joy nor sorrow, no, nor anything God ever created in time, shall be able to disturb this person, for he remains, strengthened by divine power, opposed to which creature things are insignificant and futile.

Once again, Jesus reveals himself in the soul in unmeasured wisdom, which he is. He reveals himself in the wisdom which is God's self-knowledge or his knowledge of his own fatherly power. And that Word, of which we spoke, is also wisdom and welds all those things it touches into unique oneness. When wisdom is joined to the soul, all doubt, error, and darkness fly away and the soul is set in a pure clear light, which is God himself. That is what the prophet says:[12] "Lord, in thy light, we shall see light." Thus God is known through God in the soul, and the soul, through this wisdom, comes to know itself; and thence, too, the soul knows the paternal glory in its fruitful procreation, and the real is-ness in its simple unity, in which are no distinctions.[13]

Jesus also reveals himself in unmeasured sweetness and fullness, which flows from the powerhead of the Holy Spirit, overflowing its unsearchable riches and sweetness into hearts which are sensitive to it. And thus,[14] when Jesus does unite with the soul, the soul's tide moves back again into its own, out of itself, over itself, above all things, with grace and power back to its prime origin. Then the outward man is obedient to the inner man until death and he has constant peace in the service of God for all time.[15] That Jesus may also come into us and drive out all hindrances of body and soul, and that we may be one with him, here on earth as in heaven, may God help us all! Amen.

14

Nothing above the soul![1]

CONSIDERAVIT SEMITAS DOMUS SUAE ET PANEM OTIOSA NON COMEDIT.

Proverbs 31:27

THESE words are written in the Book of Wisdom and may be used of any saintly soul, but especially of St. Elizabeth. Solomon says, in the Proverbs: "She looketh well to the ways of her household and eateth not the bread of idleness."

This household stands for the soul and the ways of the house for the agents of the soul. An old authority[2] says that the soul is made between one and two. The "one" is eternity, that remains always aloof and changeless. The "two" is time, which changes and multiplies. He means to say that, with its highest agents, the soul touches eternity—that is, God—and with its lower agents, touches time and thereby becomes changeable, degraded, and inclined to material things.

If the soul had known God as perfectly as do the angels, it would never have entered the body. If the soul could have known God without the world, the world would never have been created. The world, therefore, was made for the soul's sake, so that the soul's eye might be practiced and strengthened to bear the divine light. The sunshine does not fall directly on the earth but is first damped by the air and diffused among things: otherwise the human eye could not endure it. So it is with the divine light, which is so overpowering and clear that the soul's eye could not bear it unless it were steadied by matter and supported by likenesses, so that it is led up to the divine light and accustomed to it.

The soul touches God by means of its highest agent and thus it comes to resemble him.[3] God takes after himself; he got his own image from himself and no one else. His "idea" is self-knowledge and nothing but light. When the soul contacts him with true

161

knowledge, its "idea" is like his. If a seal is pressed into red or green wax, or onto a cloth, an imprint is made. If the seal is pressed all the way through the wax, so that no extra wax is left over un-pressed into the seal, then the shape of the wax is identical with that of the seal. The soul is thus perfectly united with God in image and likeness when it is in contact with him in true knowledge. St. Augustine says that the soul is created so much higher in rank than any other creature that no mortal thing that is to perish at the latter day can communicate with the soul, or affect it, except through mediation or messengers. These are the eyes, the ears, and the five senses; these are the ways the soul gets out to the world and, reciprocally, the world gets back into the soul. One authority says that the soul's agents carry more cargo into the soul than they take back out, but that they always carry something. One should, therefore, carefully guard his eyes so that they shall not transmit any harmful matter. I am sure that what a good man sees improves him. If he sees an evil thing, he thanks God for protecting him from it, and prays God that he may convert that in which the evil is. If he sees anything good, he will desire that it be made perfect in him.

This seeing serves two purposes. It causes one to put away what-ever does harm and to correct his faults. I have said often that those who fast much, and watch much and do great things, but fail to correct their faults or improve their ways—which alone is true progress—deceive themselves and are the devil's laughingstock. A man once had a hedgehog[4] by which he got rich. He lived by the sea. When the hedgehog sensed a change of wind, he tapped his hide and turned his back to that direction. Then the man went to the sea and said to them [i.e., the people who lived there]: "What will you give me to show you how the wind is going to turn?" And he sold them [the means of foretelling changes of] wind and got rich on it. Thus too a person may grow rich in virtue by dis-covering the point at which he is weakest and correcting it, and by turning his chief care to overcoming his weakness.

This is what St. Elizabeth did with such care. She looked well to the ways of her household. She had, therefore, no fear for the winter because her dependents were well clad. She took precautions against whatever might hurt them. Whatever she lacked, she turned to with diligence, to make up for it. She did not eat the bread of idleness. She turned the highest agents of her soul to God.

The highest agents of the soul are three.[5] The first is intuition; the second, *irascibilis*,[6] which is the upsurging agent; and the third is the will. When the soul comes to know the real truth by that simple agent through which one knows God, then the soul is called a light. God, too, is light and when the divine light pours into the soul, the soul is united with God, as light blends with light. The soul is then called the light of faith, which is a divine virtue and thence, where the soul with its senses and agents may not go, faith carries it.

The second is that upsurging agent whose proper function it is to lift man upwards. As it is the property of the eye to see form and color, and of the ear to hear sweet sounds and voices, it is the property of the soul ever to struggle upwards by means of this agent, and if it looks aside, or relents from the way upwards, that is sin.[7] The soul cannot bear to have anything above it. I believe that it cannot bear to have even God above it. If he is not in the soul, and the soul is not as good as he, it can never be at ease. God is apprehended in the soul by his agent, in so far as it is possible to a creature, and in this connection, we speak of hope, which is also a divine virtue.

By this agent, the soul has such confidence in God that it imagines that in all God's being nothing is impossible to it. King Solomon says that stolen waters are better than others.[8] St. Augustine says: "The pears I stole were sweeter than those my mother gave me, because they were forbidden me and locked up."[9] So the grace that is won by special wisdom and effort is far sweeter to the soul than the grace which is the common property of all people.

The third agent is the interior will, which, like a countenance, is always turned toward God in divine willing, and thus creates the love of God within itself. God is drawn into the soul by means of it, and the soul into God, and so it is called divine love and is also a divine virtue. Divine blessing depends on three things: knowledge, steady independence of creatures, and perfect contentment as far as self and creatures are concerned. On this, too, the soul's perfection depends: on knowing and comprehending that it knows God and on the unison of perfect love.

Do we wish to know what sin is? Sin comes of departure from this blessedness and virtue. Every soul should look well to its ways and then it will not fear the winter, for its family will then have been clothed in twofold raiment, as the Scripture says of it.[10] It will be clothed with strength to withstand every imperfection, and adorned with the truth. As for the world, this woman had apparent riches and honor; inwardly she prayed in true humility. When her outward comforts departed, she fled to that to which all things flee, disdaining the world and herself. Therefore, she overcame herself and had contempt for the contempt of man, not being led astray by it. This was the perfection she desired: to tend the sick and to wash the dirty and to get along by the virtue of her own pure heart.

That we, too, may light up the ways of our households and not eat the bread of idleness, may God help us all! Amen.

15

Into the Godhead![1]

MODICUM ET IAM NON VIDEBITIS ME.

John 16:17–19

I HAVE quoted a Latin text from the Gospel of St. John assigned for reading on this Sunday. It is something our Lord said to his disciples: "A little,[2] and ye see me no more." However small it may be, if anything adheres to the soul, you cannot see me. St. Augustine was asked what eternal life might be and, replying, he said: "You ask me what eternal life is? You had better ask eternal life itself and hear it!" No one knows better what heat is like than something hot. No one knows better what wisdom is than one who has it. No one knows better what eternal life is than eternal life itself. Our Lord Jesus Christ says: "This is life eternal that they should know thee, the only true God!"

You should understand that if the soul beheld God even at a distance, as if through some medium, such as the clouds, for example, and saw him only for a moment, it would never turn back again to this world. How then do you think it would be if a man saw God himself, as he is, without any intervening medium, in his naked essence?[1] All the creatures God ever created, or could create if he chose to, would amount to very little when compared to God himself.

You would not believe me if I told you how great and wide the sky is. If the sky were pricked with the point of a needle,[3] the area of the prick would be less in comparison to the sky and the world put together, than the world is compared to God. Therefore, it is well said: "A little, and ye see me no more." As long as the least of creatures absorbs your attention, you will see nothing of God, however little that creature may be. Thus, in the Book of Love, the soul says: "I have run around looking for him my soul loves and found him not."[4] She found angels and many other things but not him her soul loved, but she goes on to say: "After that, I went a little further and found him my soul loved." It was as if she had said: 'It was when I stepped beyond creatures [which are the trifles] that I found my soul's lover." The soul must step beyond or jump past creatures if it is to know God.

Now, you must know that God loves the soul so strenuously that to take this privilege of loving from God would be to take his life and being. It would be to kill God, if one may use such an expression. For out of God's love for the soul, the Holy Spirit blooms and the Holy Spirit is that love. Since, then, the soul is so strenuously loved by God, it must be of great importance.

In the Book of the Soul, an authority says: "If it were not for the intervening medium, the eye might distinguish an ant or a gnat in the sky." He is correct; for he refers to fire and air and all there is between the eye and the sky. Another says: "If there were no intervening medium, the eye could not see."[5] Both are right.

If there were no intervening medium, says the first, the eye could distinguish even a gnat in the sky, and he had something there. If there were nothing between God and the soul, the soul would see God at once, for God uses no media nor will he suffer any intervention. If all the shells were removed from the soul and all God's shells could be taken off too, he could give himself directly to the soul without reserve. But as long as the soul's shells are intact— be they ever so slight—the soul cannot see God. If anything, even to the extent of a hairbreadth, came between the body and the soul, there could be no true union of the two. If that is the case with physical things, how much more true it is with spiritual! Thus Boethius says: "If you want to know the straight truth, put away joy and fear, confidence, hope and disappointment." Joy, fear, confidence, hope, and disappointment are all intervening media, all shells. As long as you stick to them and they to you, you shall not see God.

The second authority says: "If there were no intervening medium the eye could not see."[5] If I lay my hand over my eyes, I do not see the hands at all. If I hold them a little distance away, I see them at once. This is due to the density of the hands, which must be rarefied in the air and light and carried into the eye as an image seen in a mirror. If you stand before a mirror, your image appears in it. The eye and the soul are also mirrors and whatever stands in front of them appears within them. Thus I do not see either my hand or a stone but, rather, I see images of them, and not by secondary images. Images are seen directly, without the mediation of other images. The image itself is always an intermediary. It has no image of its own any more than motion has motion, although motion may well cause motion. Size has no size, even though it measures bulk. Thus an image has no image by means of which it is seen and the eternal Word is itself an intermediary, image-wise, which exists without a further medium to purvey it, so that the soul may comprehend God in the eternal Word without any mediation.

In the soul, there is an agent of the first rank, the intellect, by means of which the soul detects and knows God. It has five properties. First, it is detached from the here and now. Second, it is *sui generis*, like nothing else. Third, it is pure and uncontaminated. Fourth, it is automatic and self-criticizing. And fifth, it is an image [idea].

The first: it is detached from the here and now. "Here" and "now" are symbols of place and time. "Now" is the smallest element of time. It is not a bit of time nor a part of time. It is rather a taste of time, a relative of time, or an end of time. But no matter how small it is, it must vanish. All that touches time must vanish. Furthermore, the intellect is separated from "here." "Here" is a synonym for place. The place where I am is indeed small, but however small, it must vanish if one is to see God.

The second: it is *sui generis*, like nothing else. One authority says: "God is a being like no other and who cannot be made like another." But St. John says: "We should be called children of God."[6] If we are to be God's children, we must be like him. What, then, does this authority mean? He says that God is a being like no other. However, this is meaningful. In that an agent [of the soul], such as the intellect, is like nothing else, it is like God. Just as this agent of the soul is like nothing else, so God is like nothing else. Know that, by nature, every creature seeks to become like God. If there were no search for God, the heavens themselves would not be revolving. If

God were not in everything, nature would not function and entelechy[7] would cease. Whether you like it or not, whether you know it or not, secretly all nature seeks God and works toward him. No person was ever so thirsty that he would not refuse a drink from which God was missing! Nature's intent is neither food nor drink, nor clothing, nor comfort, nor anything else in which God is left out. Covertly, nature seeks, hunts, tries to ferret out the track on which God may be found.

The third: it is pure and uncontaminated. It is God's nature that he can tolerate neither contamination nor blending. Thus, this agent of the soul, the intellect, is no mixture or blend [of other things]. It is uncontaminated and nothing impure can lodge in it. To tell a person he is both fair and dark at once would be to do injustice. The soul is not to be confused. Sew a patch on a cloak and he who wears it will wear the patch. If I wear the cloak outdoors, the patch will go with me. Whatever the spirit dwells on, or is attached to, takes the spirit with it but the person who relies on nothing and is attached to nothing will never be moved, even though heaven should turn upside down.

The fourth: it is automatic and self-criticizing. God is such a being as dwells only in the [soul's] innermost part. Thus, the intellect, seeking him [is turned inward], but the will goes out to him it loves. If I meet a friend, my love goes out to him at once and I take pleasure. Now St. Paul says that we shall know God as we are known by him,[8] and St. John says that we shall know God as he is. If I am to see color, I must have that in me which is sensitive to color but I should never see color if I did not have the essence of color already. So I may never see God except it be in the same light he sees himself. Thus a saint says that God dwells in a light to which there is no access.[9] No one will deny that it is a good thing to be on the way but to be on the way is to be still far from the truth, for the way is not God himself.

The fifth: it is an image [idea]. Pay strict attention to this point, for it is the whole sermon in brief. One idea is so like another essentially that it is impossible to distinguish between them. Of course, one can think of fire apart from heat and heat apart from fire. Or one can think of the sun apart from light and light apart from the sun, but between ideas there is no real distinction, because they are all conceived in the same way and vanish together. Of course, I do not die because my father dies, but when I do die, no one can say of me again: he is his son, but rather they must say: he was his son. Paint a wall white and its whiteness is essentially the same as all whiteness, but paint it black and it is dead to all whiteness. See, then, how it is in the intellect. If the image [idea] which is fashioned like God could die away, the image [idea] that is God's could die away too.

I want to say one thing which may mean two or three different things to you. But understand me rightly! The intellect that peers into and penetrates all the corners of the Godhead sees the Son in the Father's heart and puts him [the Son] at its own core. Intellect that presses on that far is not content with goodness, nor with wisdom, nor the truth, no, nor even with god himself. To tell the truth, it is no more content with [the idea of] God than it would be with a stone or a tree.[10] It can never rest until it gets to the core of the matter, crashing through to that which is beyond the idea of God and truth, until it reaches the *in principio*, the beginning of beginnings, the origin or source of all goodness and truth. The intellect's sister, the will, is well satisfied with God as goodness, but the intellect disdains all that and pierces to the root of the matter, to the source of the Son, from whom the Holy Spirit blossoms. That we all may understand this and eternally be blessed by it, may the Father, the Son, and the Holy Spirit help us. Amen.

16

Being is more than life[1]

IN OCCISIONE GLADII MORTUI SUNT.

(Hebrews 11:37)

WE READ of the holy martyrs, whom we are to remember today,
that "they were slain with the sword." Our Lord said to his disciples: "Blessed are ye . . . when ye shall suffer . . . for my
name's sake."[2] According to the Scripture, the martyrs suffered
death for Christ's sake, being put to the sword.

We learn three things of them. The first is that they are dead.
Whatever one may suffer in this world, there is an end to it. St.
Augustine says: "All the pain and trouble of this world have an
end but God's reward for it is eternal." Moreover, we ought to keep
in mind that since this life is mortal, we need not fear all the pain
and trouble that could come, because it is going to have an end. In
the third place [we learn that] we should be so dead to the world
that nothing will affect us, whether we like it or not.

One authority says: "Nothing can affect heaven," and by this
he means the heavenly person who is moved by nothing that
happens. Another asks: "If creatures amount to so little, how does
it happen that they so easily turn a person from God—when the
soul at its worst is better than creatures and heaven to boot?" He
says that this comes of paying too little attention to God. If a man
paid as much attention to God as he should, it would be well-nigh
impossible for him to fall. This is good doctrine. In this world,
people should behave as though they were dead. As St. Gregory
says: "No one can have as much of God as he who is dead to this
world."

But the fourth lesson is best. It says that they are dead but that
death gives them Being. An authority says that nature never
destroys anything without putting something better in its place.

When air turns to fire, that is something better, but when air turns to water, there is destruction, something gone wrong. If, then, nature does so well, how much better may God do! He never destroys without giving something better in return. The martyrs are dead. They have lost their lives but they have received Being. There is an authority who teaches that "Being, life, and knowledge rank highest but knowledge is higher than life and Being, because whoever has knowledge necessarily has both the others." According to that, life would rank ahead of Being as, for example, a tree has life, while a stone has only Being. However, if we reach down into Being pure and simple, as it really is, we should find that Being ranks higher than life or knowledge.

I shall say that they have lost a natural life and received Being. One authority says that God is like nothing so much as Being; to the extent anything has Being it is like God. Another says that Being is so high and pure that God cannot be more than Being. God sees nothing else, knows nothing else, for Being is his arena.[1] He loves nothing else, thinks of nothing else than his Being. Now I should say that creatures as a whole have only one Being.[1] However, one authority says that "Certain creatures are so near to God and so instinct with divine light that they give Being to others." That is not true, because Being is so superior in rank and purity and so much God's own that no one can give it but he—as he gives himself. Being is the property of God.

One authority says that one creature might well give another life but that whatever really is exists in Being. Being is a name above all names. To be defective is to show a decline in Being. All our lives should reveal Being and therefore, to the extent that life is Being, it is of God. As far as it is included in Being, it is related to God. Let a man's life be ever so mean, if he takes it as Being, it will rank higher than anything else life might be.[3] I am very sure that, if a soul knew the least of what Being is, its attention would never be diverted from it even for an instant. The least one knows of God as, for example, to see a flower get its Being from him, is more perfect knowledge than any other. To know the least of creatures as one of God's Beings, is better than knowing an angel.

When an angel turns its attention to creatures, night falls. St.

Augustine says that when angels attend to creatures apart from God, then it is twilight. So it is with the soul. If the soul knows God in creatures, night falls. If it sees how they have their being in God, morning breaks. But if it sees the Being that is in God himself alone, it is high noon! See! This is what one ought to desire with mad fervor—that all his life should become Being.

There is nothing so mean that to some degree it does not long for Being. Even caterpillars, when they fall off a tree, go at once to climb a wall, to regain their Being. Thus we say that it is good to die in God so that he may give us instead that Being which is better than life, a being in which our life subsists even now. One ought to be glad to give up to dying and death, so that better Being may be his portion.

I once said that wood is better than gold,[3] which is a fantastic thing to say, and yet a stone, to the extent it has Being, would be better than even God and the Godhead without Being. (Supposing that God could be abstracted from Being.) That must be a strong life in which lifeless things are made to live, in which even death is changed to life. There is no death in God, for in him everything is made alive. "They are dead," says the Scripture of the martyrs, "and are transformed to life eternal," that is, to a life in which life is Being.

We are to be so dead that neither good nor evil affect us. What we know must be known to its roots, for we shall never know anything until we know its causes. There can be no knowledge until knowing reaches the hidden reasons. Thus, too, life cannot be perfected until it has returned to its secret source, where life is Being, a life the soul receives when it dies even down to its roots, so that we may live that life yonder which itself is Being. One scholar points out what it is that hinders us from that: We are hindered by cleaving to time. Whatever cleaves to time is mortal.

An authority says: "The course of heaven is eternal, and yet it may well be that time comes from heaven by reason of a defection."[4] Heaven itself is eternal in its course and knows nothing about time. That means that the soul, too, consists of pure Being—but then, too, there are opposites in the soul. What are opposites? Good and evil, white and black are such opposites, which, however, are not part of Being.

One authority says that the soul is put in the body to be purified. If it is separated from the body, it has neither intelligence nor will. It is then One and cannot send forth agents through which it might turn to God. Nevertheless, the agents are present [in germ] in the soul's core, which is to say, in its roots rather than its activities.[5] The soul is purified in the body through its function in gathering together [all the body's] disparate elements. When [the forces] expressed through the five senses are gathered again into the soul, then the soul is one agent by means of which everything is unified.

In the second place, the soul is purified in the practice of virtues by which we climb to a life of unity. That is the way the soul is made pure—by being purged of much divided life and by entering upon a life that is [focused to] unity. The whole scattered world of lower things is gathered up to oneness when the soul climbs up to that life in which there are no opposites. Entering the life of reason, opposites are forgotten, but where this light does not fall, things fall away to death and destruction.

In the third place, the purity of the soul consists in never turning aside to anything [at which it does not ultimately aim]. To turn aside is to die and finally not to be.[6]

Let us pray our dear Lord God that he help us to mount from a life divided to a life unified. Amen.

No respecter of persons[1]

MOYSES ORABAT DOMINUM, DEUM SUUM.

(Exodus 32:11)

I have quoted a text in Latin from the lection for today and in English, it means: "Moses besought the Lord his God and said, 'Lord, why doth thy wrath wax hot against this people?' Then God answered him and said: 'Moses, let me be angry—grant me this much—permit me thus to do and do not begrudge it—allow me to be angry so that I may be avenged of the people.'[2] And God praised Moses and said: 'I will promote you and make you great and multiply your race and make you the Lord of a great people.' But Moses said: 'Blot me out of the Book of Life or spare the people.' "[3]

What is meant by the words, "Moses besought the Lord his God?" To tell the truth, if God is to be your Lord, you must really be his servant, but if you work only for your own ends, to secure your own bliss, then you are not his servant. For in that case you do not seek the glory of God but your own profits. Why does it say, "the Lord his God"? If God wills that you be sick and you wish to be well, or if God wills that your friend die but, contrary to the will of God, you wish that he live, then certainly God is not your God. If you love God, then when you are sick, it is in God's name. When your friend dies, it is in God's name. If he loses an eye, let it be in God's name. And the person who does so will be on the right track. If, however, you are sick and pray God for health, then your health is dearer to you than God, and he is not your God. He may be the God of heaven and earth, but he is not yours.

Now notice that God says: "Moses, let me be angry!" You might ask: "How can God be angry?" For the sole reason that our own eternal well-being has been hurt; he never seeks his own satisfaction,

174

and so God suffers when we act contrary to our own well-being. God could have sustained no greater wound than the martyrdom and death of our Lord Jesus Christ, his only begotten Son, who suffered for the sake of our eternal well-being.

But notice again that God says: "Moses, let me be angry!"—and observe what a good man may accomplish with God. This is a sure and necessary truth, that he who gives up to God his own will, captures God and binds him, so that God can do nothing but what that person wills! Give your will over completely to God and he will give you his in return, so fully and without reserve, that the will of God shall be your own human will. In such a case—he has sworn by himself—he cannot do otherwise than what you want done; but he cannot belong to anyone who has not first become his.[4]

St. Augustine says: "Thou canst not belong to anyone who does not first belong to thee!" We cry to God by night and day: "Lord, thy will be done!" Then, when God's will *is* done, we are often angry because it is—and that is wrong. When our wills become God's, that is good—but when his becomes ours, that is better! If your will becomes God's, and you get sick, you will not want to get well contrary to the will of God, but you may wish that it were the will of God for you to recover. So, too, when any evil overtakes you, you may wish that it might be the will of God that all were well.

When, however, God's will becomes yours, then, if you get sick, it will be "in God's name"! If your friend dies—"in God's name"! It is a certain and necessary truth that, notwithstanding all the pain of hell, purgatory, and the world, we should prefer them to our own comfort, if our wills were joined to God's, and we would let go even of the perfection of our Lady and all the saints, and gladly endure eternal pain and bitterness—never caring to run away from it even for a moment[5]—or entertaining a single thought to the contrary—for then we should be united to God with such unity that the Father in heaven would beget his own eternal Son in us as he does in himself.

Why in us as he does in himself? Because then we are one with him and cannot be excluded. In the unification, the Holy Spirit receives its being, its work, and its destiny—from me as from God! Why? Because I am [then] in God. If the Holy Spirit does not receive [its being] from me, then it will not from God. There is no way God may exclude me.

So completely had Moses' will become God's will that God's prestige among the people meant more to him than his own well-being. God made him a promise and he, Moses, paid no attention to it. Indeed, if God had promised Moses all his Godhead, still Moses would not have consented. So Moses besought God and said: "Lord, blot me out of the Book of Life!" Some authorities ask: "Did Moses love the people more than he loved himself?" They answer: "No!"—for in seeking God's honor among the people, he well knew that he was nearer to God than if he had let God's reputation go and looked after his own well-being. It is this way with a good man. Whatever he does, he must always avoid serving his own interests, or preferring one person's interest to another's, and must serve the honor of God alone. As long as you act in your own behalf, or in behalf of one person rather than another, the will of God has becomes yours only imperfectly.

Our Lord says in the Gospel: "My doctrine is not mine but his that sent me."[6] This, too, shall be the position of the good man: my work is not mine, nor is my life mine. If this is the case, then all the perfection and eternal well-being of Sts. Peter and Paul, which they attributed to their Head, and all the blessings that were apportioned to them for their devotion, I may taste as well as they, and enjoy them as they did—if I do as they did.[7]

I say that humanity and persons are not the same thing. Essentially, humanity ranks so high that, at its best, it is like angelic Being and is related to the Godhead. The ultimate union that Christ had with the Father is something to which I am eligible—if I can put off the "this and that" and be human. Whatever, therefore, God gave to his only begotten Son, he will give to me in equal measure and not less.[1] Indeed, he has given me more. He gave my humanity more completely to Jesus than he did to the Son. We should say, rather, that he never gave it to the Son at all, for the Son had it from his Father through all eternity. If I should strike you, I should be striking a Bernard or a Henry, that is to say, a person—but that is not God's way. He aims first at humanity; and who of this humanity is most human? He who takes his nature from the humanity of Jesus Christ, as our Lord indicates when he says in the Gospels: "He who touches one of these touches my soul."[8]

Now, however, I say: "Moses besought the Lord." Many people pray to God that he will do all he can for them, but they never give their all to him. They are willing to share with God—giving him the least share—and only a little at that—whereas God, giving, gives first himself.[9] When you have God, you have the whole world with him. Thus, I once said that to have God, and with him the whole world, is to have no more than if you had only God. What is more, in eternity, a thousand angels mean no more than one or two, because in eternity there is no number. Eternity is above number.

Moses besought the Lord his God. "Moses" means "one who was taken up out of the water."[10] Thus, now, I shall say something more about the will. If one were to give away a hundred pounds of gold for God, that would be a great thing and would seem important. I assert, nevertheless, that if I have the will, and a hundred marks to give, and my will to give it is perfect, then I have really given it to God as much as if I had actually handed over the money to him and he must render me an accounting. Indeed, if the Pope were struck by my hand, without my will, I could go to the altar and say the Mass none the less truly.

I say that humanity is just as perfect in the poorest, most despised person as it is in the Pope or the emperor, for humanity is really dearer to me than even the person I am myself.

That we may be so united with God, may the truth, of which I have spoken, help us. Amen.

18

Justice is even[1]

JUSTI AUTEM IN PERPETUUM VIVENT ET
APUD DOMINUM EST MERCES EORUM.

(Wisdom of Solomon 5:15)

"The just[1] shall live forever and their reward is with God." Let us look with care at this dictum. Even though it sounds trite and commonplace, it is nevertheless noteworthy and very good.

"The just shall live!" Who are the just? A Scripture says:[2] "He is just who gives to each what belongs to him." Thus, they are just who give to God what is his, to the angels what is theirs, and to their fellow men what is theirs.

Honor belongs to God. Who are they that do honor to him? Those who become selfless, caring nothing for their own rights in anything, whatever it may be, great or small, who expect nothing beneath themselves or yet above or beside themselves, who think not at all about goods, or comfort, or pleasure, or profit, or spirituality, or saintliness, or reward, or heaven. The just have finished with all these and everything else that belongs to themselves. It is such people who honor God and give him what is his own.[3]

To the saints and angels, give joy. O Wonder of Wonders! Can one who is still in this life give joy to those in eternity? Certainly, he can. No mouth can tell nor can any mind conceive how great is the joy and pleasure of every single saint in each good work done with good will or in each high desire. How is that? They love God so without measure, they hold him so dear, that they prefer his honor to their own blessedness.

And not only the saints and angels: even God himself takes pleasure in these things, just as if, blessing him, they were vital to him and his own pleasure and satisfaction depended on them. Ah!—but now look! If we are to serve God for no other reason

178

than the joy it gives to those who are in eternity, still we might well do it by preference and with all diligence. So, too, we should give help to those in hell-fire and betterment to the living.

The person who does these things is just to some degree[4] and to another degree,[4] they are just who take everything from God evenly, just as it comes, great and small, desirable and undesirable, one thing like another, all the same, and none more or less. If one thing means more than another to you, you are unjust. You must always put your own will aside.

There is something that has been much on my mind in recent days: If God does not want what I want, then I must want what he wants. Many people want their own way in everything, and that is bad. That way evil comes. There are others—a little better—who approve of God's will and who would do nothing contrary to his will but who, when they are sick, wish it were God's will for them to be healthy. These people would have God's will conform to their own rather than theirs to his. This is to be condoned but it is still wrong. The just have no will at all: whatever God wants, it is all one to them, however great the discomfort of it may be.

The just man is so in earnest for justice that, if God himself were not just, he would not care in the least for God.[5] Indeed, the just are so firmly devoted to justice and so wholly selfless that, whatever they do, they regard neither the pains of hell nor the joys of heaven. Indeed, not all the pains of hell, whether human or fiendish, nor all the pains ever suffered on earth, or to be suffered, were they heaped upon the just, would influence them one bit, so firmly established are they in God and justice. To the just person, nothing is so hard to bear or so painful as anything opposed to justice, that is to say, as not feeling impartially the same about everything that happens.

How so? If one thing makes them happy and another depressed, they are not just. What is more, if at one time they rejoice more and another time less, that, too, is wrong. He who loves justice is so firmly attached to it that, loving it, it is his being. Nothing can draw him away from it and he is concerned with nothing else. St. Augustine says: "The soul is more real in what it loves than it is in what it gives life to." Our text sounds ordinary and commonplace, but very few people understand what it really means and how deep a truth it is. Those who understand clearly about justice and the just will understand all I say.

"The just shall live." There is nothing in all the world so dear or desirable as life. Thus, no life is so bad or difficult that a person would not elect to remain alive. A Scripture says: "The nearer death comes, the more painful it is"—and yet, however bad life is, still there is the desire to live. Why do you eat? Why sleep? So that you may live. Why do you desire goods or honors? You know very well why. But why live? For the sake of living—and yet you do not know why you live. Life is so desirable in itself that one wants it for its own sake. Even those who are in the eternal pains of hell, still do not want to part with their lives, whether souls or fiends, because life is so precious, flowing immediately out of God into the soul. That is why they want to live.

What is life? God's being is my life, but if it is so, then what is God's must be mine and what is mine God's. God's is-ness is my is-ness,[6] and neither more nor less. The just live eternally with God, on a par with God, neither deeper nor higher. All their work is done by God and God's by them. Thus St. John says: "The Word was with God"—it is completely like him and immediately with him—neither deeper nor higher, but only like him.

When God made people, he made woman from the man's side, so that she might be equal to him. He did not make her from the head or the foot, to be neither man nor woman, but to be like him. Thus the just soul is to be like God, by the side of God, exactly his equal and neither above nor beneath.

Who, then, are they that are like God? It is they who are like nothing else, save God alone. There is nothing like the divine Being, for in him there is neither idea nor form. Therefore, those souls that are like God are the ones to whom God has given himself evenly, withholding nothing. All the Father can give, he gives to them evenly, when they hold to the evenness of justice and do not consider themselves as being more than others and are no more dear to themselves than others are. They shall not consider their own honor or profit, or whatever, more urgent than a stranger's. Personal rights, whether bad or good, they hold to be harmful, foreign, and alien. All the love of this world is based on self-love.[7] If you have given that up, you have given up the whole world.

In eternity, the Father begets the Son in his own likeness. "The Word was with God and the Word was God." Like God, it had his nature. Furthermore, I say that God has begotten him in my soul. Not only is the soul like him and he like it, but he is in it, for the Father begets his Son in the soul exactly as he does in eternity and not otherwise. He must do so whether he will or not.[8] The Father ceaselessly begets his Son and, what is more, he begets me as his Son—the self-same Son! Indeed, I assert that he begets me not only as his Son but as himself and himself as myself, begetting me in his own nature, his own being. At that inmost Source, I spring from the Holy Spirit and there is one life, one being, one action. All God's works are one and therefore He begets me as he does his Son and without distinction.[9] My physical father is not my real Father, except for some small bit of his nature. For I am cut off from him. He may be dead and yet I alive. Therefore the heavenly Father is my true Father and I am his Son and have all that I have from him. I am identically his Son and no other, because the Father does only one kind of thing, making no distinctions. Thus it is that I am his only begotten Son.

St. Paul says:[10] "We are always being transformed into God and changed." Consider the simile: The bread of the sacrament is changed into the body of our Lord and, however much it may still seem like bread, it is nevertheless the body of Christ. Similarly, if all the bread were to be changed into my finger, it would still be no more than one finger. Suppose, however, that my finger were changed back into bread, there would still be the same amount of bread as ever, for whatever is changed into something else becomes identical with it. If, therefore, I am changed into God and he makes me one with himself, then, by the living God, there is no distinction between us.[11] The Father ceaselessly begets his Son. Once the Son is born, he takes nothing more from the Father, for he has it all. Only while he is being born does he take anything from the Father.

The point is that we ought not ask anything from God as we would of a stranger. Our Lord said to his disciples: "I have not called you servants, but friends." Whoever asks something of another is his servant and he who grants is Master. Recently I have been wondering if I could receive or desire anything from God.[14] I must earnestly consider this matter, for if I should take anything from God then I should be his servant and he would be like a master in the act of giving. In life eternal, however, it shall not be so.

I once said, in this place (and it is true): When a man goes beyond himself to fetch or get anything, he is doing wrong. I shall not find God nor even imagine him apart from myself, but as my own and belonging to me. Neither shall I do anything or serve in any way, neither for God, nor to glorify him, nor for any cause extraneous to himself, but only for that which is his own being and the life that is in him.

Some simple people imagine that they are going to see God as if he were standing yonder and they here, but it is not to be so. God and I: we are one.[12] By knowing God I take him to myself. By loving God I penetrate him. Some people say that blessedness lies in willing rather than knowing, but they are wrong. If it were merely a matter of willing, there would never be this unity.

Action and becoming are one. If the carpenter does no work, the house is not built. When his broadax stops, the structure stops. God and I are one in process. He acts and I become, just as fire changes anything that is thrown into the fire, so that it takes the nature of fire. Wood does not change fire into wood but the fire does change wood.[13]

Thus, if we are to be changed into God, we must know him as he is,[15] says St. Paul. This, then, is to be our knowledge, that I know him as He knows me, neither more nor less, but always the same, as our text has it: "The just shall live forever and their reward is with God."

That we shall love justice for its own sake and love God without any reason for loving, may God help us all! Amen.

19

God must give himself[1]

OMNE DATUM OPTIMUM ET OMNE DONUM PERFECTUM DESURSUM
EST, DESCENDENS A PATRE LUMINUM.

(James 1:17)

St. James says in the Epistle: "Every good gift and every perfect gift is from above and cometh down from the Father of lights."

Now see! You should know that to those persons[2] who put themselves completely in God's hands, and seek with all diligence to do his will, all that God gives is best of all. Be sure, as God lives, that it is necessarily the best and that nothing could be better. Even if something there is that seems better to you, it should not; for, since God wills it this way and not otherwise, it must necessarily be best for you. Let it be sickness, or poverty, or hunger, or thirst, or whatever God ordains or denies, gives or withholds: it is best for you. Whether it be devotion or fervor, both of which you lack, sadly enough, or anything else you have or have not, let it be your way to seek the honor of God in everything, and then whatever he does to you will be best.

Now likely, you will ask: "How shall I know whether it is the will of God or not?" As for that, know that if it were not God's will it could not be. You will have neither sickness nor anything else except God will it, and when, therefore, you know that it is God's will, it will be your good pleasure and satisfaction to suffer no more pain as pain. Indeed, if you come to the extremity of pain and suffered it in any sense as misery or distress, that would mean that you were in the wrong frame of mind. You should take it from God as best, for it is necessarily best for you. God's Being depends on its being best. Therefore I should will it and then nothing could give me more comfort.

If there were a person whom I urgently wished to please, and if h knew for sure that I should please him more in gray clothing than in any others, however good they might be, then, no doubt, gray clothing would also please me more and be dearer to me than any other. Given, then, that I wished to please someone, knowing what he preferred, were it words or deeds, I should do [his pleasure] and nothing else. Ah! Judge for yourself what your love is like! If you love God, nothing would give you more pleasure than to please him, so that his will might be consummated perfectly. However hard the pain may seem, or the misery of it, if you do not delight in it you are wrong.

It is my custom to say—and it is a fact—that every day we shout and plead in the Lord's Prayer: "Thy will be done!"—and when his will is done, we grumble and are not pleased with it. Whatever he does, we should be glad, and those who are will always live in peace. Sometimes you think or say "Ah—but it would have been so much better otherwise," or "if that hadn't happened, this would have turned out so much better." As long as you see it that way there is no peace for you. You must take everything for the best. This is the first meaning of our text.

But there is another—and mark it well! He says "Every gift." Best and highest [in value] are the personal gifts—the most intimate gifts. God gives nothing so gladly as the greatest gifts. I once said here that God much prefers forgiving great sins to little sins. The bigger they are, the gladder he is to forgive them and the quicker. It is so with the graces, gifts, and virtues. The greater they are, the more he likes to give them, for it is his nature to give great things. The better anything is, the more he bestows it.[3]

I said once that, properly expressed, a matter must come out of a person, bringing its form with it.[4] It cannot get into one from without. No. It must issue from the inner man. Its true life is in the soul's inmost recess. It is all alive, active, and present within you in the best and highest sense of the word. Why are you not aware of it? Because you are not at home there. The more precious anything is, the more general it is. Senses I have in common with the animals, life in common with the trees, but Being, still more innate, I have in common with every creature. The sky is vaster than everything beneath it and therefore it is of more value. The higher anything is

in the scale of values, the more there is of it and the commoner it is.
Love is as high as it is universal.

It does seem hard that our Lord should command that we love our
fellow Christians as ourselves. Rude people usually think we ought
to love them by doing them the good their own self-love suggests.
But, no—that cannot be. One ought to love others as much as he
loves himself[5] and that is not difficult. Come to think of it, such
love is more of a reward than a command. The commandment seems
hard but the reward is something to be desired. He who loves God
as he ought to love (and must love whether he will or not), he who
loves God as all creatures love him, must "love his neighbor as
himself," rejoicing in all *his* joys as if they were his own. He must
love a stranger as he does his own relatives. In this frame of mind,
one will always find joy, honor, and profit, as much so as if he were
in the Kingdom of Heaven itself; for his joy is more frequent than
if he rejoiced only in his own good fortunes. Know ye that if your
own honor is more precious to you than someone else's, you are
wrong.

Know, too, that when you seek your own, you never find God,
for you are not seeking him with purity of heart. You are seeking
something along with God and you act as if you were using God,
as if he were a candle with which one might look for something
else and, having found it, one might throw the candle away. Take
it for granted that what you look for *with* God has no essential value,
whatever it may be, whether profit, or reward, or spirituality, or
whatever. [Using God] you are looking for nothing and that is why
you find nothing [by that means]. Creatures [by themselves] are
pure nothings.[6] I do not say that they are either important or unimportant but that they are pure nothings. What has no Being [of and
by itself] is nothing. Creatures have no Being of their own, for their
Being is the presence of God. If God withdrew from them even for a
moment, they would all perish. From time to time I have said—
and it is true—that to get all the world together with God is to get
nothing more than God alone. All creation without God could have
no more Being than a fly would have without him—just as much—
no more or less.[7]

Ah—but now, get this truth! To give a thousand marks of gold to build a church or cloister would be a great thing, but to give a thousand marks for nothing at all would be a far greater gift!

When God made creatures, they were so small and tight that he could not operate in any of them. Then he made the soul, so like himself, so convenient to himself, that he could give himself to it. Whatever he gives otherwise is nothing to the soul. God must give himself to me to be my own, just as he is his own, or I shall get nothing from him worth while or to my [soul's] taste. Always to receive him like this, one must always deny himself and be detached from self. So disposed, one will always get all God has straight from him and it will be his own as much as it was God's own, just as our Lady does, and all who are in the Kingdom of Heaven. To be so detached [objective] and to have denied self is to receive this much [from God] and no less.

The third phrase is "from the Father of lights." The word "Father" implies a Son and the phrase "Father of lights" implies an immaculate birth and a universal principle. The Father begets the Son in the eternal mind and also begets the Son in the soul as if in his own nature. He begets the Son in the soul, to be its own and his Being depends on his doing so, for better or for worse.

Once I was asked what the Father is doing in heaven. I replied that he begets his Son and that this activity is so pleasant to him and suits him so well that he never does anything else and that from the two there blossoms forth the Holy Spirit. When the Father begets his Son in me, I am that Son and no other.[8] "If we are sons, then we are true heirs." He who knows the truth knows very well that the word "Father" implies the immaculate birth and the having of sons. Thus we all are in the Son and are the Son.

Notice the phrase "cometh down from above." I said to you before that to receive gifts from above one must be beneath—that is, have true humility. This is the truth to know: not to be humble always is to receive nothing at all, however little it may be. If your eye is on yourself or anything or anybody, you are not humble and you receive nothing, but if your humility is constant, then constantly you receive, and in all fullness. It is God's nature to give and his existence depends on his giving when we are subject to him. If we are not and thus receive nothing from him, we do him violence and even kill him,[9] or if not him, we do violence to ourselves and as much as is possible to us. If you would really give your all to God, see that you are humbly subject to him and exalt him in your mind and heart. "God hath sent our Lord into the world."

I said once on this point that, in the fullness of time, God sent his Son into the soul—that is, when the soul had finished with time. When the soul is freed from time and place, the Father sends his Son into it, and this is what the words mean: "Every good and perfect gift is from above and cometh down from the Father of lights." That we may be prepared to receive the best gifts, may the Father of lights help us. Amen.

20

Purity of heart requires denial of self[1]

EGO ELEGI VOS DE MUNDO.

(John 15:19)

THE TEXT which I have quoted in Latin is read from the Gospel for today, the feast of a saint named Barnabas, to whom the Scriptures usually refer as an apostle. Our Lord says: "I have called you, I have chosen you out of the world, I have selected you out of all the world and from all created things, that you might bring forth much fruit and that your fruit might remain." It is a fine thing to be fruitful and to have your fruit permanent and your fruit will be permanent if you continue to be loving. At the end of the Gospel, our Lord says: "Love one another as I have loved you from eternity. As my Father eternally loves me, so have I loved you. Keep my commandments by continuing in my love."[2]

All God's commandments come from his love and from the goodness of his nature. If they did not spring from love, they could not be his. He who lives lovingly lives by what is good in his nature and within the love of God—a love that asks no questions. If I have a friend and love him so that he may benefit me and do what I wish, then I do not love my friend at all but rather myself. I am to love my friend for his own sake, for the goodness and virtue of him, for all that he himself is and then I shall truly love him, in the only real sense of the word. This is how it is with the person who lives in God's love, who does not seek his own welfare, either in God or himself or any other, who loves God only for his goodness, for the sake of the goodness of his nature and all that He himself is. That is true love.

The love of virtue is a flower, the ornament of all virtue, indeed, the mother of virtues and all perfection and blessing. It is God—for God is the fruit of virtue, the fruit which remains in man. When a person tries to produce fruit and at last it is his, he is very glad. Suppose a man had a vineyard or a field and let his servant work it and keep the fruit and profit of his efforts, naturally the servant would be very glad, for he would have the profits without the risks. Thus the man who lives by the fruits of virtue ought to be very glad. He has neither vexations nor worries, because he has given up selfishness and all that goes with it.

Our Lord says: "To him who shall forsake anything for me or my name, I will restore an hundredfold and he shall have life eternal"[3]—but if you forsake it with an eye on the hundredfold and to get eternal life, you have forsaken nothing. If you left it for a thousandfold reward, you would be forsaking nothing. You must deny yourself altogether and that alone is what it means "to forsake things." Not long since, a man came to me and told me that he had given up great quantities of this world's goods in order to save his soul. Then I thought: "Oh dear! How little you have given up!" [So to give up something] is all blindness and folly as long as you imagine you have really given up something worth while. If you deny yourself, that will be true self-denial.

The person who really has denied himself is so pure that this world could not tolerate him, as I said not long ago. To love righteousness is to submit to it and be possessed by it and one with it. Once I wrote in my book that the just person serves neither God nor creatures, for he is free and the nearer he is to righteousness the nearer he is to freedom, until at last he is freedom itself. Created things are not free. As long as anything other than God rules over me, it limits me, however small it may be or whatever its kind. Even if it were intelligence or love, in so far as it is created and not God himself, it would limit me, for these things are not freedom. The unjust man who serves illusions, the world, and creatures is a slave of sin, whether he likes it or not.

I have been thinking for some time that the fact that *I am a person* is something others hold in common with myself. That I see and hear and eat and drink—this I have in common with other animals, but the fact that *I am* pertains only to me and not to other men or angels, nor even to God, except as I am one with him. All of God's efforts are directed to reproducing himself. He gives [himself] to everything alike and yet they all behave differently, each seeking to reproduce itself. By virtue of God nature does what nature should do. It is thus the point of nature that I should be a father as God is a Father. All things together strive to replace themselves with their own replicas and that, too, is the common human intention. When nature, however, was diverted or hindered in its purpose, so that it could not achieve its desired goal, then there came to be women,[4] and nature ceased its efforts and God began his work of creation, for if there had been no women there could have been no men. That a child, conceived in a mother's womb, has the form, the color, and the nature [of the parents] is nature's work, which is done in the first forty days and nights. On the fortieth day, God creates the soul in less than the twinkling of an eye and all that nature can do comes to an end with the making of form, color and being. Thus the work of nature ceases, but as it does so it reappears again in the work of the intelligent soul. Man is a work of nature and a creature of God but in things created (as I have often said) there is no truth.

There is something, however, above the created being of the soul,[5] that does not touch creation, in which nothing is. Even an angel who has pure being hasn't it, because things which are pure and yet extended [in space?] cannot touch it. It is a species of the divine order, unique in itself and having nothing in common with anything else. Many priests fumble it, for it is unique, better left unnamed than given a name, more unknown than known. If one could annihilate himself even for a moment—I say less than a moment— it would all be his, together with all it is in itself, but as long as to any degree your mind is on yourself or anything else you will know as little of God as my mouth knows about color, or my eye about taste. Thus little do you know what God is.

Now Plato, that great priest who occupied himself so much with such lofty matters and spoke of them so much, refers to this. He speaks of a purity that is not of this world, which is neither in the world nor out of it, neither in time nor in eternity, which has neither outside nor inside.[6] Out of this purity, God the Father eternal derives the fullness and the emptiness of his Godhead and gives birth to his only begotten Son, so that we are at once his Son. His birth is his indwelling and his indwelling is his epiphany. It [the pure abyss of God] remains forever unique, uniform, and self-generating.

Ego, the word "I," is proper to no one but God alone in his uniqueness. *Vos* means "you" to the extent that all of you have achieved unity in [God's] uniqueness. Thus, Ego and Vos, I and you-people, together stand for the unity of which I have spoken.

That we may be unique and that our uniqueness may remain, may God help us all! Amen.

21

The will is free[1]

CONVESCENS PRAECEPIT EIS, AB IEROSOLYMIS NE DISCEDERENT, etc.

(Acts 1:4)

THE passage I have quoted in Latin is read from the Mass celebrated today. It was written by St. Luke that our Lord, when he wished to return to heaven, was with his disciples and commanded that they should not depart from Jerusalem, but wait for the promise of the Father, which they had heard from his mouth, for in a few days they were to be baptized by the Holy Spirit.

Now he speaks of the promise or vow of the Father. This vow is also made to us, that we, too, should be baptized by the Holy Spirit and thus experience what it is to live beyond time in eternity. We do not get the Holy Spirit in temporal things. When a person turns from temporal things inwards, into himself, he becomes aware of a heavenly light that does come from heaven. It is beneath heaven and yet comes from heaven. There are people who take satisfaction from this light because, they say, it is physical, it is material. Now iron, whose property it is to fall, is raised up, contrary to this property, and hangs to the lodestone by virtue of a superior power the lodestone is given by heaven. However the stone turns, the iron turns with it. It is so with the human spirit which can never be satisfied with what light it has but storms the firmament and scales the heavens to discover the spirit by which the heavens are driven in revolutions and by which everything on the earth grows and flourishes.[2]

Even then, the human spirit takes no rest. It presses on further into the vortex, the source in which the spirit originates. There, the spirit, in knowing, has no use for number, for numbers are of use only within time, in this defective world.[3] No one can strike his roots into eternity without being rid [of the concept] of number. The

192

human spirit must go beyond all number-ideas, must break past and away from ideas of quantity and then he will be broken into by God. As God penetrates me I penetrate God in return. God leads the human spirit into the desert, into his own unity, in which he is pure One and self-creating. It has no reason for being,[4] for if there could be a reason, then there would be a reason underlying the Unity [God]. Here the spirit achieves unity and freedom.

Now the authorities say that the will also is free and that only God can constrain it.[11] God, however, does not constrain the will. Rather, he sets it free, so that it may *choose* him, that is to say, freedom. The spirit of man may not will otherwise than what God wills, but that is no lack of freedom. It is true freedom itself.

There are people who say: "If I have God and God's love, I may do whatever I want to do." They are wrong. As long as you are capable of acting contrary to the will of God, the love of God is not in you, however you may deceive the world. The person who lives in God's love and by God's will takes his pleasure in what God prefers and refrains from any act contrary to his wishes, finding it impossible to omit what God wants and impossible to go contrary to him. It is like a man whose legs are tied together. He cannot walk. It is just as impossible for a man who lives in God's love to do evil. Someone has said: "Even if God should command me to do evil and shun virtue, still I could not do what is wrong." For no one loves virtue but he who is virtuous. The person who has denied himself and all else, who seeks his own advantage in nothing, and who lives without assigned reasons,[4] acting solely from loving-kindness, is one who is dead to the world and alive in God and God is alive in him.

Now other people say to me: "You say many fine things which mean nothing to us."[5] I, too, regret this fact. This knowledge is so precious and so common that you cannot buy it for a nickel or a cent! If, however, your intentions are right and your will is free, you will receive it.

The person who has let go of things here on this lowest plane where all is mortal shall receive them again in God where they are Truth. What is dead here is alive there; what is material here is spiritual there in God. For example: pour clean water into a clean basin that is fresh and bright and set it in a quiet place. Then one who holds his face over it may see the bottom just as it is, because the water is pure and quiet. So it is with people who live in peace and unity within themselves. In peace and quiet they know God and so they shall know him in trouble and unrest and thus they are well off. If, however, a man knows God less in trouble and dis-ease, he is wrong. St. Augustine says: "Let him to whom the days are dreary and the time too long, return to God in whom there is no duration and where everything comes to rest." The lover of justice is possessed by justice and inherits its strength.

Now our Lord said: "I call you not servants; for the servant knoweth not what his Lord doeth"[6]—but even my friend may know something I am not aware of and not reveal it to me. Still, our Lord said: "All things that I have heard of my Father, I have made known to you." Now I wonder about some of these priests, who have much learning and would like to be great priests, that they are so quickly satisfied and deluded, and interpret our Lord as saying: "I have told you about all I have heard from my Father"—by which they mean to say: "He has revealed to us only just so much as we shall need on our way to eternal bliss." I am not of the opinion that it is so to be understood, for then it would not be the truth.

Why did God become man? So that I might be born to be God— yes—identically God.[7] And God died so that I, too, might die to the whole world and all created things. One must understand the saying of our Lord in this sense: "All that I have heard, I have revealed to you." What, then, did the Son hear from his Father? The Father can do nothing but beget and the Son nothing but to be begotten. All the Father has and is, the whole basis of the divine being and nature, he begets at once in his only begotten Son. That is what the Son heard from the Father and that is what he has revealed to us—that we should be identical Sons. All the Son has he has from his Father, being and nature, so that we, too, might be Sons in the same sense. Also, no one has the Holy Spirit if he has not the only begotten Son. To be truly spiritualized by the Holy Spirit, that spirit must be given one by the Father and the Son and then it is permanent, for it is both real and spiritual.

It is true that you may receive gifts of the Holy Spirit [inspiration] but these do not remain—they are not permanent. For illustration: A man may blush and then blanch but these are incidental and pass away, but the person who is handsome and rosy by nature remains so permanently. It is so with one who is born the only begotten Son, for the Holy Spirit remains with him as something belonging to his nature. Thus it is written in the Book of Wisdom: "This day have I begotten thee in the reflection of my eternal light, in the fullness and clarity of the saints." He is begotten in the Now-moment and today. There is childbed in the Godhead and then we are baptized in the Holy Spirit—for that is the promise given by the Father. It is "after these days which are neither many nor few" that the "fullness of the Godhead" comes. Then there shall be neither day nor night and things more than a thousand miles from me shall be as near as the place where I stand. Thus it is with the fullness and pleasure of the Godhead. This is unity.

Mary Magdalene sought her Lord in the grave and was looking for one who was dead but found instead two living angels. Still she was not comforted. Then the angels said: "What's the matter with you? What are you looking for, woman?" It was as if they had said: "You were looking for one dead man and found two alive." She might have replied: "That is exactly my complaint and my distress, that I found two when I was looking for only one!"[8]

As long as things can make an impression on the soul, so long will the soul want comfort. I repeat what already I have said many times: As far as the soul's creature nature goes, there is no truth, but I hold that there is something more than creature nature in the soul. There are, however, some priests who do not understand this something so nearly related to God that it is one with him. It has nothing in common with anything else. Created things are nothings[9] and that Something is far from and strange to anything that could be created. Only the One is at rest in itself, receiving nothing from without.

Our Lord went up to heaven, above all light, above all understanding, and beyond reach. To be borne above all light is to live in the Unity. Thus St. Paul says: "God lives in a light to which there is no approach"[10]—a light that is itself pure unity. Thus one must be dead—quite dead—no longer himself—beyond comparison because unlike anyone else—and then he is like God, for it is God's property and nature to be incomparable and like no one.

That we may be one with the unity that is God, may God help us! Amen.

22

Good hinders the best[1]

EXPEDIT VOBIS UT EGO VADAM, etc.

(John 16:7)

WE READ in the holy Gospel that our Lord said to his disciples:
"It is expedient for you that I go away, for if I go not away, you
will not be able to receive the Holy Spirit." That is because of
three kinds of hindrances by which three kinds of people are baffled.

First are sinful people who are hindered by creature things,
enjoying them, each according to his pleasure, instead of God.
Thus St. Augustine says: "They are cursed who go astray on the
way to God." These people miss their way to God, for even creatures are ways of God. Of such people I shall say no more, for they
follow their animal senses and are thus cut off from God.

There are also certain good people who expend too much energy
on their natural needs and who take pleasure in external things.
With reference to these, God says: "He that loveth his life shall
lose it (that is, loves it sensually, too much, so that he loses his
soul) and he that hateth his life in this world shall keep it unto
life eternal"[2] (meaning those who do not follow their inordinate
lusts and desires).

The second [class of] hindrances which keep another kind of
good people from true spirituality is the Seven Sacraments. "*Sacra-
mentum*" means a symbol. The man who stops with the enjoyment
of a symbol never comes to the inward truth, for all seven of these
pieties refer to a single truth. Marriage, for example, symbolizes
the divine and human natures [joined together] and also the unity
of the soul with God. Thus, to get no further than the symbol is
to be kept from the one great truth. You must not imagine that
marriage is nothing more than the union of a man with a woman
for the indulgence of the senses and to live for lust. This is no true

197

marriage. Rather, marriage is obedience to the marriage rule and its seven occasions for deeds of tender mercy.

Furthermore, there are some good people who are hindered by too much dependence on repentance and confession. They cling to the symbol and are not in the least concerned to get at the pure truth. As for these, our Lord said: "He that is washed needeth not save to wash his feet"[3]—which is as much as to say that once washed by thoroughgoing repentance and clean confession, a man need not be always confessing his old sins anew. What would be more to the point would be that he "wash his feet," that is, his desires and his conscience, which need to be purified by daily confession of sin.

Also, some good people are hindered by being outwardly too zealous for the blessed sacrament of our Lord's body, so that they never receive it in reality. They expend too much diligence on superfluous things and are never joined to the truth—for truth is to be found within and not in visible phenomena. Therefore, they receive the body of God unworthily,[4] for all the sacraments point only to one spiritual truth. For this reason, do not cling to the symbols, but get to the inner truth! To seek the spirit of God's truth is to pray in spirit and in truth. That is what the Lord Jesus Christ himself said to the woman who was drawing water at the well of Samaria, when she asked him where one ought to pray— whether on the mountain, where her ancestors had prayed, or in the places where the Jews prayed. To which our Lord replied: "The hour cometh and now is, when true worshipers shall pray, neither on this mountain nor yet in a temple, but in the spirit and place of God."[5] This is to indicate that we ought to pray not only in temples or on the mountains, but to pray without ceasing, everywhere and at all times. Thus, too, St. Paul says: "Rejoice evermore, pray without ceasing. In everything, give thanks to God."[6]

This is the way they pray who do everything lovingly, solely for the love of God, careless of their own convenience and pleasure, and bowing humbly before him, they let God alone act. These pray without ceasing. The prayer of the lips is ordained for Christendom only that the soul may be gathered in from the senses, through which it gets scattered in a multiplicity of perishable things. When it is collected in the highest agents, that is, in the intellect, the will, and memory,[7] it is spiritualized, for when the spirit clings to God in a complete union of will, it is made divine. Then, for the first time, it is really praying, for at last its goal has been reached—the goal for which it was created. We were created only for God and that is why we were made in his image. Not to achieve oneness of spirit with God is to fail to be spiritual!

Again, good people are kept back from perfection by dwelling with holy pleasure on their images of the humanity of our Lord Jesus Christ. By the same token, they are hindered by laying stress on visions, in which they visualize the things of their souls, be they men or angels, or the humanity of our Lord Jesus Christ. They believe the messages they hear in spirit, especially when they hear that they are good people most beloved, or they hear about the faults of others or the virtues, or when they hear that God will do something they want done. They are often deceived, for God never does anything for the sake of any creature, but only for its pure good. This is the point of every Christian prayer: "Do this, O Lord, for the sake of thine only begotten son Jesus Christ!" Thus he said to his disciples: "It is expedient for you that I go away."

By that he meant to speak not only to his disciples of that time but to all who want to be his disciples now and to follow him to higher perfection. His humanity is a hindrance to them in the pleasure with which they depend on him. If they are to follow God in all his ways, they must not follow the ways of any human being, for these will put them off the road to God. Christ himself said: "I am the way, the truth, and the life: no man cometh unto the Father but by me, and he that climbeth up some other way, the same is a murderer and worthy of everlasting death."[8] He is referring to all who take it for granted that they, of themselves, may do good, or that God will do it for their sakes. Christ himself said that he was not [speaking] of himself; and the eternal wisdom: "He that created me dwells in my tent"[9]—the uncreated wisdom, for God is unborn wisdom. This is to be applied to the eternal birth, for the Son issues [from God] by way of birth, which is to say, creation.

Thus the eternal wisdom is born by the Father's power, for the Son is wisdom and the Holy Spirit is goodness. They are both love, one in nature and distinct in person—and what is this "tent" of which wisdom speaks? It is the humanity of our Lord Jesus Christ, in which the Father lives with the Son. They are of one essence, God in person, Godhead in nature. We must invoke this "tent" of the humanity of our Lord Jesus Christ only for the sake of union with the Godhead, for man is truly God and God is truly man.[10] We ought not to be bothered with any sort of creature things, but only with Jesus Christ, who is our only Father and Helper and a means to his Father.

Yet, when turning away from creatures we get on the track of truth, which is Jesus Christ, we are not wholly blessed, even though we are looking at divine truth; for while we are still looking at it, we are not in it. As long as a man has an object under consideration, he is not one with it. Where there is nothing but One, nothing but One is to be seen. Therefore, no man can see God except he be blind, nor know him except through ignorance, nor understand him except through folly. To this point, St. Augustine says: "No soul may come to God except it come to him apart from creature things and seek him without any image." That, too, is what Christ meant when he said: "First cast out the beam out of thine own eye and then thou shalt see clearly to cast the mote out of thy brother's eye!"[11] This suggests that creatures are to be compared to beams in the soul's eye and that they hinder union with God because they are creaturely. Therefore, because even the soul is a creature, even it must first be cast out. Indeed, it must cast out even the saints and angels and even our blessed Lady, because these are all creatures!

The soul should be independent and should not want anything[12] and then it would attain godly stature by reason of likeness [to him]. Nothing makes for unity as much as likeness, for God, too, is independent and needs nothing. In this way the soul enters the unity of the Holy Trinity but it may become even more blessed by going further, to the barren Godhead, of which the Trinity is a revelation. In this barren Godhead, activity has ceased and therefore the soul will be most perfect when it is thrown into the desert of the Godhead, where both activity and forms are no more, so that it is sunk and lost in this desert where its identity is destroyed and it has no more to do with things than it had before it existed. Then it is dead to self and alive to God.[13] What is dead in this sense has ceased to be. So that soul will be dead to self which is buried in the Godhead-desert. Of such people, St. Paul says: "You are dead and your life is hidden with Christ in God."[14] And Dionysius says: "To be buried in God is nothing but to be transported into uncreated life."

There are some people who imagine that they have been transmuted into the Holy Trinity, who have really never got beyond self because they are loath to deny themselves. They want chiefly their own selfish profit, enjoyment and emotional titillation—all of which they have foresworn in thought and will. They are no followers of our Lord Jesus Christ, who never once sought pleasurable excitement in anything he did, but who said: "My soul is sorrowful even unto death."[15] He is referring to his soul—the aristocrat—but he also refers to his bodily life which also was "sorrowful even unto death" until all that belongs to our salvation should be made perfect, until even our death is killed. Our souls, too, must be sorrowful unto death until all that lives in us for its own sake, for selfish profit and by self-will, is killed. When the soul is dead to the life of desire and selfish profit, and buried in God, to the degree that it is hidden from creatures and ignorant of them, then it can never again be troubled.

Now see how one may know when he is received into the Holy Trinity. In the first place, at the sight of the Holy Spirit, the soul's guilt is washed away and self and things are all forgotten. Next the soul receives from the Godhead the eternal wisdom of the Father—knowledge and understanding of all things. Thus opinion, supposition, and belief are removed, for the soul has arrived at the truth. Whatever one has believed heretofore, and known by means of clear statements and demonstrations, or by sensuous representations either from man or from spirit—he has no longer any need to mention these things, as people must who have never known the truth and who, when a pure truth is revealed to them, try to grasp with human senses what goes beyond the powers of angels. Thus, they ask others and speak of it as they have understood it, in a material sense, and those who hear also take it in a material sense as they have received it, forthwith pronouncing it distorted and incompatible with the Christian faith. They therefore hold it to be false, for they imagine it to be as they see it, when they have not understood it at all. They are deceived.

Finally, the soul, the aristocrat, when it is drawn by truth up into the Holy Trinity, receives instantly something of the Father's powers and might, so that it is able to do anything. St. Paul also speaks of this: "I can do all things through Christ which strengtheneth me."[16] Then the soul neither works, nor knows, nor loves any more, but God through the soul works and knows and loves. So Jeremiah also preached that we are really gods in knowing and loving God. May God help us to this truth! Amen.

23

Distinctions are lost in God[1]

QUI AUDIT ME, NON CONFUNDETUR.

(Ecclesiasticus 24:30)

THE eternal wisdom of the Father says: "He that heareth me is not ashamed. (If he is ashamed, it is of his shame.) He who acts in me sins not. He that reveals me and fears me shall have eternal life." There is matter enough for one sermon in any of these three statements.

I shall discuss the first—that the eternal wisdom says: "He that heareth me is not ashamed." To hear the wisdom of the Father, one must be "in," at home, and alone.[2]

Three things there are that hinder one from hearing the eternal Word. The first is corporeality, the second, number, and the third, time. If a person has overcome these three, he dwells in eternity, is alive spiritually and remains in the unity, the desert of solitude, and there he hears the eternal Word. Our Lord says: "No man heareth my word or teaching until he hath forsaken selfhood."[3] The hearing of God's Word requires complete self-surrender. He who hears and that which is heard are identical constituents of the eternal Word. What the eternal Father teaches is his own Being, Nature, and Godhead—which he is always revealing through his only begotten Son. He teaches that we are to be identical with him.

To deny one's self is to be the only begotten Son of God and one who does so has for himself all the properties of that Son. All God's acts are performed and his teachings conveyed through the Son, to the point that we should be his only begotten Son.[4] And when this is accomplished in God's sight, he is so fond of us and so fervent that he acts as if his divine Being might be shattered and he himself annihilated if the whole foundations of his Godhead were not revealed to us, together with his nature and being. God makes haste to do this, so that it may be ours as it is his.[5] It is here that God finds joy and rapture in fulfillment and the person who is thus within God's knowing and love becomes just what God himself is.

If you love yourself, you love everybody else as you do yourself. As long as you love another person less than you love yourself, you will not really succeed in loving yourself but if you love all alike, including yourself, you will love them as one person and that person is both God and man. Thus he is a just and righteous person who, loving himself, loves all others equally.[7]

Some people say: "I prefer my friends who are good to me to other people"—but they are wrong and this is not the perfect way. Nevertheless, we have to make the best of it, just as people do who have to sail over the sea with a cross wind and yet manage to get over. Well, it is like this with one who has his preferences in people, as naturally one will. If I care for other people as I do for myself, then what happens to them, whether for better or for worse, let it mean life or death, I should be glad to take it on myself. That is true friendship.

Speaking to this point, St. Paul says: "I could wish to be cut off eternally from God for my friends' sake and for God's sake."[6] To be cut off from God for an instant is to be cut off from him forever, and to be cut off from God at all is the pain of hell.[7] What, then, does St. Paul mean by saying that he could wish to be cut off from God? The authorities question whether or not St. Paul, when he made this remark, was already perfect or only on the road to perfection. I say that he was already quite perfect, for otherwise he would not have said it and now I shall explain why St. Paul could say that he could wish to be cut off from God.

Man's last and highest parting occurs when, for God's sake, he takes leave of god.[8] St. Paul took leave of god for God's sake and gave up all that he might get from god, as well as all he might give— together with every idea of god. In parting with these, he parted with god for God's sake and yet God remained to him as God is in his own nature—not as he is conceived by anyone to be—nor yet as something yet to be achieved—but more as an "is-ness,"[9] as God really is.[10] Then he neither gave to God nor received anything from him, for he and God were a unit, that is, pure unity. Thus one becomes that real person, for whom there can be no suffering, any more than the divine essence can suffer.[11] As I have often said, there is something in the soul so closely akin to God that it is already one with him and need never be united to him.[12] It is unique and has nothing in common with anything else. It has no significance [for this world?] whatsoever—none! Anything created is nothing but that Something is apart from and strange to all creation. If one were wholly this, he would be both uncreated and unlike any creature. If any corporeal thing or anything fragile were included in that unity, it, too, would be like the essence of that unity. If I should find myself in this essence, even for a moment, I should regard my earthly selfhood as of no more importance than a manure worm.

God gives to all things alike and as they proceed from God they are alike. Angels, men, and creatures all flow out of God in whom their prime origin is. Take them as they first emanate from him and you will find them all alike but, if they are alike in this temporal sphere, in eternity and in God they are the much more so. A flea, to the extent that it is in God, ranks above the highest angel in his own right. Thus, in God, all things are equal and are God himself.

In this likeness or identity God takes such delight that he pours his whole nature and being into it. His pleasure is as great, to take a simile, as that of a horse, let loose to run over a green heath where the ground is level and smooth, to gallop as a horse will, as fast as he can over the greensward—for this is a horse's pleasure and expresses his nature. It is so with God. It is his pleasure and rapture to discover identity, because he can always put his whole nature into it—for he is this identity itself.

A question is raised about those angels who live with us, serving and guarding us, as to whether or not they have less joy in identity than the angels in heaven have and whether they are hindered at all in their [proper] activities by serving and guarding us. No! Not at all! Their joy is not diminished, nor their equality, because the angel's work is to do the will of God and the will of God is the angel's work. If God told an angel to go to a tree and pick off the caterpillars, the angel would be glad to do it and it would be bliss to him because it *is* God's will.

Always to be ready to do God's will is to be ready for nothing else than what God is and wills. Such a person, being ill, would not wish to be well. Pain would be a pleasure to him and all the manifold of things would be an empty unity to him who is ready to do God's will. Indeed, if the pains of hell should follow, they would be joy and bliss—for he would be empty, having denied himself, and whatever might happen would not touch him. If my eye is to distinguish colors, it must first be free from any color impressions. If I see blue or white, the seeing of my eyes is identical with what is seen. The eye by which I see God is the same as the eye by which God sees me. My eye and God's eye are one and the same—one in seeing, one in knowing, and one in loving.[13]

To love as God loves, one must be dead to self and all created things, and have as little regard for self as for one who is a thousand miles away. His life is an identity and a unity and there is no distinction in him.[14] This person must have denied himself and the whole world. If anyone owned the whole world and gave it up as freely as he received it, God would give it back to him and eternal life to boot.

And if there were another person who had nothing but good will and he thought: "Lord, if this whole world were mine and two more with it, [or as many more as you please] I would give them up and myself too as completely as it was before I received them"— then God would return to him as much as he had given away with his own hands. There is still another person, who has nothing whatever, material or spiritual, to give away or forsake; he has given away and forsaken most of all. To him who even for one instant completely denies himself, shall all things be given, but if a person were to deny himself for twenty years and then return to selfishness even for a moment, it would be as if he had never denied himself at all. One who has denied himself and keeps denying himself and never even casts a glance on what he has given up, and remains steady, immovably and unchangeably what he is—he alone has really denied himself.

That we too may remain steady and unchangeable in the eternal Father, may God help us and the eternal wisdom too. Amen.

24

God enters a free soul[1]

INTRAVIT IESUS IN QUODDAM CASTELLUM ET
MULIER QUAEDAM EXCEPIT ILLUM . . .

(Luke 10:38)

I HAVE read a text from the Gospel, first in Latin, which means in English: "Our Lord Jesus Christ went into a little castle and was received by a virgin who was a wife."[2]

But notice this text with care! It must necessarily be that the person who received Jesus was a virgin. A virgin, in other words, is a person who is free of irrelevant ideas, as free as he was before he existed. Yet see—someone might ask: How can a person, once born and launched into rational life, be as devoid of ideas as if he did not exist? How can he be free?

Listen to the analysis I shall now make. If I were sufficiently intelligent to comprehend all the ideas ever conceived by man or God himself, and if I were detached[3] from them, so that I did not regard them as mine to take or leave, in either past or future, and if I were free and empty of them in this Now-moment, the present, as it is the blessed will of God for me to be, and if I were perpetually doing God's will, then I would be a virgin in reality, as exempt from idea-handicaps as I was before I was born.

Nevertheless, I assert that being a virgin will not deprive a man of the results of his efforts. Rather, he will be virgin and detached from them and none of them will keep him back from the highest truth—if he, like Jesus, is free and pure and himself virgin. As the authorities say, "like to like"[4] is the condition of unity, so that one must be innocent and virgin if he is to receive the innocent[4] Jesus.

Now stop, look, and listen in earnest. To remain virgin forever is never to bear fruit. To be fruitful, it is necessary to be a wife.

"Wife" is the optimum term that may be applied to the soul. It is even above "virgin." That within himself, a man should receive God is good; and receiving God, the man is still virgin. Nevertheless, it is better that God should be fruitful through him, for fruitfulness alone is real gratitude for God's gift and in fruitfulness the soul is a wife, with newborn gratitude, when it bears Jesus back again into the Father's heart.

Many good gifts, received in virginity, are not brought to birth in wifely fruitfulness by which God is gratefully pleased. The gifts decay and come to nothing, so that the man is never blessed or bettered by them. The virgin in him is useless when it does not ripen into the wife who is fruitful. Here is the mischief! It is against this that I have said: "Jesus entered a little castle and was received by a virgin who was a wife." This must needs be so, as I have shown.

Married people seldom bear fruit more than once a year, but now I shall speak of another kind of married persons—those who are married to prayers, fasts, vigils, and all sorts of external disciplines and chastisements. Any devotion to any practice that limits your freedom to wait upon God in this present moment and to follow him into the light, by which he may show you what to do and what not to do—how to be as new and free with each moment as if you had never had, or wanted, or could have another—any such commitment or premeditated practice that limits your freedom—I now call "married life."[5] In it, your soul will bring forth no fruit other than the discipline to which you are so anxiously committed and you will trust neither God nor yourself, until you are finished with it. In other words, you will find no peace, for no one can be fruitful until he is done with his own work. I put this down as an interval[5] [of effort] from which the yield is small, because it has to come out of self-designed bondage and not out of freedom. I call them married who live in this voluntary bondage. They seldom bear fruit and before God there is little profit in them, as I have explained.

A virgin who is a wife, free and unfettered in affections, is equally near both to God and to self. She brings forth much fruit and is big withal, no less and no more than God himself is. This virgin who is a wife accomplishes this birth, bears fruit every day an hundred- or a thousandfold—yes, she gives birth times without number and bears fruit from the most fertile of soils. To speak plainly, she bears fruit out of the ground[6] in which the Father begets his eternal Word. She is thus fruitful and parturient. For Jesus is the light and shine of the paternal heart (as St. Paul puts it, he is the glory and reflection of the Father's heart—the power shining through). This Jesus is united with her [the virgin soul] and she with him. She is illumined and radiates him as the One and only pure, clear light of the Father.

I have often said before that there is an agent in the soul, untouched by time and flesh,[7] which proceeds out of the Spirit and which remains forever in the Spirit and is completely spiritual. In this agent, God is perpetually verdant and flowering with all the joy and glory that is in him. Here is joy so hearty, such inconceivably great joy that no one can ever fully tell it, for in this agent the eternal Father is ceaselessly begetting his eternal Son and the agent is parturient with God's offspring and is itself the Son, by the Father's unique power.

For this reason, if a person had a whole kingdom or all this world's goods and left it all solely for God's sake, to become the poorest man who ever lived on earth, and if then God gave him as much to suffer as he ever gave any man, and if this person suffered it out until he was dead, and if then, even for the space of a moment, God once let him see what he is in this agent of the soul, all his suffering and poverty would seem like a very little thing beside the joy of it, so great in that moment. Indeed, if afterwards God never gave him the Kingdom of Heaven at all, he would feel sufficiently repaid for all he had suffered, for God himself is in that agent of the soul in that eternal Now-movement.

If the spirit were only always united with God in this agent, a man could never grow old. For the Now-moment, in which God made the first man and the Now-moment in which the last man will disappear, and the Now-moment in which I am speaking are all one in God, in whom there is only one Now. Look! The person who lives in the light of God is conscious neither of time past nor of time to come but only of the one eternity. In fact, he is bereft of wonder, for all things are intrinsic in him. Therefore he gets, nothing new out of future events, nor from chance, for he lives in the Now-moment that is, unfailingly, "in verdure newly clad." Such is the divine glory of this agent in the soul.

There is, however, still another agent, which also is not incarnate but which proceeds out of the spirit, yet remains in it and is always only spiritual. In this second agent,[7] God glows and burns without ceasing, in all his fullness, sweetness, and rapture. Truly, it holds joy so great and rapture so unmeasured that no one can tell it or reveal it. Yet I say that if there were one person who could look into it for a moment and still keep his right mind, all he had ever suffered or that God wished him to suffer would be a very little thing indeed, nothing at all. Nay—I go even further—suffering would be to him always a joy and pleasure.

If you wish to know rightly whether your suffering is yours or of God, you can tell in the following way. If you are suffering because of yourself, whatever the manner, that suffering hurts and is hard to bear. If you suffer for God's sake and for God alone, that suffering does not hurt and is not hard to bear, for God takes the burden of it. If an hundredweight were loaded on my neck and then someone else took it at once on his neck, I had just as lief it were an hundred as one. It would not then be heavy to me and would not hurt me. To make a long story short, what one suffers through God and for God alone is made sweet and easy.

As I said in the first place, at the beginning of the sermon, "Jesus went into a little castle and was received by a virgin who was a wife." Why? It must needs be that she was a virgin and a wife and I have told you how he was received, but I have not yet told you what the little castle was and that I shall now do.

I have said that there is one agent alone in the soul that is free. Sometimes I have called it the tabernacle of the Spirit. Other times I have called it the Light of the Spirit and again, a spark.[8] Now I say that it is neither this nor that.[9] It is something higher than this or that, as the sky is higher than the earth and I shall call it by a more aristocratic name than I have ever used before, even though it disowns my adulation and my name, being far beyond both. It is free of all names and unconscious of any kind of forms. It is at once pure and free, as God himself is, and like him is perfect unity and uniformity, so that there is no possible way to spy it out.[10]

God blossoms and is verdant in this agent of which I speak, with all the Godhead and spirit of God and there he begets his only begotten Son as truly as if it were in himself. For he lives really in this agent, the Spirit together with the Father giving birth to the Son and in that light, he is the Son and the Truth. If you can only see with my heart, you may well understand what I am saying, for it is true and the Truth itself bespeaks my word.

Look and see: this little castle in the soul[10] is exalted so high above every road [of approach], with such simplicity and uniformity, that the aristocratic agent of which I have been telling you is not worthy to look into it, even once for a moment. No, nor are the other agents, of which I have also spoken, ever able to peek in to where God glows and burns like a fire with all his abundance and rapture. So altogether one and uniform is this little castle, so high above all ways and agencies, that none can ever lead to it—indeed—not even God himself.

It is the truth as God lives. God himself cannot even peek into it for a moment—or steal into it—in so far as he has particular selfhood and the properties of a person.[11] This is a good point to notice, for the onefold One has neither a manner nor properties. And therefore, if God is to steal into it [the little castle in the soul] it [the adventure] will cost him all his divine names and personlike properties; He would have to forgo all these if he is to gain entrance. Except as he is the onefold One, without ways or properties—neither the Father nor the Holy Spirit in this [personal] sense, yet something that is neither this nor that—See!—it is only as he is One and onefold that he may enter into that One which I have called the Little Castle of the soul.[10] Otherwise he cannot get in by any means or be at home there, for in part the soul is like God—otherwise it would not be possible.

What I have been saying to you is true, as I call on Truth to bear witness and my soul to be the pledge. That we, too, may be castles into which Jesus may enter and be received and abide eternally with us in the manner I have described, may God help us! Amen.

25

Get beyond time![1]

IN DIEBUS SUIS PLACUIT DEO ET INVENTUS EST IUSTUS.[1]

(Ecclesiasticus 44:17)

THIS text which I have quoted in Latin may be read in honor of the saint, St. Germanus by name, whose life is being celebrated throughout holy Christendom today[2] and of whose virtuous life much has been written. The text means in English: "He pleased God in his days and was found just."

Now notice. If we say "in his days," there are more days than one. There is the soul's day and God's day.[3] A day, whether six or seven ago, or more than six thousand years ago, is just as near to the present as yesterday. Why? Because all time is contained in the present Now-moment. Time comes of the revolution of the heavens and day began with the first revolution. The soul's day falls within this time and consists of the natural light in which things are seen. God's day, however, is the complete day, comprising both day and night. It is the real Now-moment, which for the soul is eternity's day, on which the Father begets his only begotten Son and the soul is reborn in God. Whenever this birth occurs, it is the soul giving birth to the only begotten Son. Thus, the Virgin's[4] Sons are more numerous than the children of ordinary women, for they are born beyond time in eternity. Still, however many the children to which the soul gives birth in eternity, all together they are still only one Son, because it all happens beyond time, in the day of eternity.[5]

That person is just indeed who lives virtuously—who "seeketh not his own" in anything, neither in God nor in creature. He lives in God's heart and God lives in him—as I said eight days ago.[6] To such a person, disdaining things, it is a pleasure to give them up and thus to raise everything to its highest perfection. St. John says, "Deus caritas est"—God is love and love is God, so that to live in

212

love is to live in God and to be lived in by God. Without a doubt, to live in God is to be well housed, and to be God's heir, and to have God live in you is to have a good and worthy lodger. One of the authorities says that God gives the soul a gift that moves it to spiritual things, while another says that the soul is moved immediately by the Holy Spirit, for God loves me with the same love he has for himself! This is also true of the soul. It loves God with the same love it has for itself. If it were not for the love God has for himself, there would be no Holy Spirit. It is an ardor, and a blossoming of the Holy Spirit in which the soul loves God.

One of the evangelists writes, "This is my beloved Son in whom I am well pleased." A second writes, "This is my beloved Son about whom everything pleases me." The third writes, "This is my beloved Son in whom I please myself."[7] Whatever pleases God, it is in his only begotten Son, and whatever God loves, He loves in him. Therefore one should so live that he is identified with God's Son and so that he is that Son. Between the Son and the soul there is no distinction.[8]

The love of a servant is never like the love of a master. As long as I am a servant [of God] I am far from being like an only Son. It would not be right for me to see God with the same eyes that distinguish colors, for colors are temporal and the temporal is far from God and alien to him. If one considers time, even the shortest bit of it, the Now-moment, it is still time and self-consistent. As long as one clings to time, space, number, and quantity, he is on the wrong track and God is strange and far away. Therefore our Lord said: "Let him who would be my disciple deny himself, for no one can hear my word or teaching who has not denied himself." Creatures are nothing of themselves[9] and that is why I counsel you to deny them and receive perfect being, in which your will is right. Those who relinquish their own wills completely will like what I teach and understand what I say. One authority has it that creatures receive their being directly from God and that is why, in their true essence, creatures love God more than they love themselves. If the soul knew its own utter detachment, it could stoop to nothing but only remain completely detached. Therefore it is said of our holy bishop: "He pleased God in his days."

There is a difference between the soul's day and God's day but in the day most native to the soul, it perceives things from above all space and time, and finds them neither near nor far away. It is for this reason that I have said that in this day, all things are equal in rank. To say that God created the world yesterday or tomorrow would be foolishness, for God created the world and everything in it in the one present Now. Indeed, time that has been past for a thousand years is as present and near to God as the time that now is.[10] The soul that lives in the present Now-moment is the soul in which the Father begets his only begotten Son and in that birth the soul is born again. It is still one birth, however often the soul is reborn in God, as the Father begets his only begotten Son.

I have spoken of an agent in the soul whose primitive function it is, not to reach God as he is good, or to apprehend him as he is the truth, but to go further, to the foundations, to seek him and apprehend him in his uniqueness and abstraction, in the desert of his solitude, the essence of his being. Still unsatisfied, it looks further to see what he is in his Godhead and also looks to the most intimate properties of his nature. Now, they say that there is no unity more perfect than that of the three persons in God. One might say further that there is no unity more perfect than that between the soul and God. When the soul is kissed by the Godhead, it is then completely perfected and blessed and embraced by the unity [of God]. When God has touched the soul and rendered it uncreaturely, it is then as high in rank as God himself, after he has touched it. Contemplating the creature, God gives it being, and contemplating God, the creature receives its being. The soul has an intelligent, knowing essence and therefore, wherever God is, there is the soul, and wherever the soul is, there is God!

The second part of our text reads: "He was found just"—but he found justice within himself. My body is more in my soul than my soul is in my body but both body and soul are more in God than they are in themselves and that *is* justice, righteousness, and the prime cause of every thing. Truly, as St. Augustine says: "God is nearer to the soul than the soul is to itself."[11] God and the soul are so nearly [related] to each other that there is really no distinction between them. By the same [kind] of knowledge by which God knows himself, that is, detached or dispassionate knowledge, the soul receives its being from God. For that reason God is closer to the soul than the soul is to itself and therefore, God is in the soul's core—God and all the Godhead.

One authority raises the question: "Does the divine light shine as clearly in the soul's agents as in the soul's core-essence considering that the soul receives being immediately from God and its agents extend immediately from the soul?" The divine light is far too aristocratic to make common cause with the soul's agents. For all that touches creatures or can be touched by them is far from God and alien from him. As the agents of the soul touch the world and are touched by it, they lose their virginity. The divine light cannot shine in them and they can be made sensitive and holy only through purification and renunciation. This is what that authority means who says that the soul's agents are given a light which is *like* the inner light. It is like it but it is not the Light itself. In part, the soul's agents are influenced by this light, so that they may be sensitive to the inner light. Another authority says that all the soul's agents which regulate the body die with the body, with the exception of knowledge and will, but that these remain the soul's own. If the agents which affect the body die, nevertheless their roots remain.

St. Philip says: "Lord, show us the Father and it sufficeth us."[12] But no one can come to the Father except through the Son. To see the Father is to see the Son and their mutual affection is the Holy Spirit. The soul itself is so simple that it cannot have more than one idea at a time of anything. When attention is directed to the idea of a stone, the idea of an angel cannot also be entertained, and when attention is directed to an angel, no other idea is possible. Whatever the idea to which attention is directed, it must be of interest as long as it is present. To think of a thousand angels is no more than thinking of two—and even then, no more than thinking of one. Thus, a person cannot be more than single in attention.

St. Paul says: "Being now made free from sin, you ought to become servants of God."[13] The only begotten Son has freed us from our sins but our Lord speaks much more to the point than St. Paul: "I have not called you servants, but friends" and "the servant knoweth not what his Lord doeth"[14]—but friends know all, for that is the nature of friendship. "For all things that I have heard from my Father, I have made known to you."[14] All my Father knows I know and all I know, he knows, for I and my Father are one. The person who knows all that God knows is a prophet. This kind of person takes God as he is, in his own nature, his unity, omnipresence and truth, and he is on the right track. Not to be accustomed to inward, spiritual things is never really to know what God is! To have wine in your cellar and never to drink it, or even inspect it, is not to know whether it is good or not. Even so with people who live on in ignorance: they do not know what God is but they think and imagine foolish things and so they get along. That kind of knowledge is not from God.

One must have a pure, clear knowledge of divine truth. If he is always to act with true, clear conviction, God must undergird that conviction with all his pure, divine nature. Such a person finds his goal in the divine nature and it is within himself.[15]

Now, one authority says that no one is so foolish that he does not desire wisdom. Why, then, are we not all wise? Because so much is required to that end. The principal requirement is that one shall get beyond phenomenal nature and in this process he begins soon to be weary. Then he lags behind with his little wisdom, a little man. That I am a wealthy man does not mean that I am wise too, but when my nature is conformed to God's Being, so that I am wisdom itself, then only am I a wise man.

Once in the cloister I said: "The true archetype of the soul is revealed when God alone and nothing else can be described or imagined." The soul has two eyes—one looking inwards and the other outwards. It is the inner eye of the soul that looks into essence and takes being directly from God. That is its true function. The soul's outward eye is directed toward creatures and perceives their external forms but when a person turns inwards and knows God in terms of his own awareness of him, in the roots of his being, he is then freed from all creation and is secure in the castle of truth.

In this sense, I once spoke of how our Lord came to his disciples on Easter Day through a locked door and spoke to them. I meant that God does not first need to enter the person who is already free of all otherness and creature nature, because he is already there.

That we, too, may be found in the castle of truth on that Day— the time of understanding, on that Day of wisdom and justice and blessing, may the undivided Trinity help us all. Amen.

26

Like a morning star God shines[1]

QUASI STELLA MATUTINA IN MEDIO NEBULAE ET QUASI LUNA PLENA IN DIEBUS
SUIS LUCET ET QUASI SOL REFULGENS, SIC ISTE REFULSIT IN TEMPLO DEI.

(Ecclesiasticus 50:6–7)

"Like a morning star through a cloud, like the moon at its full, like
the sun in its glory, so he shone in the temple of God." Ordinarily,
these words are applied to the saints and divine teachers who, by
their virtuous lives and godly skill, have illumined human hearts—
hearts imprisoned in creature being, in the mist and cloud of darkness that ignorance is, hearts straying like the blind from the road
to their eternal salvation. The text applies especially to the holy
father St. Dominic,[2] whom we remember today as a pillar of Christendom and the founder of our preaching order, which he conceived
and established for the proclamation of the word of God, for the
help of poor sinners. He shone in the temple of God like a morning
star, says the Scripture.

What is God and what is the temple of God? Twenty-four scholars[3] got together and tried to say what God is and were unable to do
it. They met again at an appointed time and each presented what he
had to say. Let me quote two or three. One said: "God is something
compared to which all that changes with time is nothing, so that
whatever has being gets it from him and is small before him." The
second said: "God is something that must transcend being, that by
itself needs nothing and yet which all things need." The third said:
"God is intelligence occupied with knowing itself."

I shall neglect the first and third and speak only of the second and
say that God is something that must transcend being. Anything
which has being, date, or location does not belong to God, for he is
above them all and although he is in all creatures, yet he is more
than all of them.

Some authorities maintain that the soul is in the emotions[4] only but it is not so. Many great scholars make that error. The soul is whole and undivided, at once in the foot and the eye and every other member. Or take a section of time, it may be today or yesterday: the present Now-moment gathers all parts of time up into itself. That present Now in which God created the world is as near to this bit of time as any moment is and the Last Day is as near to it as yesterday.

One scholar says that God is something indivisible acting in eternity, that stays always within itself and thus needs nothing, neither any instrument or any help, but is needed by all things, being the ultimate goal toward which they strive. That goal has no path[5] which leads to it but is off any beaten path, moving at large.[6] St. Bernard says: "To love God is a way that is no way."

A physician who wants to make a sick man well has no precise kind of health in mind, or any degree of health to which he will cure him, but he has a means by which he hopes to bring health back. He does not specify how well he will make the sick, but he wants to make him as well as possible. How should we love God? As much as possible: without measure.

Each thing has its own distinctive mode and nothing can act out of character. Fire cannot do without wood. God acts at large above being, animating himself. He acts in uncreated essence. Before there was being, God was; and he is where there is no being. Great authorities say that God is pure being but he is as high above being as the highest angel is above a fly and I say that it would be as incorrect for me to call God a being as it would be to call the sun light or dark.[7]

He is neither this nor that.[8] As one saint says: "If anyone imagines that he knows God and his knowledge takes form, then he may know something but it is not God!" Thus when I say that God is not being and that he is above being, I have not denied him being but, rather, I have dignified and exalted being in him. If I find copper in gold, it is in a medium more precious than itself. St. Augustine says that God is a Way beyond ways, Good beyond goods, Power beyond powers.[9]

Teachers in the elementary schools say that of Being, there are ten kinds[10] [categories] and they deny them all to God but I say that God lacks none of these kinds of Being and yet none of them includes him. The first is substance, which includes more of being than any other category and through which everything comes to be. The last, which has least being is called "relation," but the being of the last is as great as the first in God, for all ten have the same origin or archetype in him. All things have a common prototype in God. God is neither being nor goodness. Goodness depends on being, for if there were no being there would be no goodness, and thus being is purer than goodness. But God is neither good, better, nor best.[1] To say that God is good is to falsify him as it would falsify the sun to call it dark.[7]

Yet God says that none is good save God![11] What is good? That which communicates itself. We call him a good man who, revealing himself, is of use to others. Thus a heathen scholar says that a hermit is neither good nor bad because he neither shows himself to others nor is useful to them in any way. But God is the great self-sharer. Things do not communicate being to one another for, of themselves, they are nothing. What they reveal they have had from another source. They cannot give themselves away. The sun radiates its shine and yet remains what it was. Fire gives heat and yet remains fire, but God imparts himself as he is in himself and of all his gifts he himself is ever the first. In all his gifts,[12] he gives himself to the limit of the capacity of him who is to receive. St. James says: "Every good gift comes down from above, flowing from the Father of lights."[13]

When we consider God as being, we are thinking of him in the keep of his castle where he dwells, for where God is being is and it is the stronghold of his habitation. Where, then, is God in his temple? In intelligence? Yes. Intellect is the temple of God and nowhere does he shine more holy than there. As sundry authorities say: "God is intelligence that lives only in knowledge, apart, alone with himself so that nothing disturbs him as he is there alone in the silence.

Now let us turn to the soul which contains a drop of intelligence, a spark,[14] a twig of it, and which has agents at work in the body. One agent takes care of the digestion and is more active by night than by day, such that one grows and thrives. The soul also has an agent in the eye by reason of which the eye is so sensitive, delicate, and fastidious that it does not receive things in the bulk, as they are, but first sifts them and makes them fine in the air and light and that happens because the eye has the soul in it. There is another agent of the soul by means of which it thinks. This agent conceives things not present, so therefore I may know them well, as vividly as if I could see them with my eyes, or even better. Thus I know what a rose is like in winter. It is by this agent that the soul reaches into nonbeing and follows God, who acts in nonbeing.

A heathen authority says: "The soul that loves God loves him under the veil of goodness." (Such is the thought of all the heathen masters which I have mentioned heretofore, who view things only in the light of nature; for I have not yet come to the thought of the saints who view these matters in a far higher light.) He says, then, that the soul, loving God, loves him under the veil of goodness and I say that intelligence draws aside the veil and perceives God naked, stripped of goodness, or of being, or of any name.

I said in school that intelligence is higher than the will, although both belong in this light [of nature]. Then one of the teachers in another school[15] declared that will is above intelligence, "for the will," so he said, "takes things as they are, whereas intelligence takes them only as it conceives them to be." And that is true. An actual eye is better than an eye painted on the wall. Nevertheless, I say that intelligence is above will. Willing, man conceives God in the garment of goodness. Thinking, man conceives God naked, stripped of both goodness and being. Goodness is a cloak under which he is hidden and the will is content with God so clothed. If God were not good, my will would not want him. If one were to clothe his king in drab colors on the day of his coronation, his work would be badly done. Therefore I am not blessed by the fact of God's goodness. I shall never ask God to bless me out of his goodness, for he could not do it. I am blessed only by the fact that God can be known and that I can know him! Thus one authority says: "God's mind it is, on which all angelic being depends."

It is asked where an image is, in the mirror or in the object? The image is in me, of me, and to me. While the mirror is opposite my face, I see my image in it but if the mirror falls my image is gone. Thus the being of angels depends on the presence of the divine mind in which they behold themselves, *like* a morning star shining through the cloud-mist.[16] I am always using this word "quasi," which means "like unto" and because I use it so much in my preaching, it has become a byword to the children in the school.

The most apposite reference to God in speech is the description of him as a "word" or "truth." God calls himself a Word. St. John says: "In the beginning was the Word,"[17] and means that beside this Word, man is a byword! It is like Fria's star Venus, after which Friday is named. When Venus rises before the sun and precedes the sun, it is called the morning star, but when the sun sets first and Venus follows, it is called the evening star and it moves, now above and now beneath the sun, but of all the stars it is most constant in its distance from the sun, never nearer and never farther away. Thus for one who wants always to be in the presence of God, so that nothing can estrange him, neither happiness nor unhappiness, nor any other creature, Venus is a symbol.

The text also says: "like the moon at its full." The moon rules the moist in nature. It is never nearer the sun than when it is full and then it receives its light firsthand from the sun. Still, because it is nearer the earth than any other star, the moon suffers two impairments: it is pale and flecked, and loses its light. Never is it so powerful as when it is farthest from the earth, for then it causes the ocean to rise most; but the more it wanes, the less it makes the sea rise. The more the soul rises above earthly things, the more power it has. Thus to know much creature-lore is not to need the thought-discipline of a sermon. Every creature is full of God and is a book but he who wishes to attain what I speak of (that toward which all my discourses tend) must be like a morning star, always in the presence of God, always near him, a constant distance from him, exalted above earthly things, with the Word, like a byword, like an angel among men and creatures.

There is one kind of thought which I contemplate which takes these forms: angels, creatures, men. There is another, unexpressed and unconsidered, which is never explicit but always implicit in him that expresses it, for it is ever expressed by the Father: intelligence forever at work with the man, the more effective outside him the more it affects the man within himself. In the effectiveness of intelligence God is beatified and thence the soul should be always like a byword. It should discover its own meaning in what blesses God. This is not true of corporeal things. The stronger they are, the more externally impressive, whereas intelligence, the stronger and finer it is, the more it penetrates and unites with the object of knowledge.

God's beatitude lies in what intelligence does to man within himself, the man who is inhabited by the Word that is God. The soul is thus like a byword, working together with God and finding its beatification in the same self-knowledge that exalts him. That to all time, we may be bywords of God, may the Father, the Word, and the Holy Spirit help us all! Amen.

27

Creatures seek God through me[1]

NOLITE TIMERE EOS, QUI CORPUS OCCIDUNT,
ANIMAM AUTEM OCCIDERE NON POSSUNT.

(Matthew 10:28)

"Fear not them which try to kill your body but are not able to kill
the soul." Spirit cannot kill spirit but spirit gives life to spirit.
"Them which kill" you are flesh and blood and they die together.
The highest component of man is blood—when rightly disposed—
but also it is man's worst part when ill-disposed. If the blood con-
quers the flesh, man is humble, patient, chaste, and has all the
virtues, but if flesh rules the blood, then man is haughty, irritable,
unchaste, and has all the vices.[2]

Now listen: I am going to say something I have never said before.
When God created the heavens, the earth and creatures, he did not
act. He had nothing to do. He made no effort. For God said: "We
shall make a likeness."[3] It is easy to make something, for one can
make what he will, but whatever I make, I, myself, make it—of
myself—and I put my own idea into it. "We will make a likeness"—
not of you, the Father, nor of you, the Son, nor of you, the Holy
Spirit—but *we*, in the council of the Holy Trinity—we will to make
a likeness.

When God made man, he put into the soul his equal, his active,
everlasting masterpiece. It was so great a work that it could not be
otherwise than the soul and the soul could not be otherwise than
the work of God. God's nature, his being, and the Godhead all depend on his work in the soul. Blessed, blessed be God that he does
work in the soul and that he loves his work! That work is love and
love is God. God loves himself and his own nature, being and Godhead, and in the love he has for himself he loves all creatures, not

as creatures but as God. The love God bears himself contains his love for the whole world.

Now I shall say what I never said before. God enjoys himself. His own inner enjoyment is such that it includes his enjoyment of all creatures not as creatures, but as God. His own inner enjoyment includes everything. Even the sun sheds its rays on everything and they are absorbed by all they fall upon and yet the sun does not lose its radiant power. If I take a beaker of water and lay a mirror in it and put it in the sunshine, the sun will radiate from the bottom of the beaker as well as from its own disk and be none the weaker. Really, the reflection of the sun from the mirror is also sunshine— even though the mirror is unchanged by it. Thus, the reflection of God from the soul is also God; and still the soul, like the mirror, remains what it is.

Now notice. Every creature is on its way to the highest perfection. In all, there is a movement from life toward Being. They all reach up to my understanding as if to get understanding through me. I alone prepare creatures to return to God—but be very careful how you take this—I beseech you to understand this in terms of eternal truth, the ever-receding truth, and by my soul. So I shall say something further that I have never said before.

God and the Godhead are as different from each other as heaven and earth; but let me go further. The inner and the outer man are also as different as heaven and earth—but God is many thousand miles above both! God waxes and wanes.[4] . . . Now I shall return to my argument that God enjoys himself in everything. I look at the lilies of the field with their sheens and colors and leaves but I do not see their fragrance. Why? Because their fragrance is in me. Similarly, what I am now declaring is in me and I express it to you. To my outer man, creatures taste like creatures, as do wine, bread, and meat. To my inner man, however, they taste like gifts of God rather than creatures, and to my inmost being, they are not like gifts of God but like forever and evermore![5]

God *becomes* as phenomena express him. When I existed in the core, the soil, the river, the source of the Godhead, no one asked me where I was going or what I was doing. There was no one there to ask me, but the moment I emerged, the world of creatures began to shout:

"God!" If someone were to ask me: "Brother Eckhart, when did you leave home?"—that would indicate that I must have been at home sometime. I was there just now. Thus creatures speak of God— but why do they not mention the Godhead? Because there is only unity in the Godhead and there is nothing to talk about. God acts. The Godhead does not. It has nothing to do and there is nothing going on in it. It never is on the lookout for something to do. The difference between God and the Godhead is the difference between action and nonaction.[6]

When I return to God, I shall be without form and thus my re-entry will be far more exalted than my setting out. I alone lift creatures out of their separate principles into my own, so that in me they are one. When I return to the core, the soil, the river, the source which is the Godhead, no one will ask me whence I came or where I have been. No one will have missed me—for even God passes away!

If anyone has understood this sermon, I wish him well! If no one had come to listen, I should have had to preach it to the offering box. There are, however, certain poor people who will return home and say: "[Henceforth] I shall stay in my own place and eat my own bread and serve God in peace." I say, by the eternal truth, that these people will have to remain in their errors, for they will never attain what those attain who follow after God in poverty and exile! Amen.

28

Blessed are the poor![1]

BEATI PAUPERES SPIRITU, QUIA IPSORUM EST REGNUM COELORUM.

(Matthew 5:3)

BLESSEDNESS opened the mouth that spake wisdom and said: "Blessed are the poor in spirit, for theirs is the kingdom of heaven." All the angels and all the saints and all that were ever born must keep silence when the eternal wisdom of the Father speaks; for all the wisdom of angels and creatures is pure nothing, before the bottomless wisdom of God. And this wisdom has spoken and said that the poor are blessed.

Now, there are two kinds of poverty. One is external poverty and it is good, and much to be praised in people who take it upon themselves willingly, for the love of our Lord Jesus Christ, for he himself practiced it in the earthly realm. Of this poverty I shall say nothing more, for there is still another kind of poverty, an inward poverty, with reference to which, this saying of our Lord is to be understood: "Blessed are the poor in spirit, or of spirit."

Now, I pray you that you may be like this, so that you may understand this address; for, by the eternal truth, I tell you that if you haven't this truth of which we are speaking in yourselves, you cannot understand me.

Certain people have asked me what this poverty is. Let us answer that.

Bishop Albert says: "To be poor is to take no pleasure in anything God ever created," and that is well said. But we shall say it better and take "poverty" in a higher sense. He is a poor man who wants nothing, knows nothing, and has nothing. I shall speak of these three points.

In the first place, let us say that he is a poor man who wants nothing. Some people do not understand very well what this means. They

227

are people who continue very properly in their penances and external practices of piety (popularly considered of great importance— may God pardon it!) and still they know very little of the divine truth. To all outward appearances, these people are to be called holy, but inwardly they are asses, for they understand not at all the true meaning of the divine reality. They say well that to be poor is to want nothing, but they mean by that, living so that one never gets his own way in anything, but rather so disposes himself as to follow the all-loving will of God. These persons do no evil in this, for they mean well, and we should praise them for that—may God keep them in his mercy!

I tell you the real truth, that these people are not poor, nor are they even like poor people. They pass for great in the eyes of people who know no better. Yet I say that they are asses, who understand the truth of the divine not at all. For their good intentions they may possibly receive the Kingdom of Heaven, but of this poverty, of which I shall now speak, they have no idea.

If I were asked, then, what it is to be a poor man who wants nothing, I should answer and say: As long as a person keeps his own will, and thinks it his will to fulfill the all-loving will of God, he has not that poverty of which we are talking, for this person has a will with which he wants to satisfy the will of God, and that is not right. For if one wants to be truly poor, he must be as free from his creature will as when he had not yet been born. For, by the everlasting truth, as long as you will do God's will, and yearn for eternity and God, you are not really poor; for he is poor who wills nothing, knows nothing, and wants nothing.

Back in the Womb[2] from which I came, I had no god[3] and merely was, myself. I did not will or desire anything, for I was pure being, a knower of myself by divine truth. Then I wanted myself and nothing else. And what I wanted, I was and what I was, I wanted, and thus, I existed untrammeled by god or anything else. But when I parted from my free will and received my created being, then I had a god. For before there were creatures, God was not god, but, rather, he was what he was. When creatures came to be and took on creaturely being, then God was no longer God as he is in himself, but god as he is with creatures.

Now we say that God, in so far as he is only god, is not the highest goal of creation, nor is his fullness of being as great as that of the least of creatures, themselves in God. And if a flea could have the intelligence by which to search the eternal abyss of divine being, out of which it came, we should say that god, together with all that god is, could not give fulfillment or satisfaction to the flea! Therefore, we pray that we may be rid of god, and taking the truth, break into eternity, where the highest angels and souls too, are like what I was in my primal existence, when I wanted what I was, and was what I wanted. Accordingly, a person ought to be poor in will, willing as little and wanting as little as when he did not exist. This is how a person is poor, who wills nothing.

Again, he is poor who knows nothing. We have sometimes said that man ought to live as if he did not live, neither for self, nor for the truth, nor for God. But to that point, we shall say something else and go further. The man who is to achieve this poverty shall live as having what was his when he did not live at all, neither his own, nor the truth, nor god. More: he shall be quit and empty of all knowledge, so that no knowledge of god exists in him; for when a man's existence is of God's eternal species, there is no other life in him: his life is himself. Therefore we say that a man ought to be empty of his own knowledge, as he was when he did not exist, and let God achieve what he will and be as untrammeled by humanness as he was when he came from God.

Now the question is raised: In what does happiness consist most of all? Certain authorities have said that it consists in loving. Others say that it consists in knowing and loving, and this is a better statement. But we say that it consists neither in knowledge nor in love, but in that there is something in the soul, from which both knowledge and love flow[4] and which, like the agents of the soul, neither knows nor loves. To know this is to know what blessedness depends on. This something has no "before" or "after" and it waits for nothing that is yet to come, for it has nothing to gain or lose. Thus, when God acts in it, it is deprived of knowing that he has done so. What is more, it is the same kind of thing that, like God, can enjoy itself. Thus I say that man should be so disinterested and untrammeled that he does not know what God is doing in him. Thus only can a person possess that poverty.

The authorities say that God is a being, an intelligent being who knows everything. But I say that God is neither a being nor intelligent and he does not "know" either this or that. God is free of everything and therefore he is everything. He, then, who is to be poor in spirit must be poor of all his own knowledge, so that he knows nothing of God, or creatures, or of himself. This is not to say that one may not desire to know and to see the way of God, but it *is* to say that he may thus be poor in his own knowledge.[5]

In the third place, he is poor who has nothing. Many people have said that this is the consummation, that one should possess none of the corporeal goods of this world, and this may well be true in case one thus becomes poor voluntarily. But this is not what I mean.

Thus far I have said that he is poor who does not want to fulfill the will of god but who so lives that he is empty of his own will and the will of god, as much so as when he did not yet exist. We have said of this poverty that it is the highest poverty. Next, we said that he is poor who knows nothing of the action of god in himself. When a person is as empty of "knowledge" and "awareness" as God is innocent of all things, this is the purest poverty. But the third poverty is most inward and real and I shall now speak of it. It consists in that a man *has* nothing.

Now pay earnest attention to this! I have often said, and great authorities agree, that to be a proper abode for God and fit for God to act in, a man should also be free from all [his own] things and [his own] actions, both inwardly and outwardly. Now we shall say something else. If it is the case that a man is emptied of things, creatures, himself and god, and if still god could find a place in him to act, then we say: as long as that [place] exists, this man is not poor with the most intimate poverty. For God does not intend that man shall have a place reserved for *him* to work in, since true poverty of spirit requires that man shall be emptied of god and all his works, so that if God wants to act in the soul, he himself must be the place in which he acts—and that he would like to do. For if God once found a person as poor as this, he would take the responsibility of his own action and would himself be the *scene* of action, for God is one who acts within himself. It is here, in this poverty, that man regains the eternal being that once he was, now is, and evermore shall be.

There is the question of the words of St. Paul:[6] "All that I am, I am by the grace of God," but our argument soars above grace, above intelligence, and above all desire. (How is it to be connected with what St. Paul says?) It is to be replied that what St. Paul says is true, not that this grace was in him, but the grace of God had produced in him a simple perfection of being and then the work of grace was done. When, then, grace had finished its work, Paul remained as he was.

Thus we say that a man should be so poor that he is not and has not a place for God to act in. To reserve a place would be to maintain distinctions. *Therefore I pray God that he may quit me of god,* for [his] unconditioned being is above god and all distinctions. It was here [in unconditioned being] that I was myself, wanted myself, and knew myself to be this person [here before you], and therefore, I am my own first cause, both of my eternal being and of my temporal being. To this end I was born, and by virtue of my birth being eternal, I shall never die. It is of the nature of this eternal birth that I *have been* eternally, that I *am* now, and *shall be* forever. What I am as a temporal creature is to die and come to nothingness, for it came with time and so with time it will pass away. In my eternal birth, however, everything was begotten. I was my own first cause as well as the first cause of everything else. If I had willed it, neither I nor the world would have come to be! If I had not been, there would have been no god. There is, however, no need to understand this.

A great authority[7] says: "His bursting forth is nobler than his efflux." When I flowed forth from God, creatures said: "He is a god!" This, however, did not make me blessed, for it indicates that I, too, am a creature. In bursting forth, however, when I shall be free within God's will and free, therefore of the will of god, and all his works, and even of god himself, then I shall rise above all creature kind, and I shall be neither god nor creature, but I shall be what I was once, now, and forevermore. I shall thus receive an impulse which shall raise me above the angels. With this impulse, I receive wealth so great that I could never again be satisfied with a god, or anything that is a god's, nor with any divine activities, for in bursting forth I discover that God and I are One. Now I am what I was and I neither add to nor subtract from anything, for I am the unmoved Mover, that moves all things. Here, then, a god may find no "place" in man, for by his poverty the man achieves the being that was always his and shall remain his eternally. Here, too, God is identical with the spirit and that is the most intimate poverty discoverable.

If anyone does not understand this discourse, let him not worry about that, for if he does not find this truth in himself he cannot understand what I have said—for it is a discovered truth[8] which comes immediately from the heart of God. That we all may so live as to experience it eternally, may God help us! Amen.

Fragments

1

Our Lord said to Zacchaeus: "Make haste and come down; for today I must abide at thy house." If anyone wants to see Jesus, he must outstrip the world of things; but if one does not get beyond the world of things, what does that mean? It means that one has never tasted God, for if he had, he would make haste to excel the world, to burst through creatures. One bursts through creatures when he lets go of things he has loved.

That we are not able to see God is due to the faintness of desire and the throng of things. To desire high things is to be high. To see God, one must desire high: know that earnest desire and deep humility work wonders. I say that God can do anything, but he cannot deny anything to the person who is humble and yet has high desires and so, if I cannot compel God to do what I want him to do, then I fail either in humility or in desire. I swear it, for I am certain that a man who wanted to do so, might one day be able to walk through a wall of steel, or do, as we read of St. Peter, that when he laid eyes on Jesus, he walked on water in his eagerness to meet him.

Now I say that a vessel that grows as it is filled will never be full. If a bin able to hold a cartload grew while you were dumping your load in it, you could never fill it. The soul is like that: the more it wants the more it is given; the more it receives the more it grows.

Who is Jesus? He has no name.

2

Meister Eckhart said in a sermon: God's divinity comes of my humility, and this may be demonstrated as follows. It is God's peculiar property to give; but he cannot give unless something is prepared to receive his gifts. If, then, I prepare by my humility to receive what he gives, by my humility I make God a giver. Since it is his nature to give, I am merely giving God what is already his own. It is like a rich man who wants to be a giver but must first find a taker, since without a taker he cannot be a giver; for the taker, in taking, makes the rich man a giver. Similarly, if God is to be a giver, he must first find a taker, but no one may be a taker of God's gifts except by his humility. Therefore, if God is to exercise his divine property by his gifts, he well may need my humility; for apart from humility he can give me nothing—without it I am not prepared to receive his gift. That is why it is true that by humility I give divinity to God.

3

Meister Eckhart also said: Humility exalts God and the more I have it, the more he is exalted and the more gently and sweetly his divine influence and gifts flow into me.

That God is exalted by humility, I argue thus: The more I abase myself, the higher God rises above me. Humility is like a well. The deeper the well the higher he will stand who stands on the top. Similarly, the deeper I dig down into humility the more exalted God becomes and the more gently and sweetly his divine influence pours into me. That is why I must exalt God by humility.

4

Meister Eckhart said: We should contrive not to need to pray to God, asking for his grace and divine goodness . . . but take it without asking. . . .

5

The question has been raised as to whether it is possible to make the senses obey the mind.

Meister Eckhart answered it by saying: If the mind is fixed on

God and continues so, the senses will obey it. It is like hanging a
needle on a magnet and then another needle onto that, and so on.
It might even be possible to suspend four needles from the magnet in
this way. As long as the first needle hangs onto the magnet, the rest
will hang onto it, but if the first drops off, it will lose the rest. And
so, as long as the mind is firmly fixed on God, the senses will obey
it but when the mind drops away from God, the senses drop off
from the mind and are unruly.

6

I MUCH prefer a person who can love God enough to take a handout
of bread, to a person who can give a hundred dollars for God's sake.
How do I explain that? Like this. It is the common opinion of all
authorities that honor is worth more than any fleeting good. To
give a hundred dollars for God's sake is therefore to make a big
profit in honor and glory on the money; for the giver, offering the
money with one hand, takes in more and better than he gave with
the other; but when the poor man extends his hand to beg the
bread, he trades his honor in exchange. The giver buys the honor
the receiver sells.

There is more to it than that. The poor man, by taking the handout, gets closer to God than he who gave the one hundred dollars
for God's sake. The giver is glad to be so good-natured and is proud
of it but the taker has to subdue his feelings and despise his status.
The giver is much courted for his gifts whereas the beggar is despised and rejected for being a taker.

7

MEISTER ECKHART said: The person whose attitude varies from one
thing to another, to whom God is dearer in one form than another,
is crude, uninstructed, and a child. To see God evenly in everything
is to be a man; but that person has really arrived to whom all creatures are merely bypaths to exile.

He was also asked if a person who denies himself need care at all
what happens otherwise. He replied: God's yoke is easy and his

burden is light. He asks of us only the willingness. What comes hard to the apprentice is a delight to the master. The Kingdom of God is for none but those who are thoroughly dead [to the world].

8

MEISTER ECKHART said: I shall never pray that God give me himself. I shall pray that he make me pure; for if I am pure, God must give himself and dwell in me, because it is his peculiar nature to do so.

9

MEISTER ECKHART spoke this way: One person who has mastered life is better than a thousand persons who have mastered only the contents of books, but no one can get anything out of life without God. If I were looking for a master of learning, I should go to Paris to the colleges where the higher studies are pursued, but if I wanted to know about the perfection of life, they could not tell me there.

Where, then, should I go? To [someone who has] a nature that is pure and free and nowhere else: there I should find the answer for which I so anxiously inquire. People, why do you search among the dead bones? Why don't you look for life eternal in life's holy places? The dead can neither give nor take. If an angel had to seek God without God, he would look for him in a pure, free, disinterested creature and nowhere else. Perfection depends only on accepting poverty, misery, hardship, disappointment, and whatever comes in course, and accepting it willingly, gladly, freely, eagerly until death, as if one were prepared for it and therefore unmoved by it and not asking why.

10

MEISTER ECKHART said in a sermon, when asked what the birth of God is: The birth of God in the soul is simply God revealing himself in some new bit of knowledge which has taken a new form.

Again he was asked if the soul's highest blessedness came with the spiritual birth of God in man. He replied: Even though God gets more pleasure from this act than any other thing he does to any creature in heaven or on earth, the soul is more blessed when it is reborn into him. The soul is not blessed perfectly when God is born in it but rather when, with love and praise, it follows the revelation of God back to the source from whence it came, their common origin, letting go of its own things and cleaving to his, so that the soul is blessed by God's things and not its own.

11

MEISTER ECKHART says: The Holy Scriptures shout that man should be free from self, for being freed from self, you are self-controlled, and as you are self-controlled you are self-possessed, and as you are self-possessed you possess God and all creation. I tell you the truth, as sure as God is God and I am man, if you could be freed from self —as free as you are of the highest angels—then you would have the nature of the highest angels as completely as you now have your own. By this discipline, man becomes master of himself.

12

MEISTER ECKHART said: Grace comes only with the Holy Spirit. It carries the Holy Spirit on its back. Grace is not a stationary thing; it is always found in a Becoming. It can only flow out of God and then only immediately. The function of grace is to transform and reconvey [the soul] to God. Grace makes the soul godlike. God, the core of the soul, and grace belong together.

13

MEISTER ECKHART said: To go down to death with love and knowledge makes death nobler and more precious than all the good works done of love and desire in holy Christendom from the beginning until now or all the good works that shall be done until the Last Day. Good works only serve to bring death, but from this death [in love and knowledge] life eternal springs up.

14

MEISTER ECKHART said that no person in this life may reach the point at which he can be excused from outward service. Even if he is given to a life of contemplation, still he cannot refrain from going out and taking an active part in life. Even as a person who has nothing at all may still be generous for his will to give, another may have great wealth and not be generous because he gives nothing; so no man may have virtues without using them as time and occasion require. Thus, those who are given to the life of contemplation and avoid activities deceive themselves and are on the wrong track. I say that the contemplative person should indeed avoid even the thought of deeds to be done during the period of his contemplation but afterwards he should get busy, for no one can or should engage in contemplation all the time, for active life is to be a respite from contemplation.

15

THE question was raised as to whether prayer is improved by repeated utterance. Meister Eckhart replied: The outward practice of prayer adds little virtue or none at all to prayer itself.

Prayer is good by reason of its own quality. Anything which is good because there is a lot of it has not much intrinsic worth. For example, a penny is worth little by itself, but a thousand dollars' worth of them would be considerable, simply because of the great number of pennies. Thus a penny has no great worth except in numbers. So it is with religious exercises. Repetition adds little to the value of prayer. One Ave Maria uttered sincerely is more potent and better than a thousand uttered mechanically.

Incidentally, it should be noted that no virtue depends on repetition. A virtue is just as fine and good in the least of deeds rightly done as in a thousand repetitions. Virtue does not gather merit by multiplication, for if it could, it would have small intrinsic worth. Whatever is good is good of itself and not because of many repetitions. Virtue rightly appears in the virtuous doing of the deed. No one is to be called virtuous because he does virtuous things; he alone is virtuous who acts with virtue in his heart.

To give alms for God's sake, but with reluctance and not with a glad heart, is to do a deed of virtue which has no virtue in it. So it is with prayer and all the pieties; they have virtue if done rightly but not otherwise. Apply this principle to patience. Physical suffering does not make one patient but it does tell whether or not a person is patient, just as fire will show whether a coin is made of silver or of copper. A patient person would be patient even if he never suffered. So with prayer. Having a pure heart turned toward God, even if he never prayed aloud, a man would be all right; for the heart is not made pure by prayer as a physical act, but rather the prayer is made pure by the pure heart.

16

MEISTER ECKHART asked why people are so reluctant to seek God in earnest. Then he made this comment: When one is looking for something and sees no sign that it is where he is searching, he will keep on looking there only with painful reluctance. If, however, he begins to find traces of it, then he will hunt gladly, gaily, and in earnest. The man who wants fire is cheered by feeling warmth and then joyously looks for the blaze. It is like that with people who ought to be seeking God: if they get no taste of the divine sweetness, they drag; but if a man lies in wait until he does catch the taste of the divine, ever afterwards he is a glad seeker of God.

17

EARTH cannot get away from heaven: let the earth drop downwards or rise upwards, heaven still penetrates it, embuing it with strength and making it fruitful, whether it will or no. That is how God treats man: when he thinks to escape God, he runs into God's bosom, for every hideout is open to him. God begets his Son in you whether you like it or not, whether you sleep or wake—still God is at work. That man is not aware of it is the fault of his [spiritual] tongue, which is smeared with the scum of creatures, in which there is none

of the salt of God's love. If we had God's love in us, we could taste
God in all his works and we would accept anything as from God
and finish his work along with him. In sameness [of intent] we are
his only begotten Son.

18

WHAT is truth? Truth is something so noble that if God could turn
aside from it, I could keep to the truth and let God go.

19

MEISTER ECKHART, the preacher, also said this: There never was a
struggle or a battle which required greater valor than that in which
a man forgets or denies himself.

20

I HAVE often said that a person who wishes to begin a good life
should be like a man who draws a circle. Let him get the center in
the right place and keep it so and the circumference will be good.
In other words, let a man first learn to fix his heart on God and then
his good deeds will have virtue; but if a man's heart is unsteady,
even the great things he does will be of small advantage.

21

MEISTER ECKHART asks: Who is the man whose prayers God always
hears? He answers: God hears the man who appeals to God as God.
When, however, man appeals to God, hoping for some worldly
good, he is not appealing to God at all, but to what he is asking
God for. He is trying to make God his servant. On this point, St.
Augustine says: "You pray to what you love, for true, whole prayer
is nothing but love!" Thus we pray to what we love and no one
rightly prays to God but he who prays for God and has nothing on
his mind but God.

22

SOME people want to see God with their eyes as they see a cow and to love him as they love their cow—they love their cow for the milk and cheese and profit it makes them. This is how it is with people who love God for the sake of outward wealth or inward comfort. They do not rightly love God when they love him for their own advantage. Indeed, I tell you the truth, any object you have on your mind, however good, will be a barrier between you and the inmost truth.

23

THE just man loves God for nothing, neither for this nor for that, and if God gave him wisdom or anything else he had to give, except himself, the just man would not look at it, nor would it be to his taste; for he wants nothing, seeks nothing, and has no reason for doing anything. As God, having no motives, acts without them, so the just man acts without motives. As life lives on for its own sake, needing no reason for being, so the just man has no reason for doing what he does.

24

I HAVE sometimes said that if a man goes seeking God and, with God, something else, he will not find God; but if one seeks only God—and really so—he will never find only God but along with God himself he will find all that God is capable of. If you seek your own advantage or blessing through God you are not really seeking God at all. Thus Christ says: "True worshipers shall worship the Father"—and that is well said.

If you ask a good man: "Why are you seeking God?"—he will reply: "Just because he *is* God!"

"Why are you seeking truth?"

"Just because it *is* truth!"

"Why are you seeking justice?"

"Just because it is justice!" And such people are quite right. For everything in time has a reason. For example, ask any man: "Why are you eating?" You will get the reply: "For strength." "Why do you sleep?" "For the same reason." And so it is with everything temporal.

If, however, you ask a good man: "Why do you love God?"— you will be answered: "I don't know—because he *is* God!"

"Why do you love truth?"

"For truth's sake."

"Why do you love justice?"

"For the sake of justice!"

"Why do you love goodness?"

"For goodness' sake!"

"And why do you live?"

"On my honor, I don't know—I like to live!"

25

THE will cannot be content. It does not want God as he is the Holy Spirit or as he is the Son—it flies from the Son. It does not want God as he is god. Why? Because he has a name; and if there were a thousand gods, it would penetrate them all to get into him who has no name. The will wants something of higher degree, something better than God as he is namable. What, then, does it want? It doesn't know. It wants him as he is its Father. Thus St. Philip said: "Lord, show us the Father and it sufficeth us."

26

THE heavenly Father utters a Word and utters it eternally; and in that Word he expends all his power, expressing his divine nature and all creatures. That Word lies hidden in the soul, so that man neither knows nor hears it—unless good tidings reach the center of hearing—otherwise it will not be heard of. To hear it, all voices and sounds must die away and there must be pure quiet—perfect stillness.

27

SPEAKING of knowledge and love: knowledge is better than love but the two together are better than one of them, for knowledge really contains love. Love may be fooled by goodness, depending on it, so that when I love I hang on the gate, blind to the truth about my acquaintance. Even a stone has love—for the ground! If I depend on goodness, which is God's first proffer, and accept God only as he is good to me, I am content with the gate but I do not get to God. Thus knowledge is better, for it leads love. Love has to do with desire and purpose, whereas knowledge is no particular thought, but rather, it peels off all [coverings] and is disinterested and runs naked to God, until it touches him and grasps him.

28

WHEN I pray, I often speak like this: "Lord, these are such little things for which we pray. If someone were to ask them of me, I could do them as well. But you are a hundred times more able than I and even more willing to do, so that if we asked you for something greater, you could still give it—and the more willingly, the greater what we ask for is."—For God is ready to give great things when we are ready, for righteousness' sake, to give up everything.

29

IN LIMPID souls God beholds his own image; he rests in them and they in him.

As I have often said, I like best those things in which I see most clearly the likeness of God. Nothing in all creation is so like God as stillness.

30

IT IS God's nature to be without a nature. To think of his goodness, or wisdom, or power is to hide the essence of him, to obscure it with thoughts about him. Even one single thought or consideration will cover it up. Such is the divine order of things, and when God finds this order in a soul he begets his Son, and the soul bursts into light with all its energy and from that energy, that light, there leaps a flame. That is love; and the soul, with all its energy, has penetrated to the divine order.

31

IF IT is true that God became man, it is also true that man became God . . . and so . . . you haven't got to borrow from God, for he is your own and therefore, whatever you get, you get from yourself. Before God, work that does not come from your [inmost] self is dead. . . . If a man's work is to live, it must come from the depths of him—not from alien sources outside himself—but from within.

32

GOD is love . . . and out of love he gives existence and life to every creature, supporting them all with his love. The color of the wall depends on the wall, and so the existence of creatures depends on the love of God. Separate the color from the wall and it would cease to be; so all creation would cease to exist if separated from the love that God is. God is love, so loving that whatever he can love he must love, whether he will or not. There is no creature so vile that it can love what is evil; for what one loves must either be good or appear to be so.

33

IF GOD should give my soul all he ever made or might make, apart from himself, and giving it, he stayed away even by as much as a hairbreadth, my soul would not be satisfied, for I would not be blessed. If I am blessed, the whole world is mine and God too, and where I am there is God, and where God is there I am.

34

WHEN I pray for something, I do not pray; when I pray for nothing, I really pray. . . . To pray for anything except God might be called idolatry or injustice. Right prayer is prayer in spirit and in truth. When I pray for some person such as Henry or Conrad, I pray least, but when I pray for no one in particular, I pray most of all. Really to pray, one must want nothing, for as far as God is concerned there is neither Henry nor Conrad. When one prays for what God is not, there is something wrong and faithless about the prayer and it is a sign of immaturity. As I said not long ago, when one puts something before God, he makes God nothing, and nothing, God.

35

I TELL you that the soul knows the eternal Word better than any philosopher can describe it. What anyone can set forth with words is far too little—less than the soul learns in one lesson from the eternal Word. Thus the authorities say we shall do well to hurry to that school in which the Holy Spirit is the lecturer; but I tell you that when the Holy Spirit is the teacher, his students must be well prepared if they are to understand his excellent teaching—which proceeds out of the Father's heart.

36

WHEN God laughs at the soul and the soul laughs back at God, the persons of the Trinity are begotten. To speak in hyperbole, when the Father laughs to the Son and the Son laughs back to the Father, that laughter gives pleasure, that pleasure gives joy, that joy gives love, and love gives the persons [of the Trinity] of which the Holy Spirit is one.

37

To GET at the core of God at his greatest, one must first get into
the core of himself at his least, for no one can know God who has
not first known himself. Go to the depths of the soul, the secret
place of the Most High, to the roots, to the heights; for all that
God can do is focused there.

38

THE just man lives in God and God in him, for God is born in him
and he in God. With each virtue of the just person, God is born and
made glad, and not only with each virtue, but with each deed, however trifling, done out of virtue and justice, and resulting in justice,
God is made glad—glad through and through!—so that there is
nothing in the core of the Godhead that does not dance for joy!
Ordinary persons can only believe this; but the enlightened know it.

39

I HAVE spoken at times of a light in the soul that is uncreated, a
light that is not arbitrarily turned on. I am accustomed to hint at it
frequently in my sermons, for it refers to the immediacy of God, as
undisguised and naked as he is by himself and to the [divine] act of
begetting. Thus I may truthfully say that this light is rather to be
identified with God than with any [perceptive] power of the soul,
even though it is essentially the same. You must know that within
my psyche this light takes no precedence over the least and coarsest
of my faculties, such as hearing, or vision, or any other that can be
influenced by heat or cold, hunger or thirst. This is due to the essential uniformity of the soul. Thus, if one refers the soul's agents back
to the soul's essence, the agents are alike and of equal rank, but if
the agents are referred to their functions, then some do rank above
the others.

Therefore, I say that to the extent a person can deny himself and
turn away from created things, he will find his unity and blessing in

that little spark in the soul, which neither space nor time touches. The spark is averse to creatures, and favorable only to pure God as he is in himself. It is not satisfied with the Father, nor the Son, nor the Holy Spirit, nor with all three persons together, as long as their several properties are preserved. To tell the truth, this light is not satisfied with the unity of this fruitful conception of the divine nature, but I shall go further and say what must sound strange —though I am really speaking the truth—that this light is not satisfied by the simple, still, motionless essence of the divine being that neither gives nor takes. It is more interested in knowing where this essence came from. It wants to penetrate the simple core, the still desert, into which no distinction ever crept—neither the Father, the Son, nor the Holy Spirit. It wants to get into the secret, to which no man is privy, where it is satisfied by a Light whose unity is greater than its own. This core is a simple stillness, which is unmoved itself but by whose immobility all things are moved and all receive life, that is to say, all people who live by reason and have their center within themselves. That we, too, may live so intelligently, may God help us. Amen.

40

WHEN the soul so lives in its own secret place that it is the image of God, then it has true unity that no creature can divide. God, the angels, and creatures to the contrary notwithstanding, nothing can separate this soul from the image of God. This is true unity, and true blessedness depends on it.

41

THE divine One is a negation of negations and a desire of desires. What does "One" mean? Something to which nothing is to be added. The soul lays hold of the Godhead where it is pure, where there is nothing beside it, nothing else to consider. The One is a negation of negations. Every creature contains a negation: one denies that it is the other. An angel denies that it is any other creature; but God contains the denial of denials. He is that One who denies of every *other* that it is anything except himself. (See note to this fragment.)

42

St. Paul says: "Be renewed in the spirit." If we are to be renewed in the spirit . . . the six higher and lower agents of the soul each must have a wedding ring covered with the gold of divine love. . . . The three lower agents of the soul . . . are: (1) *rationale*, reason . . . which must wear the wedding ring of light . . . (2) *irascibilis*, irascibility, which wears the wedding ring of peace . . . and (3) *concupiscibilis*, desire, which wears the wedding ring of content.

The three higher agents of the soul are (4) *memoria*, memory, on which you shall wear the golden ring of retention . . . (5) *intellectus*, intelligence which wears the ring of perception . . . and (6) *voluntas*, will, on which you are to wear the wedding ring of Love, so that you may love God.

Love God whether *he* is loving or not, and certainly not *because* he is loving, for he is nonloving, being above love and affection.

How, then, shall I love him? You are to love God aspiritually, that is, your soul shall be aspiritual, devoid of ghostlikeness, for as long as the soul is ghostlike it is a [mental] image and, being imagelike, it will lack both unity and the power to unite. Thus, it could not love God rightly, for true love is union. Your soul ought to be deghosted, void of ghosts, and be kept so. For if you love God as a god, a ghost, a person, or as if he were something with a form—you must get rid of all that.

How, then, shall I love him? Love him as he is, a not-god, a not-ghost, apersonal, formless. Love him as he is the One, pure, sheer, and limpid, in whom there is no duality; for we are to sink eternally from negation to negation in the One. May God help us to do it. Amen.

43

Our Lord cannot endure that any who love him should be worried, for fear is painful. Thus St. John says: "Love casteth out fear." Love cannot put up with either fear or pain, and so, to grow in love is to diminish in fear, and when one has become a perfect lover, fear has gone out of him altogether.

At the beginning of a good life, however, fear is useful. It is love's gateway. A punch or an awl makes a hole for the thread with which a shoe is sewed . . . and a bristle is put on the thread to get it through the hole, but when the thread does bind the shoe together, the bristle is out. So fear leads love at first and when love has bound us to God, fear is done away.

44

Envoi

MEISTER ECKHART's good friends bade him: "Since you are going to leave us, give us one last word."

"I will give you," he replied, "a rule which is the stronghold of all I have ever said, in which are lodged all the truths to be discussed or put into practice."

It often happens that what seems trivial to us is more important to God than what we think important. Therefore, we ought to take everything God puts on us evenly, not comparing and wondering which is more important, or higher, or best. We ought simply to follow where God leads, that is, to do what we are most inclined to do, to go where we are repeatedly admonished to go—to where we feel most drawn. If we do that, God gives us his greatest in our least and never fails.

Now, some people despise the little things of life. It is their mistake, for they thus prevent themselves from getting God's greatness out of these little things. God is every way, evenly in all ways, to him who has the eyes to see. But sometimes it is hard to know whether one's inclinations come from God or not, but that can be decided this way: If you find yourself always possessed of a knowledge or intimation of God's will, which you obey before everything else, because you feel urged to obey it and the urge is frequent, then you may know that it is from God.

Some people want to recognize God only in some pleasant enlightenment—and then they get pleasure and enlightenment but not

God. Somewhere it is written that God shines in the darkness where every now and then we get a glimpse of him. More often, God is where his light is least apparent. Therefore we ought to expect God in all manners and all things evenly.

Someone may now say: I should be glad to look for God evenly in all shapes and things, but my mind does not always work the same way—and then, not as well with this as with that. To which I reply: That is too bad! All paths lead to God and he is on them all evenly, to him who knows. I am well aware that a person may get more out of one technique than another but it is not best so. God responds to all techniques evenly to a knowing man. Such and such may be the way, but it is not God.

But even if God is in all ways and all things evenly, do I not still need a special way to get to him? Let us see. Whatever the way that leads you most frequently to awareness of God, follow that way; and if another way appears, different from the first, and you quit the first and take the second, and the second works, it is all right. It would be nobler and better, however, to achieve rest and security through evenness, by which one might take God and enjoy him in any manner, in any thing, and not have to delay and hunt around for your special way: *that has been my joy!* To this end all kinds of activities may contribute and any work may be a help; but if it does not, let it go!

Legends

MEISTER ECKHART met a beautiful naked boy.
  He asked him where he came from.
  He said: "I come from God."
  Where did you leave him?
  "In virtuous hearts."
  Where are you going?
  "To God."
  Where do you find him?
  "Where I part with all creatures."
  Who are you?
  "A king."
  Where is your kingdom?
  "In my heart."
  Take care that no one divide it with you!
  "I shall."
  Then he led him to his cell.
  Take whichever coat you will.
  "Then I should be no king!"
  And he disappeared.
  For it was God himself—
  Who was having a bit of fun.

2

MEISTER ECKHART spoke to a poor man.
  God give you good morning, brother!
  "The same to you, sir, but I have never yet had a bad one."
  How is that, brother?

"Because whatever God has sent me, I have borne gladly for his sake, considering myself unworthy of him. That is why I have never been sad or troubled."

Where did you first find God?

"When I left all creatures, then I found God."

Where, then, did you leave him, brother?

"In any clear, pure heart."

Who are you, brother?

"I am a king."

Of what?

"Of my flesh: whatever my spirit wants from God, my flesh is more eager and ready to take than my spirit is."

A king must have a kingdom. Where is yours, brother?

"In my soul."

How so?

"When I have shut the doors of my five senses, earnestly desiring God, I find him in my soul as clearly and as joyful as he is in eternity."

You could be holy! What made you so, brother?

"Meditation, high thinking, and union with God have drawn me to heaven; for I never could be content with anything less than God. Now I have found him and I am eternally content and happy in him and that is worth more than any kingdom, as long as we continue in time. No pious practice is so perfect that it may not be an obstacle to spirituality."

3

A DAUGHTER came to the preaching cloister and asked for Meister Eckhart. The doorman asked:

"Whom shall I announce?"

"I don't know," she said.

"Why don't you know?"

"Because I am neither a girl, nor a woman, nor a husband, nor a wife, nor a widow, nor a virgin, nor a master, nor a maid, nor a servant."

The doorman went to Meister Eckhart and said:

"Come out here and see the strangest creature you ever heard of.

Let me go with you, and you stick your head out and ask: 'Who wants me?'"

Meister Eckhart did so and she gave him the same reply she had made to the doorman. Then he said:

"My dear child, what you say is right and sensible but explain to me what you mean." She said:

"If I were a girl, I should be still in my first innocence; if I were a woman, I should always be giving birth in my soul to the eternal word; if I were a husband, I should put up a stiff resistance to all evil; if I were a wife, I should keep faith with my dear one, whom I married; if I were a widow, I should be always longing for the one I loved; if I were a virgin, I should be reverently devout; if I were a servant-maid, in humility I should count myself lower than God or any creature; and if I were a manservant, I should be hard at work, always serving my Lord with my whole heart. But since of all these, I am neither one, I am just a something among somethings, and so I go."

Then Meister Eckhart went in and said to his pupils: "It seems to me that I have just listened to the purest person I have ever known."

This example is entitled "Meister Eckhart's daughter."

4

A PRIEST once said to Meister Eckhart: "I wish that your soul were in my body." To which he replied:

"You would really be foolish. That would get nowhere—it would accomplish as little as for your soul to be in my body. No soul can really do anything except through the body to which it is attached."

5

IT HAPPENED in Meister Eckhart's time that a great priest—great not only in learning, but in life—said to him:

"Dear master and father, if you won't take it ill of me, out of divine love, I would like to talk something over with you."

To which he replied in the friendliest manner: "My dear sir, gladly; speak about anything you like!"

Whereupon the priest began by saying: "You know that I have heard a good many of your sermons—and I have liked them—and I have not liked them."

Then Meister Eckhart said: "And now, dear sir, I beg of you for God's sake to explain what you mean—for liking them and disliking them are utterly contrary to each other."

Then the good priest said: "I tell you. What I have enjoyed hearing from you were the great, adroit ideas, which by the grace of God I could understand. But thinking them over, I have also thought of the saying, 'Cast not your pearls before swine' and your sermons have become annoying to me, and I thought: these high and subtle notions should be settled for the greater part in the universities, for —and please do not be offended by this—I have become estranged from you because you say such things openly to the common, dull people in your sermons. It seems to me that there is no use in this; you might do something better and more agreeable to God, from which our fellow countrymen could derive both instruction and improvement. Your great subtle words are of no use to a beginner who does not understand them!

"And neither are they so profitable to a growing person, to whom instruction by gradual degrees of advancement is better suited. And people who are high-minded, great, perfect, and intelligent have no need for them—and no great desire for them! For as long as they are listening to them, they may be glad to hear them; but when they cease listening and come to themselves again, introspectively, and devote themselves with a great and humble abandon to the will of the Highest, sunk deep in true humility, so drowned in God's creation that they do not know whether they are in time or beyond it: in that school, in which they sit under the Highest as schoolmaster and preacher, one may acquire in a moment more instruction and knowledge than you or any other master in the external schools could impart in a hundred years.

"Therefore, dear Meister Eckhart, to these three kinds of people —the beginners, those who are making progress, and those who are perfect—your sermons and doctrines are not delivered so very helpfully or usefully. But even though I am unworthy to give you advice, nevertheless I should like to advise you, out of divine love, and with God's help, to begin now and imitate the teaching of our Lord Jesus Christ and the method he used while he walked in this world of time. His instruction in the synagogues and the temple was to the end that people should cease their unvirtuous and sinful deeds and learn to do good things well;—learn how he drove out unvirtue and put it away, until unvirtue gave place to virtue. This kind of instruction is as much needed today as it ever was: to focus the mind of Christ on the sinful, unvirtuous life of man, to preach and demonstrate to people how they may come at an orderly, virtuous Christian life.

"Now then, dear Meister Eckhart, you speak openly in your sermons about great, transcendent matters that few people understand or can use, and they are not very fruitful. And so, Meister Eckhart, you are a great priest and master of Scripture, but now you have to begin with 'A' just as you did the first day you sat down in school; but if, on that day, someone had set a big book down before you and called on you to read from it, it would have been quite useless. You yourself had to begin with the 'A' and gradually learn more and more until you have become a master of Scripture.

"Thus it is quite necessary to teach beginners and intermediate students and set forth to them how they may begin to quit their unvirtuous lives and get hold of virtue. When, by the help of God, people have found out how to lay hold of virtue, they, too, will be masters over wrong and doubtless from within, they will be instructed by the Holy Spirit, so that they will have no need of verbal teaching—and yet—they will stay within the holy church."

When he had finished this speech, the good priest said: "Dear Meister Eckhart, I have said too much and talked too long to you, forgive me. It is time now for me to go home."

Meister Eckhart turned around to him, gave him a kiss of peace, and said: "Dear sir, I tell you that for many a year I have enjoyed hearing no discourse as much as this—which I have suddenly had to listen to from you. May God be your everlasting reward! And with divine love and Christian brotherliness, I bid you and exhort you for God's sake—as I may so exhort you—to tell me plainly about your life, as God has given it you. For by the grace of God, I plainly see that you have spoken from the core of your life."

6

BROTHER ECKHART, a Master at Cologne, told what Brother Eustace, an eminent authority on the Holy Scriptures, once saw in his sleep.

Many of the brothers of his order were standing around in a circle in the dining room of the order—like a wreath. When someone joined in, he stayed and did not leave. He stood near the others, for they were all looking at something remarkable, something pleasant, enchanting.

He wanted to know what it was all about and he joined in to see what the brothers were looking at with such joy. He saw that a most beautiful little child was standing in their midst.—It was our Lord Jesus Christ, the Son of our dear Lady, the Virgin, and it was so delightful that everyone, no matter how grave or troubled, had to laugh as soon as he became aware of the child's beauty.

The child asked the brothers standing around for bread. Brother Eustace heard him and ran to the storeroom to fetch the child some bread. When he got there, and could not find a single whole loaf of fine bread, but only fragments of white bread, he was unwilling to give them to the child. He looked and looked, and finally, he found one loaf whole, but since it was not white, he was unwilling to offer that. Then his heart was anxious and he was sorely troubled because he was not able to produce a perfect loaf of white bread to give the Christ-child.

Then Brother Rupert came along—the chamberlain—and asked what he was looking for so diligently.

Master Eustace said: "I am looking for a perfect loaf of fine white bread—one that I may give to the child—our Lord Jesus Christ."

The chamberlain replied: "Don't worry. Perhaps I can find such a loaf." And at once Brother Rupert did find the desired loaf and brought it to the child, who said:

"There are many great priests, possessed of great skills, and yet when they want to bring me something at once pure and perfect they have nothing to bring. If they have something that is pure, it is not perfect; and if they have something that is perfect, it is not pure, clear, and unsoiled. Certain uninstructed people, however, are able to bring and give me things that are at once pure and clean and perfect!''

From that time on, and since this dream, Master Eustace honored Brother Rupert and was gracious to him and held him in divine love with all his heart and mind.

The Defense

(Rechtfertigungsschrift)

(From the Latin, edition of P. Augustus Daniels, Münster, 1923)

I

IN THE year of our Lord 1326, the twenty-sixth of September, on the day appointed for response on the articles drawn from books and statements of Meister Eckhart and from sermons ascribed to him, which seem to some people to contain error, and what is worse, to smack of heresy, they say:

I, Brother Eckhart, of the order of the aforesaid, after a prefatory statement, make my response.

In the first place, I protest to you, the commissioners, Master Benherus Friso, Doctor of Theology, and Brother Peter de Estate, recently custodian of the Order of Minor Brothers, that according to the liberty and privileges of our order, I am not bound to appear before you, nor to answer charges, especially as I have not been branded as a heretic, or ever been disgraced, witness my whole life and teaching, and the approval of the Brothers of the entire order, and of people of both sexes of the entire kingdom and of every nation.

Whence it is evident, in the second place, that the commission assigned to you by the venerable Father, Lord Coloniensis,[1] archbishop (may God preserve his life), is of no force, inasmuch as it proceeds from a suggestion of falsehood, an evil, root and tree. In fact, if I were of less repute among the people, and less zealous for justice, I am sure that such attempts would not have been made against me by envious men. I must, however, bear it patiently, for *Blessed are they that do suffer patiently for justice's sake,*[2] and *God scourgeth every son whom he receiveth,*[3] so that I may justly say with the Psalmist that I am prepared for the scourge,[4] especially as sometime since, in my time, certain Masters of Theology at Paris were charged by their Superior with the examination of the books of those illustrious men, St. Thomas Aquinas and Lord Brother Albertus,[5] on the ground that they were suspected of containing errors. Against St. Thomas himself, it has often been written, said and publicly preached that he wrote and taught errors and heresies.

258

By the grace of God, however, his life and teachings alike have been approved, not only at Paris, but by the Pope himself and the Roman Curia.

After this introduction, I respond to the articles brought against me. Now the aforesaid articles, of which there are forty-nine, are divided into four parts:

First: fifteen excerpts from a certain book which I wrote, which begins *Benedictus Deus.* [6]

Second: six articles taken from a certain response of mine or from statements of mine. [7]

Third: twelve articles gathered from my first commentary on Genesis. [8] I am surprised that more objections are not made to what I wrote in various books, for it is certain that I have written a hundred things, or more, which their ignorance does not grasp or understand.

Fourth: sixteen articles taken from sermons which are ascribed to me. [9]

Now as for the first, second and third of these, I state and admit that I said them and wrote them, and I think, as will be clear from my explanation, that they are all true, although many of them are rare, difficult and subtle.

If, however, anything in the aforesaid, or in other statements or writings of mine, should be false, which I do not see, I am always ready to yield to a better understanding. As Jerome says to Heliodorus, [10] "For small intellects do not sustain great matters and in the very attempt, venturing beyond their strength, they are overcome." For I am able to err, but I cannot be a heretic, since one has to do with the intellect and the other with the will.

Therefore, to make plain the meaning of the foregoing, three points should be noted:

The first is that the words "to the extent that" exclude everything other than or foreign to the sense of the term used. For though, in the case of God, being and knowing are identical, yet we say that God is not evil, although we say that he understands evil. And although, in the case of God the Father, essence and paternity are identical, yet he does not beget as essence but as Father, although essence is the root of begetting. For the performance of divine acts proceeds immediately from God, according to the qualities of his attributes, as a certain maxim of theology asserts; whence Bernard, in the fifth book of his *De Consideratione,* [11] says that God loves as charity, knows as truth, sits as equity, rules as majesty, works as virtue, reveals as light, etc.

The second is that good and goodness are one. For good, to the extent that it is good, signifies only goodness, just as white signifies only a quality, whiteness. These two, however, good and goodness, are one univocally [80] in the case of the Son, the Holy Spirit and the Father, but in the case of God and those who are good they are one analogically.

The third is that whatever begets, in fact, whatever acts, to the extent that it begets or acts, has two characteristics at the time. First, it does not naturally rest or stop until it has introduced its form into that which is acted upon or begotten. By introducing form, and thus giving it, or communicating it, it contributes reality and all that belongs to it, viz., function, and all particular properties. Hence it is, according to the Philosopher,[12] what has not been moved is not moved, and what does not touch does not act. Second:

the fact that everything that acts or begets, to the extent that it acts or begets, is innate, and not made or created, since it is not derived from something else. In fact, that which begets, to the extent it begets, and the active principle, are opposed relatively to what is begotten, the offspring, the Son, the created, or whatever is made or has its being from something else. For example, the shape of a work of art or craft, such as a house in the mind of an artisan, is a sort of offspring, begotten and made, so to speak, from something outside, such as a house or a teacher. But such is not the case with the begetter, the Father, or the producing principle. John 5:30, *The Son is not able to do anything by himself*. From this, consequently, it is evident that the begetter and the begotten are one in reality, but of opposite or distinct relation, or of real relation in divine things, where relation and reality are the same; but in created things, they are distinguished only by reason and relation. This means that "active" and "passive" are two equally prime principles but one in action. For to move and to be moved begin and end at the same time, according to the law of relations.

From these facts, therefore, I plainly infer the truth of all those statements from my books and spoken utterances which are cited as charges against me. I infer also the ignorance and impiety of those who contradict me, according to Proverbs 8:7: for the ignorance, "My mouth shall speak truth," and for the impiety, "the impious is the abomination of my lips."

1. As for the articles under the first part, therefore, when it is stated: "Wisdom and the wise, truth and the true, etc.,"[13] I say that the statement is absolutely and simply true as is evident from the third of the three premises.

2. As for the second article of the first part, when it says: "The good, to the extent that it is good, is unmade or uncreated," this must be admitted as above.

3. As for the third, when it says: "Goodness is self-begotten and all its works, etc.," I say that this is true, as is evident from the third premise, in

so far as the first part of it is concerned. Besides, it is obvious in an example, for what is white gets its white being in form from whiteness and from nothing else.

4. As for the fourth, when it says: "Goodness and the good are no more than goodness, etc.," this is true, and evident from the second and third premises, and agrees with what is said in Matthew 10:35, *I am come to set a man at variance against his father;* and Matthew 23:9, *Call no one on earth your father,* and Matthew 16:24, *Let him deny himself and follow me,* and II Corinthians 3:18, *when . . . beholding . . . the glory of God, we are changed into the same image,* and Acts 17:28, *In him we live and move and have our being . . . we are also his offspring.*

As for the statement made in the same place that the higher powers [agents] of the soul depend on the purity of the soul, apart from place and time, that is exactly what St. Thomas says[14]—that the sense powers are not in the soul, but connected with it in a subordinate rank, while the intellect and will are in the soul itself, as in a subject. And it is a fact that the intellect draws away from the here and now, from things that refer to place and time. This matter, however, and all similar matters in the book *Benedictus Deus* conduce to morality, to disinterest, and contempt for temporal and corporal things, and to the love of God, the most excellent good.

And here in this very article four, it is to be noted especially that it is stated that those higher powers [agents] are created in the soul and with it: vainly, therefore, and wickedly, or ignorantly do they charge me in another article with asserting that something *in* the soul is uncreated.[15]

5. As to the fifth, when it is stated: "A man should study, etc.," this is true and entirely ethical, and in harmony with the twelfth chapter of Proverbs:[16] *Whatever happens to the righteous man, will not make him sad.* For certainly the uncreated good, God, goodness itself, does not disturb a good man, but neither does creation, which he despises and from which he is separated and far removed.

6. As for the sixth, when it says: "My heart and my love, etc.,"[17] it is true. An outward work, done without charity, and having no moral goodness or merit, when done in charity receives being for nonbeing and is worth the whole world. The sole reward is God, according to I Corinthians 13:2, *Though I have [the gift of] prophecy, etc., and have not charity, I am nothing.*

7. As for the seventh, when it says: "Such a man is so conformed to the divine will, etc.," it must be admitted that it is true and appears clear and moral like all the rest. For how could a man be blessed or even good, if he willed what God did not will?—or if he willed otherwise than God wills? For example, how could a man be blessed if he were not willing to be blessed,

or if he willed things contrary to blessedness? Or even white, if whiteness were incompatible with him or he were unlike whiteness? The entire perfection of man consists in being conformed to the divine will, by willing what God wills and in the way God wills it; especially as everything that is good, is good because God wills it and because of the way he wills it to be. Now it is certain that a man ought always to will the good.

8. As for the eighth, when it says: "A good man, to the extent that he is good, takes on every property of goodness, etc.," it is true as stated.

9. As for the ninth, when it says: "God is more really received, etc.,"[18] it is true, as when one lacks some gift, such as being a good singer, or any other gift, because of God, then the saying is fulfilled: *From him shall be taken even that which he hath*, Mark 4:25. Concerning the teaching *Blessed are they that suffer persecution for righteousness' sake*, Matt. 5:10. Gregory teaches this [same idea]. So an eye that lacks color receives color, recognizes it and is pleased by it but a wall that has color does not know that it has color and is not pleased by it, wherefore in Matthew 5:3 the poor are said to be blessed.

10. As for the tenth, when it says: "Our Lord besought the Father, etc.," it must be admitted that it is true. For this is the word of Christ in the Gospels and the example here given about fire obviously teaches the same thing.[19]

11. As for the eleventh, when it says: "Without doubt, etc.," it must be admitted that it is true and is made sufficiently clear in the proposition, agreeing as it does with: *The Kingdom of God is within you*[20] and with *All the glory of that daughter of the king is from within*.[21] Now to deny this and assail it is extreme ignorance.

12. As for the twelfth, when it says: "A good man wishes and would always wish to suffer for God's sake, etc.," it is true and he who is not such is not a good man and does not love God perfectly nor the things that are God's.

13. As for the thirteenth, when it says: "A good man, to the extent that he is good, has divine properties," I say that it is true and that it is apparent from the first and second of the three premises above, at the beginning.

14. As for the fourteenth, when it says: "No rational soul is without God, etc.," this is the teaching and word of Seneca, in *Epistle* 74, the opinion of Cicero in the *Tusculum Disputations*, Book I, 22, and the teaching of Origen in the homily *Let them answer for themselves*. In fact, in I John 3:9, it is said *Whosoever is born of God doth not commit sin; for his seed remaineth in him*, i.e., God remains in him.

15. As for the fifteenth, when it says: "All distinctions are alien to God,

etc.," it is clear; for to deny this is to deny *God*, and his unity. Deuteronomy 6:4, *Hear, O Israel, your God is one God.* Bernard, in *De Consideratione* 5, speaks thus "God is one as nothing else is, and if it can be said, He is one-est"; and below, "Compare with this One everything that can be called one and it will not be One; yet God is a trinity"; and below, "What does it mean— number, apart from number?" In the same place, Bernard treats this subject fully.

These are the fifteen statements which they censure in the book *Benedictus Deus*—"*not knowing the scriptures nor the virtue of God*," Matthew 22:29.

II

It follows, in the second place, let us see about these matters which the unlearned censure in statements of mine in a certain response to articles attributed to me, and there are six of them:

1. The first article is: "He who should innocently believe, speak or write of anything uncreated in the soul, as a part of the soul, would not be a heretic or damned, etc.,"[22] and I say that it is true, for only a stubborn adhesion to error makes a heretic. Many thousands of good men, while they lived here, thought that God, who is a spirit, was only a man of corporal being, presiding over all things; and their idea of a distinction of persons in one essence was altogether false—and thus with many other things.

2. As for the second, when it says: "Matter and accident do not give being to a composite but the whole composite receives being only from substantial form," I say that this is true and he who does not know this is witness to his own ignorance.

3. As for the third, when it says: "A good man, to the extent that he is good, receives all his being from uncreated goodness, etc.," it must be admitted that it is true efficiently; but formally, from goodness habitually inherent. So in corporal things, a wall is colored efficiently by a painter but formally by color.

4. As for the fourth, when it says: "This is the truest and best speech with which a good man may worship goodness, a just man justice, etc.," I say that it is all true just as it stands and that it agrees with the Scripture of both Testaments, as is clear from Isaiah 1, and Psalm 49. And rebukingly, it is said in Matthew 15:8, *This people honoreth me with their lips, but their heart is far from me.* Concerning whom, the Psalm says:[23] *They have placed their mouth in heaven, and their tongue,* i.e., their interest, *has crossed the earth.*

5. As for the fifth, when it says: "Equivocals[24] are distinguished by dif-

ferent things, etc.,'' it must be admitted that this is true and is the root of
many conceptions and expositions.

6. As for the sixth, when it says: "Elementary qualities receive being
univocally from a subject, through a subject and in a subject, etc.," it must
be admitted that it is true as it stands.

So much for the second part.

III

It follows thirdly to see about the articles taken from my first exposition
of Genesis,[25] and of these there are 12.

1. In the first it says: "It is clearly evident that the holy Scriptures are
to be explained parabolically, etc."[26] It must be admitted that this is true
as it stands. Yet it is not the less true on this account that it must be explained literally and historically.

2. As for the second, when it says: "In the justification of the impious,
unbegotten justice necessarily co-operates, begetting, bearing, etc.," it must
be admitted that this is true—in divine things univocally, but in creatures
and in God analogically. This same justice or goodness, therefore, exists
simply and absolutely in divine things, but in creatures analogically, as has
been said frequently above.

3. As for the third, when it says: "Being is the very actuality of all forms"
and "Being is what everything desires, etc.," it must be admitted that this
is true. The first is the word of St. Thomas[27] and the second the word of
Avicenna[28] as it is here stated in the article.

4. As for the fourth, when it says: "Being itself does not receive the fact
of its being in anything, nor from anything, etc.," it must be admitted that
this is true but a distinction must be made between formally inherent being
and absolute being, which is God.

5. As for the fifth, when it says: "Being is God," it must be admitted that
this is true of absolute being, not of formally inherent being. The statement
is proved by five reasons in the proposition which cannot be answered in
accordance with the truth; for God himself, Truth, says: *I am who I am—he
who is hath sent me*,[29] which is fully treated by Bernard in Book V of *De
Consideratione*.

6. As for the sixth, when it says: "Every being and every single thing has
all its being from God, immediately, etc.," I say that it is true in the same
way as stated already with reference to the fifth.

7. As for the seventh, when it says: "From God alone do all things have

their being, one being, etc.," I say that it is true in the way stated in the fifth article.

8. As for the eighth, when it says: "The beginning in which God created heaven and earth is the first simple Now of eternity," it must be admitted that this is true and necessary as it stands. Creation indeed and every activity of God is the very essence of God, and yet it does not follow from this, that if God created the world from eternity, the world *is* therefore from eternity, as the uneducated think. For creation is not an eternal state, just as the thing created itself is not eternal.

9. As for the ninth, when it says: "[Things] lowest in being are first and are equal in respect to being and in being, with things highest in being," it must be admitted that this is true. The fact that all parts of the body are on a footing of equality, because on a footing of immediacy, is an example of this. For although a man can exist without arms, without eyes, and such parts, yet if there were some being which could not possibly have eyes or such parts, because of its nature, it would not be a man, according to the species of man. For there is an order of the parts with respect to their mutual relation but there is no order of them with respect to the being of the composite body, which is one: for there is no order in that which is one. Such too, for example, is the situation of the powers [agents] of the soul with respect to their mutual relation and with respect to the being of the soul, which is one, as St. Thomas teaches.[30] Hence, while Genesis 1:1 says: *In the beginning, God created heaven and earth*, in the Psalm and[31] the Epistle to the Hebrews it says: *Thou, Lord, in the beginning hast laid the foundations of the earth and the heavens are the works of thine hands.*

10. As for the tenth, when it says: "God is one in all ways, according to all reasoning, etc.," it must be admitted that this is true as it stands and is in harmony with the Scripture of the canon, of the saints, and of the teachers.

11. As for the eleventh, when it says: "In every created thing, being is one thing and derived from another; essence is something else and not derived from another," it must be admitted that this is true and it is the statement of Avicenna and of Albertus in *De Causis*.[32] Both reason and the compulsion of truth bear this out, for when it is said that "man is an animal" I do not predicate being—for the word "is" is not a predicate but a third addition—the copula of the predicate, not expressing existence but only the close connection of the predicate, which is an animal, with the subject, which is man—and also, because the fact that man *is* has a cause and is derived from something else, namely, from God, the first being, while the fact that man is an animal is derived from nothing else, for no matter what

else is unwilling, or fails to act, this remains true, that "man is an animal," even if man does not exist.

12. As for the twelfth, when it says, on Genesis: "An outward act is not really good or divine, etc.," it must be granted that this is true and its truth is evident from what has been said above, when making a distinction between the good of nature which changes with being, and the good of grace, the end of which is eternal life, according to the citation made above: *The Kingdom of God is within you.*[33] Hence, an exterior act adds nothing of the habit of goodness to that which is within, as St. Thomas teaches.[34]

So much for the third part.

Therefore, in any part of the contents of the foregoing articles, first in the book which begins *Benedictus Deus*, etc., and secondly in the contents of statements and responses of mine attributed to me, thirdly in the contents of my first exposition of Genesis, all of which I admit that I have written and said—in any part of the foregoing, I say, the truth and the reasoning of the truth is evident and also, either the definite malice or the crass ignorance of those who contradict me and attempt to measure things divine, subtle and incorporal by a material imagination, contrary to what Boethius says in his book *De Trinitate*:[35] "In divine things, one will have to apply himself intellectually and not be led aside to imaginings." I protest, however, that concerning these things, and all that I have written in different expositions of different books on whatever subject, and in many other forms, I do not have to respond to you, nor to anyone, except the Pope or the University of Paris, unless something should touch my faith, to which I always testify— which is not the case. Yet I wished voluntarily, protesting the freedom of my order, to make these remarks and offer them to you, in order that I might not seem to run away from the charges that are wrongfully put upon me.

IV

Furthermore, I should not have to reply on the other articles taken from sermons attributed to me, since now and then, even frequently, the clergy, students and learned men report incompletely and falsely what they hear. This one thing I do say, that to the extent that they sound like or imply error, or savor of heresy, I do not and have not held any such view, nor maintained nor preached it. Yet I admit that in several of them some truths are touched upon, which could be upheld by a true and sound understanding; surely there is no false doctrine which does not contain some mixture of truth, as Bede says in a homily.[36] Where, however, they imply error, or create error in the minds of hearers, I reject and abominate them, but such errors cannot and ought not to be imputed to me by envious men, according to the remark of Augustine, *De Trinitate*, Book I, Ch. 3, where he says: "I suppose that men will not be slower in certain passages of my books to form the opinion that I thought what I did not think, or that I did not think what I thought, whose error everyone would agree ought not to be attributed to me, as if, following me, but not overtaking me, they have strayed into some falsehood, whilst I was compelled to take my way through dense and shaded places, since by no means would anyone rightly attribute to the saints themselves, the authors of the divine words, so many different errors of heretics, though they all attempt to defend their false and fallacious opinions from the same scriptures."

Yet I shall reply fully to the individual articles separately.

1. So for the first, when it says: "The Father begets his Son in me, etc.,"[37] it must be understood that this article implies several things. One is that as a man stands in the knowledge and love of God the result is that he himself is God. I say that this is altogether false and that I did not say it, nor think it, nor write it, nor preach it, and that it is erroneous, and heretical if it should be rashly defended, but that without such defense no error is heresy. This is proved from Augustine:[38] "Like the apostle, avoid the heretical man after the first and second correction." "A heretic," parenthetically, "is one who stubbornly defends his error." Farther on in the same chapter, there follows: "But those who do not persistently defend their error, however false and perverse, but are ready to be corrected, are by no means to be reckoned amongst heretics." Later, in the thirty-first chapter, Augustine speaks thus: "As for those in the church of Christ, who savor of anything unwholesome or perverted, if, on being corrected, they resist stubbornly and are unwilling to emend their pernicious and deadly doctrines, and persist in defending them, they are heretics." So speaks Augustine.

As for the other things stated in the same first article, it must be realized first of all that, without doubt, God himself being One, because he is not another, is undivided in Being through power, presence and essence, the Father unbegotten and the Son begotten; for the Father is not the Father unless begetting and unbegotten and the Son is not the Son unless begotten and himself One, as being God. Hence, wherever God is the Father and the unbegotten begetter, there is the begotten Son too. Therefore, since God is in me, surely God the Father begets the Son in me, and in me the begotten Son himself is one and undivided, since there is no other Son in the divine, except this One, and he is God.

Secondly, it must be realized that in the divine, the Son himself, as well, is really One, as has been said. And he is *only begotten in the bosom*, that is, in the inmost parts *of the Father*, John 1:18. He is *the likeness of God invisible, first begotten of all creation*, Colossians 1:15, the Word in the beginning and God, John 1:1. And since he is really the Son, therefore he is properly the heir, Galatians 4:7. Hence it is that no other, except himself is the heir— unless through him and in him, he is part of him, through grace and charity; nor is any other the Son. Whence, however much we are sons, we are not heirs when we are not the Son, except in so far as the Sonship is in us and we are conformed to him, only begotten and first begotten, as the imperfect to the perfect, the second to the first, the branch to the head; wherefore, too, he is called the First Begotten. Hence it is that after the apostle had said: *If Sons and heirs*, he added the words: *Heirs of God but co-heirs of Christ*, Romans 8:17.

When, however, it is stated further on in the same article that God begets his Son in me, without distinction, that sounds bad at first sight.[39] It is true, however, because the Son begotten in me is the Son himself, undifferentiated from the Father in nature, himself One, and without distinction or differentiation; nor is he one in me and another in another man. As if he were not in me, he is undifferentiated from me, not divided or separated, for he is in all things and everywhere as being God. I think this true and sound Christian faith, and this is giving honor to God and to his only Son, through whom the Father has re-created us, and with his ineffable charity has adopted us as sons. What St. Thomas says is in harmony with the foregoing, *Summa Theologica*, II, question 108, article 1.

As for what follows at the end of the same article: "We are transformed and converted into God," that is wrong.[40] For no man, however holy and good, becomes Christ himself or First Begotten, nor are others saved through him, nor is he the likeness of God, the only begotten Son of God; but he is *after* the likeness of God, a part of him who is truly and perfectly the Son, first begotten and heir, while we are joint-heirs as has just been said, and that is the meaning of the similitude. For just as many loaves on different altars are converted into the one true body of Christ, conceived and born of the Virgin, suffered under Pilate, while the accidental qualities of the individual loaves still remain, so our minds, through the grace of adoption, and we ourselves are made one with the true Son of God, parts of the head of the church, who is Christ.

2. As for the second, when it says: "A noble man is not satisfied, etc.," it is wrong as it sounds, unless perhaps it means what Augustine says, *On the Trinity*, Book 9, Ch. 12, that from the knower and the known there issues a sort of offspring common to the knower and the known. Such too is evidently the case with the visible and vision, the sensible and sense in

operation, as the Philosopher says.[41] The likeness in us is more perfect when the soul knows God and thinks of him and loves him than it is when the soul thinks of and loves itself, as Augustine would have it,[42] and the teachers. To observe this and to teach it to the people is useful and leads to morality and the good life, so that a man may be aroused frequently and gladly to think of God and love him rather than of himself or of any other created thing.

3. As for the third, when it says: "Virtue has its root rooted in the soil of divinity," it must be said that this is true and is the very thing that Plotinus means by his four grades of virtue:[43] "social, purgatorial, of the clean soul, and exemplary," concerning which see St. Thomas, question 61, last article.[44] It is effective for commending the true virtue of charity, of which the root and the beginning is the Holy Spirit, whence, as rivers return to the place from which they go forth, a man ought to be solicitous about having love. For the root of love is God and he is love. *He that dwelleth in love dwelleth in God and God in him.*[45]

4. As for the fourth, when it says: "A humble man has as much power over God, etc.," it is wrong as it sounds, but this is true, that God gives grace to the humble, as James and Peter say.[46] In proportion as a man has grace and is the Son of God, he does have power over God and his works, because he does not wish anything different, not in a different way from what God wishes and does.

5. As for the fifth, when it says: "There is an agent in the soul that operates uniformly with God," it is wrong as it sounds, unless it should be explained as has already been said with reference to the fourth and second articles above.

6. As for the sixth, when it says: "There is an agent in the soul, such that if all the soul were like it, it would be uncreated and uncreatable," it is false and wrong. For, as another article says, the supreme powers [agents] of the soul are created in the soul and with it. Besides, I did not say that, but in commending God's goodness and his love toward man, I said that God created man from the earth in his own likeness and clothed him with virtue like his own,[47] in order that there might be intellect, just as God himself is intellect, who surely is pure intellect, uncreated, and having nothing in common with anything else. As for his only begotten Son, who is his likeness, him he clothed like himself in order that he might be uncreated and as measureless as the Father is; man, however, as a created being, he made *after* his likeness, not [in] his likeness, and clothed him not with himself but *according* to himself.

As for the statement in the same article that that which is beyond the sea[48] is as present to the intellect as the place of its own body, it is true, because intellect draws away from the here and now. Also, the thing that is imagined in the mind is not imagined more quickly or easily when present than when absent and ever so distant.

7. As for the seventh, when it says: "Human nature is in common and belongs equally to all men," it is true and to deny this is ignorance. For it is true that God, by assuming human nature, bestowed upon it, and upon all who partake of human nature, those things that were bestowed on Christ, according to Romans 8:32, *He gave all things to us with him*, and Wisdom of Solomon 7:11, *All good things came to me along with him*. 'Along with,' that is, at the same time, or 'along with,' that is, equally, or 'along with,' that is, from producing equals. For to the extent that fire produces its form in wood, it gives it all that belongs to the form of fire. *For God speaks once, but twice* . . .[49] that is, more [than one thing] is heard. According to St. Augustine: "He says all things to all men[50] but not all hear equally; each hears according to his own powers." According to Matthew 25:15: *To one he gave five talents, to another two, to another one*. Therefore it does not follow, as those ignorant men think, that I, or any other man, have all grace, and all the things that belong to grace, which apply to Christ. Yet this has force to draw us to devotion and make us grateful to God, who so loved the world that he gave his only begotten Son, and assumed flesh in Christ for my sake; for, according to the teachers, God would not have sent his Son into flesh, except for the purpose of saving man. By the fact that he assumed human nature, we are taught to serve God with humility and according to reason; for he is called man (homo) from earth (humus) with reference to the body, but rational with reference to the spirit.

8. As for the eighth, which is about the image[51] in the soul, "that the image of the Trinity in the soul is a sort of expression of itself, apart from will and intellect," the statement is obscure, except for the light thrown on it by the examples given there, whence I see no danger.

When it is said, however, at the end, that I am that image, that is an error and false, for no created thing is the image but angels, and men have been created *after* the image. For what is truly the image and likeness is not, properly speaking, made nor is it a work of nature.

9. As for the ninth, when it says: "that man can attain to this, that the outward man may be obedient to the inward man, even unto death," it is plain that this is true in the case of the holy martyrs, according to the following: *Struggle for your soul in behalf of justice and for sure justice even unto death*[52] and in John:[53] *He that hateth his soul for my sake, etc.*

10. As for the tenth, when it says: "I have wondered lately whether I

could wish to receive anything from God, or desire anything," I said this some time ago but it was misunderstood; for I did not mean to say that God is not to be prayed to, but I spoke commending the divine goodness which stands at the door and knocks, as stated in Revelation 3:20 and Isaiah 30:18, *God awaits you that he may pity you*, etc.

11. As for the eleventh, when it says: "The man who stands in love, etc.," that article contains two ideas: the first is that the perfect man ought to be dead to the world and creatures. Likewise, a perfect man ought to love his neighbor as intensely as himself. Both of these are true and agree with the passages where Matthew and Luke have[54] *sicut te ipsum* [as thyself], where Mark has *tanquam te ipsum* [as thyself], a form Augustine frequently uses. Now *tanquam* is *tantum quantum* and this surely is characteristic of perfection, for grace is higher than nature and superior to it. And he that loves God with all his heart and soul and mind and strength has nothing besides God that he loves more in one case than another. For he that loves one thing more than another loves a creature among creatures and does not love one God in all things and all things in God; for in One there is not more or less. This is what the Lord significantly says:[55] *He that loves . . . more . . . is not worthy of me.* For God is One in whom there is no number, more or less.

12. Now what is adduced in the twelfth article about Paul is equally true. Paul left god for God's sake[56] while desiring to be separated from Christ and to be with Christ, for the sake of the brothers he loved in Christ; and for God's sake he wished to live in the flesh. He left what he could receive from God and what God could give him for the sake of God himself, since otherwise he would have loved God's gift more than God. Again, the expression "for the sake of," when I say "God, for God's sake," means the final cause, which is always the best and first of all causes.

13. As for the thirteenth, when it says: "There is a certain castle in the soul, etc.," in this sermon there are many obscure and doubtful things which I never said; but it is true, as there stated, that as truth, God is comprehended by the intellect, and as good, by the will [both of which] are powers [agents] of the soul, while the reason penetrates to the essence of the soul. This makes for the teaching that man loves God and seeks him behind all concealments, with a chaste pure love, according to the statement of Genesis:[57] *I am . . . thy exceeding great reward.*

14. As for the fourteenth, when it says: "Just as the soul and body are united in being, etc.," it is true and is the word of Christ in John,[58] informing us that, divested of the love of creatures, we may be united with God,

as in the example food is divested of the form of bread and fish that it may be united in what is taken as food. There, too, it should be observed that examples are given so that he who is learning may see, as the Philosopher says.[59] As for the statement below in the article: "To be similar is evil and deceptive"—that is what Augustine says in the *Soliloquies*, Book 2: "Similitude is the mother of falsehood." For thus, a coin of gold *and* bronze is successful in misleading us and deceiving us into thinking it is gold because it is similar to gold. And Seneca, in the prologue to his *Declamations*, speaks thus: "The imitation is never quite the same. This is the nature of the case: similitude always falls short of the truth." And Cicero, *De Natura Deorum*, Book I, says this: "Nothing can imitate the skill of nature."

15. As for the fifteenth, when it says: "All creatures are pure nothing," it must be said that this is pure, devout and useful truth, leading to the formation of character, contempt of the world, love of God, and love of him alone. To believe the opposite of this is the error of inexperience and without doubt a dangerous heresy if it should be rashly defended. This is the meaning of what John 1:3 says: *All things were made by him and without him was not anything made.* That is exactly what the fifteenth article says throughout.

16. As for the sixteenth and last, when it says: "However anything may appear better or may be better, etc.," it must be said that this certainly is true. When a man fully denies himself and wholly conforms to the divine will, wishing and loving only that which, in him and in all things, is made to the honor and will of God, whatever God has given or has not wished to give, by the very fact that God has given it or wished it so, it is accepted by the true lover of God as better and certainly it is better. For the very will of God, by willing, makes a thing good. This is supported by Matthew 6:10, *Thy will be done on earth as it is in heaven.*

V

The following are articles taken from a book which Meister Eckhart sent to the Queen of Hungary, written in German. The book begins thus: *Benedictus deus et pater domini nostri Ihesu Christi.*[60]

1. First: that wisdom and the wise, truth and the true, justice and the just, goodness and the good, have a mutual relationship and are so connected because goodness is neither created nor made nor begotten, but only begetting, it begets that which is good, to the extent that it is good.[61]

2. Second: the good, to the extent that it is good, is not made or created, but is begotten, the child and son of goodness.[62]

3. Third: that goodness is self-begotten, and all its works, that is, being, knowledge, love, work [come] from the heart and soul of goodness and from that alone.[63]

4. Fourth: goodness and the good are no more than goodness in all things[64] except [that one] begets and [the other is] begotten. For goodness, to beget and to be begotten are one and the same thing in the good, and are of one being and life, and whatever belongs to the good itself is received entirely from goodness. There it is, there it lives, there it dwells, and there it knows itself. Whatever it knows, whatever it loves, it loves and operates with goodness in goodness, and with it and in it, that goodness does all its work, as it is written, and as the Son says: *The Father that dwelleth in me, he doeth the works* and *all things that my Father hath are mine* and all that is mine is the Father's, his by giving and mine by receiving.

It should be understood that this name or word that we use, "the good," includes nothing else, nothing except pure, naked goodness, neither more nor less; and yet it gives itself. When we speak of "the good," we understand that its goodness is given to it, infused and inborn from unbegotten goodness. Therefore the Gospel says: *As the Father hath life in himself, so hath he given the Son to have life in himself*. It says "in himself" and not "of himself" because the Father has given it him.

And in conclusion: whatever has been said about goodness and the good holds equally for truth and the true, justice and the just, wisdom and the wise, for God the Father and God the Son, and for all that is begotten of God and has no earthly father, and that does not beget from itself created things, and is not God, in which there is no idea other than God, pure, naked and alone—because this is what the Gospel of John says: *which were born, not of blood*, etc.

By the will of man, John understands the highest powers [agents] of the soul and person, which have nothing in common with anything else, which remain constant in purity, separate from place and time, and from all that has place and time or any reference or tendency thereto, in which man is *after* the likeness of God, in which he is of the race and blood of God. Yet because they are not God, but are created in the soul and with it, they must be stripped of their own likeness and changed by likeness into God, and begotten in God and of God, because only God is the Father there, since they are sons of God—the only begotten sons of God. And [because] of all this, I am the Son because he forms me after his own likeness and begets me in himself. Such a man is the Son of God, good and the son of goodness, just and the son of justice. In proportion as he is the Son of himself alone, unbegotten, yet begetting, the Son has this one thing that justice has and enters into every property of justice.

5. Fifth: a man should study to discount self or strip himself of his own idea [image] and of all creatures and to know no Father except God only.[65] Then nothing may sadden or disturb him, neither God nor creature, nor anything created or uncreated, and his whole being, living, perceiving, knowing and loving are from God and in God and God.

6. Sixth: my heart and my love give goodness to creatures, which is the property of God.[66]

7. Seventh: such a man is so conformed to the divine will that he wants whatever God wants and the way God wants it.[67] And when God then wishes me to have committed sin in some form, I shall be unwilling not to have committed a sin because thus the divine will *on earth* is fulfilled, that is, *in misdeeds, as in heaven*, that is, *in doing good*. Thus a man wishes to be without god for God's sake and to be separated from god for God's sake. This alone is true repentance for sin and thus do I grieve for my sins without grief. Finally, I have still greater grief for my sins because I would not have committed a sin for all creation—yet I am without grief.

8. Eighth: the good man, to the extent that he is good, takes on every property of goodness which is God himself.[68]

9. Ninth: God is more really received by [one who is] without him, than by accepting him; for when a man accepts [something], a gift has been given as a reason why man should rejoice and be comforted, but when [God] is not accepted, nothing is had, nor is anything known or hoped for that may be the material of joy—nothing but God and his will.[69]

10. Tenth: our Lord besought the Father that we might be one—one in unity—not merely united.[70] We have a clear example [illustration] of this statement in a material fact both manifest and obvious in nature. When fire goes to work on wood, kindling it to burning, it makes the wood fine and unlike itself, depriving it of its grossness, coldness, weight, dampness, and makes the wood more and more like fire; still they are both dissatisfied, fire and wood, about any heat or likeness, unless the fire begets itself in the wood and gives it its own proper nature and its own proper being, so that it is all fire equally and without the distinction of more or less. . . . And there follows, a little below: And I say in truth that the secret agent in [man's] nature secretly hates a likeness, inasmuch as it brings in a distinction and a difference. . . . And there follows immediately: therefore I say that the soul hates a likeness and does not care for a likeness for its own sake, but only for the sake of what is hidden in it and is the true Father, the

beginning without beginning in heaven and earth. This is supported by the statement in the gospel: *Philip, he that sees me, etc.*[71]

11. Eleventh: without doubt, even natural human virtue is so noble[72] and efficient that no outward work is burdensome to it, nor sufficient to prevent it from being able to manifest itself in any operation as it does in its own image. Therefore there is another work, more manifest, which neither time nor place enclose or can contain, and in this work there is something divine and similar to God, whom neither time nor place enclose, because he is everywhere and present at all times, in the same way. The result of this similarity to God, whom no creature can grasp perfectly, nor transform the divine goodness into itself, is that there must be something loftier and more intrinsic, uncreated and measureless and limitless into which the heavenly Father could infuse, reveal and represent himself wholly as in his own image. These are the Son and the Holy Spirit. The inner operation of that [divine] agent can be impeded as little as God himself. Its work shines brightly day and night, singing the praises of God, singing a new song. It follows that its work is the love of God.

12. The twelfth[73] is that a good man wishes and would always wish to suffer for God's sake and not only to have endured. By suffering, he has what he loves. He likes to suffer for God's sake and does so suffer: therefore by this very fact he is the Son of God and *after* God, transformed into God. He loves for its own sake, that is, loves for the sake of loving, acts for the sake of acting, and for this reason loves God and works ceaselessly. To work for God is his nature, his being, his life, his salvation, his blessedness, because, so says the Lord: *Blessed are they that suffer for justice's sake*, etc.[74]

13. Thirteenth: a good man to the extent that he is good has divine properties, not only from the fact that loving and working, he loves and works for God's sake—whom he loves and on account of whom he works; but also he loves and works for his own sake, because what he loves is God the unbegotten Father, while he that loves is the begotten Son of God. The Father is in the Son and the Son in the Father. Father and Son are one.[75]

14. Fourteenth: No rational soul is without God: the divine seed is in us.[76] If it has a good, wise and diligent worker and artificer, then it receives an increase and grows like to God whose seed it is, and its fruit is likewise made a nature of God. The seed of the pear grows into the pear tree, the nut into the nut tree, the seed of God into God.

15. Fifteenth: All distinctions are alien to God.[77] There is no distinction in either the divine natures or persons. Proof: nature itself is one and this is one. Any person is one: the very one that nature itself is. Whatever a person is, three persons are likewise the same one.

VI

The following are articles taken from the response of Meister Eckhart[78] to articles attributed to him in a book that begins: *Benedictus Deus et pater*, a book which he wrote.

1. The first article is: He who should innocently believe, speak or write of anything uncreated in the soul, as a part of the soul, would not be a heretic or damned. And he adds that the Master of Sentiments so died because he believed, taught and wrote that there is no created habit of charity in the soul, but the soul is moved only by the uncreated Holy Spirit.

2. The second is that matter and accident do not give being to a composite but the whole composite receives being only from substantial form.

3. The third is that a good man, to the extent that he is good, receives his entire being from uncreated goodness, and that the words "to the extent that he is good" signify only the goodness which is God, just as white signifies only whiteness.

4. The fourth is that this is the truest and best speech with which a good man may worship goodness, a just man justice, and a true man the truth: *True worshippers shall worship the Father in spirit and in truth,*[79] because God is spirit and God is truth. But as for corporal genuflection, bowing of the head and the like, which are outward [acts], and which quicken ignorant people's imaginations, there is interposed the statement: *You worship, you know not what.*

5. The fifth is that equivocals[80] are distinguished by different things, univocals by diverse differences of a thing and analogues neither by different things nor by differences of things but only by the limits of one and the same thing by number. He gives as an example of this that health is a single quality of life, from which urine, diet and things of this kind are called healthy by analogy. But in urine there is absolutely no health any more than in a stone, but it merely has the name of health because by some property of it there is an indication of that health which is in the living creature. And then, later, he adds that so throughout, in a proposition, the good, and likewise being, have an analogical relation in God and in creatures. For goodness itself, which is in God and which is God, is the quality by which all good men are good.

6. The sixth is that elementary qualities receive being univocally from a subject, through a subject and in a subject, however analogically. It is not so with justice, for example, or truth, or qualities of this sort, but contrariwise. They do not receive being from a subject but a subject receives

from them its just, true, good being, and so on: qualities which are prior to their subjects and which remain after their subjects are corrupted, as is beautifully taught by Augustine, *On the Trinity*, Book VIII, chapter 3.

VII

The following are articles taken from a certain book of Meister Eckhart, namely, from a writing of his on Genesis.[81]

1. It should be noted that it is clearly evident that the Holy Scriptures are to be explained parabolically. The saints in common with the teachers explain those statements made in the third chapter as parables by means of the serpent. Accordingly, therefore, what is here said about the serpent is explained: the serpent is the creature of sense, the woman the inferior rational creature, and the man the superior rational creature. After these premises, it would seem that without harming the other explanation of saints and teachers, historical and tropological, it could perhaps be said with probability that the tropological meaning of the serpent, the woman, and the man is indeed the historic and literal meaning, as in what is said in Judges 9:8, *The trees came together that they might anoint a king over them and they said to the olive tree: Command us*. So, too, when we say that the meadow smiles or the water runs, the literal meaning is that the meadow is in bloom and its blooming is its smile and its smile is its blooming. Accordingly, this is the explanation of what is said here about the serpent, the woman, and the man. Many doubts which are customarily raised will be done away; for example, how the serpent and the woman conversed with each other, and many such things.

2. Likewise, in the justification of the wicked, unbegotten justice necessarily co-operates, begetting, bearing and producing. Likewise, the co-operating justice would not be other than the begotten. Therefore, since no one can be just apart from justice, no one can be begotten just apart from begotten justice.

3. Being is the very actuality of all forms. Wherefore, Avicenna, *Metaphysics* VIII, chapter 6, says: "What every thing desires is being and perfection."

4. Likewise, being itself does not receive the fact of its being in anything, nor from anything, nor through anything, nor does it come after, or supervene in anything. It comes before and is prior to all things, because the being of all things comes immediately from the first or universal cause of everything. All things, therefore, come from being, through it and in it and it does not come from something else. For that which is other than being

does not exist, or is nothing. For being, to the extent that it is being, provides for all things, and supplies activity and perfection; but that which is truly desired is being. Hence it is that everything mobile and mutable falls under the consideration of metaphysics to the extent that it has being. Even matter, the root of corruptible things, and the second being of all things, to the extent it has being, is measured by eternity and not by time.

5. Likewise, being is God. This proposition is obvious, in the first place, because if being is something different from God, God does not exist and there is no God. For how can he exist, or how can anything exist, if there is another existence foreign and distinct from being? Or if God exists, does he exist in some other way, since being is different from him? No. God and being are the same—or God has being from another and thus himself is not God, as has been stated. Something different from him is prior to him and the cause of his being. Besides, everything that is has the fact of its being through being and from being. Therefore, if being is something different from God, a thing has its being from something other than God. Besides, there is nothing prior to being, because that which confers being creates and is a creator. To create is to give being out of nothing. It is a fact that all things have being from being itself, just as all things are white from whiteness itself. Therefore, if being is different from God, the creator will be something other than God. Again, in the fourth place, everything that has being is limited by something else, just as everything that has whiteness is white. Therefore, if being is something other than God, things could have come into existence without God, and thus God is not the first cause, nor the cause of the existence of things. In the fifth place, beyond being and before being there is nothing. Therefore, if being is other than God, or foreign to God, God would be nothing. Or, if something were prior to or different from him, that thing would be god to God himself and god of all. Allusion is made to the foregoing in Exodus 3:14: *I am he who is.*

6. Likewise, from God and God alone do all things have their being, one being, true being, good being. This is clear from what has already been said. For how could anything be, except from being, or be one, except from the One and through One, or through unity, or true, except through truth, or good except through goodness?[82]

7. Likewise, every being and every single thing has all its being, and all its unity, truth and goodness immediately from God. Again, it is stated thus: it is impossible for any being, or any kind or distinction of being, to be lacking or absent from being itself. For by the very fact that it is lacking or absent it is not, and is nothing. But God is being.

8. Likewise, the beginning in which God created heaven and earth is the first simple Now of eternity, the very Now, I say, in which God is from eternity, in which, too, he has been and is and will be the [source from which] persons emanate. Therefore, Moses says that God created heaven and earth absolutely, at the first beginning in which God is, without any mean or interval. Hence, when I was asked one time why God had not created the world before, I replied that he could not, [have done so] because he was not, and had not been, before the world was. Besides, how could he have created the world before, when he created it later in the same Now in which God is? For it is not to be imagined falsely that God stood waiting for some future Now in which he would create the world, for at one and the same time at which God was, in which he begot his Son, coeternal with himself, in all things his equal, he also created the world. Job 33:14, *God speaks once*. He speaks in the begetting of his Son, because the Son is the Word; he also speaks in the creating of creation. Psalm 148:5, *he spoke and they were made, he commanded and they were created*. Hence, in another Psalm [62:11] it is stated: *God spoke once; I heard these two things*. Obviously, the two things are heaven and earth—or rather, the two things are the emanation of persons and the creation of the world, things which he speaks once, has spoken once.

9. Likewise, [things] lowest in being are first and are equal in respect to being, and in being, with [things] highest in being, according to the statement (Psalm 139:8): *If I ascend up into heaven*, etc.

10. Likewise, God is one in all ways and according to every reasoning, so that in him no plurality is to be found, in mind or without mind, as Rabbi Moses [83] says in Book I, chapter 10. For he who sees any distinction clearly does not see God. For God is One, without number and above number, and he is not numbered with anything. The explanation of this he adds later as follows: being plus a being does not make number, nor, generally, form with what is formed; but being and all form are from God as from the first being and first form; therefore, no distinction can exist in him or be thought of.

11. Likewise, in every created thing, being is one thing, and derived from another [while] essence is something else and not derived from another.

12. Likewise, on Genesis: an outward act is not really good or divine, nor does God really perform it or produce it. For what the Father does, he does continually and without intermission.

VIII

The following are articles taken from sermons ascribed to Meister Eckhart.

1. The first article is: the Father begets his son in me and I am that same Son and not another. We are not heirs just because we are sons but because we are the Son we are heirs.

To the same effect elsewhere: God performs all his works for this reason, that we may become his only begotten Son.

Likewise, there follows: that man stands in the knowledge and love of God and becomes nothing other than what God himself is.

Likewise, the Father begets me as his Son, and the same Son, without distinction.

There follows: we are totally transformed and converted into God in the same way that in the sacrament the bread is converted into the body of Christ. However many loaves of bread there are, yet only one body is made of them all. Whatever is converted into something else is made one with it. Thus I am converted because he works to make me one with himself and not similar.

2. Likewise, in another place, it is maintained that a noble man [the aristocratic soul] is not satisfied that he is the only begotten Son, whom the Father begets eternally, but he also wishes to be the Father and according to that likeness of eternal paternity, to beget him by whom I am eternally begotten.

3. Likewise, that virtue has its root rooted in the soil of divinity and planted where it has its being and its essence and only there, and nowhere else.

4. Likewise, a humble man has as much power over God as God has over himself, and whatever there is in all the angels and saints, this belongs to the humble man; whatever God does he does, and whatever God is he is, one life and one being.

5. Likewise, that there is an agent[84] in the soul that operates uniformly with God. It creates and makes all things with God and has nothing in common with anything else and begets, along with the Father, the same only begotten Son.

6. Likewise, there is an agent in the soul such that, if all the soul were like it, it would be uncreated and uncreatable; but it is not so, for in another part, it [the soul] is dependent on time. There it touches creation and is created; but to that agent, namely, the intellect, that which is beyond the sea is as present as the place in which I stand.

7. Likewise, in another place, that in the soul there is an agent or power

which is not created or creatable and if the whole soul were like it, it would be uncreated, and the whole soul, to the extent it is nature, would be uncreated. But the soul replies that the soul, to the extent it is created, is nature. Since human nature is in common and belongs equally to all, the Father has given to me of human nature all he ever gave to the Son. There is no exception here. Whatever is, belongs to me, as to him. I say more: in whatever the Father gave him of human nature, he had regard for me first, and aimed more at me than at the man Christ, and gave more to me than to him. Surely, [it is so] since he gave to him for my sake—for he did not need it but I needed it. For this reason, whatever the Father gave his Son, he aimed at me and gave to me as well as to him. I made no exception to this: neither union with divinity, nor holiness, nor anything else. Whatever he gave him in human nature is no more alien to me than to him. The reason is that the Son assumed not a human personality but human nature: wherefore human nature is common, etc., as above.

8. The eighth article is about the image [idea] in the soul, that the image of the Trinity in the soul is a sort of expression of itself, apart from the will and intellect. This image in the soul belongs not to the soul, but above all to that from which the soul receives its essence and nature—not another essence but the same. This is made plain in three examples: of the image in a mirror, of a wall in the eye, and of a branch growing from a tree. Whence it is suggested of this image in the soul that it is a sort of united expression of itself, and that which there goes forth is that which remains within, and the very thing which remains there within is that which goes forth. That image is the Son of the Father, and that image is I; that image is the wisdom of the Father, and I am that image.[85]

9. Likewise, that a man can attain to this, that the outer man may be obedient to the inner man, even to death, and then he abides in peace, always in the service of God.

10. Likewise, I have wondered lately whether I could wish to receive or desire anything from God. I must deliberate very carefully.

11. Likewise, after some preliminary remarks, this statement is made: The man who stands in love should be dead to himself and to all created things, so that he may care as little for himself as for one who is a thousand miles away. That man is in equality and abides in unity.

Likewise, that a man ought to love his neighbor as himself, not only as the ignorant say, that he loves him for the same good, but in every way, and that he ought to love God as intensely as himself.

Likewise to the same effect, some people say: I love a friendly benefactor more than another man. This is imperfect; it is not loving aright; yet it is natural to love one man more than another.

12. Then follows: Paul said, I am willing to be cut off eternally from God, for my friends' sake and for God's sake. It follows that Paul stood in total perfection when he made that statement. I explain it thus: the greatest thing a man can leave—is that he leave god for God's sake. Now Paul left god for God's sake; he left everything that he could receive from God and all that God could give him.

13. Likewise, that there is a certain castle in the soul, which I have called at times the guardian of the soul, or the spark. It follows that it is very simple, even as God is One and simple, so simple and beyond all measure that not even God the Father can see it as he has characteristics or the properties of a person; and if he should see it, it would cost him all his divine names and personal properties, because it has no character or property; but inasmuch as God is One and simple and without characteristics and properties, inasmuch as he is neither the Father, the Son, nor the Holy Spirit, he can enter that which I call the castle.

14. Likewise, that just as soul and body are united in being, and just as food has one being with the nature of that eaten, so we shall be united to God according to being and not only according to function.

Likewise, there is something in the soul so closely akin to God that it is one and not united.

Likewise, to the same effect, to be similar is evil and deceptive. If I were one I should not be similar. There is nothing extraneous in oneness. Oneness permits me to be one and not similar.

15. Likewise, all creatures are pure nothing. I do not say that they are at least a little something but that they are pure nothing, because no creature has being.

16. Likewise, however a thing may appear better, or may be better, yet to a good man seeking the will of God, this is better: whatever God permits to happen to him, whether it be hunger or thirst, or sacrifice—whether he has it or not—this is better to him.

IX

The articles which follow are contained in a document shown me after I had replied to the articles given above.

Now it must be emphasized that just as in the former articles, so too in these which now follow, they are always apparently false and erroneous in the sense in which they are taken by those who charge me with them.

But if they should be understood sanely and piously, they contain the beautiful and useful truths of faith and moral instruction. They reveal the intellectual weakness or malice of my opponents, rather than their manifest blasphemy, or even heresy—if they should be defended stubbornly, as being contrary to the doctrine of Christ, the gospel, the saints, and the teachers. For example, they say that man cannot be united with God. Likewise, they say that a creature is not nothing of itself but is a little thing, as we say that a drop of the sea is a little thing.

Likewise, they say that God created the world in some other Now than the Now of eternity, when every action of God in his substance, which is eternal; but they do not understand what Augustine, speaking of God, says in his *Confession*, Book I, 10: "Thou art still the same, and all things of tomorrow, and all beyond and all of yesterday, and all behind it, Thou hast done today. What is it to me, though any comprehend not this?" The words are Augustine's and in Book XI, 13 he says: "whilst their heart fluttereth between the motions of things past and to come and is still unstable. Who shall hold it and catch the glory of that ever-fixed Eternity?" Likewise, in the fourth place, they say that an outward act can add some moral good to an inward act. Likewise, in the fifth place, they think that the Holy Spirit and its grace are given to a man who is not the Son of God, when the Holy Spirit certainly does not proceed except from the Son. Romans 8 and Galatians 4:6, *Because ye are sons, God hath sent forth the spirit of his Son into your hearts*. Why go on? The situation is similar in everything to which they object, as for example, when it is stated that God is being, which they falsely think to be false.

1. The first article in this second document comes from a sermon "I saw a lamb standing over Mt. Sion":[86] a man ought not to be similar to God but one with God.

It should be explained that creatures, except man, are created after the idea and likeness of something within God, or something which is God's, but that man is created after the image and likeness of the entire substance of God himself. Whence a man ought to be very grateful to God and devoted to him. For *to the place from whence the rivers come, thither they return again*, Ecclesiastes 1:7, but man goes forth after the likeness of the substance of God. Besides, the root of likeness is oneness and on account of that, the like pleases, is to the taste, and delights; the unlike displeases. A virtuous man, therefore, ought to stop at nothing or be content with nothing, except only God, who is One and oneness.

2. The second article is: The heavenly Father begets in me his likeness and from that likeness there comes to us love, or charity. This is the Holy Spirit.

Statement: he that denies this knows little of the Scriptures, or of truth; he knows too little of God, has too little of God.

3. The third article is: There is an agent[84] in the soul such that if the soul were wholly this, it would be uncreated.

Statement: If it should be stated and thought that any part of the soul is uncreated and uncreatable, it would be an error, but if it should be understood as has been explained above, it is a beautiful truth, moral and devout, kindling the love of God.

4. The fourth article in the sermon "Elizabeth's full time came that she should be delivered"[87]—runs thus: If anything other than the Son is begotten or born in you, or if the image [idea] of anything other than the Son is in you, then you have not the Holy Spirit, nor is there grace in you.

Statement as before: He that denies this knows little, for the Holy Spirit proceeds only from the Son. If you wish, therefore, to have the Holy Spirit, the gifts of God, the charity through which the Spirit is diffused in our hearts, be the Son. Son [filius] is derived from "philos," which is love. Work, therefore, in what you do, from love and not from fear. Likewise, secondly, he is called a Son who becomes another person, not another thing. Therefore, love nothing that is other than or foreign to God, for everything that a person loves is his father and begets itself in him. Likewise, in the third place, *the Son of man hath not where to lay his head*, Matthew 8:20. See, therefore, that you have nothing earthly on which to rest, and be the Son, and many similar things, which teach a man to live a holy, pious life.

5. The fifth article is: In man there is an agent which is so high and noble that it receives God in his own naked being or essence, and not in his garment, as he is compassion or truth, but receives him in his own marrow, to the extent that he is exposed.

It should be stated that God falls into the intellect as truth, into the will as goodness, but glides into the very essence of the soul and unites with it in so far as he is God and to the extent he is being or essence.

6. The sixth article runs thus: Without the above-mentioned agent God acts not at all. Whatever God gives, he gives through it, and if God should give us himself without that agent, we would not accept him nor would he be to our taste.

O slow in heart to believe the scriptures, as Christ says, in Luke 24:25. For who doubts that God would *not* suit the taste of a holy man, or that he would not be content with God as he knows him and accepts help or anything pertaining to the senses?

7. The seventh article reads thus: The agent operates uniformly with God; it makes all things, creates all things with God.

This is false as it sounds, for the creature is not a creator, but creation belongs to God alone. It is true that the union of the Word in Christ the man was so great that its peculiarities, its properties, were communicated to him to such a degree that that man, that offspring created the heavens, and is said to be dead and is.

8. The eighth article states that a certain agent in the soul is uncreated [and that] if the whole soul were such, it would be uncreated and un-creatable.

It is false [to say] that any part of the soul is uncreatable but it is true that the soul is intellectual after the image [idea] and species of God, Acts 17:29. But if it were pure intellect, such as God alone is, it would be uncreated and would not be soul. So, too, if a man were entirely soul, then man would be immortal: but then he would not be man. As it is, it is true absolutely, that man is mortal. This ought to summon man to devotion, the love of God and deeds of grace, since God *created man after his own likeness and clothed him according to himself*, that he might be intellectual from the garment of pure intellect, Ecclesiasticus 17:1ff. But the natural son whom he begot, he clothed not only according to himself, but with himself, that he might be god from God, uncreated from Uncreated, and so on; for example, pure intellect from pure intellect, according to the statement of Tobit 1:9, *he begat a son and put his name upon him*.

9. The ninth article states: Nothing is true that does not include all truth.

It must be said that to deny this is to be ignorant, for a half-truth is not truth. Besides, God is truth, John 14:6, and he is in a proposition altogether or not at all. In such matters one ought to proceed intellectually and not be sidetracked by imaginations, as Boethius says.

10. The tenth article says: Wherever we find ourselves among things we enjoy or do not enjoy, things pleasing or displeasing, to whatever we find ourselves inclined, we ought to report and discover it truly to him. If we do this—to God, that is—he will discover or reveal truly to us all that he has: his secret, his divinity, his wisdom.

It must be said that this is all true. Surely the affection of man should be separated from the love of the world in order that he may be united with God by the love of charity. For, as Augustine says, *Questions* 36, "complete desire, that is of earthy things, no love; little desire great love; no desire, perfect love." Now it is a fact that God gives himself wholly to whomsoever he gives himself, for it is impious to expect of God anything halfway, or imperfect; but it is true that not all men receive all things.

11. The eleventh article runs thus: He that seeks nothing cannot com-

plain if he finds nothing. He finds what he has sought. He that seeks and aims at anything except God seeks and aims at nothing and therefore receives what he seeks by receiving nothing. He that seeks nothing nor aims at anything except God, pure and purely, to him God gives, discovers or reveals every secret that God has in his divine heart, and it becomes as much his as it is God's, neither more nor less—if only he seeks it without intermission.

This is true, devout and moral, and is clear from what has already been said. As to what is said at the end, that God belongs to a divine man as much as to himself, this is an emphatic expression, according to the statement, Psalm 63:1, *O God, my God*, he said, *early will I seek thee*; for otherwise the works of God in us would not be ours unless our God were in us; for no work is ours, unless the beginning of the work should be ours in us. As it is, Isaiah 26:12 says *thou hast wrought all our works in us*. "Our," he says, and "in us." For it should be understood that the Scripture, the saints, and the preacher frequently and conveniently employ such emphatic ways of speaking, as the speaker's heart suggests, and the hearers are more aroused to the love of virtue and of God, according to the remark of Jerome: "O tear, yours is the power, yours is the kingdom, you do not fear the judge's tribunal; you impose silence on the accusers of your friends. There is no one who would forbid you to enter, if you enter alone, but you do not leave alone and empty. You torture the devil more than the punishment of hell. Why go on? You conquer the unconquerable; you bind the all-powerful; you bend the son of the virgin."

12. The twelfth article runs thus: There is a certain agent in the soul, uncreated, etc., as above.

13. The thirteenth article runs thus: All creatures are nothing in themselves.

To deny this is to be ignorant and blaspheme God, as if God were not the creator and the creature was not created. For creation is from nothing: not so making.[88] John 1:3 says: *All things were made by him and without him was not anything made.*

14. The fourteenth article says: All things are perfected in the humble man. A humble man and God are not two but one. Let God beware lest he fail to pour himself into a really humble man. A humble man does not need to ask God: he can command God. A humble man has power over God as he, God, has power over himself. If that man were in hell, God would have to come to hell, and hell would have to be the Kingdom of Heaven. God must needs do this. He is compelled to it . . . since that man's being is divine and divine being is his also.

It must be said that this is all true, moral and devout, however emphatic, as has been said above about the tear. As for the statement that such a man and God are not two but one, it is evident from the fact that in John 17, the Saviour prays to the Father for us. For a humble man, in so far as he is humble, is not two with humility—for two implies division and is the root of division. How could anyone be one [humble?] if separated from humility, or white, if separated from whiteness and without whiteness? Therefore, wherever a humble man might be in hell, there would necessarily be humility. It is obvious, too, that in the same way that God is God, man is divine by analogy. For no one is divine without God, as nothing is white without whiteness.

15. The fifteenth article, in the sermon which begins "He that heareth me is not ashamed,"[89] runs thus: If a man should consider himself the only begotten Son, to him would belong all that belongs to the only begotten Son. God performs all his works to this end, that we should be the only begotten Son.

It must be said that this is true. The work of nature and creation is arranged according to the work of grace and re-creation. Likewise, we should be sons of God in vain, except through him who is truly the Son of God—naturally, since he is first-born among many brothers and first-born of all creation.

Also this: God makes haste to come to a good man, as if the divine being or divine essence would burst unless it should reveal to us the whole depth of its divinity.

It is true and emphatic, and often the saints say that God grieves about the sin of man as if the sin hurt and saddened him more than it does the sinner. It is a fact that equality detests everything unequal, when compared with equals. So humility opposes and detests, through its essence, anyone more proud than a humble man; for the latter hates, through participation in humility itself, everything proud; and "because one is more than the other."

As for the statement at the end of the article that a divine man is nothing other than what God is, that is false and error.[90]

16. The sixteenth article runs thus: As long as you love any man less than you love yourself, you have never loved yourself in truth. A good man loves all men as himself. Some men say: I love a friendly benefactor more than other men. This is not right and it is imperfect. If I really loved another as myself, whatever happened to him in the way of comfort or disturbance, whether death or life, would please me as much as if it happened to me: this would be true friendship. Therefore St. Paul says: *I could hope for anathema,*

that is, to be cut off from God, *for my brothers' sake* and for God's sake. For the perfect man, to be separated from God for an instant would be as hard as to be separated from him eternally. To be separated from God is the punishment of hell.

It must be said that all this is true according to I Corinthians 12:26, *If one member be honored, all members rejoice. Now are ye the body of Christ and members in particular.* And I Corinthians 3:22, *Whether this world or life or death, or things present, or things to come: all are yours, and ye are Christ's.* The explanation is that charity loves all in one and one God in all. Admittedly, it is the punishment of hell to be separated from God, as to see God in his essence, to have him, to be united with him is the essential prize. Moreover, charity is for all that has ever been created, and would not dismiss God even for a moment, even as it would not dismiss him eternally.

17. The seventeenth article says that Paul says: I desired to be anathema, etc. He said this out of his perfection; otherwise he would not have been able to say this truly. And as for Paul's leaving god, for God's sake, he left all that he could receive from God and all that God could give him, and then God remained for him, not by [the fact of] giving or receiving, but by the fact that God was in him.

It must be said that this is true and clear from a former article.

18. The eighteenth says that no suffering can come to a man united with God; as little as in the divine essence.

It must be said that this is true according to the statement: *Whatever happens to him will not make a just man sad,* Proverbs 12:21. I took notice of this in dealing with the first article of the first document.

As to the addition made here that there is something in the soul akin to God, as it is one [with him] and not united, something unique and having nothing in common with anything else:

It must be said that this is true according to the statement: *We are his offspring,* Acts 17:28, and John 16:33 says, *In the world ye shall have tribulation,* and before that, *in me peace,* and in John 17:21, the Son prays that we may be one even as he is one with the Father. The things the article objects to are to be explained by these statements.

As for the statement that there is something uncreated in the soul, that has been explained several times above.

19. The nineteenth article says: The eye with which I see God is the same eye with which God sees me. My eye and God's eye are one eye, and one vision or seeing, and one knowing and one loving.

It must be said this is true according to what Augustine teaches in *On the Trinity,* Book IX, chapter 12, about the offspring begotten by the knowable and the knowing. And the Apostle says: *Then shall I know even as also I am known*, I Corinthians 13:12.

20. The twentieth article runs thus: A man who stands in the love of God ought to be dead with respect to himself and all creatures. For example, he should care as little for himself as for one who is beyond the sea. That man remains in equality and in unity.

It must be said that this is all true according as he remains more or less in charity.

21. The twenty-first, in the sermon "When Herod was dead,"[91] says this: The mind alone is free.

It must be said that, although there is some question about this among the teachers, yet it is truer that by virtue there is freedom in the mind, as if in its root; but formally [freedom] is in the will, because all the freedom of the will is from the mind descended; but the rational powers [agents] meet opposition. The mind pertains to the rational by essence, [whereas] the will pertains to the rational by participation, according to what is said by the Philosopher: the will is in the reason.[92]

22. The twenty-second, in the sermon "He pleased God,"[93] runs thus, after some preliminaries: That is all one truth, because everything that is true is true in one truth and there is only one truth.

It must be said that this is all true as has been explained above.

23. The twenty-third article runs thus: A hundred men are many and numbered; a thousand angels are many and without number; but the three persons in the Trinity are neither many nor numbered. If they were many, they would not be one.

It must be said that this is true, according to I John 5:7, *these three are one*. For deprivation is the beginning of number, but the beginning of multiplicity is negation, but in God there is no deprivation nor yet negation, since there is fullness of being.[94]

24. The twenty-fourth article, in the sermon "In this was manifested the love of God, because that God sent his only begotten Son into the world," goes thus:[95] Ever since the Son of God assumed human nature he has made my own all that he has in himself, because human nature is common to all men, belonging and related equally to all. And below: He gave me all that he ever gave to his Son; I except nothing.

25. The twenty-fifth article runs thus: I say that in all he ever gave to his only begotten Son, the Father had regard for my human nature before him, and aimed more at me, and gave to me sooner than to him. He gave to him for my sake. And below: all that he gave to him in human nature is no more foreign, or extraneous. or more remote, or distant from me than from him.

26. The twenty-sixth article runs thus: God does not give unless he gives the whole and gives everything. God does not know how to give a little. He would either give [himself] wholly or give nothing at all. To all things he gives, neither in vain nor in part; his giving is quite simple and perfect.

It must be said with regard to these three articles that they are all true and moral, giving rise to devotion, to the love of God, and to acts of grace, according to Romans 8:32, *with him, he gave us all things;* and Romans 5:5, *the love of God is shed abroad in our hearts by the Holy Ghost which is given unto us and dwelleth therein.* For he gives all things to all, but not all receive all things; he gives equally but we receive unequally, as has often been said.

27. The twenty-seventh article reads thus: God gives nothing outside himself; he always gives from eternity and not in time. God has nothing to do with time but he gives and works only from eternity.

It must be said that this is true according to Jeremiah 31:3: *I have loved thee with an everlasting love.* And the gloss: *He chose us before the foundation of the world.* Still, it is true that we receive in time.

For evidence on the four previous articles and of many other things in Scripture, it should be noted:

First, that God, himself one, as the first being, does not depend for being or for the consequences of being on anything but, conversely, all things that are later than he, and after him, depend on him for being and the consequences of being. Otherwise, the first [cause] would not be rich in itself, as *De Causis* says. Hence it is that from God all being descends, the being of nature as well as of cognition, or the intellectual being of art and nature. This is what John 13:13 truly says: *You call me master,* with respect to the being of knowledge and doctrine, *and Lord,* with respect to the being of nature; then follows: *and ye say well,* that is, you speak the truth. He supplies an explanation saying: *for so I am. I am* refers to being; and perhaps for this reason, very appropriately, the expression *I am* is used twice in Exodus 3:14: *I am who I am,* on account of the twofold being that descends from him. And this supplies an appropriate explanation of Genesis 1:1, *In the beginning God created the heaven and the earth.* By *heaven* may be understood spiritual or intellectual being; by *earth,* material being, the work of nature. Again, by *heaven* is understood the work of re-creation and grace; by *earth,* the work of creation and nature.

I take, secondly, what is said in Romans 13:1, *things which are of God are ordered.* Hence it is that the work of creation of nature is ordered to the work of re-creation and grace, material to formal, matter to form, passive to active, woman to man. I Corinthians 11:9, *Neither was the man created for the woman; but the woman for the man.* Whence it is significant that the heaven is put first. *In the beginning,* he says, *God created the heaven,* and the Master says, in John 13:13, *ye call me Master and Lord.* It is true that they occur together in time, and in effect, according to the statement, Genesis 2:24: *there will be two in one flesh,* man and woman, active and passive, heaven and earth. *Two,* he says, for otherwise they would not be ordered, for order is of plurals; but of one flesh: in effect, together, at one time. Whence Thomas [Aquinas], in the last question of Book VI, of his *Quodlibet,* carefully considering the matter, says that the watery sky and the whole universe of nature is ordered to the empyreal sky. For things which are from one are necessarily ordered to one; but in ordered things the prior always flows into the inferior, for the first is rich in itself. Augustine indicates this clearly, *Confessions,* Book XII, chapter 2, where he says of that *heaven of heavens, O Lord, of which we hear in the words of the Psalm:* "Heaven, earth and all that we see is earth to the heaven we do not see."

From these arguments it follows, in the third place, that in the work of nature and creation there shines forth the work of re-creation and grace.

Therefore, after these preliminary statements, it should be said that just as in nature, we see that a particular agent intends some particular like itself, yet the nature of the species, which is the root and beginning of action for the particular, intends something like itself according to its own species and nature, by which nature works secretly in these things. For in the generation of the particular, she intends the species.[96] So, in divine things, the Father does not beget the Father but the Son, one God in nature, because nature is the beginning of begetting in the Father. Hence too among creatures, woman is beyond the intention of nature, in particular and by accident; but by herself [she comes of] the intention of nature in general, which is a force planted in heaven, according to Avicenna (*Metaphysica,* Tract. 9, chapter 6).

Therefore, all that is stated in the above four articles is abundantly clear, namely, that the Word assumed human nature from the first intention but this nature, namely, in Christ, [was assumed] for the sake of humankind. Therefore, by assuming nature in himself and by himself, he bestowed the grace of sonship and adoption on all men, on me, on you, on anyone who participates univocally and equally in nature, according to the statement: *The Word was made flesh,* John 1:14, in Christ, *and dwelt amongst us.* And before that, *to them gave he power to become the Sons of God, that he might be the first-born among many brothers,* Romans 8:29. He assumed human nature, natural and not irrational. Therefore, if you wish the Word made flesh to dwell in you, to become a Son of God, to receive this grace bestowed on nature, be a man: live according to reason, according to the spirit and not according to the flesh. For *that which is born of the flesh is flesh and that which is born of the spirit is spirit*, John 3:6. *For they that are after the flesh do mind the things of the flesh. For if ye live after the flesh, ye shall die, but if through the spirit ye shall live. For as many as are led by the spirit of God, they are the sons of God. For the Spirit itself beareth witness with our spirit that we are Sons of God; and if sons, then heirs, heirs of God, and joint-heirs with Christ*, for there follows: *whom he did predestinate to be conformed to the image of his Son, that he might be the first-born among many brethren*, as has been said (Romans 8:5, 13, 14, 16, 17, 29). *For flesh and blood do not reveal but the Father which is in heaven*, Matthew 16:17. "The Father," he says. The Father as father, has regard only for his Son or sons: he reveals to them. The more you have been the Son, conformed to the image of the Christ, the more you will receive. Be a Son and you will see. Take a lover: he knows the things that are of a lover, as Augustine says (*The Gospel of John*, Tracts. 124 and 26): "The Saviour says that he that shall leave all things shall receive a hundredfold, but surely he has not left all things who expects a hundredfold."

From the foregoing it is plain that God gives to all abundantly; he gives to all things; he gives beyond time; in everlasting love he chose us in himself before the foundation of the world; but we receive *in* time when we *are*, and are sons. Whence the apostle says significantly: *He chose us in himself*, that is, in the Son, *that we should be holy and without blame*, Ephesians 1:4. Therefore, be holy and without blame and you will see. God the Father and the Son have nothing to do with time. Generation is not in time, but at the end and limit of time. In the past and future movements of things, your heart flits about; it is in vain that you attempt to know eternal things; in divine things, you should be occupied intellectually, as has been said above.

God, the Word made flesh, in Christ, assumed the human nature common to all men, *for he will have all men to be saved*, I Timothy 2:4, and so, according to the harmony of nature, in which the work of grace is reflected, he has secretly worked our salvation, as has been said. Whence, whatever he bestowed on *him*, he has given to all men with him. For what would he not give, who gave his only begotten Son, God and Holy Spirit, in whom are given all things, because they are by essence given?

Finally, it should be noted that God, by first intention, assumed Man, nature, that is, and not a person, teaching us that if we wish to be sons of God we should love whatever man is nearest, not *this* man, nor what belongs to this or that one, or to myself, according to Matthew 20:14, *take what is thine own. He came to his own and his own received him not*, John 1:11. Therefore he came among those that belonged to him, who did not ask what things are theirs but what things are God's. The Saviour says: *Thou shalt love thy neighbor as thyself.* Surely, if you love your father, mother, brothers and sisters, because they are *your* father, mother, brothers and sisters, *you are holden with the cords of sin,* Proverbs 5:22. *A threefold cord is not quickly broken,* Ecclesiastes 4:12. The first rope is that you love your own; the second that you love your father on earth, whose son you are; the third is that you do not love your neighbor as yourself.

For you are not your father, mother, brother or sister. Therefore, love them because they are men: for you, too, are a man. The Word assumed Man, nature itself, first naturally, but this Man in Adam, in a person, for nature's sake. Hence it is that he purged it of the original sin which mars nature, but not of the actual sin that is in us, which concerns the person and mars it, as it is aptly explained in Ezekiel 18:20, *The son shall not bear the iniquity of the father.* "Iniquity," he says, that is, sin, for often the son bears the penalty of his father's sin, according to the statement, Exodus 20:5, *I am God, punishing the iniquity of the fathers in the sons to the third and fourth generations.* There is an example of the foregoing in nature, as has been said above. In addition, we see it in art as follows: a housebuilder first and within himself plans a whole house; he conceives it and its appearance; the house takes form and is united with him; but the parts of the house are secondary, and as if by accident and at first he works them out separately. Therefore, if you wish to love your neighbor as yourself, take away what is yours, as above. Yours is what is your own; Man, or human nature, you have in common with every man. God himself is common to all. Again, he is seen, he is loved and possessed, and he is united with us. "Remove the *this* and *that* in creatures and you will see God," says Augustine in *On the Trinity,* Book VIII, chapter 3. Remove what is yours; yours is sin, falsehood and universally evil, according to the statement, Psalm 116:11, *all men are liars;* and Romans 3:4. Yours is what is your own and no one else's. *For a man's foes shall be they of his own household,* Matthew 10:36. For the more a thing is a part of one's household or one's own, so much the more is it an enemy to Man. Remove him because he is this or that person; love him because he is Man, which is in common.[97]

As for the statement that God gives nothing outside of himself, he always gives from eternity, not in time—but he gives and works only from eternity. It must be said that he that denies this knows little. Speaking of God, Augustine mentions this in *Confessions* I, 10: "All things of tomorrow, and all beyond, and all of yesterday, and all behind it, thou hast done today. What is it to me, though any comprehend not this?"

As for the statement that God has nothing to do with time, it is true, because God is not in time and is not affected by time but his activity is his substance. There is, however, a truer and more penetrating explanation of why God is not in time and has nothing to do with time, namely, that time does not exist, as is clear from the Philosopher, the Commentator, and Augustine.[98] Therefore, God is not in time, just as being is not in that which has no being; for God is being. In fact, this is the whole reason why time does not exist—because God, that is, being, is not in time—just as he is not in evil, privation, negation, sin, and in parts which do not exist as such beyond and outside the whole. For such things as have no being are recognized by not knowing them, according to Matthew 25:12, *I know you not*, and in Psalm 15:4, *in whose eyes a vile person is contemned*. The meaning is that a vile or bad man does not come under the knowledge of God,"in his sight." And again, by the very fact that a thing is not perceived by God, it is nothing. For just as that which is not perceived as warmth is not warm, that which is not perceived by being itself is nothing.

28. The twenty-eighth article says: God does not see any evil.[99] Whenever I sin I am in evil, and then God does not see me or know me.

It must be said that this is true and clear from what has already been said about time and from what follows in an article to the effect that he looks only upon himself; but in him there is no evil.

29. The twenty-ninth article states that all the works of Christ belong to a just man and all the merits of the saints and their rewards belong to me as if I did those things myself.

It must be said that this is true according to the statement: *I believe in the communion of saints*, and it says in Psalm 119:63, *I am the companion of all them that fear thee*; Augustine also teaches this in many places, and it is clear from what has been said above by way of illustration.

30. The thirtieth article runs thus: All creatures are pure nothing; there is no creature which is anything.

It must be said that this is true, as has been explained above, according to the statement: All things were made through him and without him was not anything made.

31. The thirty-first article runs thus: We ought not to know about any "for what reason" or "why?" outside of ourselves, neither God nor creature, neither for our own sake, nor for the sake of anything outside of ourselves, because to whatever we are moved, otherwise than from within, it is all an act of moral sin.

Solution: It must be said that this, like countless other statements, appears meaningless to the stupid, yet it is obvious truth that a work is not perfect or divine unless a man works from the God within him, according to the following: *the Father that dwelleth in me, he doeth the works*, John 14:10, and unless he should work from the condition existing within, according to the following: *The Holy Ghost shall come upon thee*, Luke 1:35. "Upon thee," it says.

32. The thirty-second article reads thus: There are some people to whom God is pleasing in one form and not in another. This is absolutely wrong; whoever accepts God should accept him equally in all things.

Solution: It is true that the reason for loving God is God and a Way without a way.

33. The thirty-third article runs thus: David says, Psalm 2:7, *this day have I begotten thee*. What is today? Eternity. "I beget me thee, and thee me, eternally."

Solution: It should be said that these are the words of Augustine, *Confessions* XI, 16, and the teachers take it to mean that God begets himself God.

34. The thirty-fourth article reads thus: An aristocrat is not satisfied with this, that he is that only begotten Son whom the Father begets eternally, but he also wants to be the Father and enter into the likeness of eternal Fatherhood, to beget him who begets me eternally.

Solution: I have said what Augustine says in *On the Trinity* IX, 12, that between a thing known and him that knows it an offspring is begotten, common to both; likewise [it is so] between a thing thought and him who thinks it, between one who loves and the thing loved; wherefore a man ought to be anxious to know God and frequently, at least, to think of him and love him.

35. The thirty-fifth article, in the sermon "The just shall live forever,"[100] reads thus: Those who aim neither at riches, nor honors, nor advantage, nor delight, nor utility, nor inner devotion, nor holiness, nor reward, nor the Kingdom of Heaven, but have renounced all these things and all that is their own—they honor God.

Solution: This is all true and to deny it is to be ignorant and to err; for the perfect man is satisfied with nothing and relies on no reward or gift of God, but on God himself, who is, and is sufficient reward for him according to the following, II Corinthians 3:5, *Our sufficiency is of God*; Genesis 15:1, *I will be your reward*; Exodus 33:15, *If thy presence go not with me, carry us not up hence*, he says, to whom it was said: *I will show you all good*.

36. The thirty-sixth article reads thus: My living is the being of God, or my life is the essence of God: whatever is God's is whatever is mine.

It must be said that this is false and error as it sounds. It is, however, true, devout and moral that all the being of a just man, to the extent that he is just, is from the being of God—but analogically. Likewise, no one is truly divine except by God within him; see above, IX, 14. For, obviously, no one is just except from justice, as no one is white except from whiteness, according to the following: *For me to live is Christ*, Philippians 1:21; and again, *I live, yet not I; but Christ liveth in me*, Galatians 2:20. Wherefore, a man ought to be anxious to be just, and to act justly. This has been mentioned above.

37. The thirty-seventh article runs thus: The just soul is to be with God, by the side of God, exactly his equal, neither beneath nor above him. Who are they that are thus equal [to God]? Those who have no likeness, in whom there is no image [idea] or form. They are all like to God, because the being of God has no likeness, the essence of God has no likeness, and in him there is no image [idea] or form. To those souls who thus stand even, the Father gives evenly, withholding nothing which he would not give them. All the Father has he gives to them evenly—if they stay even and are not more for themselves than for others. [The just soul] ought not to be closer to itself than to another, desiring or caring for its own honor and its own advantage and whatever belongs to it, more than for what belongs to a stranger; whatever belongs to anybody should not be foreign to it or distant from it, whether it is good or evil.

Solution: The meaning is clear from the above. For, obviously, he who loves God ought to deny himself, remove whatever is his own, love his neighbor as himself, and to be so conformed to the divine will that he wants whatever God wants, and evenly this and that; for if unevenly, then no longer does he love only God or God's will, or God in all things, or all things in God.

38. The thirty-eighth runs thus: The Father begets his Son in the soul in the same way that he begets him in eternity and not otherwise. He must do so whether it pleases him or displeases him.

It must be said that this is true because the Father does not beget different sons, nor does he beget differently in me than in eternity. For in God there is no "different" or "differently," nor has he a Son in eternity, except the one who is *first-born among many brethren*, Romans 8:29, who is transformed into the same image [idea], since he is not divided among the many but unites the many in himself, seeing that he is God, who is in all by essence.

As for the words "he must do so," they are true, but it is an emphatic expression, commending God's goodness and love. He is wholly good by essence and his goodness does not allow him to be without offspring as [Pseudo-] Dionysius says.[101] Wherefore, he gives both himself and all that he has according to the following: *With him he gives us all things*, Romans 8:32, provided we are ready to receive; Revelation 3:20, *I stand at the door and knock*; and Isaiah 30:18, *The Lord waits that he may have compassion on you.*

It is his essence to give, according to the following, Matthew 23:37, *How often would I have gathered thy children together and ye would not*—for first he himself is rich—as Augustine says on that passage.[102]

39. The thirty-ninth article reads thus: The Father begets his Son without intermission. I say more: he begets me his Son and the same Son. All that God does is one; therefore he begets me as his Son without distinction. And below: For this reason, the heavenly Father is truly my Father, because I am his Son and from him I have all that I have, and because I am the same Son and not another, because the Father does only one thing, therefore he makes me his one Son without distinction. We are transformed and changed into him even as in the sacrament the bread is changed into the body of Christ; and however many loaves there may be, yet they become one body of Christ. Whatever is changed into something else becomes one with it; so I am changed into him because he makes me one with his being—not like him—by the living God. It is true that there is no distinction there.

Solution: All that has been said is false and ridiculous, according to the imagination of my opponents, but it is true according to the true meaning, that that same Son is God himself in each one of us, and that with him and in him, he gives all things to himself. It is he through whom he does all that he does and without him he does nothing. An example has been given above, from nature. The example of the sacrament on the altar is also clear, except that every "just as" is as exact as possible. For in the sacrament on the altar the whole is changed into the whole, but it is not so in us. Whence it does not follow that we are God, as in Christ the first-born man is God, begotten the idea and likeness of the Father-God—for we are *after* the idea and likeness, and created.

40. The fortieth runs thus: I have been wondering whether I should be willing to receive or desire anything from God, because where I could be receiving from God I should be under God or below God, like a servant or a slave, and he like a master in giving; for so we ought not to be in life eternal.

Solution: It is plain that in eternal life, God will be all, and *all things in all*, I Corinthians 15:28. But in addition, all we faithful are one body with Christ, the first-born, I Corinthians 12:12ff. and 27. But of the whole and its parts, there is one being and one function. If one suffers, all suffer with it; if one rejoices, all rejoice; in fact, on the words, *for their sakes, I sanctify myself*, John 17:19, Augustine speaks thus: "Because they are I in the present." The perfect man does not rest short of or under God: he is not a slave. John 15:15, *Now I call you not slaves but friends.* "Love knows no rank," as Bernard says, "for it either finds equals or makes equals." And according to the Philosopher,[103] "There is no love between slave and master." For "master" is a term of superiority and "slave" a term of subjection, wherefore God is called our Father but the master of those that are beneath man, Matthew 11:25, *I confess to thee, Father, master of heaven and earth.*

41. The forty-first, in the sermon "All good gifts,"[104] runs thus: To that man who commits himself to God and diligently seeks his will, whatever God gives is best and must, of necessity, be best, and there could be no other way which could be better, although something else might appear to be better, or even be better, yet it would not be so good for you because God wishes it that way and not otherwise. And whether it be ill-health or poverty, or hunger, or whatever it may be—whatever God permits to be done or to happen in your case, or does not permit—this is best, whether it be devotion or inner delight, or whatever you have or have not.

Solution: It must be said that he who feels differently does not truly love God only and in all things and all things in him, nor is he perfectly conformed to the divine will, especially as, by the fact that God wishes anything, it is good, and what he does not wish is evil. Augustine, *Confessions* X, 37, "He is thy best servant, Lord, who looks not so much to hear from thee, that which himself willeth; as rather to will that which from thee he heareth."

42. The forty-second article reads thus: A man ought to love his neighbor as himself, not that a man should love his neighbors for the same good or in the same degree as the God whom he loves for his own sake, but he ought to love them as intensely as himself, in every way.

The solution is clear from what has been said: For he who loves God alone and all things in him, has no "more or less," according to Matthew 10:37, *He that loveth more is not worthy of me.* Again, he that loves God with all his heart, with all his soul, and with all his mind and all his strength, surely has nothing to love outside of God, where "more or less" occurs among creatures. Wherefore, Mark 12:31, has *Thou shalt love thy neighbor as thyself.* "Tanquam," it says, that is, as much as (tantum quantum) and Augustine often uses that form.

43. The forty-third article reads thus: All creatures are pure nothing. Whatever does not have being is nothing. No creature has being because the being of creatures depends on God's presence. If God should turn away for an instant, creatures would be reduced to nothing. From time to time I have said—and it is true—he who should receive the whole world along with God would have no more than if he had God alone.

Solution: It must be said that to deny this is to blaspheme God and to deny him. For if, without God, a creature has any being, however small, then God is not the cause of all things. Besides, a creature would not be created, for creation is the receiving of being from nothing. Again, two means a division and is the root of all division. Whence, if God is divided, and two, with something else, that will not be a thing with being; for God is being and the immediate cause of all being. Besides, God is One without one, and beyond number, whence he does not come into number with anything that has number. Notably evident, therefore, is the shortness and weakness of understanding of those who object to the foregoing. Besides, according to them, there is no infinite good, for infinite is that outside of which there is nothing. Besides, the creature would not be something to be despised but something to be loved as good, in and of itself.

44. The forty-fourth article reads thus: The virtue which a perfect man possesses has its root rooted and planted in the ground of deity, where, alone, it has its being or essence.

Solution: This is true according to the following. Psalm 24:10, *The Lord of virtues, he is the king of glory*. Thomas teaches this, *Summa Theologica* II, 1, question 65, article 4, distinguishing virtues social, purgatorial, of the clean soul, and exemplary. And this is what the apostle says, Ephesians 3:17, *rooted and grounded in love*. Romans 5:5, *The love of God is shed abroad in our hearts by the Holy Ghost*.

45. The forty-fifth article runs thus: All things are perfected in the humble man.

Solution: Explained above.

46. The forty-sixth article reads thus: All created things are nothing in themselves.

Explained above.

47. The forty-seventh article, in the sermon which begins, "Thou wilt have mercy on the people that are thine,"[105] reads thus: My body and my soul are united in one being, not as in one function, as the soul is united with the eye in one function, that is, in seeing. So it is too with the food I eat: it becomes one in being with my nature and not merely united with it in one function. As an example, this represents that great union which we ought to have with God in one being, not only in one function, and that is why the Pharisee asked the Lord to eat with him.[106]

Solution: It is true, devout and moral, according to the words of Augustine, *Confessions* VII, 16: "Grow, and thou shalt feed upon me: nor shalt thou convert me, like the food of thy flesh, into thee, but thou shalt be converted into me."

48. The forty-eighth article, in the sermon which begins "They were

slain with the sword,"[107] reads thus: God recognizes only being, knows only being; God loves only his being, thinks only being.

Solution: Obviously, God knows all things and loves them in himself and through his essence. Wherefore, we ought to be anxious to love, by which we remain in God and God in us. Likewise, again, that we may be sons of God, according to the following, John 1:12, *To them gave he power to become the sons of God*. For the Son is in the Father and the Father in the Son, but son [filius] is from "philos," which is love, which works by love and not by fear. Likewise, the Son is he who has no place outside of God where he may lay his head, according to the example of the dove which is spoken of in Genesis 8:9. Compare also, Psalm 16:2, *Thou art my Lord, since my goodness extendeth not to thee*, [of which] another translation reads: *since it is not well with me without you*. Likewise, the son is he who becomes another, not another thing, who does not have as father anything other than or foreign to God, according to the following: *Call no man your father upon the earth; for one is your Father*, Matthew 23:8.

As for the second statement in the same article: "I say that all are one being," it sounds bad and is false thus: It is true that they are one in being, just as they are one in God who is being, of whom all things are and have their being immediately. Wherefore, let man be anxious to avoid evil, which is deprivation of being, and consequently deprivation of truth and good, and so outside of God and the communion of saints.

49. The forty-ninth article runs thus: There is no life so mean but that if it is taken as being, it will rank higher than anything else which ever had being or life. And below: I said sometime that a coal is nobler than gold. This is an exceedingly strange [thing to say]. A stone, to the extent it has being, would be better than God and his Godhead without being, if being could be abstracted from him.

Solution: He who denies this is ignorant, for, without being, all things are nothing and certainly, without being, God would not be, nor could he be God. Wherefore, morally, a man should be anxious to avoid sin and evil, which is deprivation of being, as has been said above.

50. The fiftieth, in the sermon "Now I know of a surety that God hath sent his angel,"[108] runs thus: Everything that is, is God.

Solution: This is false and error. But it is true that *from him, through him, and in him are all things*, Romans 11:36. And Tobit 10:5, *Having all things in you alone*. And according to this, all things without God are to be despised, and he is to be loved in all things and all things in him.

51. The fifty-first, in the sermon "Jesus entered a certain castle,"[109] reads thus: I have sometimes said about that castle that it is an agent in the soul

which alone is free. Sometimes I have called it the guardian of the soul or spirit. Sometimes I have called it the Light of the soul or spirit. Sometimes I have said that it is a kind of spark. But now I say that it is neither this nor that, and yet it is this or that, or above this or that, higher than heaven above earth. Therefore, I call it now by a more aristocratic name than I have ever named it; [but] it lies in wait to contradict this name, for it is above it. It is free of all names and naked, apart from all forms and of itself. It is quite simple, just as God is simple and One, since there is no way to look upon it.

Solution: It must be said that in the sermon presented to me some time ago, I have found many things which I never said. Many things, too, are written there without understanding, obscure and confused like dreams, on account of which I have thoroughly blamed them [the copyists]; but as for matters which are touched on here, it is true that God, in the conception and guise of truth, enters the understanding. He enters the will in the conception and guise of good; but through his naked essence, which is above any name, he enters and penetrates into the naked essence of the soul, which also has no name of its own, and is higher than understanding and will, as being essence by its own powers. That is the castle which Jesus enters with respect to being, rather than with respect to function, bestowing on the soul divine and Godlike being, through Grace, which regards essence and being according to the following: *By the grace of God I am what I am*, I Corinthians 15:10. This is moral, teaching man to renounce all things and to be made bare, to become poor, to have no love of earthly things, to be him who truly wishes to be a disciple of Christ, and to love God without measure or any property that includes measure.

52. The fifty-second article, in the sermon which begins "Jesus went into the temple of God and drove out all those that bought and sold,"[110] runs thus, about a certain perfection to which the soul or man can attain in this life: Then the outward man is obedient to the inner man until death and he has constant peace in the service of God for all time.

Solution: It should be said, as above, that he who denies this is immature, as the Philosopher says, and he does not deny himself.

53. The fifty-third article, in the sermon which begins "I will pour clean water upon you,"[111] runs thus: The soul departs from itself and God enters it, and there God begets his only begotten Son; there the soul undergoes regeneration in God, that is, the Holy Spirit.

The solution is clear from the above, and it is moral, arousing man, who is *after* the image of God, to the love of God, particularly as between the lover and the beloved an offspring is begotten, common to both, which is love, that is, charity, and the Holy Spirit, the love with which the Father loves his Son and us. And, surely, we love him through the Holy Spirit dwelling in us. I John 4:19 is pertinent to this: *Let us Love God, since he first loved us.*

54. The fifty-fourth article, in the sermon which begins "Like a morning star through a cloud,"[112] runs thus: God is neither good, better, nor best. So I speak ill whenever I call God good, as if I were calling white black.

Solution: It should be said that God, since he is above any name that we can give him, is more excellent than white or black. This is worth setting forth, or setting before men, in order to commend God's excellence, that in his name *every knee may bow, of things in heaven, and things in earth, and things under the earth,* Philippians 2:10.

55. The fifty-fifth article, in the sermon "He pleased God in his days,"[113] runs thus: As St. Augustine says, God is nearer to the soul than it is to itself.[114] God and the soul are so near together that there is really no distinction between them. That same recognition or knowledge in which God knows himself is the knowing, or knowledge, or recognition of every abstract spirit.

Solution: Everything that is distinct from God is distinct from being, for from him, immediately, all being is.

As for the statement that God knows himself in the same way that he knows us, that is what the apostle says, I Corinthians 13:12, *Then shall I know even as also I am known,* and what is said in Psalm 36:9, *in thy light we shall see light,* for each thing is known in its own kind and by no means in another.

56. The fifty-sixth runs thus: When a man has right intentions in all that he does, God is the initiator of that intention. This is the actuality of the intention and it is pure, divine nature, which finds its goal in divine nature itself.

Solution: It should be said that the end and beginning of every good work and right intention is the divine, pure substance of God. But as for the statement that "the actuality of the intention is the divine essence," it is not well put, partly because an act is produced by an object and nothing can produce itself, partly because an act pertains to a creature, but God is the creator.

57. The fifty-seventh article reads thus: The soul is reborn in God. Whenever this birth occurs, it is the soul giving birth to the only begotten Son. Thus the Virgin's sons are far more numerous than those of other women, for they are born beyond time in eternity. Still, however many the children

to which the soul gives birth in eternity, they are only one Son, because it all happens beyond time, in the day of eternity.

Solution: It should be said that the truth of the foregoing is clear from Galatians 4:27 and Isaiah 54:1, *More are the children of the desolate woman, more than of her that hath a husband*. Origen teaches well and clearly about this in a gloss on the words *a conspiracy has been found*, Jeremiah 11:9. Augustine says: "To the extent that we grasp the eternal with our minds we are no longer in this world," and again, he says that "doers of good works in God are made Sons, they are the progeny and offspring of the holy soul." As for the statement: "However many are the children to which the soul gives birth in eternity, they are only one Son," it should be said that either works or doers are sons of God, by the one Son, who is God. He is the image [idea]; we are sons after the image. He is the likeness; we are after the likeness. He is the natural Son; we are adoptive sons, transformed into the same image that he might be the first-born among many brothers. He is the heir; we are joint-heirs in so far as we are sons and members of him, for the sake of which he is the one Saviour.

58. The fifty-eighth article runs thus: The man who lives virtuously is on the right track, because, as I said eight days ago, virtues are of the very heart of God.

This is true, as has been said above about the exemplary virtues.

59. The fifty-ninth runs thus: A man ought so to live that he is identified with God's Son and so as to be the only begotten Son. Between the only begotten Son and the soul there is no distinction.

Solution: This article states three things:

1. "Man ought so to live as to be identical with the only begotten Son." This is true; for a man ought to live in love; but *he who abides in love abides in God*, I John 4:16, and later in 5:20 he says, *Let us be in his true Son*.

2. "to be the only begotten Son." If this should be taken to mean that I am God, this is false; but if it should be taken to mean that I am God, as being a member of him, it is true, as Augustine frequently says, and by the words, *for their sakes I sanctify myself*, John 17:19. It says that "they" are "I."

3. "Between the only begotten Son and the soul there is no distinction." This is true. For how could anything white be distinct from or divided from whiteness? Again, matter and form are one in being; living and working. Yet matter is not, on this account, form, or conversely. So in the proposition. A holy soul is one with God, according to John 17:21, *That they all may be one in us, even as we are one*. Still, the creature is not the creator, nor is the just man God. Nor should it be thought that just men, in each

case, are sons of God, by one son of God after another, but just as all good men are good by analogy from one and the same goodness. And just as God is one in all things by essence, so the Son is one God in all sons-by-adoption, and they through him, and in him, are sons-by-analogy, as has been shown often above.

An example is found in the images produced in many mirrors by the face of one person looking therein, where all those images, in view of the fact that they are images, are from the one image which is the face of the person looking. Again, none of them existed or remains except through and in that one, wherefore the apostle significantly says: *We are joint-heirs of Christ*, Romans 8:17. Since this is the case, he is the heir and abides in the house forever, John 8:35, because he is the natural son. So, too, an image or likeness cast into a mirror always remains while the natural object remains. For "natural" is by and from nativity. Hence it is that we, in so far as we are many, or distinct sons, are not heirs of the kingdom [of God] but in so far as we are from, through, and in the Son himself, according to the following, *If the Son therefore shall make you free, ye shall be free indeed*, John 8:36, and 17: *I in them and thou in me that they may be made perfect in one.*

Therefore, it should not be thought that there is one Son, by whom Christ is God's Son and another by whom we are called and are sons of God but it is the same thing and the same person, who is Christ the Son naturally born, while we are sons of God by analogy, by cohering to him with whom we are joint-heirs. Nor should it be thought that God, the Son of God, is something outside or distant from us, to which we are likened, as the image cast into the mirrors, but that he, God, undivided and One by essence, is inmost and closest to each one of us. *In him we live and move and have our being*, Acts 17:28.

Conclusion

Finally, it should be noted that, although the ignorance and shortness of understanding of those who strive to despoil them is evident in some of the articles that I have preached, taught and written, yet there is also evident from the foregoing clarifications the truth of the things spoken and written by me.

But, first of all, in this they err, that they regard as an error all that they do not understand; and again, they regard every error as heresy, even though only stubborn adherence to error makes heresy and a heretic, as the laws and teachers say.

2. While they call themselves inquisitors of heretical depravity, they turn to my books and object to things that are purely natural.

3. They take objection to things as heretical which St. Thomas clearly states in the solutions of certain arguments which they have not seen or do not remember, as about the distinction in nature between univocals and equivocals and analogues and the like.[80]

4. Where I have quoted the words of Cicero, Seneca, the gloss of Origen, they take objection to these as wrong, as, for example, about the divine seed in the soul. I John 3:9, *whosoever is born of God doth not commit sin, for his seed,* that is, God's seed, *remaineth in him.*

5. They object to a number of things as erroneous which are the common opinion of the teachers, for example, that an external act has no moral goodness of itself and consequently adds nothing to the goodness of an inner act, except by accident. Likewise they think that God exists and creates in another Now-moment of eternity, although the world was created in time—because they do not know what Augustine says about God. *Confessions* I, 10: "All things of tomorrow, and all beyond, and all of yesterday, and all behind it, thou hast done today. What is it to me, though any comprehend not this?"

6. They object to certain things as false and heretical [implying] that man cannot be united to God—contrary to the teaching of Christ and the gospel, John 17:21, *Thou, Father, art in me and I in thee, that they also may be one in us.*

7. They say that a creature, or the world, is not nothing in itself except for God, which is contrary to the gospel, John 1:3, *All things were made by him; and without him was not anything made.* Besides, to say that the world is not nothing in itself but that it is some slight thing is obvious blasphemy. For if it were so, God would not be the first cause of all things, and creatures would not have been created by him—not having being from him.

8. They make it an accusation that deiform man may do the works of God, contrary to the teaching of Christ and the gospel, John 14:12, *He that believeth on me, the works that I do shall he do also, and greater works shall he do.* Again they deny that deiform man by love receives those things that are nothing without love, things made by love—contrary to what the apostle says, I Corinthians 13.

That is enough for the present.

A Short Bibliography

TEXTS

FRANZ PFEIFFER: *Meister Eckhart*, herausgegeben in *Deutsche Mystiker des vierzehnten Jahrhunderts*, II (Leipzig, 1857).

JOSEPH QUINT: *Meister Eckharts Predigten*, herausgegeben in *Meister Eckhart: Die deutschen und lateinischen Werke, Erster Band*. Kohlhammer, (Stuttgart-Berlin, 1936). Incomplete but marvelously done.

P. AUGUSTUS DANIELS: *Eine lateinische Rechtfertigungsschrift*, in Baeumker's *Beiträge zur Geschichte der Philosophie des Mittelalters*, Band XXIII, Heft 5 (Münster, 1923).

TRANSLATIONS

F. SCHULZE-MAIZIER: *Meister Eckharts deutsche Predigten und Tractate* (Leipzig, 1938). The best single-volume collection I have seen.

HERMANN BUTTNER: *Meister Eckharts Schriften und Predigten*, two volumes. Painstaking, and somewhat laborious.

GUSTAV LANDAUER: *Meister Eckharts mystische Schriften* (Berlin, 1903). Charming in its simplicity but very incomplete.

ALOIS BERNT: *Meister Eckharts Buch der Göttlichen Tröstung* (Leipzig). One of the most readable.

C. DEB. EVANS: *Meister Eckhart by Franz Pfeiffer*, Vol. I (Watkins, London, 1924); Vol. II (1931). Complete but difficult to read.

ARTICLES ABOUT ECKHART

S. M. DEUTSCH: *Eckhart*, in *The New Schaff-Herzog Encyclopedia of Religious Knowledge*. An excellent but technical summary.

RUFUS JONES: *Meister Eckhart—the Peak of the Range*, in the *Flowering of Mysticism* (Macmillan, 1939). An excellent summary.

JOSIAH ROYCE: *Meister Eckhart*, in *Studies in Good and Evil* (Appleton, 1906).

ALOIS DEMPF: *Meister Eckhart, Ein Einführung in seiner Werke* (Leipzig, 1934).

PREGER: *Meister Eckhart*, in *Geschichte der deutschen Mystiker*.

RUDOLF FAHRNER: *Wortsinn und Wortschöpfung bei Meister Eckhart*; No. 31, in *Beiträge zur deutschen Literaturwissenschaft* (Marburg, 1929).

IN GENERAL

RUFUS JONES: *Studies in Mystical Religion* (Macmillan, 1909). Especially valuable for chapters on Christian mysticism preceding his essay on Eckhart—and following it.

EVELYN UNDERHILL: *Mysticism* (Dutton, 1912).

G. C. COULTON: *Studies in Medieval Thought* (Nelson, 1940).

PAUL SHOREY: *Platonism, Ancient and Modern* (Univ. of Calif. Press, 1938).

ETIENNE GILSON: *The Spirit of Mediaeval Philosophy* (Scribners, 1936).

B. JOWETT: *The Dialogues of Plato* (Random House, 1937).

RICHARD McKEON: *The Basic Works of Aristotle* (Random House, 1941).

STEWART and RAND: *Boethius* (Harvard Univ. Press, 1936).

The "Summa Theologica" of St. Thomas Aquinas, translation by the Fathers of the English Dominican Province (Washburne, London, 1911).

The Summa Contra Gentiles of Saint Thomas Aquinas, translated by the English Dominican Fathers (Benziger Brothers, 1924).

The Nicene and Post-Nicene Fathers, edited by Philip Schaff (Christian Literature Company, 1887). This includes the works of Augustine and Jerome and many others.

Notes

Notes

INTRODUCTION

[1] This, however, was a practical necessity, owing to the decay of Latin as a living language. Especially in the nunneries, if the religious were to be taught, the teaching had to be done in the vernacular but it required the genius of an Eckhart to express the great abstractions of medieval theology in the homely tongue. See G. C. Coulton, *Studies in Medieval Thought*, Ch. VI, Limitations, and on pp. 162–164, the Dominicans' problem of education.

[2] Franz von Baader, *Werke*, Bd. XV, S. 159, quoted by Alois Dempf, *Meister Eckhart —Eine Einführung in seine Werke* (Leipzig, 1934).

[3] "If you want the kernel, you have to break the shell." Sermon 11.

[4] See Legend 5, p. 253.

[5] See T. S. Eliot's quotation and comment in *The Idea of a Christian Society*, pp. 71–72 (Harcourt, 1940). Schulze-Maizier also stresses the German *ethos* and the *furor teutonicus* in Eckhart! (Einführung, p. 28).

[6] On the Cologne school see Helen A. Dickinson, *German Masters of Art*, Ch. VII (Stokes). The pictures of this school hark back to the Byzantine style, with gold backgrounds and symbolic figures. Says Mrs. Dickinson: "The Virgin is the central object of interest . . . with her air of sweet detachment from the world. . . . [She] who would inspire the poet to devotion. Yet even his spiritual offering would lie all unnoticed by these saints, who heed not at all what transpires in this earthly world, but are lost in the contemplation of divine love and a heavenly country. . . . They are the direct expression of that mystic philosophy which was preached with such ardor and received with such sympathy at Cologne . . . by Meister Eckhart."

It is noteworthy, however, that a contemporary parallel existed in the school of Siena in Italy. See F. J. Mather, *A History of Italian Painting*, Ch. II (Holt, 1923). Between these two schools of art there is this difference: in Cologne, some human touch is preserved in the Virgin, whereas in Siena, she represents a wholly unworldly being.

[7] See Sermon 24, p. 211.

[8] See *The Aristocrat*.

[9] Alois Bernt in his introduction to *Meister Eckhart's Buch der Göttlichen Tröstung*.

[10] The Inquisition did not cite it. Furthermore, the initial paragraph on "Obedience" is significant of the earlier Eckhart.

[11] The debate, of course, ran on and on over several related topics, viz., Dominican "realism" versus Franciscan "nominalism," the Immaculate Conception, the will versus the reason. After Eckhart had returned to Cologne, covered with glory, the Franciscans sent their champion to Paris—the "subtle doctor" John Duns

Scotus. Later, as if he were shock troops, Duns Scotus was sent to the college at Cologne—Eckhart's seat—to inveigh against the "Beghards" which means, of course, Meister Eckhart. Whether the two champions ever met in formal debate is not known.

[12] Pfeiffer, p. 169, line 30, in the sermon "*Et quaerebat videre Jesum.*"

[13] See Coulton, *Studies in Medieval Thought*, Ch. VIII.

[14] For example, see Sermon 19, page 185. Or, *Defense* VIII, 15; IX, 30, 46. See also Eckhart's reply in IV, 1: "that he [a man] himself is God, I say that this is altogether false." See also IX, 39.

[15] Sermon 24, page 210.

[16] Now excellently edited by Konrad Weis in *Meister Eckhart—die lateinischen Werke* (Kohlhammer, Stuttgart-Berlin).

[17] *Defense* IV, opening paragraph, and conclusion.

[18] Schulze-Maizier's *Meister Eckhart*, Einführung. See, for example, the promissory confidence in Sermon 4, page 120.

[19] Sermon 28. "Therefore I pray God that he may quit me of god."

[20] *The Book of Divine Comfort*, page 73.

[21] Josiah Royce, *Studies in Good and Evil*, essay on Meister Eckhart (Appleton, 1906). Rufus Jones, *The Flowering of Mysticism*, chapter on Meister Eckhart—the Peak of the Range (Macmillan, 1939).

[22] Insel Verlag, Leipzig.

[23] *Talks of Instruction* 10, page 14.

[24] See *The Book of Divine Comfort*, note 1.

[25] *Defense* I, Benherus Friso, and Peter de Estate.

[26] *Platonism, Ancient and Modern*, p. 105, in Ch. IV, Platonism and the Middle Ages.

[27] Coulton, *Studies in Medieval Thought*, p. 89.

[28] Etienne Gilson, *The Spirit of Mediaeval Philosophy*, p. 54. See especially his excellent note on p. 449, on Eckhart.

[29] *Ibid.*, pp. 69 ff.

[30] *Defense* IX, 30, 46, etc.

[31] Gilson, p. 209 ff.

[32] *Defense* VIII, 6; IX, 38, 12, 8, 5, 3. See Sermon 6, note 2.

[33] *Essay on Criticism*, Pt. II, line 97.

[34] *Defense* VI, 4. John 4: 22.

THESE ARE THE TALKS OF INSTRUCTION

[1] St. Jerome, Latin father of the church (340–420).

[2] This was Confucius' chief advice also. He put it in two words: "Wu pên"—"Attend to the fundamentals." See any good edition of the *Analects of Confucius*.

[3] "blôzheit," lit., bareness. A word evidently pressed into service in place of the technical Latin "esse." These talks were not given to learned people—but to "children"—the often illiterate nuns and monks.

[4] "krefte"—"powers, faculties." See list of arbitrary translations in the Preface.

[5] Cf. II Corinthians 12:9 and 13:4.

[6] This paragraph probably reflects Boethius's *Consolations of Philosophy*, IV, Ch. II. Like many a learned medieval, Eckhart was fond of Boethius, sometimes quoting him explicitly and sometimes implicitly. Eckhart, however, has more confidence in the will than Boethius.

7 Possibly meaning ". . . when it is nonpartisan."

8 Such an illumination as Dante sees in the *Paradiso*, as symbolic of the indescribable presence of God. But probably Eckhart had to deal with hysterics seeing "lights" under the effects of religious excitements or raptures. See, however, *Paradiso*, Canto XXXIII, 49 ff.

9 Acts 9:3–9.

10 Matthew 19:29.

11 Romans 9:3.

12 Acts 9:6.

13 Luke 1:38.

14 Romans 8:28.

15 I John 4:18; possibly also in II Timothy 1:7.

16 I Peter 4:8; James 5:20.

17 Luke 7:47.

18 "krefte" again—which elsewhere, referring to human beings, I have translated as "agents" and, rarely, "faculties." But see Fragment 42.

19 Cf. Dante, *Paradiso*, Canto XXVIII, 22–34. *Convivio*, treatise II, Ch. VI.

20 Luke 11:17 and Matthew 12:30.

21 Luke 14:11 and 18:14.

22 Matthew 23:11.

23 Diogenes, Greek Cynic (412–323 B.C.).

24 Matthew 5:10.

25 See Wisdom of Solomon 1:13–14.

THE BOOK OF DIVINE COMFORT

1 Written for Agnes, daughter of King Albert of Hungary. Agnes was at least a "fellow traveler" with the German mystics. In 1305 her sister-in-law, the French Princess Blanche, died. In 1308 her father was murdered. In 1313 her mother died. This *Book of Divine Comfort* was offered as consolation to Agnes and is Meister Eckhart's most completely authenticated work and the one to which the Inquisition took most frequent objection, as fifteen articles in the *Defense* bear witness.

2 This world is a place of exile from heaven. See Dante's *Convivio* III, 13, 11.

3 This whole work reflects a thoughtful reading of Boethius's *Consolations of Philosophy*. For this opening passage, see, for example, *Consolations* III, 10–11 (Loeb edition, Harvard, 1936). This is also the first passage condemned by the Inquisition. *Defense* V, 1, and Eckhart's reply in I,

4 *Defense* V, 2; I, 2. See Sermon 6, note 2

5 *Defense* V, 3; I:3.

6 *Defense* V, 4; I, 4.

7 John 14:10, 5:17, 16:15, 17:10.

8 John 5:26.

9 John 1:12–13.

10 "krefte"—"faculties."

11 Cf. Sermon 18.

12 Wisdom of Solomon 3:1.

13 *Defense* V, 5; I, 5.

14 I Corinthians 10:13–14.

15 Cf. Ecclesiastes 7:14.

[16] Cf. *Confessions of St. Augustine* X, 66, p. 246 (Everyman's Ed.).

[17] Cf. Exodus 33:15.

[18] Matthew 12:34.

[19] Cf. Ecclesiastes 6:7.

[20] Psalm 42:3.

[21] Romans 9:3.

[22] I Corinthians 13:12.

[23] Matthew 5:3.

[24] *Defense* V, 7; I, 7.

[25] *Defense* V, 8; I, 8.

[26] Matthew 18:9.

[27] Matthew 19:29.

[28] John 1:5.

[29] II Corinthians 12:9.

[30] *Defense* V, 9; I, 9.

[31] Galatians 5:22.

[32] "Its father in the sky." According to the Ptolemaic astronomy current in the Middle Ages, if one could ascend, as Dante did in his dream, from the earth, he would pass first through the air, and then through a layer of fire before reaching the first heaven. See Dante, *Purgatorio*, Canto IX, 28–34: "He snatched me up as far as the fiery sphere . . . and I did burn . . . so scorched that needs was my slumber broken." The earth, said Aristotle, is composed of four elements: earth, water, air, fire. Thus earth falls to the bottom and fire rises to be on top, because earth is heaviest and fire lightest. This accounts for the sphere of fire above the atmosphere and under the first heaven. See Aristotle, *On the Heavens*, Book IV (*Basic Works of Aristotle*, ed. McKeon, Random House, 1941). The recurrent illustration about fire burning up wood is taken from Plato, *Timaeus* 57.

[33] Possibly Isaiah 7:10–16.

[34] *Defense* V, 10; I, 10.

[35] John 16:21.

[36] John 15:11.

[37] Lamentations 3:22.

[38] *Defense* V, 11; I, 11.

[39] Psalms 48:10, 98:1.

[40] Psalm 33:9.

[41] John 4:14.

[42] Matthew 3:17.

[43] Cf. Spinoza's *Ethic*, Fifth Part, Propositions XV–XX, pp. 379–380 (John Wild: Scribners').

[44] I Corinthians 2:10.

[45] II Peter 1:21.

[46] Cf. I Corinthians 2:11.

[47] *Defense* V, 12; I, 12. See again note 43.

[48] *Defense* V, 13; I, 13.

[49] Matthew 16:24.

[50] Cf. John 17:24.

[51] Hosea 2:14.

[52] John 12:26.

[53] Hebrews 12:6.

[54] Proverbs 17:3.
[55] Acts 5:41.
[56] Psalm 91:15.
[57] Wisdom of Solomon 7:11.
[58] Cf. Psalm 97:3.
[59] *Defense* V, 15.
[60] Psalm 38:17.
[61] Job 4:7.
[62] Wisdom of Solomon 3:1.
[63] Hebrews 11:38.
[64] II Samuel 16:5–12.
[65] II Maccabees 7.
[66] *Confessions* I, 10.
[67] See Introduction, page xxiii.
[68] Mark 2:17.

THE ARISTOCRAT

[1] *The Aristocrat* has long been regarded as a piece separate from *The Book of Divine Comfort*. It could hardly have been addressed to Agnes, and Pfeiffer omits it. Hence it has a separate title. Recently, however, early manuscripts have been unearthed in which the two pieces form a single work entitled *The Book of Benedictus*. Furthermore, the larger piece mentions the smaller (p. 63) and the Inquisition attacked both as if they were one work. See note 5.
[2] Luke 19:12.
[3] Romans 7:21–24.
[4] Galatians 5:17–23.
[5] *Defense* V, 14; I, 14.
[6] Origen is noted for his allegorical treatment of the Scriptures. There is, however, a difference between Origen's method and Eckhart's. The Bible is no "allegory" to Eckhart, but it does contain enormously useful similes, and symbols. See Genesis 21:30, 26:15.
[7] Matthew 13:44.
[8] Possibly Psalm 17:9–15.
[9] Song of Solomon 1:5–6.
[10] Proverbs 25:4.
[11] Revelation 22:13.
[12] II Corinthians 11:2.
[13] Genesis 2:7. Equate "name" to "nature."
[14] The upshot of this intricate piece of reasoning appears to be that self-conscious knowing is second rate at best and particularly bad when God is the supposed object of knowledge.
[15] John 17:3.
[16] Ezekiel 17:3–4.
[17] Hosea 2:14. A favorite quotation!

ABOUT DISINTEREST

[1] *Von Abgescheidenheit*—about detachment, but following Eckhart's own clue—that when one has given up self and self-interest, he has given up all the world—I assume

that our word "disinterest" translates his meaning more exactly than "detachment." But note carefully that *disinterest* does not mean *uninterest*. Quite the reverse. Eckhart would say that no one can be truly interested in anything until he is disinterested.

In this short work, Meister Eckhart is carrying out the principal theme of his *Book of Divine Comfort*—the ultimate conclusion of which is to be found in Sermon 28.

2 Luke 10:42. "But one thing is needful."

3 I Corinthians 13:1.

4 Cf. Boethius's *Consolations* III, 10, 85 and III, 10, 140. "God and true blessedness are one and the same thing."

5 Lit., "dem nihte." But Eckhart is by no means talking about nothing. The mathematical notion of zero is much more instructive. There is no such thing as nothing. Zero is either a position or an infinitesimal difference. With Eckhart, his "nihte" is now one and now the other. For example: between variable man and the constant God the difference may be made as small as you please.

6 Modern relativity?

7 "Inne bleiben" again . . . "to be within."

8 Psalm 45:13.

9 Cf. Sermon 28.

10 Luke 1:48.

11 Admittedly a specious argument, perhaps intended only as an offset to the argument of the next paragraph.

12 Psalm 85:18.

13 Boethius *Consolations* II, 5, 70.

14 Latinization of "ibn-Sina," Mohammedan physician and philosopher (980–1037).

15 Galatians 2:20.

16 Marcus Julius Philippus, Emperor of Rome 244–249? The Christian writers say he was a convert to Christ.

17 Isidore of Seville, Spanish bishop (560–636). His work is now known as the *Sentences*—extracts, mostly, from Augustine and Gregory the Great. Very popular in the Middle Ages.

18 Mark 14:34.

19 John 19:25.

20 Surely this would be a shocking disclosure! But it goes with the idea of the "Immaculate Conception," then being upheld by Eckhart's Dominican brethren against the objections of the Franciscans.

21 In the sense of "absence of creatures."

22 Galatians 1:15.

23 Pseudo-Dionysius (fifth century), Neoplatonist mystic and author of *Celestial Hierarchies*. One of Eckhart's favorites.

24 Possibly Ecclesiasticus 24:7.

25 Romans 13:14.

26 John 16:7.

THE SERMONS

1. This is Meister Eckhart, from whom God hid nothing

1 Title supplied by Eckhart disciple. Evidently, Eckhart wrote this and the following three sermons in full. For the substance of it compare St. Augustine, *Confessions* XI, 8; Plato, *Timaeus* 44–47, 50–51, 72.

[2] Two passages identify this sermon. See *Defense* IX, 39, and then 38.

[3] Christmas.

[4] See *Defense* IV, 1; VIII, 1. See Fragment 10, p. 236.

[5] Eckhart seems never to quote by copying and hence his quotations are difficult to identify precisely.

[6] Omitting, after "God," "the Father"—to avoid monotony, which seems not to offend German ears.

[7] "Inne sîn"—lit., "to be within."

[8] "krefte"—lit., "powers."

[9] "bilde"—lit., "images." See Preface. See, for background of this passage, Plato, *Timaeus* 61-65.

[10] Boethius, *Consolations* III, 10, 140.

[11] See Legend 5, p. 253.

[12] II Corinthians 12:3.

[13] Pseudo-Dionysius, see *About Disinterest*, note 23.

[14] Augustine, *Confessions* XI, 9. The following criticism of Moses has its parallel in Book XII of the *Confessions*.

[15] I.e., my idea of a bird does not reproduce the bird nor will it be God's idea of the bird.

[16] Augustine, *Confessions* XI, 11.

[17] II Corinthians 12:2-4.

[18] Romans 8:38-39.

[19] The Song of Solomon was Eckhart's "Book of Love." This passage may be a summary of 5:2-7.

[20] Matthew 19:29, 16:24.

[21] John 1:12.

2. THIS IS ANOTHER SERMON

[1] The title is supplied by an editing disciple. The key word in this sermon is "unwizzen"—lit., unknowledge, which I have translated variously as ignorance, unself-consciousness, unconsciousness. It is difficult to say all that it meant to Eckhart: the ignorance Socrates professed, the mystic trances, the absorption of the scholar in his study, etc. The sermon is well analyzed and the whole matter excellently discussed in Evelyn Underhill's *Mysticism*, Ch. VI.

[2] *Defense* IX, 38; IV, 1; VIII, 1.

[3] Augustine, *Confessions* XII, 29.

[4] Lit., "image," i.e., God's image, as in Genesis 1:26. See Preface.

[5] *Confessions* IV, 18. A noble passage.

[6] "krefte"—lit., "powers." See Preface.

[7] Matthew 10:37, 34, 35.

[8] "in lîdenne"—lit., "in passivity."

[9] Bearing in mind that the sermon is on the text Matthew 2:2, it is probable that Eckhart was thinking of the sixteenth verse as a simile. The children Herod slew are the senses, the soul's agents, etc.

3. THIS, TOO, IS MEISTER ECKHART
WHO ALWAYS TAUGHT THE TRUTH

[1] Title, again, by the editing disciple of Meister Eckhart. For the psychology in this sermon, see Aristotle. *On the Soul* III 4-5 (McKeon, Ed.).

[2] A misuse of divine sarcasm: Matthew 11:12.
[3] John 16:16.
[4] Matthew 17:4.
[5] Luke 10:38-42.
[6] II Timothy 4:2.
[7] Matthew 5:16.
[8] Matthew 13:8 and 7:19.
[9] Philippians 4:13.
[10] Romans 8:26.
[11] I Corinthians 12:3.
[12] I Corinthians 13:10.
[13] II Corinthians 3:6.
[14] Matthew 6:7.

4. ETERNAL BIRTH

[1] John 4:42.
[2] See Sermon 2, note 1.
[3] This is a characteristically Eckhartian, not to say German, confidence capable of giving comfort and aid to what I have called Cain-mysticism. See Introduction, page xv.
[4] Not Jeremiah, as Pfeiffer misprints it, but Hosea 2:14—a favorite quotation.
[5] Psalm 55:6.
[6] Psalm 84:10, marginal reading.
[7] Revelation 3:20.
[8] John 3:8.
[9] Song of Solomon 8:6.

5. THE LOVE OF GOD

[1] There are two versions of this sermon, one of which got more notice in the *Defense* than the other, calling for all the articles IX, 24-32. The version given here is undoubtedly a revision of this and more like Eckhart at his best. Therefore, I have chosen it for this collection. All the pertinent passages of the other version can be read in the eight articles of the *Defense* referred to above.
[2] The bracket is mine but the enclosed words are Eckhart's. Evidently he wanted to add Romans 11:36 to his text.
[3] Aquinas, *Summa Theologica* III, quest. 57, art. 5.
[4] *Defense* IX, 24 and 29.
[5] "jensît mers"—"beyond the sea"—departed. *Defense* VIII, 11; IV, 11; and IX, 20.
[6] Lit., "you may have seen the truth as an abstract idea or simile."
[7] This is literal, probably meaning "want of" or "lack." Compare the parable of the ten virgins in Matthew 25:1-13. The five foolish virgins suffered for their lack of, or want of "oil." But it must be read also in the light of the oft-repeated "All creatures are pure nothing," cited in connection with this sermon in *Defense* IX, 30. Thus "not" may mean "nothing" and therefore "creatures."
[8] For example, the famed *Theologica Germanica* of the fifteenth century, which so impressed Luther, must be quoting a long-established opinion: "Nothing burns in hell but self-will."

NOTES

319

9 See the discussion of "grunt" in the Preface. See also the long discussion of the *Defense* IX, 27 anent a statement taken from the other version of this sermon. Possibly "being" is what Eckhart here means by God's core and mine.

10 Lit., "Here I live, on my own, as God lives, on his own."

11 The substance of this is: "Act without rationalizing, or reasons, or objects foreign to your act." See Fragment 23 and *Defense* IX, 31.

12 "wîse"—lit., "modes, methods, means," but specifically, "ritual" or "artifice." This must have been extremely offensive to Eckhart's fellow ecclesiastics.

13 Lit., "that you get out of yourself, as you are creaturely." This is Eckhart's colloquial for self-denial as Christ described it. He sees the human ego as an obstacle to God, just as a divine ego would be (and is!) an obstacle to man.

14 John 3:13.

15 See note 7 above. The accepted definition of creation was "ex nihilo." Emptiness asks to be filled!

16 The rank of the will or anything else depended on its relation to God. All men were equal as God created them—in his own likeness.

6. THE KINGDOM OF GOD IS AT HAND

1 The authenticity of this sermon is vouched for by early manuscripts, its relatedness to other sermons, and Eckhart's touch.

2 This is a special use of "kraft"—"agent." It will appear as such in Sermons 7, 12, 13, 15, 20, 24, and 25. It is cited in the *Defense* many times: VIII, 5, 6, 7 and IX, 3, 5, 7, 8, 12, where the Latin word used is "virtus"—"virtue," meaning "an active quality or capacity to produce a given effect." Thus Eckhart tried to be more specific about the divine "Something" in the soul—the spark, the light, the "little castle." Moreover, the word "virtue" was appropriate because of its moral connotation. Apart from this "Something," which comprised justice, truth, goodness, and like virtues, no word or deed could be just, true, or good. Nevertheless, I have kept to "agent" in English as Eckhart kept to "kraft" in German, whether he was referring to "potentia," the purely human agents of the soul, or to "virtus," the divine source of moral virtues. In the sense here used, "agent" translates "virtus" quite as well as "potentia."

3 Genesis 28:16.

4 Cf. the illustration of Venus in Sermon 26.

5 Cf. Plato, *Timaeus* 38.

6 A free paraphrase of Augustine's breath-taking apostrophe. See *Confessions* X, 38, page 227 (Everyman's Ed.).

7. YOUTH REMAINS IN THE SOUL

1 Evidently, and sorrowfully, this is only a brief of the sermon Eckhart must have delivered. Its style and thought, nevertheless, identify it as authentic.

2 See Defense VIII, 6; IV, 6.

3 See Sermon 6, note 2.

4 John 1:1.

5 Lit., "dwell within." See "inne bleiben" in Preface.

6 See Sermon 24, note 10; *Defense* VIII, 13; and *Timaeus* 69 and 72.

8. The fruits of good deeds live on!

[1] This sermon is well certified by much repetition in early manuscripts and by Eckhartian thought and style.

[2] Lit., "[how the deeds] may be resurrected to living again." Living "under mortal sin" means to have committed a mortal sin and not yet to have been restored to the grace of God through the sacrament of confession and absolution.

[3] Grace: "the divine unmerited favor of God toward man; the mercy of God, as distinguished from his justice; also any benefits his mercy imparts; divine love or pardon." Cf. Romans 5 and 6.

[4] A challenge? Apparently, it was not noticed.

[5] To understand the following argument, note that "deeds" and "time" rank as creatures, which are, says Eckhart, pure nothings.

[6] Cf. *Defense* IX, 37.

9. Now I know

[1] For identification of this sermon see *Defense* IX, 50. As for the translation of the text, Eckhart usually paraphrases rather than translates his Latin. He was seldom speaking to scholars as such. The statement objected to in the *Defense* does not appear exactly in the sermon except as noted in the last two paragraphs. When Eckhart says, in comment on the charge, "this is false and error," he must mean that his accusers have made the error.

[2] Cf. *Summa Theologica* I, quest. 79, art. 1. Note the careful difference, that Aquinas says: "In God alone is his intellect his essence; while in other intellectual creatures, the intellect is a power, (i.e., an agent of the soul)." On this point Eckhart went beyond Aquinas and laid himself open to the charge of heresy.

[3] Matthew 11:27.

[4] The Aristotelian rule was "like is known by like." See *On the Soul*, I, 404b. See also III, 431b: "the soul is in a way all existing things."

[5] *Summa Theologica* I, quest. 39, art. 8.

[6] I Timothy 6:16. I Corinthians 13:8.

[7] Cf. the parallel treatment of ideas and angels by Aquinas. *Summa Theologica*, I, quest. 15 and the *Treatise on the Angels*, 50–64.

[8] *Summa Theologica* I, quest. 16, art. 3.

[9] Thus, the sermon as we have it ends.

10. God laughs and plays

[1] See note 5 below for identification of this sermon. Also Legend 1, p. 251.

[2] But see Sermon 28 to get Eckhart's real meaning.

[3] Plato, *Timaeus* 60.

[4] Augustine, *Confessions* III, 19: "O Thou Good omnipotent, who carest for every one of us, as if thou carest for him only; and so for all, as if they were but one!"

[5] Cf. *Defense* VIII, 2.

[6] Cf. the marvelous passage in Augustine, *Confessions* X, 8 and 9.

[7] Cf. *Confessions* I, 1.

11. Honor thy father

1 This sermon is identified as Eckhart's by its style and content.
2 "In German"—of course.
3 Exodus 20:17.
4 Exodus 20:19.
5 Exodus 20:24.
6 Exodus 19:16-20.
7 "gelîchnesse"—"likeness"; but since this word refers back to "one in essence" I have translated it "uniformity." This may seem like too great a liberty but is due, I think, to the fact that Eckhart was making new language.
8 Aquinas, *Summa Theologica* I, quest. 20, art. 4: "God loves Christ not only more than he loves the whole human race but more than he loves the entire created universe."
9 *Ibid*. I, quest. 12, art. 2. The Latin parentheses appearing in the text are Eckhart's and they equate "bilde" to "formae" to "ideas" in the Platonic sense. Interestingly the passage equates this sequence of words to "Son" also. See P. E. More, *Platonism*, Ch. VI.
10 The key sentence to Eckhart himself.
11 Referring to the concatenation of physical and chemical change. See Plato, *Timaeus* 59.
12 Obviously, several points of the original sermon are missing.
13 II Maccabees 7:22-23. Quoted also in *The Book of Divine Comfort*.
14 Possibly Luke 12:3.
15 *Timaeus* 49, 50, 58.

12. When God shows himself

1 For identification, see *Defense* IX, 4.
2 Philippians 4:4.
3 Cf. Augustine's *Confessions* X, 66 (Everyman's Ed., p. 246) "I, through my covetousness, would not indeed forego Thee, but would, with Thee, possess a lie." See also X, 40.
4 *Defense* IX, 4.
5 *Defense* IX, 26, and Plato, *Timaeus* 57.
6 Ephesians 3:18.
7 *Defense* IX, 5, and Sermon 6, note 2.
8 Romans 11:36.
9 *Defense* IX, 9.
10 I Corinthians 11:7.
11 Matthew 10:26.
12 Lit., "nothings," i.e., creatures.
13 *Defense* IX, 13.
14 *Defense* IX, 10.
15 *Defense* IX, 11.
16 "stucke," lit., "items."
17 Revelation 14:4.

13. TRUTH IS NOT MERCHANDISE

[1] For identification, see *Defense* IX, 52.
[2] Genesis 1:26.
[3] See Sermon 1, 2nd par., and Legend 5.
[4] John 15:5.
[5] "Nu"—see Preface.
[6] Sermon 6, note 2; also cf. *The Aristocrat*.
[7] "âne wîse"—lit., "without manner." See *Defense* IX, 8.
[8] "ungemüschte"—"unmixed."
[9] "nihtes niht"—see Preface.
[10] This is to be understood with Eckhart's "*Esse est Deus*"—"being is God," as set forth in his Latin commentary on Genesis. See also Introduction. As for the rest of the passage, Eckhart writes in his commentary on John: "*Et hoc est quod Graecus habet: in principio erat verbum, id est logos, quod Latine est verbum et ratio.*" Thus, he equates the "Word" to reason, wisdom and idea.
[11] John 1:14.
[12] Psalm 36:9.
[13] *Defense* VIII, 1d; IV, 1d. "Is-ness" = "istikeit" = "being," see note 10, and also Sermon 18, note 6, and Sermon 23, note 9.
[14] Omitting a clause of peculiarly German redundancy.
[15] *Defense* IX, 52 and VIII, 9; IV, 9.

14. NOTHING ABOVE THE SOUL

[1] This sermon is identified by style and content and much copying in oldest and best manuscripts. Josef Quint: *Meister Eckhart, Neue Handschriftenfunde*, Kohlhammer, Berlin, 1940.
[2] The "old authority" is, of course, unidentifiable, but it is startling to find a close parallel to Eckhart's citation in ancient China. Lao Tzu (circa 340 B.C.) has a well-known sentence: "I shêng êrh, êrh shêng san, san shêng wan wu"—"One begat two, two begat three, three begat all things." This is a Chinese way of saying that the Creator is a Trinity (Lao Tzu, *Canon of Reason and Virtue*, Section 42). A Chinese dictionary, the *Shuo Wên*, dating from A.D. 200, states that the Chinese number three, which consists of three parallel horizontal strokes, symbolizes the trinity of creation. The upper stroke is "yang," the heaven-father; the lower stroke is "yin," the earth-mother; while the middle stroke is "jen," man, i.e., Eckhart's soul, thus made "between one and two" (San, shu ming, t'ien, ti, jên chih tao yeh). Whether any of this had filtered through "old authorities," to Europe, who can say? Or was it something inherent in man spontaneously expressed in many places?
[3] Aquinas, *Summa Theologica* I, quest. 12, art. 2, "The divine essence is united to the created intellect, as the object actually understood." *Ibid.*, I, quest. 14, art. 2, "The intelligible idea itself is the divine intellect itself and thus he [God] understands himself by himself."
[4] "Igele"—"hedgehog" is also medieval German slang for "arrow" or "dart" and it is a temptation to make this passage an account of a weathervane, and thus more intelligible. It may refer, however, to some primitive legend of the hedgehog's

powers as a weather or wind prophet, which its owner was acute enough to make profitable.

⁵ Cf. *Summa Theologica* I, quest. 79, and also *Fragment* 42. Eckhart's ratings of the "soul's agents" evidently varied from time to time.

⁶ Aquinas rated "*irascibilis*" among the lower or sensitive agents of the soul, as Eckhart does in *Fragment* 42. I understand Eckhart to mean by it that "something" in the soul that makes a good man strive for unity with God. The contemporary Nazi claimants of Eckhart like best to refer to his and Germany's (!) "*irascibilis*" as an inability to tolerate bounds. Certainly, in some sermons, Eckhart used the word in a novel sense. In Plato, it is the irrational element of the soul, giving rise to such emotions as courage, fear, pride and anger. See Plato, *Phaedrus* 246, 253; *Republic* 411; *Timaeus* 70–71.

⁷ Cf. Luke 9:62.

⁸ Proverbs 9:17.

⁹ *Confessions* II, 9 ff.

¹⁰ Proverbs 31:25.

15. INTO THE GODHEAD!

¹ The genuineness of this sermon has much internal evidence. It is based on the idea of "*irascibilis*" of Sermon 14. It recalls Eckhart's saying: "When I preach, I usually speak . . . of the purity of the divine nature." It also illustrates Eckhart's fondness for Boethius. I should judge that he had just reread Boethius's *Consolations*, Books II and III, when he preached this sermon.

² Certainly a cavalier interpretation of this text!

³ Boethius, *Consolations*, II, 7, 10.

⁴ Song of Solomon 3:2 and 4. The erotic analogy of spiritual love is common among medieval mystics who bend everything to their one aim. The erotic note is more common among the Sufis of Islam.

⁵ Aristotle, *On the Soul*, Book II, ch. 7, 419a. See also *The Book of Divine Comfort*, note 32.

⁶ I John 3:1.

⁷ Aristotle's word. Literally the passage reads: "If God were not in all things, nature would not function nor would desire be in anything." Cf. *Consolations* III, 11, 107 ff.

⁸ I Corinthians 13:12. I John 3:2.

⁹ I Timothy 6:16. Aquinas, *Summa Theologica* I, quest. 12, art. 11.

¹⁰ This is "*irascibilis*." See Sermon 14, note 6. See also *Defense* IX, 34; VIII, 2.

16. BEING IS MORE THAN LIFE

¹ For identification, see *Defense* IX, 48.

² Matthew 5:11.

³ *Defense* IX, 49.

⁴ Plato, *Timaeus* 37.

⁵ Aquinas, *Summa Theologica* I, quest. 77, art. 6.

⁶ It is clear that this sermon is sadly abbreviated.

17. NO RESPECTER OF PERSONS

[1] In early manuscripts, this sermon was much copied. It is identified by citation in the *Defense* as indicated below.

[2] Exodus 32:10.

[3] Exodus 32:32—but an extraordinary arrangement.

[4] *Defense* VIII, 4; IV, 4, cf. IX, 14.

[5] See *The Book of Divine Comfort*, at note 47. *Defense* V, 12; I, 12.

[6] John 7:16.

[7] *Defense* IX, 29, then IX, 25, and latter part of IX, 27.

[8] Possibly Matthew 25:40. Cf. *Defense* VIII, 7.

[9] *Defense* IX, 27.

[10] Exodus 2:10.

18. JUSTICE IS EVEN

[1] For identification of this sermon, see *Defense* IX, 35. I have preferred "just" to the more literal "righteous."

[2] A translation of the *Institutes of Justinian*, 1:1: "*Justitia est constans et perpetua voluntas uis suum cuique tribuens.*"

[3] *Defense* IX, 35.

[4] An arbitrary translation of "wîse" and "sinne" which seems better to fit the sense of the passage.

[5] Eckhart is unwilling that God should be defined by the name man gives him.

[6] "istigkeit"—a coined, but interesting and oft-quoted word with varied spellings Nevertheless, the Inquisition objected to the idea. See *Defense* IX, 36. See Sermon 13, note 10.

[7] *Defense* IX, 37.

[8] *Defense* IX, 38.

[9] *Defense* VIII, 1d.

[10] II Corinthians 3:18.

[11] *Defense* VIII, 1e. IX, 39.

[12] The idea of this paragraph is that if God and I *are* one, then it remains only for me to know it—but if I must will to do the will of God, this implies a distinction which John 10:30, as a premise, denies.

[13] Cf. Plato, *Timaeus* 57, from which, undoubtedly, Eckhart draws this simile.

[14] *Defense* IV, 10 and IX, 40.

[15] II Corinthians 3:18; I Corinthians 13:12; I John 3:2.

19. GOD MUST GIVE HIMSELF

[1] For identification of this sermon, see *Defense* IX, 41. Since the Inquisition took so much objection to it, it is interesting to see how Eckhart's contemporary, Dante, treated this text in the *Convivio*, Fourth Treatise, Ch. XX.

[2] *Defense* IX, 41. VIII, 16.

[3] Omitting two interpolated sentences about angels. See *Defense* IX, 26.

[4] Goethe says: "Gehalt bringt die Form mit" ("Matter brings form with it").

[5] *Defense* IX, 42 and VIII, 11.

[6] *Defense* VIII, 15; IV, 15; IX, 43.
[7] *Defense* IX, 43; IX, 30—an oft-repeated objection by the Inquisition.
[8] *Defense* VIII, 1; IV, 1; IX, 25.
[9] Characteristic of Eckhart's "heresy of degree." Cf. Sermon 15, p. 166.

20. PURITY OF HEART REQUIRES DENIAL OF SELF

[1] This sermon is sufficiently identified by its reproduction of thought from *The Book of Divine Comfort* and also by a familiar reference to statements condemned by the Inquisition. See note 5 below.
[2] John 15:12, 9.
[3] Matthew 19:29.
[4] Cf. *Timaeus* 91. See also Aquinas on "The Production of Women" *Summa Theologica* I, quest. 92.
[5] *Defense* IX, 3 and 12. See Sermon 6, note 2.
[6] Sounds like *Timaeus* 28.

21. THE WILL IS FREE

[1] This sermon is identified by its thought and style. See notes below.
[2] "*irascibilis*"—see Sermon 14, note 6.
[3] Because number means multiplicity which is the tendency away from unity, i.e., God.
[4] "Dirre geist hat kein warumbe"—lit., "this spirit has no why." See Sermon 5, note 11. Also *Defense* IX, 31 and Fragment 23.
[5] Legend 5.
[6] John 15:15.
[7] *Defense* IX, 25, 29. Also IX, 3, 8.
[8] John 20:11—but an extraordinary interpretation!
[9] *Defense* IX, 30, 46.
[10] I Timothy 6:16.
[11] Aquinas, *Summa Theologica* I, quest. 83, art. 1.

22. GOOD HINDERS THE BEST

[1] Identified as authentic by style and content.
[2] John 12:25.
[3] John 13:10.
[4] I Corinthians 11:29.
[5] Cf. John 4:21ff.
[6] I Thessalonians 5:16–18.
[7] Cf. Fragment 42 with which this sermon agrees, in contrast to Sermon 14.
[8] John 14:6, 10:1.
[9] Possibly Ecclesiasticus 24:9–10.
[10] *Defense* IX, 14.
[11] Matthew 7:5.
[12] *Defense* IX, 11.
[13] *Defense* IX, 20.
[14] Colossians 3:3.

[15] Mark 14:34.
[16] Philippians 4:13.

23. DISTINCTIONS ARE LOST IN GOD

[1] For identification, see *Defense* IX, 15.
[2] Cf. Matthew 6:6a.
[3] Cf. Luke 14:26.
[4] *Defense* IX, 15a and VIII, 1b.
[5] *Defense* IX, 15bc.
[6] Romans 9:3. *Defense* VIII, 12; IV, 12.
[7] *Defense* IX, 16.
[8] Obviously, "god" means a human conception of God. This is a distinction Eckhart did not make explicit and his statements therefore sounded blasphemous to his contemporaries, even though they were intended in all piety. See Preface.
[9] "isticheit"—Cf. Exodus 3:14, "I am what I am." See Sermon 18, note 6, and Sermon 13, note 13.
[10] *Defense* VIII, 12 and IX, 17.
[11] *Defense* IX, 18a.
[12] *Defense* VIII, 14b and IX, 18bc.
[13] *Defense* IX, 19.
[14] *Defense* IX, 20 and VIII, 11.

24. GOD ENTERS A FREE SOUL

[1] For identification, see *Defense* IX, 51; VIII, 13; IV, 13.
[2] Admittedly, a cavalier rendering of the text in German and English.
[3] "âne eigenschaft"—lit., "without proprietorship," according to Quint, but the phrase has the same effect as "abgescheidenheit"—"disinterest." However, here, "detached" seems better.
[4] See Sermon 9, note 4. "megetlichen"—"virginal," but more appropriately "innocent."
[5] "ein jar," lit., "a year," but Quint says that it means the nine-month period of pregnancy. Eckhart is comparing the labors of the "I-bound, purpose-bound, time-bound" person with pregnancy and the child to be born or stillborn with the fruits of their labors.
[6] "grunt"—which elsewhere I translate as "the core"—of the soul—but here, as "ground," better to carry out the simile.
[7] *Defense* IX, 3 and 12. VIII, 5, 6, 7. A recapitulation of passages to the same purpose: Sermons 6, note 2; 7, 2; 12, 16; 14, 5; 15; 20, 5; 25.
[8] "vünkelîn"—the inner light of all mystics.
[9] Cf. the Hindu phrase "Neti, neti." Or Plato, *Timaeus* 49.
[10] This is "heresy of degree." See *Defense* VIII, 1 and 13. *Defense* IX, 51.
[11] "sich habende ist nach wise"—God, as conceived in some particular manner or characteristic of human thinking.

25. GET BEYOND TIME!

[1] That is, this text is comparable to Ecclesiasticus 44:17. The actual wording is believed to come from the Roman Missal, Dominican edition. Roger Bacon (1214 -

1294) made loud complaint about the corruption of various Biblical texts used in his time. See *Defense* IX, 55–59 on this sermon.

² The Feast of St. Germanus was for July 31.

³ The soul's day is psychological time—the flowing sense of future, present, and past. God's day is eternity—the "Now-moment." See Augustine, *Confessions* XI, 16. See *Timaeus* 38. *Defense* IX, 33.

⁴ i.e., the soul's, of which the Virgin Mary is a parable.

⁵ See *Defense* IX, 57.

⁶ See *Defense* IX, 58, 44 and also VIII, 3.

⁷ But compare Matthew 3:17, Mark 1:11, and Luke 3:22.

⁸ See *Defense* IX, 59.

⁹ See *Defense* IX, 13 and 46.

¹⁰ Psalm 90:4. See Augustine, *Confessions* XI, 12–14; *Timaeus* 37.

¹¹ *Defense* IX, 55.

¹² John 14:8.

¹³ Romans 6:22.

¹⁴ John 15:15.

¹⁵ *Defense* IX, 56.

26. LIKE A MORNING STAR, GOD SHINES

¹ For identification, see *Defense* IX, 54.

² Domingo de Guzmán, Spanish (1170–1221).

³ Referring to the *Liber 24 Philosophorum*, the *Book of 24 Philosophers*, by Pseudo-Hermes Trismegistus, edited by Denifle.

⁴ Galen, Greek physician (130–200?) as cited by Aquinas, *Summa Contra Gentiles*, Ch. 68.

⁵ Again "wise"—"means," "technique," or "ritual."

⁶ "gat in die breite"—"goes in wide places"—like the wind that "bloweth where it listeth and thou hearest the sound thereof, but canst not tell whence it cometh, and whither it goeth." John 3:8.

⁷ Lit., white or black. See *Defense* IX, 54. Anticipating Hume, the objection seems to be that these are physiological or psychological reactions of which the sun itself is quite innocent. Aquinas had made this point too. This whole passage may appear to be quite a step beyond or away from the *Esse est Deus* of Sermon 13, note 10, but it was not so in Eckhart's meaning: being is God but God is more than being.

⁸ Sermon 24, note 9.

⁹ Reproduces the essential thought of Lao Tzu, in *The Canon of Reason and Virtue*: tao k'ê tao, fei ch'ang tao, i.e., the Way about which man can think is not the Way of eternity.

¹⁰ "Expressions which are in no way composite signify substance, quantity, quality, relation, place, time, position, state, action, or affection." Aristotle, *The Categories*, Ch. 4 (McKeon, Ed.).

¹¹ Matthew 19:17.

¹² Here, too, see *Defense* IX, 26 and 27.

¹³ James 1:17.

¹⁴ "vünkelîn"—the light of the soul. See Evelyn Underhill's *Mysticism*, pp. 64 ff.

¹⁵ Thought to refer to the Franciscan General Gonsalvus, a natural adversary of Eckhart. See Introduction, note 11.

[16] Or, as St. Paul puts it, "through a glass darkly."

[17] John 1:1.

27. CREATURES SEEK GOD THROUGH ME

[1] Quint shows that this sermon is widely quoted in early manuscripts as being Eckhart's. It reveals the Eckhart of the later years. Quint, *Neue Handschriftenfunde . . . Meister Eckharts . . .* (Kohlhammer, 1940).

[2] See Plato, *Timaeus* 84 and 86. See also Genesis 4:10, 9:4; Leviticus 17:10. The Biblical notion is that the blood is the seat of the life or soul. I Corinthians 10:16, "the blood of Christ" is the life or soul of Christ—but now used metaphorically.

[3] This is Genesis 1:27 and the *Timaeus* 28 pressed close together.

[4] Becomes and unbecomes. See *Talks of Instruction*, section 11. The presence of God is not steady but intermittent.

[5] I.e., eternity.

[6] Once more, reminiscent of Lao Tzu. The Eckhart "Godhead" answers to Lao Tzu's description of the Tao: *Wei wu wei*, it acts without acting.

28. BLESSED ARE THE POOR!

[1] This sermon bears such unmistakable earmarks of Eckhart's touch that external evidence is hardly required. As Quint shows, it occurs in all the earliest and best manuscripts. It harks back to Sermons 1–4 but is obviously the work of an older man under great stress. It is the logical outcome of Eckhart's central idea, of the unity of God and man: "God and I are one." John 10:30. It is the complete expression of this great idea.

[2] "in mîner êrsten ursache," lit., "in my prime origin."

[3] The reader of this sermon will be bothered by the not unusual distinction between God and god. I judge that this reflects the reading of Plato's *Timaeus*, where the divine name is spelled both ways, with the upper- and lower-case G. The *Timaeus* tells about the "created gods," who were responsible for the soul. There is, however, the other distinction in Eckhart, perhaps more important: God is beyond my thinking; god is what I think he is.

[4] Sermon 24, note 7. *Defense* IX, 3, 12.

[5] The meaning of this sentence is that we should be very humble indeed about what we think we know about God.

[6] I Corinthians 15:10.

[7] Probably Plato, again, in the *Timaeus* 40–41. The phrase "bursting forth" refers, I believe, to the "eternal birth" in which one gets out of self, space, and time into eternity, the habitation of God; "efflux" means the birth of the individual out of undifferentiated eternity. Thus Eckhart means to say: I was not blessed by being born in the first place, but I am blessed by a second and more glorious birth. Which is good Johannine doctrine: John 3:3.

[8] "discovered" or "uncovered" truth—that is to say, a truth Eckhart found himself uttering without premeditation in the course of a sermon as he delivered it. It was this kind of "truth" that really got him into trouble with the Inquisition—the utterances in which he "went too far" and said things "which might easily lead his listeners into error." But Eckhart obviously had great respect for the "discovered" truth. It came immediately from the heart of God! See discussion of sermons in the Introduction.

FRAGMENTS

The numbers below are the serial numbers of the Fragments.

[1] From the sermon *"Et quaerebat videre Jesum,"* Luke 19:3-5. See Pfeiffer, pp. 168, 17 to 169, 3.

[2] Pfeiffer, Fragment 46, p. 614.

[3] Pfeiffer, Fragment 47, p. 614.

[4] Pfeiffer, Fragment 48, p. 614 (in part).

[5] Pfeiffer, Fragment 37, p. 608.

[6] Pfeiffer, Fragment 15, p. 601.

[7] Pfeiffer, Fragment 11, p. 600.

[8] Pfeiffer, Fragment 16, p. 601.

[9] Pfeiffer, Fragment 8, p. 599.

[10] Pfeiffer, Fragment 1, p. 597.

[11] Pfeiffer, Fragment 5, p. 598.

[12] Pfeiffer, Fragment 6, p. 599.

[13] Pfeiffer, Fragment 17, p. 602.

[14] Pfeiffer, Fragment 33, p. 607.

[15] Pfeiffer, Fragment 43, p. 611.

[16] Pfeiffer, Fragment 38, p. 609.

[17] From the sermon *"Ave, gratia plena,"* Luke 1:28. Pfeiffer, p. 287, line 34.

[18] *"Mulier, venit hora . . ."* John 4:23. Pfeiffer, p. 57, line 31.

[19] Pfeiffer, Fragment 24, p. 604.

[20] *"Fluminus impetus . . ."* Psalm 45:5. Pfeiffer, p. 200, line 20.

[21] Pfeiffer, Fragment 39, p. 610.

[22] *"Quasi vas auri,"* Ecclesiasticus 50:9. Pfeiffer 70, 16.

[23] *"Beati qui esurient,"* Matthew 5:6. Pfeiffer 146, 16. Cf. Sermon 5.

[24] *"Mulier, venit hora . . ."* John 4:23. Pfeiffer 58, 8.

[25] *Ibid.*, Pfeiffer 59, 16.

[26] *"Dominus dicit,"* Jeremiah 7:1-2. Pfeiffer 120, 28.

[27] *Ibid.*, Pfeiffer 121, 16.

[28] *"Beati qui esurient,"* Matthew 5:6. Pfeiffer 149, 16.

[29] *"In omnibus requiem,"* Ecclesiasticus 24:11. Pfeiffer 152, 20, 33.

[30] *"Ecce, ego mitto angelum meum,"* Matthew 11:10. Pfeiffer 160, 30.

[31] *"Haec est vita aeterna,"* John 17:3. Pfeiffer 158, 7.

[32] *"Deus caritas est,"* I John 4:16. Pfeiffer 31, 1.

[33] *Ibid.*, Pfeiffer 32:10.

[34] *Ibid.*, Pfeiffer 32, 38.

[35] *"In principio erat verbum,"* John 1:1. Pfeiffer 77, 13.

[36] *"Scio hominem in Christo,"* II Corinthians 12:2. Pfeiffer 79, 18.

[37] *"Haec est vita aeterna,"* John 17:3. Pfeiffer 155, 21.

[38] *"Justus in perpetuum vivet,"* Wisdom of Solomon 5:15. Pfeiffer 189, 7.

[39] Sermon LX, Pfeiffer 193, 16.

[40] *"Adolescens, tibi dico surge,"* Luke 7:14. Pfeiffer 256, 8.

[41] From Schulze-Maizier, p. 391. The method of the mystic is often negation. Here is a double negation. The "negation of negations" is fullness of being. The reason for this seeming circumlocution is to avoid putting a verbal description on something words do not describe. See *Defense* IX, 23, Eckhart's reply.

[42] "*Renovami spiritu mentis,*" Ephesians 4:23. Pfeiffer pp. 319–320.

[43] "*Expedit vobis,*" John 16:7. Pfeiffer 235, 18.

[44] It has been debated whether or not this piece should be classified as a Legend or a Fragment. Probably it was written posthumously but of the genuineness of its contents there is no question. Its chief message was forbidden as the contents of *Defense* IV, 16; VIII, 16 indicates. It is memorable for the sentences which say: "the evenness of God—his ubiquity—*that has been my joy!*"

THE DEFENSE

The discovery of Meister Eckhart's Latin *Defense* and its publication in 1866 did indeed mark the beginning of the present era of Eckhart studies. This document, signed by Eckhart himself, became the means of certifying the authenticity of the German works he did not sign.

Something more, however, is claimed for it. In his introductory essay to the Daniels edition (*Beiträge zur Geschichte der Philosophie des Mittelalters,* Bd. XXIII, Heft 5), Baeumker says that since the discovery of the *Defense,* we may know exactly what Eckhart did say. Is this true? The careful reader who checks up on the cross-references will note discrepancies between the passages translated from the German and the same passages translated from the Latin.

My own explanation of these discrepancies is twofold. First, the Latin of Sections V-VIII is itself a translation, made presumably by Eckhart's accusers. Secondly, what Eckhart said in the heat of his vernacular preaching probably did differ from what he would have been prepared to say to an unsympathetic court of the church. He admitted that his German preaching often contained "discovered truths," which the Latin would not be likely to contain. And then, his reporters were not always accurate. Eckhart sometimes denies outright that he ever said what his accusers attributed to him. See below, note 40, or the introductory paragraph of Section IV.

In the notes that follow, references to Aristotle may be checked in the excellent *Basic Works of Aristotle,* edited by McKeon, Random House, 1941; the references to St. Augustine and Jerome in *The Nicene and Post-Nicene Fathers* (NPNF) published by the Christian Literature Society, Buffalo, 1887. The references to Thomas Aquinas are easiest for the American reader in *The Summa Theologica of St. Thomas Aquinas,* a Dominican translation, published by Washburne, London.

I

[1] Heinrich von Virneberg, archbishop of Cologne.

[2] Matthew 5:10.

[3] Hebrews 12:6.

[4] Psalm 37:8.

[5] Albertus Magnus (1193?–1280).

[6] The complete article in Section V; Eckhart's reply Section I.

[7] The complete article in Section VI; Eckhart's reply Section II.

[8] The complete article in Section VII; Eckhart's reply Section III.

[9] The complete article in Section VIII; Eckhart's reply Section IV.

[10] Jerome, letter 60, NPNF, Second Series, Vol. VI, p. 123.

[11] Chapter V.

[12] Aristotle, *Physics* III, 2 and VII, 1.

[13] For the full statement of this and the following fifteen articles under Section I, see Section V, under the corresponding serial.

[14] *Summa Theologica*, Pt. I, quest. 77, art. 5, p. 64.

[15] But Eckhart did seem to say that. See Sermon 24, note 7, and *Defense* VIII, 6 and 7, IX, 3, 12.

[16] Proverbs 12:2.

[17] See V, 6. I cannot identify this passage; possibly it is a paraphrase of *The Book of Divine Comfort*, pp. 48–49.

[18] Again, possibly a paraphrase; see V, 9.

[19] "the example about fire" is from Plato, *Timaeus* 57.

[20] Luke 17:21.

[21] Cf. Psalm 45:13.

II

[22] For the full statement of this and the following five articles under Section II, see Section VI, under the corresponding serial.

[23] Cf. Psalm 73:9.

[24] See note 80, in Section VI.

III

[25] *Expositio Libri Genesis*. Published in *Meister Eckhart: Die lateinischen Werke*, 1, Lief. (Kohlhammer, Stuttgart-Berlin, 1937).

[26] For the full statement of this and the following eleven articles of Section III, see Section VII, under corresponding serial.

[27] *Summa Theologica* I, quest. 3, art. 4, p. 36.

[28] *Metaphysics* 8, 6.

[29] Exodus 3:14.

[30] *Summa Theologica* I, quest. 77, art. 4.

[31] Psalm 102:25 and Hebrews 1:10.

[32] Avicenna, *Metaphysics* 5, 1; Albertus, *De Causis* I, 8.

[33] Luke 17: 21.

[34] *Summa Theologica* I, Pt. II, quest. 20, art. 4.

[35] Chapter II, lines 17–18 (Loeb).

IV

[36] Not Bede, but Augustine: *Quaestionum Evangeliorum* II, 40.

[37] For a full statement of this and the following fifteen articles of Section IV, see Section VIII, under the corresponding serial.

[38] Augustine, says Daniels, is here cited at second hand from the *Decretum Gratiani*.

[39] Eckhart's own words!

[40] Whose error? Eckhart's? The German reporters'? The Franciscan inquisitors, who cited the supposed erroneous passages?

[41] Aristotle, *On the Soul* II, Chs. 5 and 12.

[42] Augustine, *On the Trinity*, Bk. 14, Ch. 12.

[43] Quoted at second hand from the following passage of Aquinas, note 44.

[44] *Summa Theologica* II, quest. 61, art. 5.

[45] I John 4:16.
[46] James 4:6; I Peter 5:5.
[47] Ecclesiasticus Ch. 17—?
[48] "beyond the sea"—i.e., absent or departed. See Sermon 5.
[49] Psalm 62:11.
[50] *Confessions* X, 37.
[51] Augustine taught that there is an image or replica of the Trinity in the soul. *O the Trinity*, Bk. IX, Ch. 3 ff.
[52] Ecclesiasticus 4:28.
[53] John 12:25.
[54] Matthew 22:39; Mark 12:31; Luke 10:27.
[55] Matthew 10:37.
[56] Romans 9:3; Philippians 1:23.
[57] Genesis 15:1.
[58] Probably referring to John 6:56 (Flesh—body, blood—soul).
[59] *Prior Analytics* I, 41.

V

[60] *The Book of Divine Comfort*, hereafter abbreviated to BDC.
[61] BDC, p. 43 at note no. 3.
[62] BDC, p. 43 at note no. 4.
[63] BDC, p. 44 at note no. 5.
[64] BDC, p. 44 at note no. 6.
[65] BDC, p. 46 at note no. 13.
[66] BDC, possibly p. 48.
[67] BDC, p. 50 at note no. 24.
[68] BDC, p. 51 at note no. 25.
[69] BDC, p. 51 at note no. 30.
[70] BDC, p. 55 at note no. 34.
[71] John 14:9.
[72] BDC, p. 58 at note no. 38.
[73] BDC, p. 62 at note no. 47.
[74] Matthew 5:10.
[75] BDC, p. 63 at note no. 48.
[76] *The Aristocrat*, p. 75 at note no. 5.
[77] BDC, p. 68 at note no. 59.

VI

[78] This response of Eckhart is probably the verbal defense he made in the church at Cologne. See Introduction, p. xxiv.
[79] John 4:23.
[80] Cf. Aristotle, *The Categories*, Ch. 1: "Things are said to be named 'equivocally when, though they have a common name, the definition corresponding with the name differs for each. . . . On the other hand, things are said to be named 'univocally' which have both the name and the definition, . . . in common." And *Prior Analytics*, Bk. II, Ch. 24: "We have an 'example' [paradigm, analogue] when the major term is proved to belong to the middle by means of a term which resembles the third."

VII

51 See note 25.

52 In either III or VII, articles 6 and 7 have been interchanged so that they do not correspond.

53 Moses ben Maimun, Spanish rabbi, philosopher, and writer (1135–1204).

VIII

84 "virtus," see Sermon 6, note 2. See also Preface, on "kraft."

75 See note 51.

IX

86 Sermon 13 in Quint, *Meister Eckhart: Die deutschen Werke.* It is not among the twenty-eight in this book.

87 Sermon 12.

88 This probably means that creation is not the mere rearrangement of things already created—as this book is.

89 Sermon 23.

90 Cf. note 40.

91 I have not seen this sermon.

92 Aristotle, *On the Soul*, III, 9 (432b, 5).

93 I have not seen this sermon. Cf. above, IX, 9.

94 See Fragment 41.

95 Sermon 5.

96 "So careful of the type she seems,
   So careless of the single life." —Tennyson, *In Memoriam*.

97 The foregoing paragraph is the kind of passage, as I mentioned in the Introduction, that the Nazis might well seize with delight.

98 Aristotle, *Physics* IV, 10, 219a; Averroes, *Physics* IV, 89; Augustine, *Enarratio in Psalmum* 38, 7, and *Confessions* XI, 17.

99 Aquinas, *Summa Theologica* I, quest. 14, art. 10.

100 Sermon 18.

101 *On the Celestial Hierarchy* 4, 1. *On the Divine Name* 4, 1.

102 *Quaestionum Evangeliorum*, Bk. 1, quest. 36.

103 Aristotle, *Nicomachean Ethics* 1161 b.

104 Sermon 19.

105 Sermon 7 in Quint. It is not among the twenty-eight in this book.

106 Luke 7:36.

107 Sermon 16.

108 Sermon 9.

109 Sermon 24.

110 Sermon 13.

111 I have not seen this sermon. The text is Ezekiel 36:25.

112 Sermon 26.

113 Sermon 25.

114 *Enarratio in Psalmum* 74, 9.

Revised January, 1970

harper ✦ torchbooks

† The New American Nation Series, edited by Henry Steele Commager and Richard B. Morris.
‡ American Perspectives series, edited by Bernard Wishy and William E. Leuchtenburg.
a History of Europe series, edited by J. H. Plumb.
§ The Library of Religion and Culture, edited by Benjamin Nelson.
‖ Researches in the Social, Cultural, and Behavioral Sciences, edited by Benjamin Nelson.
Σ Harper Modern Science Series, edited by James A. Newman.
° Not for sale in Canada.
+ Documentary History of the United States series, edited by Richard B. Morris.
# Documentary History of Western Civilization series, edited by Eugene C. Black and Leonard W. Levy.
∧ The Economic History of the United States series, edited by Henry David et al.
¶ European Perspectives series, edited by Eugene C. Black.
** Contemporary Essays series, edited by Leonard W. Levy.
* The Stratum Series, edited by John Hale.

CLEMENT EATON: The Freedom-of-Thought Struggle in the Old South. *Revised and Enlarged. Illus.* TB/1150

CLEMENT EATON: The Growth of Southern Civilization, 1790-1860. † *Illus.* TB/3040

ROBERT H. FERRELL, Ed.: Foundations of American Diplomacy, 1775-1872 + HR/1393

LOUIS FILLER: The Crusade against Slavery: 1830-1860. † *Illus.* TB/3029

WILLIM W. FREEHLING: Prelude to Civil War: *The Nullification Controversy in South Carolina, 1816-1836* TB/1359

PAUL W. GATES: The Farmer's Age: *Agriculture, 1815-1860* Δ TB/1398

THOMAS JEFFERSON: Notes on the State of Virginia. ‡ *Edited by Thomas P. Abernethy* TB/3052

FORREST MCDONALD, Ed.: Confederation and Constitution, 1781-1789 + HR/1396

JOHN C. MILLER: The Federalist Era: 1789-1801. † *Illus.* TB/3027

RICHARD B. MORRIS: The American Revolution Reconsidered TB/1363

CURTIS P. NETTELS: The Emergence of a National Economy, 1775-1815 Δ TB/1438

DOUGLASS C. NORTH & ROBERT PAUL THOMAS, Eds.: *The Growth of the American Economy ot 1860* + HR/1352

R. B. NYE: The Cultural Life of the New Nation: 1776-1830. † *Illus.* TB/3026

GILBERT OSOFSKY, Ed.: Puttin' On Ole Massa: *The Slave Narratives of Henry Bibb, William Wells Brown, and Solomon Northup* ‡ TB/1432

JAMES PARTON: The Presidency of Andrew Jackson. *From Volume III of the Life of Andrew Jackson. Ed. with Intro. by Robert V. Remini* TB/3080

FRANCIS S. PHILBRICK: The Rise of the West, 1754-1830. † *Illus.* TB/3067

MARSHALL SMELSER: The Democratic Republic, 1801-1815 + TB/1406

JACK M. SOSIN, Ed.: The Opening of the West + HR/1424

GEORGE ROGERS TAYLOR: The Transportation Revolution, 1815-1860 Δ* TB/1347

A. F. TYLER: Freedom's Ferment: *Phases of American Social History from the Revolution to the Outbreak of the Civil War. Illus.* TB/1074

GLYNDON G. VAN DEUSEN: The Jacksonian Era: 1828-1848. † *Illus.* TB/3028

LOUIS B. WRIGHT: Culture on the Moving Frontier TB/1053

American Studies: The Civil War to 1900

W. R. BROCK: An American Crisis: *Congress and Reconstruction, 1865-67* ° TB/1283

T. C. COCHRAN & WILLIAM MILLER: The Age of Enterprise: *A Social History of Industrial America* TB/1054

W. A. DUNNING: Reconstruction, Political and Economic: 1865-1877 TB/1073

HAROLD U. FAULKNER: Politics, Reform and Expansion: 1890-1900. † *Illus.* TB/3020

GEORGE M. FREDRICKSON: The Inner Civil War: *Northern Intellectuals and the Crisis of the Union* TB/1358

JOHN A. GARRATY: The New Commonwealth, 1877-1890 † TB/1410

JOHN A. GARRATY, Ed.: The Transformation of American Society, 1870-1890 + HR/1395

HELEN HUNT JACKSON: A Century of Dishonor: *The Early Crusade for Indian Reform.* † *Edited by Andrew F. Rolle* TB/3063

WILLIAM G. MCLOUGHLIN, Ed.: The American Evangelicals, 1800-1900: An Anthology ‡ TB/1382

JAMES S. PIKE: The Prostrate State: *South Carolina under Negro Government.* ‡ *Intro. by Robert F. Durden* TB/3085

FRED A. SHANNON: The Farmer's Last Frontier: *Agriculture, 1860-1897* TB/1348

VERNON LANE WHARTON: The Negro in Mississippi, 1865-1890 TB/1178

American Studies: The Twentieth Century

RICHARD M. ABRAMS, Ed.: The Issues of the Populist and Progressive Eras, 1892-1912 + HR/1428

RAY STANNARD BAKER: Following the Color Line: *American Negro Citizenship in Progressive Era.* ‡ *Edited by Dewey W. Grantham, Jr. Illus.* TB/3053

RANDOLPH S. BOURNE: War and the Intellectuals: *Collected Essays, 1915-1919.* ‡ *Edited by Carl Resek* TB/3043

A. RUSSELL BUCHANAN: The United States and World War II. † *Illus.*
Vol. I TB/3044; Vol. II TB/3045

THOMAS C. COCHRAN: The American Business System: *A Historical Perspective, 1900-1955* TB/1080

FOSTER RHEA DULLES: America's Rise to World Power: 1898-1954. † *Illus.* TB/3021

HAROLD U. FAULKNER: The Decline of Laissez Faire, 1897-1917 TB/1397

JOHN D. HICKS: Republican Ascendancy: 1921-1933. † *Illus.* TB/3041

WILLIAM E. LEUCHTENBURG: Franklin D. Roosevelt and the New Deal: 1932-1940. † *Illus.* TB/3025

WILLIAM E. LEUCHTENBURG, Ed.: The New Deal: *A Documentary History* + HR/1354

ARTHUR S. LINK: Woodrow Wilson and the Progressive Era: 1910-1917. † *Illus.* TB/3023

BROADUS MITCHELL: Depression Decade: *From New Era through New Deal, 1929-1941* Λ TB/1439

GEORGE E. MOWRY: The Era of Theodore Roosevelt and the Birth of Modern America: 1900-1912. † *Illus.* TB/3022

GEORGE SOULE: Prosperity Decade: *From War to Depression, 1917-1929* Δ TB/1349

TWELVE SOUTHERNERS: I'll Take My Stand: *The South and the Agrarian Tradition. Intro. by Louis D. Rubin, Jr.; Biographical Essays by Virginia Rock* TB/1072

Art, Art History, Aesthetics

ERWIN PANOFSKY: Renaissance and Renascences in Western Art. *Illus.* TB/1447

ERWIN PANOFSKY: Studies in Iconology: *Humanistic Themes in the Art of the Renaissance. 180 illus.* TB/1077

OTTO VON SIMSON: The Gothic Cathedral: *Origins of Gothic Architecture and the Medieval Concept of Order. 58 illus.* TB/2018

HEINRICH ZIMMER: Myths and Symbols in Indian Art and Civilization. *70 illus.* TB/2005

Asian Studies

WOLFGANG FRANKE: China and the West: *The Cultural Encounter, 13th to 20th Centuries. Trans. by R. A. Wilson* TB/1326

L. CARRINGTON GOODRICH: A Short History of the Chinese People. *Illus.* TB/3015

Economics & Economic History

C. E. BLACK: The Dynamics of Modernization: *A Study in Comparative History* TB/1321

GILBERT BURCK & EDITOR OF *Fortune:* The Computer Age: *And its Potential for Management* TB/1179

SHEPARD B. CLOUGH, THOMAS MOODIE & CAROL MOODIE, Eds.: Economic History of Europe: *Twentieth Century* # HR/1388

THOMAS C. COCHRAN: The American Business System: *A Historical Perspective, 1900-1955* TB/1180

HAROLD U. FAULKNER: The Decline of Laissez Faire, 1897-1917 △ TB/1397

PAUL W. GATES: The Farmer's Age: *Agriculture, 1815-1860* △ TB/1398

WILLIAM GREENLEAF, Ed.: American Economic Development Since 1860 + HR/1353

ROBERT L. HEILBRONER: The Future as History: *The Historic Currents of Our Time and the Direction in Which They Are Taking America* TB/1386

ROBERT L. HEILBRONER: The Great Ascent: *The Struggle for Economic Development in Our Time* TB/3030

DAVID S. LANDES: Bankers and Pashas: *International Finance and Economic Imperialism in Egypt. New Preface by the Author* TB/1412

ROBERT LATOUCHE: The Birth of Western Economy: *Economic Aspects of the Dark Ages* TB/1290

W. ARTHUR LEWIS: The Principles of Economic Planning. *New Introduction by the Author*° TB/1436

ROBERT GREEN MC CLOSKEY: American Conservatism in the Age of Enterprise TB/1137

WILLIAM MILLER, Ed.: Men in Business: *Essays on the Historical Role of the Entrepreneur* TB/1081

HERBERT A. SIMON: The Shape of Automation: *For Men and Management* TB/1245

Historiography and History of Ideas

J. BRONOWSKI & BRUCE MAZLISH: The Western Intellectual Tradition: *From Leonardo to Hegel* TB/3001

WILHELM DILTHEY: Pattern and Meaning in History: *Thoughts on History and Society.*° *Edited with an Intro. by H. P. Rickman* TB/1075

J. H. HEXTER: More's Utopia: *The Biography of an Idea. Epilogue by the Author* TB/1195

H. STUART HUGHES: History as Art and as Science: *Twin Vistas on the Past* TB/1207

ARTHUR O. LOVEJOY: The Great Chain of Being: *A Study of the History of an Idea* TB/1009

RICHARD H. POPKIN: The History of Scenticism from Erasmus to Descartes. *Revised Edition* TB/1391

MASSIMO SALVADORI, Ed.: Modern Socialism # HR/1374

BRUNO SNELL: The Discovery of the Mind: *The Greek Origins of European Thought* TB/1018

History: General

HANS KOHN: The Age of Nationalism: *The First Era of Global History* TB/1380

BERNARD LEWIS: The Arabs in History TB/1029

BERNARD LEWIS: The Middle East and the West ° TB/1274

History: Ancient

A. ANDREWS: The Greek Tyrants TB/1103

THEODOR H. GASTER: Thespis: *Ritual Myth and Drama in the Ancient Near East* TB/1281

MICHAEL GRANT: Ancient History ° TB/1190

History: Medieval

NORMAN COHN: The Pursuit of the Millennium: *Revolutionary Messianism in Medieval and Reformation Europe* TB/1037

F. L. GANSHOF: Feudalism TB/1058

F. L. GANSHOF: The Middle Ages: *A History of International Relations. Translated by Rémy Hall* TB/1411

ROBERT LATOUCHE: The Birth of Western Economy: *Economic Aspects of the Dark Ages* ° TB/1290

HENRY CHARLES LEA: The Inquisition of the Middle Ages. || *Introduction by Walter Ullmann* TB/1456

History: Renaissance & Reformation

JACOB BURCKHARDT: The Civilization of the Renaissance in Italy. *Introduction by Benjamin Nelson and Charles Trinkaus. Illus.* Vol. I TB/40; Vol. II TB/41

JOHN CALVIN & JACOPO SADOLETO: A Reformation Debate. *Edited by John C. Olin* TB/1239

FEDERICO CHABOD: Machiavelli and the Renaissance TB/1193

THOMAS CROMWELL: Thomas Cromwell: *Selected Letters on Church and Commonwealth, 1523-1540.* ¶ *Ed. with an Intro. by Arthur J. Slavin* TB/1462

FRANCESCO GUICCIARDINI: History of Florence. *Translated with an Introduction and Notes by Mario Domandi* TB/1470

WERNER L. GUNDERSHEIMER, Ed.: French Humanism, 1470-1600. * Illus.* TB/1473

HANS J. HILLERBRAND, Ed., The Protestant Reformation # HR/1342

JOHAN HUIZINGA: Erasmus and the Age of Reformation. *Illus.* TB/19

JOEL HURSTFIELD: The Elizabethan Nation TB/1312

JOEL HURSTFIELD, Ed.: The Reformation Crisis TB/1267

PAUL OSKAR KRISTELLER: Renaissance Thought: *The Classic, Scholastic, and Humanist Strains* TB/1048

PAUL OSKAR KRISTELLER: Renaissance Thought II: *Papers on Humanism and the Arts* TB/1163

PAUL O. KRISTELLER & PHILIP P. WIENER, Eds.: Renaissance Essays TB/1392

DAVID LITTLE: Religion, Order and Law: *A Study in Pre-Revolutionary England. § Preface by R. Bellah* TB/1418

NICCOLO MACHIAVELLI: History of Florence and of the Affairs of Italy: *From the Earliest Times to the Death of Lorenzo the Magnificent. Introduction by Felix Gilbert* TB/1027

ALFRED VON MARTIN: Sociology of the Renaissance. ° *Introduction by W. K. Ferguson* TB/1099

GARRETT MATTINGLY et al.: Renaissance Profiles. *Edited by J. H. Plumb* TB/1162

J. H. PARRY: The Establishment of the European Hegemony: 1415-1715: *Trade and Exploration in the Age of the Renaissance* TB/1045

PAOLO ROSSI: Philosophy, Technology, and the Arts, in the Early Modern Era 1400-1700. || *Edited by Benjamin Nelson. Translated by Salvator Attanasio* TB/1458

R. H. TAWNEY: The Agrarian Problem in the Sixteenth Century. *Intro. by Lawrence Stone* TB/1315

H. R. TREVOR-ROPER: The European Witch-craze of the Sixteenth and Seventeenth Centuries and Other Essays ° TB/1416
VESPASIANO: Rennaissance Princes, Popes, and XVth Century: The Vespasiano Memoirs. Introduction by Myron P. Gilmore. Illus. TB/1111

History: Modern European

MAX BELOFF: The Age of Absolutism, 1660-1815 TB/1062
D. W. BROGAN: The Development of Modern France ° Vol. I: From the Fall of the Empire to the Dreyfus. Affair TB/1184
Vol. II: The Shadow of War, World War I, Between the Two Wars TB/1185
ALAN BULLOCK: Hitler, A Study in Tyranny. ° Revised Edition. Illus. TB/1123
JOHANN GOTTLIEB FICHTE: Addresses to the German Nation. Ed. with Intro. by George A. Kelly ¶ TB/1366
ALBERT GOODWIN: The French Revolution TB/1064
H. STUART HUGHES: The Obstructed Path: French Social Thought in the Years of Desperation TB/1451
JOHAN HUIZINGA: Dutch Civilization in the 17th Century and Other Essays TB/1453
JOHN MCMANNERS: European History, 1789-1914: Men, Machines and Freedom TB/1419
FRANZ NEUMANN: Behemoth: The Structure and Practice of National Socialism, 1933-1944 TB/1289
DAVID OGG: Europe of the Ancien Régime, 1715-1783 ° a TB/1271
ALBERT SOREL: Europe Under the Old Regime. Translated by Francis H. Herrick TB/1121
A. J. P. TAYLOR: From Napoleon to Lenin: Historical Essays ° TB/1268
A. J. P. TAYLOR: The Habsburg Monarchy, 1809-1918: A History of the Austrian Empire and Austria-Hungary ° TB/1187
J. M. THOMPSON: European History, 1494-1789 TB/1431
H. R. TREVOR-ROPER: Historical Essays TB/1269

Literature & Literary Criticism

JACQUES BARZUN: The House of Intellect TB/1051
W. J. BATE: From Classic to Romantic: Premises of Taste in Eighteenth Century England TB/1036
VAN WYCK BROOKS: Van Wyck Brooks: The Early Years: A Selection from his Works, 1908-1921 Ed. with Intro. by Claire Sprague TB/3082
RICHMOND LATTIMORE, Translator: The Odyssey of Homer TB/1389

Philosophy

HENRI BERGSON: Time and Free Will: An Essay on the Immediate Data of Consciousness ° TB/1021
H. J. BLACKHAM: Six Existentialist Thinkers: Kierkegaard, Nietzsche, Jaspers, Marcel, Heidegger, Sartre ° TB/1002
J. M. BOCHENSKI: The Methods of Contemporary Thought. Trans by Peter Caws TB/1377
CRANE BRINTON: Nietzsche. Preface, Bibliography, and Epilogue by the Author TB/1197
ERNST CASSIRER: Rousseau, Kant and Goethe. Intro by Peter Gay TB/1092
WILFRID DESAN: The Tragic Finale: An Essay on the Philosophy of Jean-Paul Sartre TB/1030

MARVIN FARBER: The Aims of Phenomenology: The Motives, Methods, and Impact of Husserl's Thought TB/1291
PAUL FRIEDLANDER: Plato: An Introduction TB/2017
MICHAEL GELVEN: A Commentary on Heidegger's "Being and Time" TB/1464
G. W. F. HEGEL: On Art, Religion Philosophy: Introductory Lectures to the Realm of Absolute Spirit. ‖ Edited with an Introduction by J. Glenn Gray TB/1463
G. W. F. HEGEL: Phenomenology of Mind. ° ‖ Introduction by eGorge Lichtheim TB/1303
MARTIN HEIDEGGER: Discourse on Thinking. Translated with a Preface by John M. Anderson and E. Hans Freund. Introduction by John M. Anderson TB/1459
F. H. HEINEMANN: Existentialism and the Modern Predicament TB/28
WERER HEISENBERG: Physics and Philosophy: The Revolution in Modern Science. Intro. by F. S. C. Northrop TB/549
EDMUND HUSSERL: Phenomenology and the Crisis of Philosophy. § Translated with an Introduction by Quentin Lauer TB/1170
IMMANUEL KANT: Groundwork of the Metaphysic of Morals. Translated and Analyzed by H. J. Paton TB/1159
IMMANUEL KANT: Lectures on Ethics. § Introduction by Lewis White Beck TB/105
QUENTIN LAUER: Phenomenology: Its Genesis and Prospect. Preface by Aron Gurwitsch TB/1169
GEORGE A. MORGAN: What Nietzsche Means TB/1198
H. J. PATON: The Categorical Imperative: A Study in Kant's Moral Philosophy TB/1325
MICHAEL POLANYI: Personal Knowledge: Towards a Post-Critical Philosophy TB/1158
WILLARD VAN ORMAN QUINE: Elementary Logic Revised Edition TB/577
JOHN E. SMITH: Themes in American Philosophy: Purpose, Experience and Community TB/1466
MORTON WHITE: Foundations of Historical Knowledge TB/1440
WILHELM WINDELBAND: A History of Philosophy Vol. I: Greek, Roman, Medieval TB/38
Vol. II: Renaissance, Enlightenment, Modern TB/39
LUDWIG WITTGENSTEIN: The Blue and Brown Books ° TB/1211
LUDWIG WITTGENSTEIN: Notebooks, 1914-1916 TB/1441

Political Science & Government

C. E. BLACK: The Dynamics of Modernization: A Study in Comparative History TB/1321
KENNETH E. BOULDING: Conflict and Defense: A General Theory of Action TB/3024
DENIS W. BROGAN: Politics in America. New Introduction by the Author TB/1469
LEWIS COSER, Ed.: Political Sociology TB/1293
ROBERT A. DAHL & CHARLES E. LINDBLOM: Politics, Economics, and Welfare: Planning and Politico-Economic Systews Resolved into Basic Social Processes TB/3037
ROY C. MACRIDIS, Ed.: Political Parties: Contemporary Trends and Ideas ** TB/1322
ROBERT GREEN MC CLOSKEY: American Conservatism in the Age of Enterprise, 1865-1910 TB/1137
JOHN B. MORRALL: Political Thought in Medieval Times TB/1076

5

EDWARD CONZE et al, Editors: Buddhist Texts through the Ages TB/113
H. G. CREEL: Confucius and the Chinese Way TB/63
FRANKLIN EDGERTON, Trans. & Ed.: The Bhagavad Gita TB/115
SWAMI NIKHILANANDA, Trans. & Ed.: The Upanishads TB/114

Religion: Philosophy, Culture, and Society

NICOLAS BERDYAEV: The Destiny of Man TB/61
RUDOLF BULTMANN: History and Eschatology: *The Presence of Eternity* ° TB/91
LUDWIG FEUERBACH: The Essence of Christianity. § *Introduction by Karl Barth. Foreword by H. Richard Niebuhr* TB/11
ADOLF HARNACK: What Is Christianity? § *Introduction by Rudolf Bultmann* TB/17
KYLE HASELDEN: The Racial Problem in Christian Perspective TB/116
IMMANUEL KANT: Religion Within the Limits of Reason Alone. § *Introduction by Theodore M. Greene and John Silber* TB/67
H. RICHARD NIERUHR: Christ and Culture TB/3
H. RICHARD NIEBUHR: The Kingdom of God in America TB/49

Science and Mathematics

W. E. LE GROS CLARK: The Antecedents of Man: *An Introduction to the Evolution of the Primates.* ° *Illus.* TB/559
ROBERT E. COKER: Streams, Lakes, Ponds. *Illus.* TB/586
ROBERT E. COKER: This Great and Wide Sea: *An Introduction to Oceanography and Marine Biology. Illus.* TB/551
F. K. HARE: The Restless Atmosphere TB/560
WILLARD VAN ORMAN QUINE: Mathematical Logic TB/558

Science: Philosophy

J. M. BOCHENSKI: The Methods of Contemporary Thought. *Tr. by Peter Caws* TB/1377
J. BRONOWSKI: Science and Human Values. *Revised and Enlarged. Illus.* TB/505
WERNER HEISENBERG: Physics and Philosophy: *The Revolution in Modern Science. Introduction by F. S. C. Northrop* TB/549
KARL R. POPPER: Conjectures and Refutations: *The Growth of Scientific Knowledge* TB/1376
KARL R. POPPER: The Logic of Scientific Discovery TB/576

Sociology and Anthropology

REINHARD BENDIX: Work and Authority in Industry: *Ideologies of Management in the Course of Industrialization* TB/3035
BERNARD BERELSON, Ed., The Behavioral Sciences Today TB/1127
KENNETH B. CLARK: Dark Ghetto: *Dilemmas of Social Power. Foreword by Gunnar Myrdal* TB/1317

KENNETH CLARK & JEANNETTE HOPKINS: A Relevant War Against Poverty: *A Study of Community Action Programs and Observable Social Change* TB/1480
LEWIS COSER, Ed.: Political Sociology TB/1293
ALLISON DAVIS & JOHN DOLLARD: Children of Bondage: *The Personality Development of Negro Youih in the Urban South* || TB/3049
ST. CLAIR DRAKE & HORACE R. CAYTON: Black Metropolis: *A Study of Negro Life in a Northern City. Introduction by Everett C. Hughes. Tables, maps, charts, and graphs* Vol. I TB/1086; Vol. II TB/1087
PETER F. DRUCKER: The New Society: The Anatomy of Industrial Order TB/1082
CHARLES Y. GLOCK & RODNEY STARK: Christian Beliefs and Anti-Semitism. *Introduction by the Authors* TB/1454
ALVIN W. GOULDNER: The Hellenic World TB/1479
R. M. MACIVER: Social Causation TB/1153
GARY T. MARX: Protest and Prejudice: *A Study of Belief in the Black Community* TB/1435
ROBERT K. MERTON, LEONARD BROOM, LEONARD S. COTTRELL, JR., Editors: Sociology Today: *Problems and Prospects* || Vol. I TB/1173; Vol. II TB/1174
GILBERT OSOFSKY, Ed.: The Burden of Race: A Documentary History of Negro-White Relations in America TB/1405
GILBERT OSOFSKY: Harlem: The Making of a Ghetto: *Negro New York 1890-1930* TB/1381
TALCOTT PARSONS & EDWARD A. SHILS, Editors: Toward a General Theory of Action: *Theoretical Foundations for the Social Sciences* TB/1083
PHILIP RIEFF: The Triumph of the Therapeutic: *Uses of Faith After Freud* TB/1360
JOHN H. ROHRER & MUNRO S. EDMONSON, Eds.: The Eighth Generation Grows Up: *Cultures and Personalities of New Orleans Negroes* || TB/3050
ARNOLD ROSE: The Negro in America: *The Condensed Version of Gunnar Myrdal's* An American Dilemma. *Second Edition* TB/3048
GEORGE ROSEN: Madness in Society: *Chapters in the Historical Sociology of Mental Illness.* || *Preface by Benjamin Nelson* TB/1337
PHILIP SELZNICK: TVA and the Grass Roots: *A Study in the Sociology of Formal Organization* TB/1230
PITIRIM A. SOROKIN: Contemporary Sociological Theories: *Through the First Quarter of the Twentieth Century* TB/3046
MAURICE R. STEIN: The Eclipse of Community: *An Interpretation of American Studies* TB/1128
FERDINAND TONNIES: Community anα Society: *Gemeinschaft und Gesellschaft. Translated and Edited by Charles P. Loomis* TB/1116
W. LLOYD WARNER and Associates: Democracy in Jonesville; *A Study in Quality and Inequality* || TB/1129
W. LLOYD WARNER: Social Class in America: *The Evaluation of Status* TB/1013
FLORIAN ZNANIECKI: The Social Role of the Man of Knowledge. *Introduction by Lewis A. Coser* TB/1372